□ □ □ **Henri Lefebvre on Space**

Henri Lefebvre on Space

Architecture, Urban Research, and the Production of Theory

Łukasz Stanek

MINNESOTA

UNIVERSITY OF MINNESOTA PRESS
MINNEAPOLIS | LONDON

THIS BOOK IS SUPPORTED BY A GRANT FROM THE
GRAHAM FOUNDATION FOR ADVANCED STUDIES IN THE FINE ARTS.

Portions of the text were published in Łukasz Stanek, "Lessons from Nanterre," in
"Aftershocks: Generation(s) since 1968," a special issue of *Log* 13/14 (Fall 2008); in
Łukasz Stanek, "Productive Crisis: Henri Lefebvre and the European City after the
Welfare State," *Quarterly Architecture Essay (QAE)* 3, no. 3 (Spring 2008), http://
www.haecceityinc.com; and in Łukasz Stanek, "Collective Luxury: Architecture and
Populism in Charles Fourier," *Hunch* 14, ed. Salomon Frausto (NAi Publishers/Berlage
Institute, 2010). A version of chapter 3 appeared previously as Łukasz Stanek, "Space
as Concrete Abstraction: Hegel, Marx, and Modern Urbanism in Henri Lefebvre," in
Stefan Kipfer, Richard Milgrom, Kanishka Goonewardena, and Christian Schmid, eds.,
Space, Difference, Everyday Life: Reading Henri Lefebvre (London: Routledge, 2008).

Published by the University of Minnesota Press
111 Third Avenue South, Suite 290
Minneapolis, MN 55401-2520
http://www.upress.umn.edu

Printed in the United States of America on acid-free paper

The University of Minnesota is an equal-opportunity educator and employer.

Library of Congress Cataloging-in-Publication Data

Stanek, Łukasz.
 Henri Lefebvre on space : architecture, urban research, and the production of theory
/ Łukasz Stanek.
     p. cm.
 Includes bibliographical references and index.
 ISBN 978-0-8166-6616-4 (hardcover : alk. paper)
 ISBN 978-0-8166-6617-1 (pbk. : alk. paper)
 1. Social sciences—Philosophy. 2. Space and time. 3. Lefebvre, Henri, 1901–1991.
 I. Title. II. Title: Architecture, urban research, and the production of theory.
 H61.15.S73 2011
  304.2′3—dc22   2011011284

18 17 16 15 14 13 12 11   10 9 8 7 6 5 4 3 2 1

□□□ **Contents**

□□□ Introduction

THIS BOOK ADDRESSES THE ENCOUNTER among sociology, architecture, urbanism, and philosophy in 1960s and early 1970s France in view of the shifts in the postwar processes of urbanization at every scale of the social reality, from that of the neighborhood to the global level. The work of Henri Lefebvre (1901–91) was central to this encounter, and his theory of production of space, published between 1968 and 1974, contributed both to an understanding of these processes that have staked out the tendencies of the global urban condition until today and to a redefinition of the identities of the disciplines involved, their subject matters, and their conceptual frameworks, but also their social obligations and political ambitions.

To argue that Lefebvre's theory was formulated from within an engagement with sociology, architecture, and urbanism is at odds with the prevailing view on the theory of production of space as a projection of his philosophical positions. "He developed a very interesting reflection about the city," wrote Paul-Henry Chombart de Lauwe, one of the pioneers of French postwar urban sociology, about Lefebvre, "but, no doubt, he lacked a fieldwork experience, a direct knowledge of the terrain and sufficiently deep exchange with architects."[1] More recently, Manuel Castells stressed the weakness of Lefebvre's *La production de l'espace (The Production of Space)* on the level of empirical research: "Frankly, I do not believe that it is possible to offer a theory of production of space on a strictly philosophical basis, without a profound knowledge of the economic and technological data about the processes of urbanization and about their social and political organization."[2]

The statements of Chombart and Castells are symptomatic of much of urban sociology still today, which appreciates Lefebvre as an *inspiring* philosopher, that is to say, accepts his writings on the condition of their relegation beyond the realm of sociology proper. Yet while Lefebvre's theory cannot be understood without accounting for his philosophical readings, I argue in this book that neither can it be grasped without acknowledging what was largely forgotten in his work: a number of empirical studies he carried out and supervised within a range of French research institutions, as well as his intense exchanges with architects, urbanists, and planners. The focus on these studies and on Lefebvre's engagement with French architectural culture is intended not to diminish the relevance of philosophy in his thinking but to argue that it cannot be understood from a single disciplinary perspective, including a philosophical reading, which, even if most sympathetic, tends to reverse the gesture of Chombart in order to celebrate Lefebvre as an *inspiring* sociologist.[3] This is why in this book I discuss the production of Lefebvre's theory by juxtaposing, bringing together, and pulling apart his critical reflections on the general condition of modernity, his research on the processes of urbanization, and his project of spaces for a transforming society.

These are three voices in Lefebvre's writings: research, critique, and project. They were developed in a dialogue with the voices distinguished by Maurice Blanchot in the work of Marx—the scientific discourse, the words of the philosophical logos, and the political speech—which Blanchot described as constantly breaking itself into multiple forms, heterogeneous, divergent, noncontemporaneous; being always and at once tacit and violent, political and scholarly, direct and indirect, total and fragmentary, lengthy and almost instantaneous.[4] The attention to this polyphony governed Lefebvre's readings of Marx's work, which opposed, more often than not, its dominant interpretations, whether the official doctrine of the Stalinist Soviet Union adopted by the French Communist Party (PCF) during the immediate postwar period or the structuralist Marxism of the 1960s. At the same time Lefebvre's research, critique, and project are embedded in specific French discussions in 1960s and 1970s philosophy, urban sociology, architecture, and urbanism while also reflecting an international ferment of ideas, including Anglo-American sociology and planning, German philosophy, Italian architectural theory, and dissident revisions of Marxism, both Western and Central European.

These debates reverberate in the empirical studies Lefebvre was involved in, or rather in his "concrete" research—the term that he preferred and that the authors of the comprehensive *Méthodes des sciences sociales* (Methods of Social Sciences, 1964) defined as aiming at either a "practical application" or a "theoretical discovery" but distinguished from a "theoretical and abstract reflection."[5] This included his studies on the Pyrenean communities commissioned by the Musée national des arts et traditions populaires (MNATP) during the Second World War; his research in rural and urban sociology at the Centre d'études sociologiques (CES) from the 1940s until the early 1960s; the interdisciplinary research projects headed by him as a professor in Strasbourg (1961–65) and

Nanterre (1965–73); and the studies on practices of dwelling carried out by the Institut de sociologie urbaine (ISU), which Lefebvre cofounded in 1962 and over which he presided until 1973.

It is from within these engagements that his understanding of space was developed by means of three main theoretical decisions: the shift of the research focus from space to processes of its production; the embrace of the multiplicity of social practices that produce space and make it socially productive; and the focus on the contradictory, conflictual, and, ultimately, political character of the processes of production of space. While dwelling on a range of empirical and historical studies, this understanding of space was formulated in opposition to much of French sociology of the 1950s and early 1960s and its quantitative and statistical methods. Rather, Lefebvre aimed at a qualitative approach with particular attention to the irreducible and singular lived experience: an approach that not only posed the question of generalization as a major theoretical challenge for his theory but also prevented him from formulating a fully operative method of sociological research. This resulted, until very recently, in the scarcity of empirical studies developed along the lines of his theory, in France as much as elsewhere.[6]

Examining the relationships among the three voices making up Lefebvre's work allows us to distinguish it from the discourse of what he identified as his main ideological opponents: the planning state and postwar functionalist urbanism. Lefebvre's theory needs to be contextualized within the efforts of the French state since the 1960s to refound the procedures of urban planning on a new type of knowledge about processes of urbanization, a knowledge that is not only operative but also self-critical. With the introduction of procedures of inhabitants' participation in urban planning, an increasing politicization of its operations, and an active stimulation of critical urban research, including Marxist research, French planning institutions embarked on a process of institutionalization of critique: the very condition that Michel Foucault began to examine at the end of the 1970s in his genealogy of liberalism.[7]

This book shows that these processes not only paralleled the formulation of Lefebvre's theory of space, published in six books between 1968 (*Le droit à la ville, The Right to the City*) and 1974 (*The Production of Space*), but also constituted both its condition and its target: its *condition* because Lefebvre's courses and seminars in urban sociology during his professorships in Strasbourg and Nanterre contributed to the academization of urban sociology in France and because almost all of the urban empirical studies he was involved in were commissioned by state institutions aiming at developing alternatives to the postwar functionalist urbanism; its *target* because much of his work addressed the incorporation of critical concepts into the increasingly self-critical French state planning discourse, including Lefebvre's concepts as well, such as the postulate to grant the "right to the city" and "centrality" to the inhabitants by accounting for their "everyday life" and "lived space." In other words, what was at stake was not just a co-optation of critical discourse about the city and its transformation into a "stimulus of capitalism," as it was argued at that time by such Marxist theorists of architecture as Manfredo Tafuri,[8] but also a decisive step in a constitution of a regime of governance based on institutionalized critique. What distinguishes Lefebvre's writings from a more operative and more direct cooperation with architects, planners, and administrators, which characterized the work of Chombart since the early 1950s, was his attempt to rethink the production of space at this stage of the historical process of entanglement between power and knowledge—from within which his own theory was formulated—and his attempt to challenge the institutionalization of the translations among research, critique, and project by identifying the gaps between them as possible sites for a politics of space.

These translations were at the core of Lefebvre's attacks on modern architecture and functionalist urbanism and their promise to develop a general account of the inherited modes of urbanization into a critique of unacceptable social, technological, political, and aesthetic conditions and, in the second step, their attempt to derive from this critique a design of a new space for a new society. Much of this redefinition of architecture as a heteronomous discipline whose operations cannot be based on preexisting aesthetic norms was developed within the CIAM (Congrès internationaux d'architecture moderne), the organization founded in 1928 that gathered a rising group of architects and planners committed to the modern movement.[9] In particular, Lefebvre targeted the main document of the prewar CIAM: the Athens Charter (1933), which defined the "functional city" by means of four main functions of urbanization: living, working, and recreation, linked by transportation.

Much of Lefebvre's critique of the CIAM was prefigured by the discussions between its members and sympathizers since the 1940s, such as Lewis Mumford, who argued that cities cannot be conceived without accounting for political, cultural, and educational functions. During the postwar congresses in the late 1940s and early 1950s the doctrine of functionalism was complemented by attention to urbanity, monumentality, collective public spaces, and historical centers of cities, and the relationship between research and design was complicated by a declared opening of architectural practice toward a critique, both "rational" and "affective," by individuals, the general public, and the authorities.[10] Yet Lefebvre's critique did not register much of this evolution of the CIAM discourse, even when it shared some of his own concerns, as was the case with the younger generation of members (Team 10), who, in the course of the 1950s, had been moving away from the doctrine of the four functions and the global and universalist perspective in order to address the practices of dwelling within the Western welfare states and the consumer societies. Rather, the primary target of Lefebvre's writings during the mid-1960s and the early 1970s was the prewar doctrine of the CIAM and its influence on the production of space in Europe and beyond. In that sense, his work was inscribed into a climate of a wholesale revision of modern architecture and functionalist urbanism: a revision not always sufficiently informed and itself subsequently questioned by historiographies of both the CIAM and the modern movement's "other traditions."[11] This suggests that Lefebvre's writings on architecture and urbanism need to be understood within their specific historical condition, including the general shift in French urbanism away from the mass housing estates of the postwar period (*grands ensembles*) and also coinciding with the experience of formal and theoretical experimentation in French architectural culture between the death of Le Corbusier in 1965 and the mid-1970s, when various paths within, beyond, and against the legacy of the modern movement were tested.

At the same time, it was in the course of these debates that the disciplinary identity of architecture, its formal techniques, conceptual frameworks, and social obligations were revised, providing orientation points for discourses and designs until today. Lefebvre's call for a unitary knowledge about urban space coincided with the attempts of French architects to redefine their disciplinary competence and political responsibility as producers of such knowledge. Consequently, when in 1971 he compared his work to that of an architect who is "an intellectual, . . . brought to pose problems which are the same as those I pose,"[12] this statement pointed to a shift in architectural culture, with the architects claiming the position of intellectuals speaking on behalf of urban space. Lefebvre's contributions to architectural culture in the course of the 1960s prefigured this role, going far beyond the publication of his books, including contributions to architectural journals and catalogues of design exhibitions and the supervision of PhD dissertations focused on architecture and urbanism, as well as his participation in the reorganization of architectural education around 1968, his jury participation in architectural competitions, his editorial policies attentive to architectural themes, and his organization of interdisciplinary research projects.

The figure of research, critique, and project was chosen to structure the following chapters, because of its central role in Lefebvre's work, but also because such reading captures the relevance of this work for urban research and design today. Yet to read Lefebvre today requires accounting for the historical continuities and ruptures between the processes of urbanization as he analyzed them and the current conditions of production of space. In particular, it requires coming to terms with the undermining of the credibility of his theory by the increasing co-optation of his concepts into the discourses of dominant agents of the production of space in France as much as beyond and the crisis of Marxism after the end of state socialism in Central and Eastern Europe. In the first chapter of this book both challenges are historicized in order to argue that the co-optation of critical discourse and the necessity to revise Marxism in view of the development of postwar capitalist and state socialist societies were major stimuli for Lefebvre's studies in rural and urban sociology, as well as his contributions to French architectural culture. A review of these engagements not only reveals the impact on Lefebvre's concepts and research methods of the institutional contexts in which they were developed but also allows interrogating the interdependencies between the formulation of his theory of space and the disciplinary transformations of architecture, urbanism, and urban sociology in the late 1960s and early 1970s. Chapter 1 shows that Lefebvre's theorizing of space aimed at explaining the transformation of regimes of governance, the restructuring of class composition of Western societies, and a change of the regimes of production of knowledge that condition the processes of urbanization beyond the Fordist–Keynesian welfare state.

In chapter 2, I argue that the fundamental theses of Lefebvre's work, including the concept of space being socially produced and productive, are directly related to the research on the practices of dwelling in the studies of the ISU. These studies were focused on the *pavillon,* or the suburban house, and the *grands ensembles,* or the collective housing estates—two spatial forms considered symptomatic of French postwar urbanization, with the former often linked to the privatization of the everyday life in the emerging consumption society, and the latter seen as a result of the state intervention in the postwar housing crisis and as a framework of forthcoming forms of spatial segregation among social groups. These studies are considered in light of Lefebvre's account of the new town of Mourenx in southwestern France, his review of a series of urban designs (including the functionalist new town of Furttal near Zurich), and his engagements in the architectural debates of the 1960s and '70s inscribed into the revision of the modern movement. Chapter 2 also argues that the practices of dwelling investigated by the ISU—the appropriation of space and its consumption—and the critique of ideology of the *pavillon* pursued by the *institut* were direct sources for Lefebvre's understanding of space as perceived, conceived, lived, and produced by material practices, practices of representation, and everyday practices of appropriation. With the consumption of space and the practice of its appropriation becoming two paradigmatic practices for theorizing the production of urban space today, this reading of Lefebvre's work allows an understanding of the emergence of these two antithetical paradigms and their theoretical and political consequences.

What allowed Lefebvre to generalize the results of his specific studies and to relate them to an account of the historical development of capitalism was the main philosophical argument of his theory of space: that space is a *concrete abstraction.* For Lefebvre, this argument became the basis of a critical knowledge of space, in the double sense that "critique" took on in Western philosophical culture since Kant: as an eradication of error and as a research on the limits of faculty or practice—in this context, the limits of thinking and producing space.

In chapter 3, I argue that a reading of Hegel and Marx, in particular the latter's discussions of labor, commodity, and money, allowed Lefebvre to examine space as the general form of social practice in capitalist modernities, characterized by distinctive features, such as its simultaneous homogenization and fragmentation and its blend of illusion and reality. Lefebvre's take on concrete abstraction staked out his research program on space and opened up its two perspectives: a deductive account of the most general principle of social space unfolding in history, and a historical and empirical study about specific conjunctures of practices producing space. It is in the tensions between these two research perspectives and in the attempts to mediate between them that the core concepts of the theory of production of space were developed.

In chapter 3, I argue that Lefebvre's theorizing of space as a whole produced by multiple social practices opened new prospects for a transdiciplinary research on space, which still awaits its development. If Lefebvre's theory allows linking the efforts of various disciplines focused on specific practices of production of space, it is because the understanding of space as a concrete abstraction shifts the discussion from an ontology of space to an "epistemology of the urban": a broad theoretical framework for studying the "compete urbanization of the society."[13] At the same time this theorizing of space as a whole, with its underlying dialectics of singularity, particularity, and universality, has the potential to inform current research on transnational urbanization, postcolonial spaces, and global restructuring of statehood—areas in which Lefebvre's work has been recently used most fruitfully.[14]

In chapter 4, I discuss the "project" of Lefebvre, understood as research on the possible tendencies of social and spatial development based on an investigation into the emerging "urban" society. Lefebvre saw these tendencies being manifested in protorevolutionary conjunctures of urban practice, such as the Commune of 1871 and the Parisian May 1968: moments in which the concepts of centrality, dwelling, difference, and scale were experienced as presentiments of a different society. This chapter reads these concepts together with several architectural designs, including such seemingly disparate ones as the "unitary architecture" of Charles Fourier; the City in Space, by Ricardo Bofill and the Taller de arquitectura; the New Babylon, by Constant Nieuwenhuys; and the project for New Belgrade, developed in the mid-1980s by Serge Renaudie, Pierre Guilbaud, and Lefebvre himself. This does not mean that Lefebvre's project can be approximated by specific architectures or that his concepts can offer a common denominator for architectural designs. Rather, his project is discussed as consisting of an operation proceeding "from the (given) real to the possible,"[15] which was recognized by several architects in the late 1960s as the specific competence of architectural practice. Through a reading of the discussions between Lefebvre and Manfredo Tafuri, this chapter suggests that such understanding of the "project" goes beyond the impasse of the Marxist critique of architecture, which is still today overshadowed by Tafuri's argument that the architectural practice is unable to transcend its position within the capitalist division of labor.

In this perspective, the confrontation between architectural projects and Lefebvre's writings aims at questioning them in view of urbanization tendencies, which he himself described and yet which seem to undermine the emancipatory potential of his concepts. This involves discussing Lefebvre's praise of urban centrality in the context of the exacerbating social and spatial segregation between the center of Paris and the suburbs as he experienced it in Nanterre; revising his belief in dwelling as the paradigmatic practice of production of space in view of the increasing privatization and gentrification of urban spaces modeled according to domestic interiors; challenging his theorization of difference in the face of the cultural logics of consumption as differentiation; and questioning the possibility of a politics of scale in a situation in which the traditional homologies between spatial forms and social groups are undermined by the increasing mobility of urban populations, the multiplication of modes of belonging, and the crisis of traditional political associations. These discussions situate architecture and urban planning of the 1960s and 1970s within a broad account of the urban condition of that period, but they also suggest how to discuss architecture today in view of sociospatial marginalization and exclusion in metropolitan areas; the transformation of the urban sphere into a productive resource, its valorization by capital, and its appropriation by the dominant social classes; but also in view of counterhegemonic strategies and urban protest movements.[16]

By devoting a chapter to research, critique, and project, this book does not address distinct parts of Lefebvre's theory but rather suggests three starting points from which the relationships among these three voices are negotiated within a transdisciplinary research on space. The basis for such research was provided by the concept of production of space itself, and thus one way of reading this book is to consider it as an extended commentary on this concept: from an account of its formulation in the course of his various "concrete" studies discussed in chapter 1, through the analysis of practices of dwelling as practices of production of space in chapter 2 and a critical account of production of space as a decisive step in the historical development of capitalism in chapter 3, to the research on the emancipatory possibilities of socially produced space finally in chapter 4.

By focusing on the empirical research of Lefebvre and on his exchanges with architects and urbanists, I advance the vibrant discussion of historical and theoretical relevance of his work in general and specifically his theory of space. This discussion has been marked by the essays of Michel Trebitsch;[17] Rob Shields's *Lefebvre, Love and Struggle: Spatial Dialectics* (1996), the intellectual biography of Lefebvre that followed Rémi Hess's *Henri Lefebvre et l'aventure du siècle* (Henri Lefebvre and the Adventure of the Century, 1988); Edward Soja's *Postmodern*

Geographies: The Reassertion of Space in Critical Social Theory (1989) and his *Thirdspace: Journeys to Los Angeles and Other Real-and-Imagined Places* (1996); Stuart Elden's philosophically oriented *Understanding Henri Lefebvre: Theory and the Possible* (2004); Christian Schmid's conceptual reconstruction of Lefebvre's theory of space in *Stadt, Raum und Gesellschaft: Henri Lefebvre und die Theorie der Produktion des Raumes* (City, Space, and Society: Henri Lefebvre and the Theory of Production of Space, 2005); Andy Merrifield's broad overview *Henri Lefebvre: A Critical Introduction* (2006); and the recent volume edited by Kanishka Goonewardena, Stefan Kipfer, Christian Schmid, and Richard Milgrom, *Space, Difference, Everyday Life* (2008), to mention just a few.[18]

This book shares with the last volume the attention to empirical urban research: both Lefebvre's own research and the case studies that reveal the epistemic value of his theory beyond the formulation of its author. This focus is, according to the editors of *Space, Difference, Everyday Life,* one of the main characteristics of what they see as the current, "third constellation of Lefebvre's readings," in distinction to two previous ones in Anglo-American scholarship, including the urban political–economic readings centered on David Harvey since the 1970s and the introduction of Lefebvre's work into the "postmodern geographies" of Edward Soja within the spatial, cultural, and linguistic turn in social sciences and the humanities in the 1980s.[19] But what seems to be specific for this turn to empirical studies in the recent readings of Lefebvre is their explicitly global scope, which accounts not only for a striking multiplicity of centers of urbanization and the variety of its patterns today but also for an equal multiplicity and variety of centers of production of knowledge about urbanization. Following this sensitivity, this book departs from the Anglo-American discussions and extends them by accounting for the theory of production of space in French, German-speaking, and Central European contexts—an attempt that clearly does not exhaust the receptions of Lefebvre's work today, and thus needs to be read as program for further research.[20]

Henri Lefebvre
The Production of Theory

T HE INCREASING INTERNATIONAL INTEREST in the theory of production of space in urban research since the late 1980s appears somehow paradoxical in the face of the historical conditions that seem most unfavorable for a rereading of Lefebvre's work. First, what does it mean to read Lefebvre's Marxist theory in the course of the symbolic liquidation of socialism; after the end of the Soviet Union and other socialist states in Europe and the evolution of China; in the face of the vanishing of the international communist movements and the decline of the communist parties; and given the gradual dismantling of the postwar institutional compromises in Western Europe, which stemmed from socialist inspiration and for which Marxism was a major theoretical reference?[1] More specifically, what is the relevance of Lefebvre's work for urban research today, after the political and economic end of the regimes that instrumentalized Marxist rhetoric and, to a certain extent, realized some Marxist postulates, such as that of undoing, or at least limiting, the commodification of space?[2] While the economic, financial, and social crisis at the end of the first decade of this century challenged the intellectual delegitimization of Marxism, which became, again, attractive to an increasing number of readers both in the former East and in the "former West," this challenge was not followed by a theoretical and political reassessment of twentieth-century socialism, a theme increasingly handed over from the discipline of "transitology" to that of history of the "century of totalitarianisms." Where the readings of Lefebvre are concerned, this omission feeds into the routine of legitimizing his work as having nothing to do with popular democracies in Central and Eastern Europe—as if the greatest possible achievement for a Marxist intellectual would have been to ignore the historically unprecedented attempt to realize socialism that he witnessed during his life, however disappointing this realization might have been. Yet, in fact, Lefebvre himself was much more thoughtful about the end of socialist states in Europe, which he witnessed just before his death in 1991 and whose importance for his work he admitted without having enough time to reflect upon.[3] It is thus necessary to interrogate the cognitive value of Lefebvre's theory in today's postsocialist urban condition, which is not limited to the situation of the countries behind the former Iron Curtain but which encompasses both a state of mind and the all-too-real deconstruction of Fordist–Keynesian national welfare states with the concomitant shift in patterns of urbanization, urban morphologies, and development policies around the globe.

But this apparent "failure" of the philosophical and political foundations of Lefebvre's theory is not the only challenge for its reading today. With the concepts coined or shaped by Lefebvre, such as "centrality," "monuments," "urban everyday," and even "the right to the city," having been increasingly incorporated into dominant discourses of architects, planners, administrators, and developers, his work seems to be at least equally undermined by its own "success." Thus, Lefebvre's theory would share the fate of what Luc Boltanski and Eve Chiapello in *The New Spirit of Capitalism* (1999) described as "artistic critique," focused on demands of autonomy, creativity, and authenticity, put into crisis in the course of the 1970s and 1980s by "its seeming success and the ease in which it found itself recuperated and exploited by capitalism."[4] The situation in his native France is particularly symptomatic in this respect, where the presence of Lefebvre's concepts in mainstream discourse on architecture and urbanism during the last forty years is countered by an almost equally long tendency toward erasing his name from this discourse,[5] an erasure effectuated often by those influenced by Lefebvre's work to such an extent that they have no choice but to deny it in order to preserve their own identity. Does this mean that Lefebvre's theory has been suppressed—or rather "superseded" and reduced to mere slogans, with the concept of the "right to the city," to continue with one example, becoming an empty battle cry when detached from its specific historical context of the late 1960s and the social and spatial struggles around the French welfare state?

This double challenge is addressed in this chapter from within a historical account of the formulation of Lefebvre's theory of space. This requires contextualizing the formulation of his theory in his involvements in urban sociology, architecture, and urbanism. These engagements, stretching from the 1940s to the 1980s, reflect the transformations of the French society during the *trente glorieuses,* the period between the Liberation in 1944 and the oil crisis in 1973. Starting with the Reconstruction and rapid postwar urbanization paralleled by demographic and economic growth, the period addressed in this chapter continues through the emergence of the society of consumption over the course of the 1950s, to the processes of decolonization resulting in the shift of the target markets from the colonies toward advanced countries, followed by an effort at economic and social modernization.[6] Within a wide overview of Lefebvre's work, this chapter focuses on the decade between the mid-1960s and mid-1970s, when his main books about space were published and when the questions of the city and urban space were given an unprecedented importance in France. This was paralleled by the critical urban sociology entering academia, the broad interest in qualitative methods of urban research, the beginnings of architectural research, the politicization of urbanism and the simultaneous introduction of urban questions into French politics, the shifts in French planning from the postwar collective estates toward the concept of the new towns, and the transition away from the concepts, images, and criteria coined by the architectural avant-gardes of the early twentieth century.

After a general introduction to Lefebvre's contribution to research in rural and urban sociology and to architecture and planning culture in France, this chapter develops a reading of his theory in view of the crisis of Marxism and the institutionalization of critique seen not as recent shifts in the context of its reception but rather as two essential conditions in which this theory itself was formulated. The review of Lefebvre's research projects shows that these studies were what made him aware of the necessity to revise such Marxist categories as class struggle, alienation, division of labor, and commodity fetishism and the urgency to complement and transform them by a critique targeting new themes, such as everyday life, consumption, and technocracy.[7] This was paralleled by his critique of state socialism in Central and Eastern Europe, which stemmed from a political disappointment but also brought about a theoretical challenge concerning the understanding of the "socialist city" as a reality and as a project. At the same time, in view of the transformations of the institutional context in which Lefebvre's research on space was carried out in the late 1960s and early 1970s, his theory is to be understood as a constant negotiation of his critical discourse with the self-critical discourse of the French state and its planning institutions. Thus, while this chapter contextualizes the theory of the production of space within the Fordist–Keynesian planning state in France of the 1950s and 1960s associated with what Lefebvre called the "bureaucratic society of controlled consumption," it also discusses his attempt to rethink the condition of this society moving beyond Fordism.[8]

Empirical Research, Urban Sociology, Architectural Practice

If one were to draw a diagram connecting the sequential places of Lefebvre's life and work, it would resemble the railway network in France; that is, it would look like a star centered on Paris with its arms reaching to the provinces. His journey across this diagram started and ended in southwestern France, at the foot of the Pyrenees, where he was born in 1901 in Hagetmau, in the old Département des Landes, and where he died in 1991 in the maternal house in Navarrenx, fifty kilometers south of Hagetmau, in the ancient Département de Béarn. After passing through Saint Brieuc, in Bretagne, Lefebvre was sent to Paris, where he attended the Lycée Louis-le-Grand and later studied philosophy at the Sorbonne, writing his thesis under the idealist philosopher Léon Brunschvicg. Until the end of the 1930s, Lefebvre left Paris several times either to recover his poor health, which led him to study for two semesters in Aix-en-Provence under the Christian philosopher Maurice Blondel, or to take temporary jobs as a professor in the secondary school in Privas, in southern France, and later in Montargis, east of Paris, during which time he returned periodically to work in the Citroën factories at the Quai de Javel and as a taxi driver. After the Second World War and the often dramatic moves from Paris to Aix and later to Marseille, the Béarn, and the Pyrenees, Lefebvre passed through Toulouse on his way back to Paris, where he was employed in various research and teaching institutions, including the Centre national de la recherche scientifique (CNRS) beginning in 1948 and, after a professorship in Strasbourg (1961–65), at the university in Paris Nanterre (1965–73). For this period the train diagram needs to be superimposed with a chart of his flights from Parisian airports, which account for his numerous journeys to all the continents where he was invited to teach, lecture, advise, and research.[9]

The 1920s and 1930s were the formative years for Lefebvre, with his adherence to the dadaists and surrealists; his cofounding of the Philosophes group (with Pierre Morhange, Georges Politzer, and later Norbert Guterman and Georges Friedmann); his translations of the early philosophical writings of Marx, undertaken with Guterman; and his joining of the French Communist Party (PCF) in 1928.[10] In the course of these exchanges with others in his world, the main tenets, interests, aims, and styles of his writing were established: the anti-systematic way of thinking, the attempt to relate heterogeneous philosophical traditions, the conviction about the necessity of linking lived experience and philosophical thought to concrete social practice, and the interest in everyday life.[11]

Also at that time, however, Lefebvre carried out his first empirical studies, developing them in various locations as he was changing jobs. To the first of them belonged the *rabcors*—the studies carried out by the "workers–surveyors" on demand of the Third Internationale. He examined the Lafarge cement factories, the silk industry in the Lyon region, the switchyard Dutel, and a telephone exchange in Paris, where he carried out interviews and statistical analyses.[12] As professor in Privas he investigated the social structure in the Département de l'Ardèche on the request of one of the trade unions.[13] The results of this research, based on official statistics, were published in a local journal of the teachers' trade union, presenting data about the composition of social groups, with special attention to agricultural and industrial workers, and charting gender structure as well as the size and type of factories. Aware of the insufficiency of these data, Lefebvre called for the workers' contributions to the research, which he considered necessary for political action: he argued that knowledge about the specificity of each location and its social structure is indispensable for "steering revolutionary action" and for translating ideas and general concepts into claims relevant for particular local conditions and immediately understandable to the masses.[14] Another experience that might have been relevant to his future work on space and the urban society was his membership in the municipal council in Montargis; elected from a pro-Communist list (1935–39), Lefebvre was directly involved with the decisions concerning schooling, the supply of water and gas, and street lighting.[15]

From the Rural to the Urban

The first empirical research that can be shown to have significantly influenced Lefebvre's theory of the production of space was the study of the peasant communities in the Campan Valley, in the Pyrenees, for which he gave up his initial project of a philosophical dissertation planned under the title "La pensée française et l'individualisme" (French Thought and Individualism).[16] The study on Campan was commissioned in 1943 by the ethnographer Georges-Henri Rivière, the director of the Musée national des arts et traditions populaires in Paris, founded in 1937 under the Popular Front, the alliance of left-wing movements that had won the parliamentary elections in the previous year. At the time when the question of folklore and its relationship to national identity became a profoundly political issue in prewar Europe, Rivière's take on ethnography differed from the conservative understanding of Frenchness, which was rooted in rural landscapes and peasantry as the residuum of the nation's culture. Rather, he was convinced of the heterogeneity of preindustrial popular civilizations in France, which he intended to investigate in the course of their transformation under the impact of contemporary processes of urbanization and modernization.[17] This is also how he saw the study of the Campan Valley; Albert Soboul, the future author of the Marxist history of the French Revolution and a member of the team of Rivière, explained to Lefebvre that the research should "encompass all aspects of one type of rural civilization in its historical evolution and specific geographical context" and stressed that what was interesting for the *musée* was a "study of a specific environment *[milieu]* in its current condition, informed by its historical evolution."[18]

Lefebvre developed his research in the framework of the *chantiers intellectuelles* (literally: intellectual work sites). The *chantiers* were intended to provide

SECRÉTARIAT D'ÉTAT AU TRAVAIL

COMMISSARIAT
A LA LUTTE CONTRE LE CHÔMAGE
4, Rue de Presbourg
PARIS (16ᵉ)

RÉGIE DE DÉPENSES
21, Rue de Berri - PARIS (8ᵉ)

Modèle N° 46

QUESTIONNAIRE

Nom **LEFEBVRE** Prénoms *Henri-François-Marie* Nationalité *Française*

Adresse *chez Mᵉ Gaubert chemin Henri ?, Gerde (Hᵗᵉˢ Pyrénées)*

Date et lieu de naissance *Hagetmau (Landes) 16 juin 1901*

Situation de famille : *2*

Nom, prénoms, religion et nationalité de votre père *Lefebvre, René, nationalité française, religion catholique.*

Nom de jeune fille, prénoms, religion et nationalité de votre mère *Darracq, Jeanne, nation. française, religion catholique.*

Etes-vous célibataire, marié, veuf ou divorcé ? *Divorcé et remarié.*

Si vous êtes marié , nationalité de votre mari / femme } *française*

Quel est son nom de jeune fille ? *Valet, Henriette*

Nombre et date de naissance des enfants à charge ? *Quatre dont deux entièrement à ma charge*

Avez-vous d'autres personnes à charge ? *(nés le 10-10-25 ; à 26-9-26 ; à 20-1-28 ; à 27-1-30.*

Appartenez-vous à la religion juive ? *Néant* *Non*

Avez-vous appartenu à une association secrète (cf. Loi du 13 août 1940) ? *Non*

Etes-vous immatriculé aux Assurances Sociales ? *Non* N° d'immatriculation

Situation militaire, Grade *Sanitaire ?-classe* Arme *6ᵉ comp. secret État major.*

Service Armé ? Auxiliaire ? Exempté ? Réformé ? Non appelé ? ~~~~~~ *Service armé*

Bénéficiez-vous d'une pension, d'une retraite civile ou militaire ? *Non*

Degré d'instruction *Etudes d'enseignement supérieur.*

Quels diplômes possédez-vous ? *Baccalauréat, Licence, diplôme études supérieures.*

Quelles langues étrangères connaissez-vous ? *Allemand*

Etes-vous comptable ? *Non*

Etes-vous titulaire d'un permis de conduire ? *Oui*

Motocyclette . Tourisme *Oui.* Poids Lourds

Quels étaient vos derniers appointements ? *19.600*

Votre mari est-il employé ? femme est-elle employée ? } *Oui*

Dans l'affirmative, dans quelle entreprise ? *Central Téléphonique Moulins (Allier)*

Quels sont ses appointements ? *21.400.*

Etes-vous inscrit : A un Office départemental de placement ? *Non* Lequel ?

A une Caisse de chômage ? *Non* Laquelle ?

Imp. du Centre—462—9-42.

Divorced and remarried, father of four, university graduate, staff officer, fluent in German, unemployed—this is how Henri Lefebvre described his personal situation when taking up his research position at the Musée national des arts et traditions populaires. Questionnaire of the Commissariat à la lutte contre le chômage, 26 October 1943. Courtesy of the Archives of Musée national des arts et traditions populaires, Paris, dossier Henri Lefebvre.

employment for intellectual workers who had lost their jobs in the economic disorder caused by defeat and the occupation. (Lefebvre's personal situation was particularly precarious: he was responsible for four children, constantly losing jobs in secondary education because of his Communist affiliation, and arrested twice by the German occupiers and their Vichy allies.)[19] The *chantiers* offered the possibility of carrying out research projects not normally funded by republican governments, at the same time giving the researchers the chance to be spared forced labor in Germany.[20] Rivière organized four *chantiers,* dealing with rural architecture (*chantier* no. 1425); traditional rural furniture (no. 909); crafts and traditions of peasantry, such as pottery, metallurgy, weaving, and techniques of wood and basketry (no. 1810); and one whose task was to process the reports, drawings, photographs, and documentation produced by other *chantiers* (no. 1817).[21]

Lefebvre participated in the *chantier* 1810 from 1943 to 1946, in the section of physical and human geography and economic and social history. Like every other researcher he was required to keep a daily journal of his scientific activities and, on the 25th of each month, to submit a review of his archival research carried out in the archives of Campan and larger cities of the region.[22] Lefebvre, who envisaged turning the research into a dissertation under the supervision of Maurice Halbwachs,[23] consulted Rivière intensely about it, but also consulted Soboul, who participated in the same section of the *chantier* 1810, and Charles Struys, who had investigated rural architecture in Campan.[24] This work was contextualized in one of the most controversial debates in avant-garde architecture of the 1930s, to which Rivière, a friend of Le Corbusier, contributed: the debate over the relationship between modern and vernacular architecture, understood as a manifestation of the universal human condition and a poetic inspiration for modern civilizations rather than a shrine of national values.[25]

The letter exchange with Rivière reveals Lefebvre's ambition to enlarge the scope of the research beyond a set of local studies and to present the Campan Valley as nested in the general historical, social, and economic development of the region.[26] Thus, one of the first aims of the study was to explain the particularism of the valley by reference to the general history of France and the region, its "general laws," and its "rhythms of development."[27] Accordingly, in the report about June and August 1945, Lefebvre informed Rivière that in response to the "problems of generalization" of his research in Campan, he had launched two new investigations: one focused on Navarrenx, a fourteenth-century *bastide* (fortified new town) and a small commercial center, where his mother owned a house; the other focused on the vestiges of agrarian communities in the Basque region of Soule, between the settlements of Mauléon and Tardets.[28] This scope was broadened still further in the months to come.[29] After one year, Lefebvre reported to Rivière: "The local polls in Campan, vallée de Lais de pays d'Albert, Bourbonnais, Mayenne, that I have worked on are still insufficient in order to establish

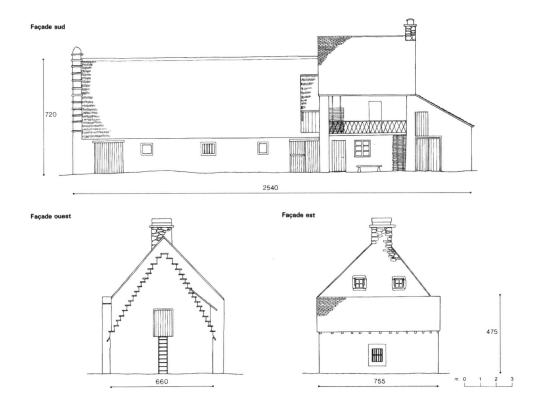

House in Haut Adour, in the Campan Valley. The architecture of the valley was inventoried in the 1940s by Charles Struys, Lefebvre's colleague at the Musée national des arts et traditions populaires. This drawing was made in 1980 and published in Bidart et al., *Pays aquitains,* 215.

well-founded conclusions." The framework that these conclusions were aimed at supporting was envisaged as truly monumental: Lefebvre wanted to address "dialectically" what he called the "grand laws of evolution of folklore" as a part of a work on "the relationships between the rational and the irrational in history," and he planned the *History of the Rural Community,* the first volume of the *Rural History in France,* prepared with Soboul.[30] This ambition to contextualize specific studies within larger historical processes, combined with the awareness of the dangers of illegitimate extrapolation, became an idiosyncrasy of Lefebvre's research on space in the 1960s and 1970s.

Lefebvre resigned from his position at the Musée national des arts et traditions populaires in 1946 and, after an episode in Radio Toulouse with Tristan Tzara and a short return to secondary education, he was employed in 1948 by the Centre national de la recherche scientifique, the main institution responsible for scientific research in France. It was in the newly created Centre d'études sociologiques (CES) of the CNRS that his research on the Campan Valley was broadened, developed, and defended as a *doctorat d'État* in 1954 at the Sorbonne.[31]

The dissertation was supervised by the sociologist Georges Gurvitch, because Maurice Halbwachs, initially envisaged as the supervisor, had been detained by the Gestapo and died in the Buchenwald concentration camp in 1945. It was based on the archival research developed within the framework of the *chantier* 1810 as well as on 150 surveys, interviews, and observations on the ground carried out during Lefebvre's affiliation with the CES.[32] Developing the plan sketched for Rivière, Lefebvre enlarged the scope of the research to all of the Pyrenean communities, which are the focus of the principal dissertation, while the complementary dissertation was devoted specifically to Campan. The latter, together with the gathered archival documents, was formally published in 1963 under the title *La vallée de Campan: Étude de sociologie rurale* (The Campan Valley: Study in Rural Sociology).[33]

Lefebvre was employed at the Centre d'études sociologiques until 1961, with one year of expulsion for his Communist affiliation (1951–52),[34] and this period was essential for the development of his thinking in general and specifically for the development of this theory of space and the urban society. Founded in 1946 on the initiative of Georges Gurvitch, the CES was to become a facilitator of the renewal of sociology in France, together with other institutions set up in this period, including the Institut national des études démographiques, and Section IV of the École pratique des hautes études, founded by the historian Lucien Febvre.[35] With Gurvitch, Febvre, the sociologists Marcel Mauss, Louis Massignon, and Georges Friedmann (whom Lefebvre knew from the prewar Philosophes group); the anthropologist Paul Rivet; the psychologist Henri Wallon; and the jurists Gabriel Le Bras and Henri Lévy-Bruhl passing through the CES, the *centre* functioned as a meeting point of established researchers and the new generation of sociologists, particularly important in view of the weak institutionalization of French sociology in the 1940s and 1950s.[36]

Among the most active researchers at the *centre* was Paul-Henry Chombart de Lauwe, whose Groupe d'ethnologie sociale developed a series of empirical studies focused on popular neighborhoods and suburbs of Paris with the improvement of housing policy in view beginning in the early 1950s, and it continued with commissioned research on worker's housing and new housing typologies.[37] This was complemented by the work of its spin-off, the Bureau d'études sociotechniques, created in 1953 by Chombart as a private nonprofit organization and renamed the Centre d'étude des groupes sociaux (CEGS) one year later, which carried out commissioned research projects in several French cities.[38] In his studies Chombart developed the concept of everyday life that had been worked on by Lefebvre since the 1930s, at the same time introducing themes that became important for Lefebvre in the years to come. They included the concept of a "sociogeographic space of multiple dimensions," which can be restricted neither to a geographic space nor to a social space detached from the material framework, and an interest

Plan d'une étude sur
La communauté rurale (pastorale) dans les Pyrénées.

I) Les forces productives.
  a) Technologie générale (agricole, pastorale, domestique) et rapport actif de l'homme au sol, au climat. Brève étude.
  b) La division du travail { biologique (sexes, âges)
  (L'économie dite "naturelle" patriarcale } sociale

II) Le mode de production
  a) Les rapports sociaux. Régime et structure de la propriété. Propriété collective et réglementation communautaire de eaux, pâturages, forêts, parcours du bétail.
  b) Propriété privée. Rapports avec la propriété collective. La Maison héréditaire et le patrimoine familial dans les Pyrénées.
  c) Fonction de la vie pastorale dans la formation et la conservation de cette structure sociale.

III) Organisation sociale. La communauté politiquement organisée. Le "voisin" et le droit de voisinage dans les Pyrénées. La "réunion" ou assemblée de communauté. Son fonctionnement. Les pouvoirs. Les rapports avec les autres pouvoirs.

IV/ _des conditions individuelles dans_
la communauté

    a) Serfs et hommes libres au moyen âge.
    b) des cadets dans la famille.
    c) condition des femmes.
    d) le clergé. Les seigneurs.
    e) les "notables" (à partir du XVI siècle)

V/ _La différenciation dans la communauté_
(et sa dissolution interne)

~~Différenciation des individus et des groupes d'individus.~~

Cohésion de la communauté. Sa
résistance aux premiers externes ; sa lutte
contre les pouvoirs féodaux, monarchiques, etc.

Sa dissolution interne. Conditions de
la formation d'une bourgeoisie locale
(et "notables")

L'histoire générale de cette différenciation
et de la dissolution et décadence de
la communauté ancienne, jusqu'à nos
jours.

First two pages of Lefebvre's research project "La communauté rurale (pastorale) dans les Pyrenées." The first page describes the focus of the initial sections of the planned study: forces of production, mode of production, and social organization. The second page describes the study's last two sections, dealing with the internal differentiation of the community. Courtesy of the Archives of Musée national des arts et traditions populaires, Paris, dossier of Henri Lefebvre, attached to letter to Georges-Henri Rivière, 23 January 1944.

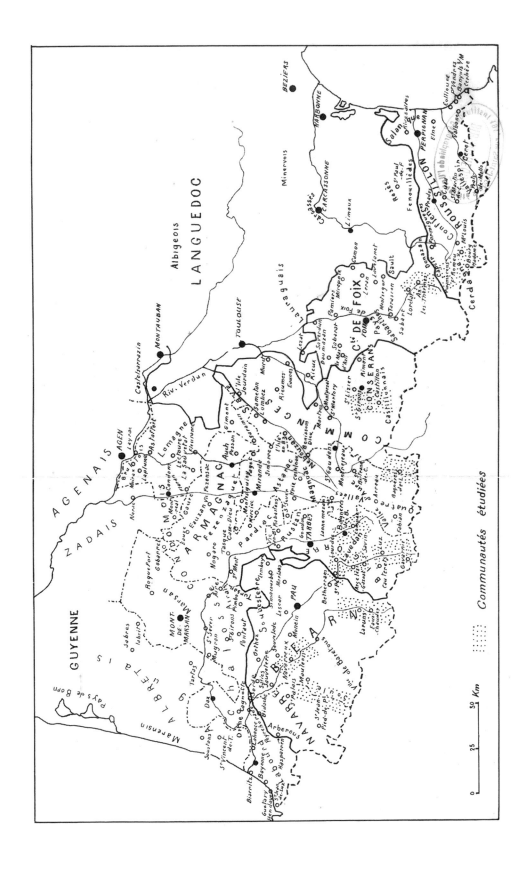

Communautés étudiées

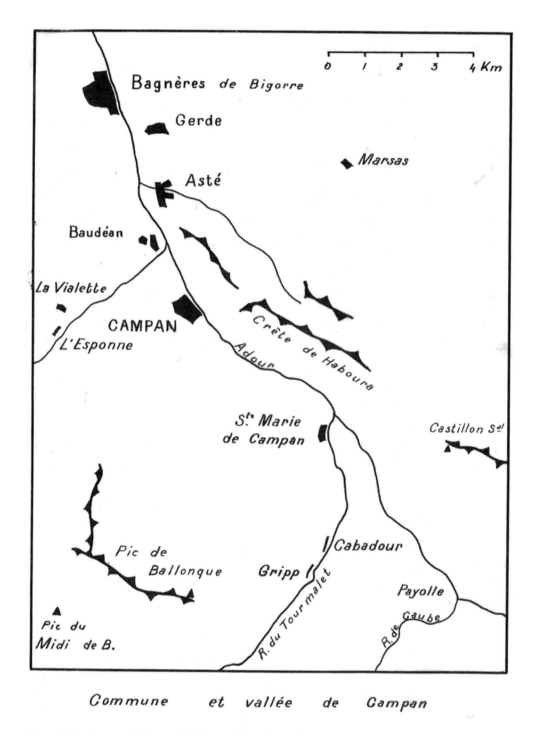

Commune et vallée de Campan

(*above*) The Campan Valley studied by Lefebvre in his dissertation. From Lefebvre, "Une république pastorale." Courtesy of Catherine Régulier.

(*opposite page*) The Pyrenean communities studied by Lefebvre in his dissertation. From Lefebvre, "Une république pastorale." Courtesy of Catherine Régulier.

Henri Lefebvre *(right)* in Navarrenx. Courtesy of Norbert Guterman Archive, Butler Library, Columbia University, dossier Henri Lefebvre, 1939–49.

in the large social transformations expected from the new, collective forms of dwelling.[39] These shared interests were discussed by Chombart and Lefebvre within the CES, without being reflected in references of their publications.[40]

Other sociologists employed by the CES included Henri Raymond, who became a close collaborator of Lefebvre, and his future colleagues at the Nanterre university: Alain Touraine, François Bourricaud, and Michel Crozier. Several unclassifiable figures passed through the CES, such as Pierre Naville, Roland Barthes, and Edgar Morin, who, together with Kostas Axelos and Pierre Fougeyrollas, belonged to the founders of the journal *Arguments* (1956–62). The journal called for the questioning of Marxism by means of empirical research and introduced to the French debates such authors as Georg Lukács, Karl Korsch, Theodor W. Adorno, Herbert Marcuse, and Max Horkheimer. (Lefebvre was closely attached to the group while not belonging to it nominally.)[41] The Marxist geographer, member of the PCF, and Sorbonne professor Pierre George was also linked to the CES, and so was the art historian Pierre Francastel.[42]

As a testing ground of new methods and in complement to the prewar French experiences with American quantitative sociology, the CES was among the first research institutions to launch a systematic program of empirical research with the aim of drawing "an image of the social structure of the liberated France," much in accord with Lefebvre's postulate from his 1948 article published in *Cahiers internationaux de sociologie* to establish an institute of scientific sociology that would launch empirical research on the "reality of France in its totality and its future."[43] With Friedmann working in the sociology of labor, Chombart in urban sociology, and Lefebvre in rural sociology,[44] they were all grappling with the problem of generalization of empirical material, each of them developing an original approach to this problem, carried out by the teams of researchers around them. The CES offered a privileged place for methodological discussions, which took place in seminars focused on techniques of research, with special attention to empirical research.[45] Lefebvre's work from that time combined numerous discussions of methodological questions in rural sociology with investigations of specific case studies. His research in the Pyrenees continued, extending toward research of agrarian policies with an international perspective, including the transformation of the agrarian structure in the socialist states, such as Hungary (1950), and in agricultural cooperatives in Central Europe and in the Mediterranean (1954).[46] In spite of very meager resources made available, Lefebvre traveled to Tuscany to investigate the system of sharecropping, which, begun in the thirteenth century, continued weighing on the social and economic organization of the region. (In a letter written to Norbert Guterman at the beginning of Lefebvre's employment at the CES, he expressed his frustration with the contradiction between the requirement of empirical research and the lack of resources.)[47] This sharecropping research led to Lefebvre's "Traité de sociologie rurale" (Treatise in Rural Sociology), which he claimed to have lost; the finished manuscript was stolen from Lefebvre's car and never reconstructed.[48]

But his activities at the CES were not nearly limited to rural sociology; the leaflets, posters, and programs of the *centre* in the course of the 1950s reveal Lefebvre as an active participant in multiple discussions, seminars, and conferences focused on "industrialization and technocracy," the composition of the contemporary family, and the relationship between cities and coutryside (1951).[49] Within the *centre,* Lefebvre gave talks on the sociology of the mass media (1950, 1955), debated the sociology of Marx with Gurvitch and Naville (1951); discussed the relationship between philosophy and sociology with Maurice Merleau-Ponty (1952), spoke on leisure and the everyday together with Jean Dumazedier (1955), and lectured on society and language (1954)—all themes that reverberate in his later work.[50]

In the autobiographical *Le temps des méprises* (The Time of Mistakes, 1975), Lefebvre looked back at the genesis of his research on space "as the guiding line

Norbert Guterman and Henri Lefebvre. Courtesy of Norbert Guterman Archive, Butler Library, Columbia University, dossier Henri Lefebvre, 1939–49.

through the complexification of the modern world" and noticed that he had "arrived at the problematic of space in many ways."[51] Among the most important of these ways was through his agrarian sociology research on land rent and his questioning of the mutual conditioning between land economies and social relationships. The step yet to be made was to leave behind the concepts of territory or milieu, as employed in French rural history, sociology, human geography, and ethnography, in order to develop the concept of socially produced space by advancing the French discussions of social space: a concept introduced by Maurice Halbwachs in response to the work of Émile Durkheim and Marcel Mauss.[52]

A second perspective from which Lefebvre developed his theory of the production of space was the research on the everyday life of the *trente glorieuses*. At the end of his life, Lefebvre explained his interest in the everyday as stemming from the phenomena he had already witnessed between the world wars: the receding importance of the family, the emerging influence of the global dimension of social practice on the individual life, the growing programming and ordering of the everyday life, and the dominance of the division of labor. Surrealism, he added, was a reaction to these conditions: "Surrealism was a way of life beyond the everyday."[53] At that time the philosophical inspiration for the critique of everyday life came from the tradition of German Romanticism (Friedrich Hölderlin, Novalis, and Ernst Theodor Amadeus Hoffmann), which was extended by a reading of Georg Lukács and Martin Heidegger[54]—even if Lefebvre distinguished his position from the last two.[55] The spatial determinations of everyday life were the focus of the three volumes of his *Critique de la vie quotidienne (Critique of Everyday Life,* first published in French in 1947, 1961, 1981) as well as his *La vie quotidienne dans le monde moderne (Everyday Life in the Modern World,* 1968),[56] discussing the postwar spaces of consumption, the retreat from politics to the domestic interior, the bureaucratic control of urban spaces, and the functionalist refraction of cities into spaces for work, housing, leisure, and transportation.

The First Urban Studies

Lefebvre's research on the everyday as the "rest" that "remains" when the salient aspects of the human world are subtracted was not welcomed by the Communist Party, since it appeared to be external to the fields of political, ideological, and economic struggle of the proletariat, on behalf of which the PCF claimed to be speaking.[57] Consequently, Lefebvre could have continued developing these ideas only after his suspension in 1958 from the PCF—a suspension that, although issued for one year, became permanent:

> It was only after 1956, the year of the famous Khrushchev report, when I decided to study the urban life in its concrete environment. By leaving the Communist Party in 1956 *[sic]*, I could give myself free rein to what had been mere premonitions, intuitions until then.[58]

These two sources of Lefebvre's research on space—the agrarian question and the critiques of everyday life—came together in his experience of the construction of the new town of Mourenx in the Département des Pyrénées Atlantiques. In *Le temps des méprises* Lefebvre described his visit to Mourenx as the singular event that triggered his interest in urban society:

> Next to the village where I have spent several months per year since my childhood, a new town was founded, in Lacq: oil, gas, sulphur. . . . I saw bulldozers razing the forest, I saw the first stones placed for the new city, which became a small laboratory. . . . Since then I became interested in the city: I suspected that this irruption of the urban in a traditional rural reality was not a local coincidence but that it was linked to urbanization, to industrialization, to worldwide phenomena.[59]

Lefebvre's first published account about Mourenx was the 1960 article "Les nouveaux ensembles urbains" (New Urban Estates), a result of the research and interviews carried out by him in the new town,[60] but he had already discussed the "consequences of the implantation of an industrial environment in the rural environment" in Lacq at the CES during the 1957–58 academic year.[61] In the course of the late 1950s, drawing conclusions from these studies, Lefebvre shifted the focus of his research "from the rural to the urban," as the title of his 1970 omnibus goes.[62] Since the late 1940s he had participated in seminars, colloquia, and conferences that focused on questions of rural and urban sociology, the most relevant of which was the 1951 colloquium "Villes et campagnes," organized by Georges Friedmann.[63] Among the participants were sociologists (Chombart, Lefebvre); historians (Fernand Braudel and other members of the Annales School); and geographers (Pierre George) discussing the transition of French society from the rural civilization to the urban civilization.[64] This conference became one of the key events for the institutionalization of urban sociology in France, a process to which, in the course of the 1950s, the works of Pierre George, Louis Chevalier, and Chombert's Centre d'étude des groupes sociaux (and later the Centre de sociologie urbaine), contributed as well.[65]

The turn in Lefebvre's interests was reflected in his affiliation with the CES, which shifted toward urban sociology in the course of the late 1950s. Henri Mendras became the new head of the group of rural sociology, and in 1960 Lefebvre created the Group of Sociological Research on Everyday Life. (Since the late 1950s his research themes included the sociology of everyday life and the question of the "birth of the city," with the focus on Mourenx and Lacq.)[66] Within the new research group Lefebvre employed Guy Debord for a short time,[67] and the group also included Christiane Peyre working on the domestic work of women; Michel Clousard discussing "marginal time"; the writer and philosopher Georges Auclair; and the future members of the Institut de sociologie urbaine (ISU), including Henri Raymond and Nicole Haumont. Georges Perec was also a part of the group, paying special attention to stammering, silences, unfinished sentences, and gestures of the interviewed persons, all of which he noted rather than selecting and cleaning the phrases as professional interviewers were required to. Perec carried out two research projects: one on the everyday life of a miners' community in Normandy; the other on the peasant community in the rich agricultural zone of the Département de l'Oise.[68]

The journeys to New York, Teheran, Osaka, and later to Los Angeles and San Francisco, and his exchanges with municipal planning offices in Montreal and Tokyo allowed Lefebvre to investigate the convergence of such phenomena as urban sprawl, urbanization of the countryside, consumption of historical cities by tourism, and the fragmentation of cities planned according to the doctrine of functional division proclaimed by the architects and urbanists gathered in the CIAM.[69] All these phenomena added to the "urban crisis," one of the aspects of the crisis of North Atlantic Fordism in general.[70] According to Lefebvre, this crisis was a double one—theoretical and practical—and this process can be studied only by means of research that relates empirical studies with philosophical analysis, historical investigation, and an understanding of the planning practices of architecture and urbanism. This interdisciplinary perspective was reflected in his work from that time, including his critiques of the methodology of historical research ("What Is Historical Past?" 1959), developed in his book on the Paris Commune (*La proclamation de la Commune, 26 mars 1871* [The Proclamation of the Commune, March 26, 1871], 1965) and in his first review on urban design ("Utopie expérimentale: Pour un nouvel urbanisme" [Experimental Utopia: For a New Urbanism], 1961).

Institut de sociologie urbaine

The study on Mourenx, the first writings about urbanism, and the postulate of research about space as simultaneously empirical, philosophical, historical, and design-oriented, coincided with the creation of the Institut de sociologie urbaine. The *institut* was established by Lefebvre, Monique Coornaert, Antoine Haumont, Nicole Haumont, and Henri Raymond in 1962 as an independent organization designed to carry out studies commissioned by various research and planning institutions.[71]

A central role in the *institut*'s creation was played by Monique Coornaert, a philosopher and sociologist who collaborated at the beginning of the 1960s with the architect and urbanist Jean Coignet at the Institut d'urbanisme de l'Université de Paris (IUUP). In preparation for Coignet's preliminary study of the new town of Cergy-Pontoise, they carried out research on the possibilities of urban development north of Paris, with the focus on the plateau of Montmorency. This research was considered important by the District de la Région de Paris (founded in 1961), which suggested its development in collaboration with Henri Lefebvre, a contact that Coornaert helped to establish.[72] Following the agreement, a research project focused on the relationship between the material structures and the "ways of life" was worked out by Lefebvre and Coornaert, who were joined by the Haumonts and Raymond;[73] since the district was entitled to sign contracts only with institutions, at the end of 1962 or at the beginning of 1963 the ISU was created, recalled Coornaert.[74] This reveals that the origins of the *institut* were conditioned by a direct engagement with urban planning in the transitory period in French urbanism in the mid-1960s, when the increasingly criticized scheme of the *grands ensembles* was replaced by the concept of the new towns *(villes nouvelles),* introduced by the urbanistic plan of Paris of 1965 in order to accommodate the growth of the capital.[75]

The study that defined the themes of the ISU for years to come was focused on Choisy-le-Roi, the suburban settlement north of Paris. It was commissioned by the Centre de recherche d'urbanisme, headed by Jean Canaux.[76] Raymond recalls that its results inspired him to suggest to Canaux a new research on the *pavillon,* or the detached house with the garden—a suburban housing form already addressed by Lefebvre in the 1958 introduction to the first volume of *Critique of Everyday Life.*[77] Canaux, who was interested in the "exploration of the consciousness of the petit bourgeois," accepted the proposal,[78] and the ISU launched research on the practices of dwelling, comparing the individual house with collective housing estates.

"It was a situation," said Raymond, "constructed out of the resources available at the moment."[79] Nicole Haumont was responsible for the recruitment of the pollsters, whom she had chosen from the recent graduates specializing in psychosociology. In order to limit the impact of the researcher's influence on the interviewees, the "method of undirected interviews" was developed by Raymond and spelled out in his *thèse 3ème cycle* (1968) and subsequent publications.[80] Besides Nicole Haumont, her husband, Antoine, and Monique Coornaert, the team was joined by Claude Bauhain and Marie-Geneviève Raymond (later Dezès-Raymond), a graduate of the Institut d'études politiques in Paris, later married for a short time to Henri Raymond.[81] The research was consulted by external experts, including Pierre George.

The ISU worked as a team; thus, the attribution of credits for the study of the *pavillon,* published in three volumes in 1966, is not an easy task. *L'habitat pavillonnaire* (The Pavillon Habitat) contains the summary of the study and was credited to Antoine Haumont, Nicole Haumont, Henri Raymond, and Marie-Geneviève Raymond, with a preface by Lefebvre; *La politique pavillonnaire* (The Politics of the Pavillon), a historical study of the political and legal conditions of suburbanization in France and the discourse around it, was credited to Marie-Geneviève Raymond; and *Les pavillonnaires* (The Inhabitants of the Pavillon), which presents the results of the interviews and their interpretation, was signed by Nicole Haumont.[82] According to Henri Raymond, Lefebvre was not directly involved in the research, "following it from Sirius," and his interest in the study was doubted by Raymond—an opinion challenged by some of his former colleagues, including Maïté Clavel.[83]

From Strasbourg to Nanterre

The "Sirius" that Raymond referred to was Strasbourg, where Lefebvre was appointed professor of ethics in October 1961 and of sociology two years later.[84] (During that time he still lived in the capital: "I knew all the trees near the rail tracks between Paris and Strasbourg," he said once to Rémi Hess).[85] Lefebvre's work in Strasbourg was inspired and influenced by his contacts with several colleagues, students, and artists. They included the philosopher Georges Gusdorf and the mathematician René Thom, professor in Strasbourg until 1963 and the founder of catastrophe theory. Assembling his team in Strasbourg, Lefebvre invited Henri Hatzfeld to teach the sociology of work and religion, and the electrical and acoustic engineer Abraham Moles, a former teacher at the Hochschule für Gestaltung in Ulm,[86] to lecture on the methodology of social sciences ("He is the number, I am the drama," said Lefebvre about Moles).[87] It was at that time that Lefebvre's contacts with the situationists were most intense; since the late 1950s he had known Guy Debord, whom he put in touch with Raoul Vaneigem after receiving from Vaneigem his essay of "poetry and revolution," and Théo Frey, Jean Garnaud, and Mustapha Khayati were his students in Strasbourg.[88] It was also during his professorship in Strasbourg that he met the artist Constant Nieuwenhuys and arranged several trips to Amsterdam to discuss his project "New Babylon."[89]

Looking back at his teaching in Strasbourg, Lefebvre believed that he was "one of the first in France who was addressing urban questions."[90] He offered two types of courses: one in urban sociology specifically for the students of sociology (and interested students of psychology or philosophy) and the other, "public courses" open to everybody. The themes of both courses changed every year and developed previous writings of Lefebvre about the city, including, first, the "right to the city" and the understanding of urban space as that of everyday life to be "decolonized"; second, the distinction between the city and "the urban" as the new form of the modern society; and third, the criticism of functionalist urbanism and its founding document, the Athens Charter (1933, published in 1941), and of the transition from the "city as an oeuvre" to the "city as a spectacle."[91] Finally, an important theme was the affirmation of the street as the gathering of activities, objects, and commodities; the interest in the monuments; and the role of *bistrot* clubs as "kernels" of social life absent in the *grands ensembles*.[92] The bibliography edited by Lefebvre under the title "Urban Sociology and Urbanism" in preparation of his lectures shows that the bulk of references for his later books about space were gathered at that time, including the Anglo-American sources (Kevin Lynch, Christopher Alexander), Martin Heidegger, and the description of the city in literature (Eugène Sue, John Dos Passos, John Steinbeck, Malcolm Lowry).[93]

A crucial part of the student's curriculum introduced by Lefebvre was the participation in research studies supervised by him. They included the first nationwide demographic study of the *grands ensembles,* launched by the CRU and assigned to the Institut national d'études démographiques (INED) in 1964.[94] The most comprehensive study was launched by the Direction de l'aménagement, du foncier et de l'urbanisme (DAFU) at the Ministère de l'équipement, aiming at "establishing a dialogue between urbanists and sociologists in order to find social and cultural meaning of city planning."[95] The group in Strasbourg, created around Lefebvre, was a partner in the network that consisted of urbanists investigating various cities—Aix-en-Provence, Montpellier, Bordeaux, Paris, Le Havre, and Toulouse—and included François Bourricaud, Georges Granai, and Raymond Ledrut, the last being among the first in France to address the question of the *grands ensembles* in terms of social space.[96] The research resulted in a study of the uneven growth of cities, the circuits of decision in urban planning, and the participation of inhabitants and associations in the processes of production of space. The report about Strasbourg, submitted under the title "Étude de sociologie urbaine" (Study in Urban Sociology, 1967), was followed by research on the ZUP (*zone à urbaniser en priorité*, urban development zone) Haute-Pierre, commissioned by the planning office of the city of Strasbourg (1967).[97]

The synthesis of DAFU's work by Jean-Paul Trystram served as the introduction to the colloquium "Sociologie et urbanisme" in Royaumont (Sociology and Urbanism, 1968), which gathered urbanists (Robert Auzelle, Guy Lagneau, Marcel Lods, Michel Ecochard), sociologists (Lefebvre, Chombart, Trystram), and engineers together with administrators and representatives of the "users"— a collective subject emerging in the course of the 1960s debates in architecture and urbanism in France.[98] This coming together of various parties involved in the processes of the production of urban space was programmatic for the seminar, and it was the focus of the session "The Interdisciplinary Research and the Urban Sociology," which was chaired by Lefebvre and revolved around the question that would be fundamental to all his books on space: the possibility of a multidisciplinary science on urban space. A few days before the Parisian events of May 1968, Lefebvre urged for a systematic critique of the concept of the "city" as a social object, thus announcing the main argument of his *Révolution urbaine (The Urban Revolution)*, to be published two years later.[99]

The studies of DAFU and the Royaumont colloquium itself were inscribed in the intellectual and institutional reorganization of the spatial planning of the Fifth Republic, whose centralized and technocratic character reached its peak in the mid-1960s, to become challenged at the end of the decade. The interventionist tendencies of the French policy of spatial planning, reinforced by the Vichy regime, had gained the upper hand in the 1950s through a series of financial, managerial, organizational, and administrative regulations that facilitated the postwar reconstruction and the palliation of the housing crisis.[100] While the functionalist urbanists provided the formal and technological means for this policy, the central planning administration in France was dominated by the engineers educated at the École nationale des ponts et chaussées (ENPC) and by the ideology of technological rationality and political neutrality.[101] The domination of planners over other professionals involved and over the local policy makers and regional administration was confirmed by the 1963 foundation of the Délégation à l'aménagement du territoire (DATAR) as the central coordinator of spatial planning in France and, for Lefebvre, "a new step of production of space," which he followed closely.[102] This was followed by the merger of the Ministère des travaux publics, responsible for engineering works, with the Ministère de la construction, focused on housing, into the Ministère de l'équipement (1966).[103]

However, this apogee of "the golden age of planning" (Gérard Chevalier) and "the era of technocrats" (Jean-Claude Thoenig) was also its turning point. Since the mid-1960s, French spatial planning had become a scene of a constant negotiation between the tendency toward liberalization, which accepted the social inequalities as a natural datum of economic order and limited itself to the correction of particularly acute situations, and the critique of liberalism, stemming from Marxists, progressive Catholics, and reformist bureaucrats.[104] In the words of Lefebvre, French urbanism of the late 1960s hovered between two tendencies: "neoliberalism" and "neomanagerialism."[105] The tension between them was expressed in a series of legislative shifts: the Commissariat général du plan, the main French institution responsible for economic planning, was regionalized, and new research institutes focusing on urban and regional planning were created (among them the OREAMs, Organisations d'études d'aménagement des aires métropolitaines). These initiatives were synthesized in new legal instruments that ordered the relations between procedures and institutions of spatial and economic development,[106] complemented by research projects in architecture, urbanism, and housing launched in the course of the 1970s by the newly founded 1972 architectural research and development committee (Comité de la recherche et du développement en architecture, CORDA).[107]

These changes channeled the demand of state planning institutions for a new type of critical knowledge of the processes of urbanization, a demand that was answered, in the late 1960s and early 1970s, from a range of positions, Marxist and others. Besides the group around Lefebvre and the ISU, others involved included Manuel Castells and the structural Marxists; the Centre d'étude des mouvements sociaux (CEMS), headed by Alain Touraine; the Foucauldian structuralists of the Centre d'études, de recherches et de formation institutionelle (CERFI); and also the Centre de sociologie urbaine (CSU) of Chombart.[108] The evolution of the last group was most symptomatic of the changes undergone by French urban sociology at that time: while in the 1950s Chombart was one of those "humanists of the reinforced concrete" targeted by the situationists,[109] by the end of the 1960s the focus of the CSU had shifted from psychosociology and preliminary studies of urban planning to a Marxist critique of planning.[110]

Lefebvre contributed to this intellectual reorientation in his new affiliation: in October 1965 he was appointed professor of sociology at the recently opened (in 1964) Faculty of Humanities at the University Paris 10–Nanterre. The director of the Department of Sociology in Nanterre was Alain Touraine, and Lefebvre's colleagues included the political scientist and sociologist Michel Crozier.[111]

Henri Raymond returned from Vienna, where he had been organizing a center of research and meeting for sociologists from Western and Eastern Europe, to become senior assistant to Lefebvre and deputy director of the Faculty of Sociology; Lefebvre's other assistants included Jean Baudrillard and René Lourau.

Both Baudrillard and Lourau wrote their dissertations under Lefebvre's supervision, the former on the "system of objects," the latter on institutional analysis.[112] At the university in Nanterre, during his tenure (1965–73) and during the first years after his retirement, Lefebvre supervised forty-seven dissertations (including the *thèses 3ème cycle* and the theses of doctorate). Among a bewildering variety of topics, the themes relating to rural and urban sociology played a crucial role. They included specific studies of selected cities, both in France (Montauban, Le Havre, Antony) and abroad (in Iran, Argentina, and Turkey) and were complemented by studies of rural sociology in France and Africa.[113] Many of Lefebvre's collaborators and students in sociology, some of them linked to the ISU, defended theses related directly to architecture and urbanism, including comparative research on the "silence and revolts of users" in the United States, France, the United Kingdom, and Italy; research on architecture built by nonarchitects; and critical accounts of representations of space with a special focus on architecture, including the work of Le Corbusier.[114] Spatial planning in France was addressed as well, including the thesis by Maïté Clavel, who based this research on her previous experience as a researcher in the OREAM of the Lorraine region.[115] Much later (in 1980) Henri Raymond defended his *doctorat d'État* on "architecture as a concept."[116]

The most interesting theses Lefebvre supervised belonged to those he was involved with as professor at the Institut d'urbanisme de l'Université de Paris (with Hubert Tonka as his assistant, and later Monique Coornaert).[117] They included a study of the relationship between housing typologies and juvenile delinquency in the twentieth arrondissement in Paris by Paul Orville (1967).[118] In the same year Robert Cattiau submitted the dissertation "Histoire générale des festivals et essai d'une phénoménologie des festivals français" (General History of Festivals and an Essay in Phenomenology of French Festivals). The study was divided into two parts: "General History of Festivals" followed by "Contemporary French Festivals," which examined urban festivals from four perspectives: morphological, technological, aesthetic, and sociological.[119] A thesis that linked historical research to an urbanistic project in a most direct way was submitted by A. Y. Solinas, focusing on the village of Castelsardo, in Sardinia.[120] With the locale facing a "brutal confrontation between the traditional society and the modern society," the aim of the study was to develop spatial planning of tourist facilities that would allow preserving this medieval city and its exceptional site.[121] Thus, after sociological research on contemporary tourism and a historical monograph on Castelsardo, the thesis proposed an urban plan for the city that was intended to facilitate exchanges between the population and the tourists, for example, by opening up the facilities of the planned holiday village to the inhabitants of the city. The description of the project combines Lefebvre's vocabulary (the leisure facilities are described as a possibility of a "rupture of the rhythm" in the everyday) with a curious pedagogical project, in which the tourists are supposed to help the inhabitants "to pass smoothly from a traditional life to a modern life."[122] Lefebvre also took part in the examining committee of Philippe Boudon, whose thesis on Le Corbusier's neighborhood in Pessac, published in 1969, was an important contribution to the rethinking of modern architecture in France and a point of reference for Lefebvre's own work.[123]

It was during his tenure at Nanterre that Lefebvre formulated his theory of the production of space in six books. The first of them was *The Right to the City* (1968), which became one of the most influential books in the French architectural and urbanistic debates of the late 1960s.[124] Other books followed: *The Urban Revolution* (1970), as well as two omnibuses of previously published articles and delivered speeches: *Du rural à urbain* (From the Rural to the Urban, 1970) and *Espace et politique* (Space and Politics, 1972), called also the second volume of *The Right to the City*. Lefebvre's next book, *La pensée marxiste et la ville* (Marxist Thinking and the City, 1972), contained the most extensive analysis of the instrumentalization of space in capitalist economy, thus preparing for *The Production of Space* (1974). These six books were later complemented by discussions about space in *De l'État* (On the State, 1976–78) and the articles gathered in the posthumously published *Éléments de rhythmanalyse* (Rhythmanalysis, 1992).

With Lefebvre's arrival at Nanterre, the work of the ISU, which had slowed down during his stay in Strasbourg and during Raymond's in Vienna, was resumed. In 1968 the ISU published the essay "Propositions de recherches sur la vie urbaine" (Suggestions concerning Research on Urban Life), which spells out the program of the *institut,* presents its general theoretical framework, examines the current state of research in urban sociology, and launches a series of questions pursued by the *institut* in the years to come. Combining the lucid style of Nicole Haumont, the playfulness of the texts by Henri Raymond, and a set of Lefebvrean ideas, the essay argued for relating the research on the "ways of life" of differentiated social groups to studies of urbanization:

> The expression of Henri Lefebvre that "the city is a projection of the social relationships on the ground" points out a method of analysis that takes into account all the aspects of the society: ways of life, history, economic organization, technical and social divisions, et cetera.[125]

The authors concluded by identifying three research themes: the adaptation of the city to the ways of life, the decision-making processes that condition the

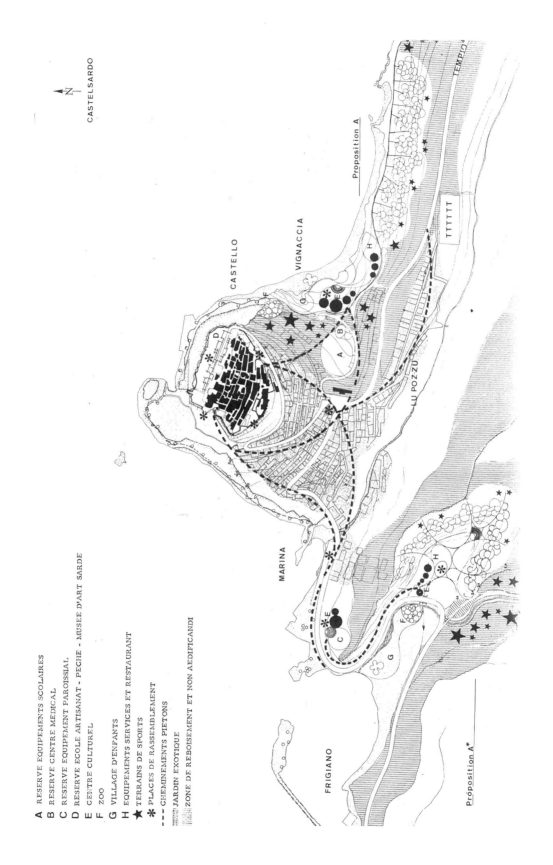

A RESERVE EQUIPEMENTS SCOLAIRES
B RESERVE CENTRE MEDICAL
C RESERVE EQUIPEMENT PAROISSIAL
D RESERVE ECOLE ARTISANAT - PECHE - MUSEE D'ART SARDE
E CENTRE CULTUREL
F ZOO
G VILLAGE D'ENFANTS
H EQUIPEMENTS SERVICES ET RESTAURANT
★ TERRAINS DE SPORTS
✻ PLACES DE RASSEMBLEMENT
- - - CHEMINEMENTS PIETONS
JARDIN EXOTIQUE
ZONE DE REBOISEMENT ET NON AEDIFICANDI

CASTELSARDO

N

CASTELLO

VIGNACCIA

Proposition A

LU POZZU

TEMPIO

TTTTT

MARINA

FRIGIANO

Proposition A*

social production of space (on the levels of both institutions and inhabitants), and the images of the city and of social life.[126] These themes were the focus of numerous books and research reports of the ISU, produced until Lefebvre's retirement from his position in Nanterre in 1973, which was followed by his withdrawal from the *institut*. They included *La copropriété* (The Co-ownership, 1971); *Habitat et pratique de l'espace* (Habitat and Practice of Space, 1973); *L'espace du travail dans la ville* (The Space of Work in the City, 1973); and *Les locataires* (The Tenants, 1976).[127]

The research in France was complemented by Lefebvre's engagements abroad, including in Spain (between 1972 and 1975), where he participated in a research project on tourism, invited by the urbanist and sociologist Mario Gaviria, his former student from Strasbourg and editor of *Du rural à l'urbain*. The study focused on new tourist towns in Spain, with particular attention to Benidorm, and included an analysis of the urban plan and research on the everyday in this city and its transformation into a center of international mass tourism. The team of researchers numbered around forty people, among them sociologists, urbanists, and students of architecture, for whom Lefebvre gave a seminar on the processes of urbanization.[128]

Lefebvre and the Architects

What distinguishes the studies of the ISU was their ambition to engage in the discussion of architecture and urbanism, expressed in another programmatic paper, "Ville, urbanisme et urbanisation" (City, Urbanism, and Urbanization, 1968), published by Lefebvre with Monique Coornaert in a book devoted to the memory of Georges Gurvitch. The paper embraced Gurvitch's postulate: to analyze the society "in becoming" in order to unveil the antinomies and tensions that are intrinsic to the "totality of the social phenomenon."[129] According to Lefebvre and Coornaert, the process of urbanization, rather than the city, is such a total social phenomenon. Announcing the argument that Lefebvre made later in *The Urban Revolution,* the authors write that urbanization is not an emanation of the city but a result of socioeconomic development as a whole, and it encompasses both the countryside and the city itself, linking them in new ways.[130] Thus, the city cannot be thought of as autonomous but as part of a larger whole that reaches from the neighborhood to the global hierarchy of urbanization.[131] The authors conclude that rather than programming the future of the city on the basis of restricted

(opposite page) Thesis by A. Y. Solinas, project of tourist development of the village Castelsardo, in Sardinia, supervised by Henri Lefebvre. From Solinas, "Essai d'organisation touristique à Castel Sardo [Sardaigne], Italie."

and reductive data, an urban analysis should start from the present situation and reveal the various tendencies at stake—a procedure of a "constant movement between theory and application."[132]

Such exchange between theory and application is what characterized Lefebvre's contacts with architects and urbanists. These contacts were most intense around 1968, a moment when the interests of the architectural students of Beaux-Arts and the sociologists of Nanterre converged, with the concept of social space as a way to bridge the gaps between architectural practice and the social sciences, humanities, and political engagement.[133] At that time Lefebvre participated in the "commissions Querrien," responsible for the reform of architectural education in France,[134] and he was lecturing at the École normale supérieure des Beaux-Arts and later at the Unité pédagogique 7, when, after the closure of the section of architecture at the École des Beaux-Arts in December 1968, five, and soon nine, *unités pédagogiques* (UP) in Paris were created.[135] Lefebvre was also a frequent guest at the UP8, where Henri Raymond developed an advanced program of research on the structure of space across various societies (the Bororos, the Nuers, the Eskimos, and the Chinese).[136] The contacts with students and junior faculty at the *unités* allowed Lefebvre a glance into the energetic contestation not only of architectural education but also of the disciplines of architecture and urbanism themselves, with "lectures on the street," the organization of citizens' advice bureaus for information on housing matters, visits to building sites, and the construction of a community center in Villeneuve-la-Garenne (1970) by the students of the UP6. This contestation not rarely included a critique of Lefebvre's ideas themselves.[137] Together with the UP8 and the Groupe de sociologie urbaine (formed in Nanterre around Manuel Castells), Lefebvre's collaborators organized a series of seminars focused on architectural space and the anthropology of space (Oliva, 1968), architectural theory and the social sciences (Port-Grimaud, 1968), and the relationships among politics of space, urban design, and architectural space (Cogolin, 1970).[138] Dan Ferrand-Bechmann, at that time a student and today a professor of sociology in Nanterre, recalled that architecture was a significant theme during the seminars, most importantly in Port-Grimaud, with Manfredo Tafuri debating with Lefebvre.[139] Tafuri was also a frequent visitor at the UP8, invited by Bernard Huet; during these stays he saw Lefebvre, who himself traveled several times to the Venice School of Architecture in the late 1960s.[140]

The publication of Lefebvre's books on space in the late 1960s and early 1970s coincided not only with the reorientation in French urbanism and spatial planning policies but also with a period of transition and experimentation in French architecture, between the death of Le Corbusier in 1965 and the establishment of the French "urban" or "postmodern" architecture around 1973 and 1974, marked by such events as the Maubuée competition (1973); Bernard Huet's becoming the editor-in-chief of *L'architecture d'aujourd'hui* (1974); the formulation of the "groupe des sept," which included Christian de Portzamparc, Roland Castro, and Antoine Grumbach; and the increasing influence of Italian architectural theory on French architectural practice, teaching, and research.[141]

The variety of architectural discussions and tendencies of the late 1960s and early '70s in France can be studied exemplarily by focusing on the multiple readings of the ISU study of the *pavillon* by the architects and urbanists at that time. In the opinion of Henri Raymond, this study was much better received by the architects than by the sociologists, and it significantly influenced the architectural discussion.[142] It received the attention of several architects (Paul Chemetov, Jean Deroche, Paul Bossard) turning since the 1950s to traditional forms and building techniques of the *banlieue pavillonnaire,* considered to be a resource for an architecture critical to the economic and intellectual reorganization of France of the late Gaullist era. The tiled roofs and cobblestone walls became a reservoir of forms referred to, for example, in the housing complex in Vigneux built by Paul Chemetov (1960–64) and the home for elderly people in La Courneuve by Chemetov and Jean Deroche (1961–65). Among the most influential examples of this trend was the housing Les Bleutes in Créteil, by Paul Bossard (1959–62), characterized by the intentional imprecision of concrete surfaces resulting from workers embedding schistose stones within the elements poured on the building site: the intensification of the visual and tactile features of the building materials and the emphasis on their joints highlight the concrete dimension of labor, which avoids the abstraction of the industrialized ways of construction.[143] This reading was paralleled by the reception of the populist embrace of the American suburbs by Robert Venturi and Denise Scott-Brown, in particular in their research project and 1970 Yale design studio "Learning from Levittown," excerpts of which were published in French.[144] In the context of the revision of architecture and urbanism of the modern movement in France in the course of the 1960s, the study of the *pavillon* was read as a profound critique of the most fundamental functionalist concepts, including those of "function" and "need."[145] Bernard Huet retrospectively argued that the study was an eye-opener, for the first time relating the anthropological reflection on space, which Claude Lévi-Strauss and Pierre Bourdieu developed about the Bororo and the Kabyle people, to Lefebvre's critique of everyday life in postwar France. At the same time Huet's own work from the early 1970s linked the study of the *pavillon* to the emerging interest in typology and urban morphology, under the growing influence of the Italian schools of architecture in France after 1968 and Italian architectural discourse in general.[146]

Lefebvre's doctoral students and the ISU contributed to this rethinking and reevaluation of the architecture of the modern movement by investigating the appropriation by the inhabitants of Le Corbusier's flagships: the Pessac neighborhood (1926) and the Unité d'habitation in Marseille (1952). These studies tested and developed Lefebvre's critique of functionalist urbanism, going beyond the

Paul Bossard, housing Les Bleutes, Créteil, 1959–62; detail of the wall. Photograph by Łukasz Stanek, 2008.

French debates since the late 1950s that were focused either on an accusation of urbanism's alleged totalitarian instrumentality (with Pierre Francastel's description of Le Corbusier's masterplans as "the universum of concentration camps") or on the functional and aesthetic dissatisfaction of the inhabitants, as discussed by the researchers of the Centre d'étude des groupes sociaux and by Françoise Choay in the long introduction to her anthology *L'urbanisme: Utopies et réalités* (Urbanism: Utopias and Realities, 1965).[147] In contrast to these approaches, Lefebvre analyzed postwar functionalist urbanism as a part of the Fordist reorganization of society, which, in the second part of the twentieth century, was dated both technologically and socially.[148]

This critique of functionalism was followed by the urbanists in an appeal for "open structures" allowing spontaneity, liberty, openness, and change. The answers to this appeal ranged from the technological utopia of the "spatial urbanism" or "prospective architecture" (Yona Friedman, Walter Jonas, Paul Maymont, Ionel Schein, and Nicolas Schöffer); through the anti-monumental urbanism of the Faculty of Humanities in Toulouse-le-Mirail by Candilis–Josic–Woods (1963) and the urban designs of the Atelier Montrouge for Saint-Denis (1964–65); to a

Paul Bossard, housing Les Bleutes, Créteil, 1959–62. Photograph by Łukasz Stanek, 2008.

unité d'habitation de marseille de le corbusier

propositions
de l'architecte

L'ART D'HABITER

solutions
des habitants

Ci-contre : cinq cartes postales vendues à
l'unité d'habitation de Marseille communiquées
par un de nos lecteurs.

Editées par la Société Editions de France.

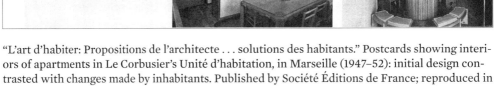

"L'art d'habiter: Propositions de l'architecte . . . solutions des habitants." Postcards showing interiors of apartments in Le Corbusier's Unité d'habitation, in Marseille (1947–52): initial design contrasted with changes made by inhabitants. Published by Société Éditions de France; reproduced in *L'architecture d'aujourd'hui* 125 (1966): lv.

new monumentality based on an opposition between the heavy structure of housing and the light, modifiable structure of facilities, as in the scheme for the ZUP in Toulouse-le-Mirail by Candilis–Josic–Woods (1961) or in the quartier de l'Arlequin in Grenoble by Atelier d'urbanisme et d'architecture (AUA) of 1966.[149] The ISU engaged in these discussions by investigating new approaches to urbanism.[150] One of them was the Village-Expo in Saint-Michel-sur-Orge (1966), on the southern periphery of Paris, a celebrated *habitat intermédiaire*—an attempt at dense housing typology that preserves the qualities of an individual house, being an intermediary between collective housing and the *pavillon*.[151] Another one was the neighborhood La Grande Borne in Grigny, by Émile Aillaud (1964-71), aimed at creating a sequence of recognizable urban spaces differentiated in dimensions, forms, and ambience in the conditions of the industrialized building techniques and extreme unification of means.[152]

These interactions among sociologists, architects, and urbanists in the late 1960s came together in the question of multidisciplinary research, facilitated by the state's stimulation of innovation in the building industry and housing typologies, supported by several architects at pains to break away from their professional isolation, and prefigured by some offices such as the AUA.[153] Opposed to the concept of an "architectural space understood as the preserve of a particular profession within the established social division of labour,"[154] Lefebvre was convinced that social space can be grasped only by an effort of all disciplines; accordingly, he not only theorized the methodology of multidisicplinary research but also took part in multidisciplinary design teams, including the work with Mario Gaviria, Ricardo Bofill, and later Jean Renaudie and his son Serge.[155]

Lefebvre's most relevant contribution to multidisciplinary research was his co-organization of a series of studies, seminars, and colloquia, which gathered sociologists, architects, urbanists, philosophers, and psychologists. The largest of them addressed human needs in the context of the practice of architects ("Les besoins fonctionnels de l'homme en vue de leur projection ultérieure sur le plan de la conception architecturale") and was organized between 1968 and 1970 by the Centre de recherche d'architecture, d'urbanisme et de construction (CRAUC). The project, headed by Michel Dameron, the director of CRAUC, Paul Sivadon, professor at the Free University Brussels, and Lefebvre himself, was carried out by means of four seminars (between March 1968 and October 1969) and seven research projects.[156] Lefebvre and his collaborators (Jean Baudrillard, Maïté Clavel, Antoine Haumont, Nicole Haumont, Martine Hargous, Henri Raymond) were joined by other sociologists, including Henri Coing, and intellectuals such as Roland Barthes, as well as many architects and urbanists (Bernard Huet, Ricardo Porro, Georges-Henri Pingusson, Jean Boris, Bernard Duprey, Claude Genzling, Anatole Kopp). Lefebvre gave several talks during the seminars, and he actively participated in the debates.[157]

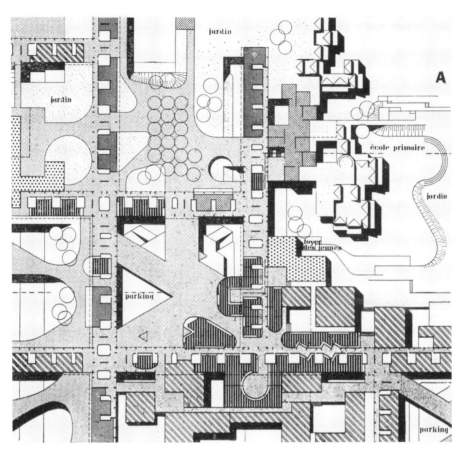

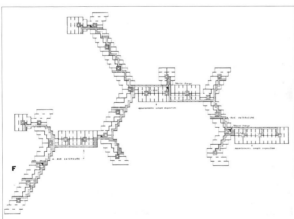

(top) Atelier Montrouge (Jean Renaudie, Pierre Riboulet, Gérard Thurnauer, Jean-Louis Véret), design for Francs-Moisins, Saint-Denis, 1964–65. An attempt at a non-hierarchical urban space. Published in *L'architecture d'aujourd'hui* 130 (1967): 20.

(left) Alexis Josic, study of a program of a thousand flats near Paris. Published in *L'architecture d'aujourd'hui* 130 (1967): 19.

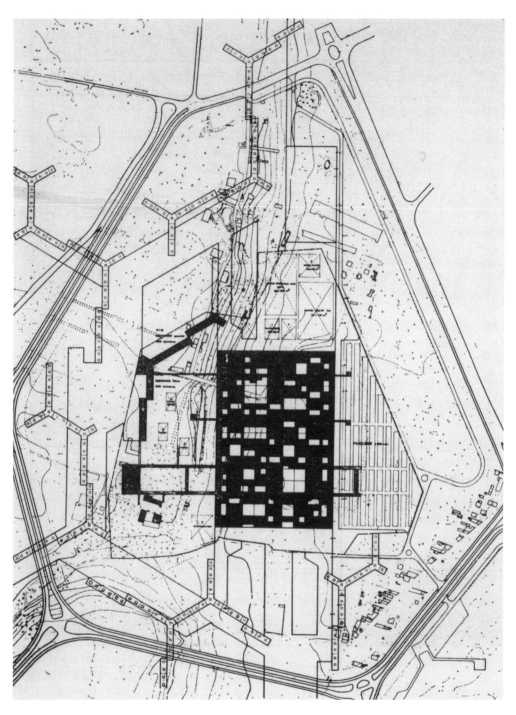

Antimonumental urbanism of Georges Candilis, Alexis Josic, and Shadrach Woods (with Fabien Castaing and Paul Gardia), Faculty of Humanities, Toulouse-le-Mirail, 1967–75. Published in *L'architecture d'aujourd'hui* 137 (1968): 58.

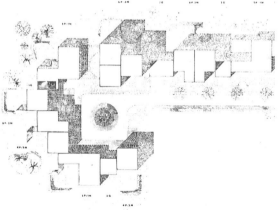

Michel Andrault and Pierre Parat, master plan, Village-Expo, Saint-Michel-sur-Orge, 1966. This "intermediary habitat" aimed at combining qualities of the individual house (such as privacy or direct access to the garden) with the economic advantages of collective estates, including high density and prefabrication. Published in *L'architecture d'aujourd'hui* 128 (1966): xli.

Émile Aillaud, La Grande Borne in Grigny, 1964–71. A sequence of recognizable urban spaces differentiated in dimensions, forms, and ambience, designed within the constraints of industrialized building techniques. Photograph by Ákos Moravánszky, 2009. Courtesy of Ákos Moravánszky.

Jean Renaudie, complex of housing, shops, and offices "Jeanne Hachette," Ivry sur Seine, 1969–75, on the main street in Ivry. Photograph by Łukasz Stanek, 2008.

According to the final report of the project, "Les besoins fonctionnels," its aim was to investigate the "relationship between the human being and the external world" by determining "human needs on all levels (physical–chemical, physiological, psychological, social)" in a way that would result in a series of conclusions useful to the architects.[158] Rejecting the functionalist concepts of need and function, the participants of the seminar challenged the procedures of translation between the needs and the design and argued that "one has to demystify, according to the current state of knowledge, the concept of an ideal organization for a given program."[159] The sensitivity to the differentiation of space resulted in embracing the role of decision and judgment in the design process, which do not result from scientific knowledge. ("There is no place for a fear of a judgment of value," said Lefebvre in one of the discussions.)[160]

The acknowledgment of the social, cultural, and ethnic differences in the city highlights the relationship among architecture, urbanism, and politics. In the wake of May '68, the seminar revealed a series of positions concerning the possibility of a subversive potential of architecture. While Bernard Huet envisaged the architect as a critical commentator who "cannot change things to a large extent, but he might make people more aware of the phenomena that are covered up by his architecture,"[161] Georges-Henri Pingusson, a member of the Union des artistes modernes in the 1930s and former collaborator of Le Corbusier, opposed him by claiming that architects should try to serve the people in the small margin of freedom that is available,[162] and Anatole Kopp, the author of the influential book *Town and Revolution* (1967), which popularized the Soviet architectural avant-garde in France, stated that architects cannot transgress the social structures in which they work. While the "architects oscillate between two extreme opinions: not being able to do anything, being able to do everything,"[163] it is necessary to delineate the specific field of their intervention: a task that would be addressed in Lefebvre's writings about space in the 1970s.

The multidisciplinary approach, as exercised during the CRAUC seminar, was also the focus of the journal *Espaces et sociétés,* which Lefebvre founded in 1970 with Anatole Kopp.[164] Even if Lefebvre's books on space rarely footnoted the articles from the journal, the influence of those articles on the theory of the production of space is evident. The relationships among space, economy, and politics were explicitly addressed in articles about the urban renewals of the 1970s, most important those in Paris (Les Halles, Place d'Italie, Nanterre, cité d'Aliarte), as well as in the issues devoted to social marginalization in the cities (no. 3), immigrant workers (no. 4), social urban movements (nos. 6 and 7), production of the built environment (nos. 6 and 7), and socioeconomic contradictions and urban structures (no. 8).[165] The journal included a series of essays about land rent and analyses of urban economies, written from a Marxist perspective.[166] The focus of the journal was international: until 1974, when the original French version of

The Production of Space was published, the journal featured several articles about processes of urbanization in Latin America (no. 3) and "environment and space in Africa" (nos. 10 and 11) but also articles about the United States.[167] The ninth issue focused on the two disciplines that are at the center of Lefebvre's discussion about the production of space: anthropology and the semiology of space.[168]

Lefebvre's contribution to the professional debates by means of *Espaces et sociétés* was complemented by his interventions in the popular mass media. At the time of the rapid rise in the number of TV sets and the heyday of cultural weeklies and paperbacks since the beginning of the Fifth Republic,[169] Lefebvre gave many interviews and took part in multiple debates addressing a range of themes. Together with Louis Althusser, Kostas Axelos, Alexandre Koyré, Edgar Morin, Jean-Pierre Vernant, and Jean Wahl, he discussed philosophy; he debated sociology with Jean Duvignaud and Georges Gurvitch; his views on fashion were juxtaposed to those of Roland Barthes and Michel Foucault; and, together with Albert Soboul, he talked about history. Besides art, pornography, theater, and literature, Lefebvre commented on current political events and his recently published books.[170] In the course of the 1960s he was acknowledged as an authority concerning questions of urban space. In this role he gave numerous interviews in popular weekly journals and on the radio and TV, speaking of Fourier's phalanstery; the spatial planning of the French Enlightenment; the Director's House in Claude-Nicolas Ledoux's Arc-et-Senans; reflecting upon everyday life in the *grands ensembles* together with Pierre George and Jean Balladur; and debating architecture with Fernand Pouillon and Ricardo Bofill.[171] Exhibitions in architecture and design were a specific field of public mass media, and Lefebvre contributed to catalogues of several shows, including *Matériau/technologie/forme* (Material, Technology, Form, 1974), and later *Paris—Paris 1937–1957* (1981), *Construire pour habiter* (Building for Dwelling, 1981), and *Architectures en France: Modernité, post-modernité* (Architectures in France: Modernity, Postmodernity, 1981).[172]

Lefebvre's role as a public intellectual speaking about and on behalf of urban space (rather than an "urban sociologist," in which role Chombart appeared on TV in interviews in the late 1950s)[173] was acknowledged and reflected in numerous invitations to conferences about architecture and urbanism, juries of architectural competitions,[174] and debates about the urban development of Paris. For example, he participated on the jury of the 1980 competition over Les Halles, organized by the Syndicat de l'architecture in the protest against the decision of the mayor of Paris, Jacques Chirac, to reject the broad democratic debate about the future of the city center. Lefebvre's vote represented a plea for a complex urban centrality, including space for dwelling in the center of Paris, and the symbolic dimension of architecture. The selection he voted for included the project of Franco Purini and his team, which was a design focusing on the historical memory of the French Revolution and its architectural symbolism; the project

(top) Henri Lefebvre in discussion with Fernand Pouillon. From *Oratorio reportage*. Institut national de l'audiovisuel, Paris.

(bottom) Henri Lefebvre comments on the Palais Royal. From his interview on *Un certain regard: Charles Fourier*. Institut national de l'audiovisuel, Paris.

cannes 6

(top) The jury of the Grand Prix d'Urbanisme et Architecture during the discussion about the project by Eilfried Huth and Günther Domenig, Cannes, February 1969: Jean Abasse, Serge Antoine, Jaap Bakema (1), Jürgen Joedicke (2), Louis Kahn (3), Henri Lefebvre (4), Robert Le Ricolais (5), Horia Maicu, Zygmunt Stanisław Makowski (6), François Mathey (7), Pierre Piganiol, Jean Prouvé, Karl Schwanzer (8), Heikki Siren (9), and Bruno Zevi. Published in Zach, ed., *Eilfried Huth,* 35. Courtesy of Eilfried Huth. The author thanks Jesko Fezer for information about this photograph.

(right) The project for Les Halles submitted by Franco Purini and his team in 1980 (no. 848) referred to French "revolutionary" architecture of the late eighteenth century. From *Architectural Design* 9–10 (1980): 49.

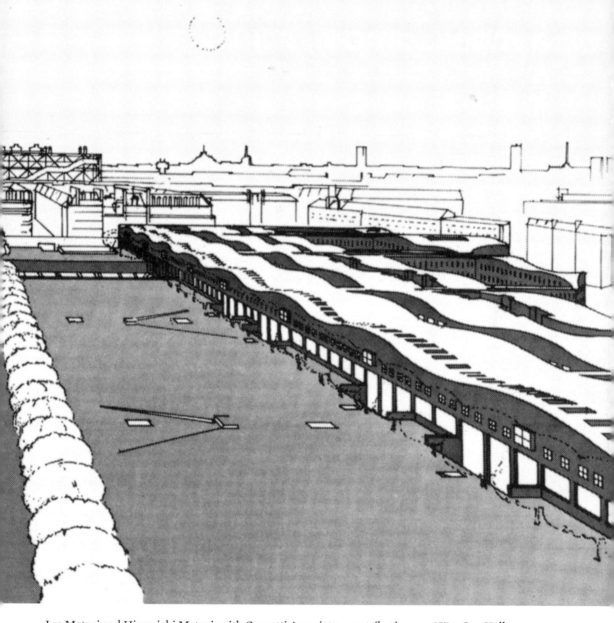

Jun Matsui and Hiromichi Matsui, with Gregotti Associates, contribution no. 657 to Les Halles competition, 1980. Lefebvre valued this entry for reintegrating housing and production into the center of the city. Published in *L'architecture d'aujourd'hui* 208 (1980): 10.

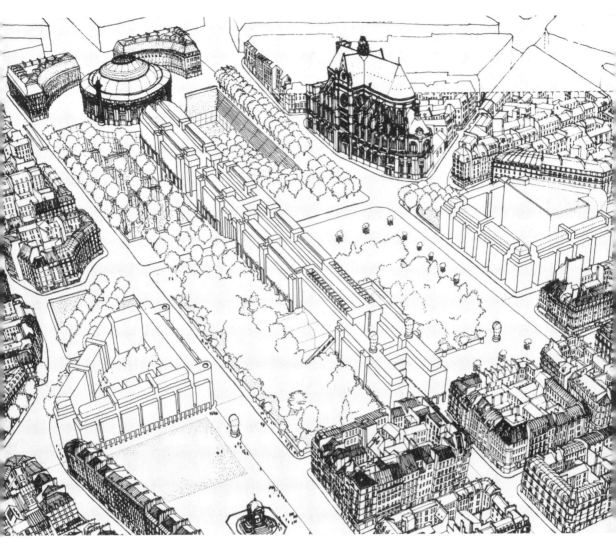

The project for Les Halles submitted by the team of Yves Lion in 1980 (no. 313) introduces housing into the center of Paris. From Lion, *Yves Lion: Études, réalisations, projets 1974–1985*, 16.

Discussion during Les Halles competition between Henri Lefebvre and Philip Johnson (in profile with dark-rimmed glasses in the right foreground). Published in *L'architecture d'aujourd'hui* 208 (1980): 40.

of Yves Lion and collaborators, which argued for an introduction of housing into the heart of Paris; and the project of Jun Matsui and Hiromichi Matsui with Gregotti Associates, which Lefebvre saw as linking the site of Les Halles to the Beaubourg and reintegrating habitation and productive activities into the center of the city.[175]

The discussions about urban space continued on a private level, and Lefebvre's extraordinary broad social circle included many architects and urbanists: the members of the Situationist International (IS) in the late 1950s and early 1960s; and the Utopie group around 1968 (Jean Baudrillard, Hubert Tonka, and the architects Jean Aubert, Jean-Paul Jungmann, and Antoine Stinco).[176] At the Unité pédagogique 7, Lefebvre met the architects Jean Prouvé and Henri Ciriani, as well as Paul Maymont (the director of the UP7) and Nicolas Schöffer.[177] He befriended architects sympathizing with the Left, including Pierre Riboulet and Paul Chemetov, but Fernand Pouillon as well, whom he visited several times in Algeria. His circle of friends also counted architects of the younger generation, such as Claude Parent, Paul Virilio, and Bernard Huet.[178] In the 1970s he cultivated intense contacts with several architects abroad as well, mainly in Spain (Óscar Tusquets, Ricardo Bofill) and Italy (Giancarlo de Carlo). With Lefebvre, De Carlo published the Italian translation of *Espaces et sociétés,* which after two issues continued as *Spazio e Società.*[179] According to Mario Gaviria, contacts with people were Lefebvre's essential source of information: "This was his way of learning about the world: through the people he worked with—and he worked with people whom he liked."[180] The productive character of these contacts was reflected in the schedule of his working day: getting up before 7:00 A.M., Lefebvre used to read and write until lunch and then go out to meet people, to lecture, and to engage in discussions.[181]

The Late Projects

It was at a dinner at the home of the architect Ciriani in the late 1970s that Henri Lefebvre met Jean-Pierre Lefebvre, who would soon become the director of the Sodédat.[182] The Sodédat (Société anonyme d'économie mixte d'équipement et d'aménagement du territoire) had been created in 1975 by the Département de la Seine-Saint-Denis and eventually became an important actor in the processes of construction of public facilities in the Paris region. Within thirty years, it was responsible for the management of almost forty ZACs (*zones d'aménagement concerté,* integrated development zones), including such important locations as the urban restructurization of the centers of the city of Saint-Denis and Villetaneuse, as well as the quartier de la Maladrerie in Aubervilliers. The Sodédat, cooperating with many innovative French and international architects, was entrusted with the construction of fifty colleges in the *département*.[183]

In the late 1970s and '80s the Sodédat became a platform for Lefebvre to engage with the practices of architecture and urbanism in the Paris metropolitan region. Jean-Pierre Lefebvre, who had worked for the Sodédat since its creation and was its director between 1984 and 1994, wrote that the ideas of Henri Lefebvre were very influential for the *société* and that "between 1981 and 1987 a very fruitful collaboration between Lefebvre and the Sodédat took place."[184] Henri Lefebvre (together with Robert Lion, Jean-Pierre Duport, Yves Dauge, and Roland Castro) participated in colloquia organized by the Sodédat.[185] In the mid-1980s Lefebvre and the Sodédat submitted a collaborative research proposal for a comparative study between France and California (where he traveled regularly at that time, accompanied by Serge Renaudie, at the invitation of several universities).[186] Jean-Pierre Lefebvre explained that the main hypothesis of Henri's research proposal, which never took place, aimed at examining the residues of poverty in the capitalist city, comparing Watts and Saint-Denis.[187]

Jean-Pierre Lefebvre recalls that Henri was invited several times to sit on the juries of architectural competitions organized by the *société,* where his voice was often decisive in discussions with representatives of the socialist and communist communes, such as Bagnolet and Saint-Ouen, and the juries often followed the opinion of "the interesting guy."[188] Henri's engagement in the activities of the Sodédat included his contributions to the journal *Archivari,* in which he discussed the projects built by the *société,* such as the development of Jean Renaudie's renovation project in the Maladrerie in Aubervillers, but also the work of Atelier Renaudie in Givors and Saint Martin d'Hères.[189]

Lefebvre's engagements in architectural debates continued until the late 1980s. In 1986 he supported the foundation of the journal *M, Mensuel, Marxisme, Mouvement,* which postulated the unification of "the producers of objects, spaces, ideas, theories, and information" and which often addressed questions of the city and architecture.[190] In August 1985 he cofounded the Groupe de Navarrenx, which included philosophers, historians, sociologists, psychiatrists, engineers, economists, and psychoanalysts as well as architects (Serge Renaudie and Lucia Martini-Scalzone).[191] Catherine Régulier, Lefebvre's companion at that time, recalls many trips they made together to visit new architecture, usually accompanied by the designers: in Marseille with Paul Chemetov; in Barcelona with Ricardo Bofill; in Ivry and Saint Martin d'Hères, near Grenoble, with Serge Renaudie; and in Marne-la-Vallée with Henri Ciriani.[192] "He was fascinated with the act of building," said Régulier, "and his disappointment with much of the postwar architecture did not undermine this fascination."[193]

Lefebvre's Theory of Space and the Crisis of Marxism

In his sympathetic review of Lefebvre's autobiographical *La somme et le reste* (The Sum and the Remainder, 1959), Maurice Blanchot did not ask why Lefebvre left the PCF; he asked why he had stayed so long. By Lefebvre's appearing as a "representative" of Marxism, Blanchot speculated, it was possible for him "to maintain an interpretation of Marxist thought that he believed most open to the future, one that brought difficulties to the fore, that clarified questions and showed that truth was not yet settled." By "expressing this thought while remaining under the discipline of official Marxism," Blanchot continued, "he was making the latter responsible for his open interpretation and thereby enriching it with this responsibility."[194]

Lefebvre perceived this openness as the only possibility of developing Marxism in the face of its crisis; first proclaimed by Masaryk at the end of nineteenth century and continually announced since then, the "crisis of Marxism" was a recurring theme in Lefebvre's thinking.[195] In his lectures in Strasbourg in the early 1960s, he analyzed three phases of this crisis: the first at the end of nineteenth century, when the proletariat did not bring the capitalist society to an end and became divided between the reformist and revolutionary currents; the second after the 1917 October Revolution, when the center of revolution shifted to underdeveloped countries, challenging Marx's argument about the industrial proletariat as the agent of revolutionary change; and the third when the advent of Stalinism contrasted with Marx's understanding of socialism as the withering of the state.[196] Much of Lefebvre's work can be considered an attempt to come to terms with this sequence, from *La conscience mystifiée* (Mystified Consciousness, 1936), written with Norbert Guterman in the face of the rise of Nazism in Germany,[197] to his accounts of space in the late 1960s and early 1970s.

The latter period coincided in France with a particularly profound step in the sequence of the "crises" of Marxism, linking the disenchantment with state socialism in Central and Eastern Europe; the widespread disappointment with the policies of the PCF in the wake of May '68; and a strong theoretical reaction against both orthodox and structural Marxism, which ranged from post-structuralism, psychoanalysis, and Foucault's work to the anti-Marxist, post-*gauchiste,* "postmodern" *nouvelle philosophie*.[198] The massive changes that French society underwent since the late 1950s only reinforced the doubts about the explanatory value of Marxism: with the rapid growth of disposable incomes; the reduction of working hours and prolongation of paid holidays; new credit instruments stirring consumption; the widening access to education; and the improvements in housing conditions and standards of living, French society began to perceive itself as a society without classes and without social conflict.[199]

In response, many French Marxists, beginning in the 1950s, stressed the role of empirical research, including anthropology, psychology, and sociology, and moved away from the orthodoxy of the DiaMat (the dialectical materialism) as a doctrine of the Communist Party that Stalin identified with Marxism Leninism (1931) and codified in his *Dialectical and Historical Materialism* (1938).[200] Lefebvre's theory of space contributed to this intellectual ferment, and in *The Production of Space* he argued, "We cannot rely solely on the application of 'classical' categories of Marxist thought" if both state capitalism and state socialism are to be left behind on the path toward "the collective management of space, the social management of nature, and the transcendence of the contradiction between nature and anti-nature."[201]

Toward a Revision of Marxism

The incompatibilities between Lefebvre's theory of space and a large part of Marxist positions came to the fore in the polemics against his theory, of which Manuel Castells's *The Urban Question* (1972) was most influential. The book by Castells starts with counting Lefebvre among "the greatest theoreticians of contemporary Marxism" and as someone who "has opened up what is perhaps a crucial direction in the study of 'the urban'" by recognizing new contradictions in the cultural sphere and linking the urban question to the process of the extended reproduction of labor power.[202] However, Castells argues that Lefebvre (who in the early 1970s was his colleague at the university in Nanterre) has immediately closed off this direction by succumbing to what is called in *The Urban Question* "the ideology of urbanism," meaning: "that specific ideology that sees the modes and forms of social organization as characteristic of a phase of the evolution of society, closely linked to the technico-natural conditions of human existence and, ultimately, to its environment."[203]

Similarly to the "housing question" addressed by Engels, to which the title of his book alludes, Castells argues that the urban question is not an isolated problem but an aspect of general social processes. Thus, he claims that the city must be defined in relation to the processes of industrialization, as the unity of collective consumption. Accordingly, he rejects the concepts of a specific "urban culture"—referring to Georg Simmel and the Chicago School of Sociology—and of an "urban society" as ideologies that relate a particular way of life to the specific ecology of the city instead of linking them to capitalist industrialization.[204] For Castells, urban ideologies—a paradigm of them being the definition of the city by Louis Wirth from his essay "Urbanism as a Way of Life" (1938)—are based on the claim of causal connections between the spatial forms of the city and the characteristic social content of urban culture. Castells considers Lefebvre's theory "a 'left-wing' version of the ideological thesis of urban society," derivative of the urban ideology.[205]

As an ideology of urbanism, Lefebvre's theory is in discord with Marxism, so Castells says. By relating the urban both to the emerging transformations of the contemporary city and to the vision of the future society as "emancipated creative spontaneity," Lefebvre violates Marxist premises by suggesting that this new society is engendered by the "form of the city," understood as a "simultaneity of concentration" of goods, people, and ideas, rather than being produced by social and political practice.[206] Another alleged "paradox" put forward by Castells is Lefebvre's claim that urban space facilitates social change, on the one hand, and his description of it as an expression of everyday life, on the other: "Whereas one makes urban practice the centre of social transformations, space and urban structure are pure transparent expression of social actors."[207] Castells claims that Lefebvre leaves Marxism by attributing to the city and urban space the agency that should be attributed to the social practices conditioned by economic and political relationships. Thus, he concludes, "Having set out from a *Marxist analysis of the urban phenomenon*, [Lefebvre] comes closer and closer, through a rather curious intellectual evolution, to an *urbanistic theorization of the Marxist problematic*."[208]

After its quick translation into English (1977), *The Urban Question* misguided much of the Anglo-Amercian reception of Lefebvre's theory until its "postmodern" rediscovery at the end of the 1980s: what Castells took for "paradoxes" was, in fact, Lefebvre's fundamental decision at a dialectical theorizing of the social production of space.[209] As several authors have pointed out, this misreading resulted from Castells's Althusserian Marxism and its hostility toward the Hegelian sources of Marx, which Lefebvre explored in his theorizing of dialectics.[210]

But Lefebvre's work was equally rejected by those subscribing to the orthodoxy of the DiaMat. A case in point is a 1981 review of the then-recent West German translations of several of Lefebvre's books, published in the East German architectural journal *Architektur der DDR*.[211] The authors reproached Lefebvre for what they perceived as his belief in a scientific–technological revolution that replaces the social–political revolution, a belief that "negates the fundamental thesis of the primacy of the economic social formation as the key to social development" and thus "has nothing in common with a Marxist position."[212] While Lefebvre is praised for describing urbanization as a global process, he is criticized for negating the "qualitative opposition between social–economic conditions in capitalism and socialism."[213] Rather than addressing Lefebvre's argument about the striking similarities between the space of state socialism and postwar capitalism, the authors accuse him of having an "idealist" concept of space, which led to his condemnation as a "bourgeois ideologist" who uses Marx's theses in order to disguise an idealistic theory and as a "modern revisionist" for whom the urban society is a "third way" between capitalism and socialism.[214] These statements render rather fairly the official reception of Lefebvre's books in state socialist countries, reflected in the abrupt end of translating his writings into Central and Eastern European languages after his suspension from the PCF. In a similar vein, the accusations against Lefebvre for an "activity of breaking away" and "blatant fractional activity," with which the PCF substantiated this suspension, conflate with the title of the 1964 review of *La somme et le reste* that was published in the Soviet Union, which in English translation is "Balance of a Renegade."[215]

If these discussions seem dated today, it is also because several of these critiques have since been withdrawn. And so, in *The City and the Grassroots* (1983) Castells employed Lefebvre's concepts, in particular that of the "urban revolution," which he earlier dismissed as "a play of words," just to admit in a recent interview, "I was right that Lefebvre was not very Marxist, but he was right not to be so."[216] The question, however, is not of the degree of Lefebvre's Marxism but rather of its specificity as opposed to both Althusser and DiaMat, which, in what follows, will be argued to have been developed from within Lefebvre's research on rural and urban sociology. These studies allowed him to address the most controversial themes of postwar Marxist debates, such as the theorizing of historical change, the question of class composition, and the critique of state socialism: three themes that set the theoretical and political stakes for the theory of the production of space.

The Pyrenees and Historical Change

The kernels of Lefebvre's revision of the Marxist understanding of historical change can be found as early as his study on the Pyrenees. Attracted by the image of the Campan Valley as a "pastoral republic," an egalitarian "valley of happiness," and the "new Arcadia," Lefebvre was interested in the social, political, and economic processes as well as the practices of everyday life that led to the emergence and the subsequent dissolution of this specific social formation. This is why the study encompasses almost three millennia, from the origins of the settlement in the valley to the present day, examining the conflicts between collective and private property and between the modes of life and the juridical systems as they are accompanied by political and economic shifts.[217] Lefebvre stressed that none of these perspectives is fundamental; rather, his approach was to "clarify" one type of facts ("economic," "historical," "juridical") by examining their dependence on others in order to grasp the relationship between "moments" of the process in question—a procedure that would be applied, thirty years later, in *The Production of Space*.

With the objective of discovering the persistent tendencies beyond the sequence of facts and events, Lefebvre's study was related to the work of the historians of the Annales School, grouped around the *Annales d'histoire économique et sociale* (Marc Bloch, Lucien Febvre, and later Fernand Braudel among others),[218] many of whom he knew personally.[219] Not unlike the Annales, Lefebvre's study rejected economic determinism and conceived social transformation in terms of possibilities rather than as determinations, structured by the historically specific lived daily experience. Like the Annales, Lefebvre stressed that social change is never restricted to the economy and ideology but also involves everyday life. Thus, for example, Lucien Febvre wrote in his doctoral dissertation, *Philippe II et la Franche-Comté* (Philip II and the Franche-Comté, 1911), that the struggle between the two social classes he had analyzed—the declining nobility and the rising bourgeoisie of merchants and lawyers—was not merely an economic conflict but a conflict of ideas and feelings as well. Similarly, Marc Bloch's influential *Feudal Society* (1939–40) was not restricted to an analysis of the relationships among land tenure, social hierarchy, warfare, and the state but studies what Bloch called "modes of feeling and thought." These attempts were explicitly developed in Braudel's *Capitalism and Material Life* (1967) in the project of the historicization of everyday life.[220]

Clear inspirations for the Pyrenees study came from the regressive method systematically introduced by Bloch.[221] Writing about Campan, Lefebvre argued that in order to understand the valley today and to envisage its future development, it is necessary to interrogate rural ways of life, uses, and ownership relations not only under the ancien régime but also under feudalism and earlier stages of social and economic development. While the starting point of his research is "descriptive and empirical," he felt it was necessary to complement the observations and interviews by means of a *regressive method* in order to go back from the traces and 'sociological fossils'—from what is contemporary—to the past": a method developed in his "Problèmes de sociologie rurale" (Problems of Rural Sociology, 1949).[222] This is why Lefebvre departs from "traces" or "splitters" of disappeared social structures that persisted until the twentieth century, such as the right of primogeniture of girls, strong neighborhood relationships, and a large share of collective property.[223] Since these "sociological fossils" are nonsynchronous with the current mode of production, their investigation cannot suppose a deterministic relationship between the economic base and ideological, legal, and cultural "superstructures," as the DiaMat would require.

Consequently, the study begins with a "provisory" definition of a rural community, which is qualified in the course of the investigation. A rural community is described as a social association that organizes, around the historically determined modalities, a group of families attached to land.[224] This is specified by three factors that define a rural community: the presence of both private and collective property (arable land, pastures, forests, waters, roads); the essential role of families in the structure of the village; and the delegation of tasks to representatives, who are directly responsible to the community ("direct democracy").[225] Lefebvre studied the changing relationships among these three factors in a long perspective stretching from the prehistorical period, through the Roman times, the Middle Ages, and the early modern period, to the revolution in 1789 and the introduction of the Napoleonic Civil Code, which put an end to the communities by privileging private property over collective property and individuals over families.[226]

Such a definition of rural communities—"provisory," "incomplete," "a hypothesis and an instrument of work"[227]—was developed and modulated by investigating the specific historical development of the Pyrenees. These investigations included research on geographic conditions, transhumance (livestock movement to higher pastures in summer and to lower valleys in winter), neighborhood relations, hereditary laws, taxation, family structure, and division of labor, as well as individualization and differentiation of social groups. None of these aspects is understood as determining the others, and what was investigated is the network of interrelationships rather than linear causal relations. It is the multiplicity of the interactions of these phenomena that constitutes the process of emergence, assertion, weakening, and dissolution of rural communities. Lefebvre reconstructed these processes through an analysis of archival documents, among which the "Cahiers de délibérations" were a privileged source: minutes of discussions held in the assembly of the village and by the elected representatives of the community. Their study offers a glance into "concrete everyday life," with its rhythms of rituals, gatherings, and transhumance; at the same time Lefebvre argues that these "small facts" needed to be linked to "more general perspectives."[228]

The rural community as a transhistorical social structure defined by the changing constellations of property relationships, family structure, and institutions of direct democracy cannot be thus inscribed into the rigid narrative of the subsequent modes of production, one taking over another. Rather, the community persists within the subsequent modes of production by adapting to the changing conditions and benefiting from the conflicts within the feudal and early capitalist systems as well as by using changing religions, ideologies, and legal systems to its advantage.[229] This is demonstrated, in particular, in the Campan study, which describes the struggles of the community for recognition by and autonomy from neighboring villages, feudal lords, cities, the Catholic Church, and the kingdoms of France, England, Aragon, and later Spain.

As a consequence, Lefebvre described Campan as a node of multiple times—much in accordance with Braudel's distinction among the history of relationships between man and environment; the gradually changing history of economic and political structures; and factual history (l'histoire événementielle).[230] All three "histories" were discussed in the Pyrenees study: the shaping of the geographical conditions (the expansion of arable land, the formation of routes by commodity circulation and transhumance); the slow transformation of economic, political, legal, and fiscal structures; and the history of events, such as wars, battles, and treaties.

In that sense, Lefebvre's "sociological history" is an attempt to relate the sequence of facts to a sociological research about long-term processes of reproduction and transformation of social structures:

> One could try to write, for every country (nation or region), a sociological history that avoids anecdote without omitting an explication of events (the "factual" history); that gives an account of the continuities and the most stable sociological elements without adopting the hypothesis of immutable substrates; that would be thus a history and give an account of the changes, of the discontinuities.[231]

Lefebvre's concern here is not to oppose one to another but rather to show their relationships without privileging any of them, to reveal persistent tendencies without losing the empirical character of the study.[232] This might be the reason why in his book the term sociological history is often exchanged with historical sociology, applied in the subtitle of his dissertation and described as a "dialectical movement between research on history and research on sociological reality."[233]

This approach prevents the recourse to geographical determination as an explanatory model for social development. Space in itself cannot be an explanatory factor, argues Lefebvre, because societies transform in a considerable way without significant changes in the environment. He stressed that the geographical environment *(milieu)* is "a necessary condition of social development, but it influences this development rather than accelerating it or slowing it down."[234] (This was already posited in his outlines of the Campan study submitted to Rivière in May 1944, in which Lefebvre argued, "Geography, just as geology, determines the conditions that, in themselves, are abstract in relationship to concrete development.")[235] Rather than trying to speculate about the consequences of topography in the history of mountain communities—a primary example used in geodeterministic literature of the late nineteenth century[236]—Lefebvre focused on archival research on the transactions concerning the particular use of singular pieces of land in determined historical circumstances. The study examined what Lefebvre would later call "spatial practices" of the community, such as transhumance and the management of commons (pastures, systems of routes). He gave particular attention to the struggles for the integration of the territory *(territoire)* of the community within the geographical borders of the valley by examining specific use agreements in regard to heredity regulations, fiscal contracts, and enfeoffment acts among the community of Campan, feudal lords, neighboring villages, the monastery of Escaladieu, the city of Bagnères, and the royal administrations.[237] Lefebvre stresses that this process cannot be separated from the formulation of the institutions of the community: the recognition of the territorial integrity of the valley since the fourteenth century, even if never fully accomplished, marks the transition from the "real" community (a community sustained every day in social practices) to a "legal" community, recognized by other actors of the feudal system but increasingly detached from the lived everyday.[238] The production of the territory and the production of community were interdependent and not separable from each other—a thesis that will return in Lefebvre's argument about the social production of space.[239]

In view of Lefebvre's later books about space, the study of the Pyrenees suggests that the introduction of this concept into the research of long-term processes challenges the reductive understanding of causality, power, and intentionality. This potential of Lefebvre's work was recently discovered by historians of the medieval and early modern city, who advance his understanding of historicity of space as a multifaceted and multivalent product of apprehension, experience, and reification and who develop his analysis of space as a physical, ideological, and symbolic reality.[240] Such "spatial history" suspends narratives that attribute structural changes to individuals by shifting attention to the historical processes that produced them. It rejects the reduction of cities to outcomes of processes generated by "the market," "political self-determination," or "the state" and thus allows an understanding that these abstractions are the products of spatial histories rather than their generators, even if these concepts are indispensable for a historical understanding of European cities, in particular of the period in question. In that sense, Lefebvre's work is read against the tendency to reductivism, which characterizes orthodox Marxist historical materialism, putting aside the determinative power of the market by revealing the agency of discursive and symbolic spatial practices, discovering rivalry among different elements of the citizenry where previous scholars have seen nothing but class struggle, and complicating the thesis about the homogenizing power of capitalism by discovering inside it a constant negotiation, dispute, and compromise over spaces.[241]

Farmers, Workers, Suburbanites

The two volumes on the Pyrenees, while dedicated to the memory of Engels, set the orientation points for Lefebvre's research on space and society by questioning orthodox Marxism and its account of the determination of social organization, ideologies, and ways of life by economic structures and modes of production. But at the same time this study engaged with current debates on the Left by raising questions about the possibility of autonomy and the self-management of a community and about collective ownership of land and its relative modalities irreconcilable with the capitalist concept of absolute individual ownership. This fed into Lefebvre's conviction that "among the branches of sociology, rural sociology is perhaps more than others intertwined with life, practical action, efficacy."[242] This argument was forged in the course of his postwar empirical studies, linked directly to political issues of class composition and the possibility of struggle against capitalism. His contacts with Bernard Lambert, the leader of the movement of *paysans–travailleurs* (farmers–workers) in the early 1960s,[243] his discussion of the position of the farmers within the apparent depoliticization of French society,[244] and the fact that the authorities of the USSR, Algeria, and Cuba denied him permission to carry out empirical research on agrarian policies in those countries made him aware of the political significance of the question of land.[245]

The political questions around the concept of class became central to Lefebvre's paper on Tuscany ("Les classes socials dans les campagnes" [Social Classes in the Countryside], 1951), developed within the Centre d'études sociologiques and focused on another "sociological fossil": the *métayage* system in agriculture, which is a form of sharecropping. On the basis of his interviews and analysis of statistical data related to landownership, professional structures, and production outputs, Lefebvre argued that the investigated rural population has no homogeneity; that is, it consists of several classes and groups rather than one single class. Distinguishing the classes of agricultural workers, small independent farmers, *métayers,* and landowners, Lefebvre investigated the conflicts among them and their specific forms of struggle.[246]

The question of class was very much discussed by the researchers of the CES,[247] and the sense of theoretical and political concerns with the transformation of class struggle in postwar society and its specific occurrences at that time was pertinent in the climate of opinion in which Lefebvre was immersed in the course of the 1950s and early '60s. Among the first radical leftist groups that investigated these topics was Socialisme ou barbarie, created in 1946 by Cornelius Castoriadis, Claude Lefort, and several other activists as an oppositional current within the Trotskyist Parti communiste internationaliste, with which the group broke in 1948. Between the late 1940s and late 1950s Socialisme ou barbarie developed an analysis of the transformations of the working class in the Fordist society, which the group characterized by the fundamental contradiction between management and subordinate labor, specific to both postwar capitalism and state socialism. This contradiction was investigated by the members of Socialisme ou barbarie who were sent to analyze workers' strikes and paid special attention to forms of organization and to political demands as well as to the conditions of daily life.

Thus, Claude Lefort, in his essay "L'experience proletarienne" (The Proletarian Experience, 1952), called for an analysis of classes as understood not only according to places assigned to them within the processes of production but also according to subjective modes of relationships in the course of historical development. The proletariat requires a specific approach that allows grasping its subjective development, argued Lefort, because the practice of the proletariat is not a simple consequence of its conditions of existence, but rather these conditions trigger a constant struggle for their transformation and thus a permanent distancing of the proletarian from his or her daily life: an experience that is constitutive for the proletariat as a class.[248] This experience ought to be examined, so says Lefort, by a specific analysis of the workers' appropriation of industrial work, the development of specific relationships among the workers, their own perception of these relationships, and the extension of these relationships to the whole society. What coincided with Lefebvre's attention to the lived experience was Lefort's stress on empirical research combined with skepticism toward a quantitative approach: what is necessary are studies about "concrete individuals" who are irreducible to a quantifiable average and yet share both the position of producers—operators of machines—and the condition of alienation.[249] Within this perspective, the research of Socialisme ou barbarie during the late 1950s focused on the possibility of an autonomous workers' movement in the circumstances of a destructuralization of the proletariat; a critique of the trade unions becoming institutionalized as a mediator between workers and management; the crisis of Marxist discourse dominated by Stalinism; and an analysis of mass culture, mass consumption, and the privatization of daily life—the last theme of which was developed by Guy Debord, a member of the group for a short time.[250]

The question of social class was at the center of not only numerous articles that Lefebvre published in the late 1940s and early 1950s but also his first paper on urban sociology focused on Mourenx, "Les nouveaux ensembles urbains."[251] The subtitle of the paper, "Lacq-Mourenx et les problèmes urbains de la nouvelle classe ouvrière" (Lacq-Mourenx and the Urban Problems of the New Working Class, 1960), reveals that it was inscribed into the debate of the "new working class," developed by the group around the journal *Arguments* and, in particular, the Club de la gauche: the groups that contributed to the emergence of the French New Left, including the Parti socialiste unifié (PSU). Spelled out since the late 1950s by Serge Mallet, Pierre Belleville, and Alain Touraine,[252] the thesis about the new working class aimed at accounting for the changes in class composition in industrialized countries after the Second World War. These authors argued that the automatization in advanced industries implied a new type of labor related to surveillance, control, management, intensification of specialization, and integration of the workers into the factory and an increase of responsibility of workers over the processes of production. This made wage calculation more complex (the workers have no individual skills beyond those required in the firm into which they are integrated) and a change in trade unionism, of which the basic unit tends to be the firm itself. Consequently, in *La nouvelle classe ouvrière (The New Working Class,* 1963), Mallet argued that while the workers of heavy industry could no longer envisage an alternative society, the new working class restores issues of autonomy and control to the center stage of the struggle between labor and capital, surpasses the wage demands of precedent movements, and assumes the revolutionary role that Marxism attributed to the proletariat.[253]

These discussions suggest that Lefebvre's "discovery" of Mourenx was not just a happy accident during one of the trips to the Pyrenees; the new town was built in order to house the staff of one of the most advanced petrochemical industrial complexes in postwar France and was thus a privileged place to test the hypothesis about the new working class. This is how Lefebvre discussed Mourenx during a conference in Dijon (1960), with Mallet and Touraine participating: as "a small social laboratory, a test tube in which the play of current social forces becomes visible and observable."[254] Lefebvre's analysis of this city aimed at examining the role of urban space and everyday life as modes of socialization of the "new workers," who indicated their potential to self-organization and political agency—a theme of which some of the designers of the new town were very much aware.[255] The cohabitation of people belonging to the same socioprofessional categories in the same buildings was seen by Lefebvre as a condition of the possibility of an enhanced class consciousness of the "new working class," in contrast to the fragmentation of the proletariat in the city of Aix-en-Provence.[256]

Henri Lefebvre commenting on the new town of Mourenx. From *Het Internationaal Filosofen Project*. Nederlands Instituut voor Beeld en Geluid, Hilversum.

Henri Lefebvre in front of the petrochemical factory in Lacq. From *Het Internationaal Filosofen Project*. Nederlands Instituut voor Beeld en Geluid, Hilversum.

The turn toward empirical research on the working and living conditions of workers, initiated by Socialisme ou barbarie, became central for many Marxist groups in Western Europe that in the course of the 1960s undertook a revision of Marxist categories. Among the most original was the Italian operaismo (worker-ism), whose theoretical and empirical work, including studies on the FIAT and Olivetti factories, advanced the question of class composition, a concept that aimed at capturing the combination of political and material characteristics of both the historically given structure of labor power and the determinate level of solidification of needs and desires that define the working class.[257] Both the technical aspect of class composition (the ways in which workers are brought together in the process of production and reproduction) and its political aspect (the forms of self-organization and struggle) make the question of the spatial composition of class particularly important, dictating workerism's political strategies and its theoretical valence.[258] In France, the question of class composition was addressed by Marxist urban sociologists, who interrogated the possibility of a convergence between urban and workers' struggles, in view of the increasing importance of individual and collective consumption in the economy as a whole, and the emergence of the urban protest movements of tenants in the *grands ensembles,* as well as those of workers in new industrial towns, squatters, users of public transport, and students.[259]

The team of the Institut de sociologie urbaine contributed to this discussion. One of the initial motivations for the research of the suburban house was to investigate the hypothesis of the *pavillon* as a class phenomenon—the specific habitat of the petite bourgeoisie, in contrast to the collective housing that was considered by many at that time a site for the emerging new working class. This hypothesis was decisively refuted, and one of the most important conclusions of the study was that no correspondence can be established between social class and the preference for the *pavillon* among the French population. This conclusion was confirmed by subsequent critical accounts, among the most influential of which was the paper "Proximité spatiale et distance sociale" (Spatial Proximity and Social Distance, 1970), by Jean-Claude Chamboredon and Madeleine Lemairelien. Oriented against the "prospective technocracy" of planners, the "populist utopia" of Chombart, and also the "urban prophecies" of Lefebvre (by which they might have meant the Mourenx study), the authors rejected the argument that spatial proximity facilitates social cohesion; rather than the shared conditions of dwelling engendering solidarity, the collective housing estates elicited the social differences among people of various social backgrounds and thus of different prospects for changing their accommodation. Yet Lefebvre never argued that spatial proximity alone creates social bond; rather, he aimed at theorizing dwelling as a practice that allows identifying the collective political subject (the "inhabitant") and redefines the working class by its deprivation of the "right of the city."[260]

The variety of the case studies chosen by Lefebvre and his collaborators, which straddled the peasant communities in the Pyrenees and Tuscany, the workers in Lacq–Mourenx, the inhabitants of *grands ensembles,* and suburbanites, contributed to rethinking class composition beyond Marx's atomistic vision of the proletarians as restricted to workers (and thus excluding as "lumpenproletariat" the unproductive parts of deprived populations: thieves, beggars, prostitutes).[261] Breaking with Marx's early vision of the proletariat as defined by its lack of property *(Eigentum)* and thus without qualities *(Eigenschaft),*[262] this research draws attention to the conditions of life of these populations conveyed by such concepts as urban space and the everyday. In that sense, Lefebvre's work is situated as research, unfinished until today, that develops a Marxist understanding of classes beyond its Eurocentric limitations and, in particular, breaks with Marx's image of the proletarian as "free" to sell "his" labor on the market within a nation-state.[263]

The Crisis of Marxism and the Socialist City

Lefebvre's dissociation from orthodox Marxism was paralleled by his disenchantment with state socialism in Central and Eastern Europe. His rejection of the Soviet model of socialism was shared by many intellectuals on the French noncommunist Left, who had become increasingly disillusioned in the wake of the Korean War of 1950–53, Budapest 1956, Prague 1968, and Solzhenitsyn's *Gulag Archipelago,* which was published in French in 1973 and marked the final shift of the majority of French intellectuals to an anti-totalitarian stance. This was paralleled by a golden age of a noncommunist "French Marxism," whose proponents included writers such as Kostas Axelos, Cornelius Castoriadis, François Châtelet, Lucien Goldmann, André Gorz, Claude Lefort, and Edgar Morin.[264]

In Lefebvre's contributions to these discussions were stirred by his exchanges with Marxist heterodox thinkers behind the Iron Curtain. He cultivated contacts in Hungary (he met Lukács in 1947) and Poland (he participated in philosophical congresses in Warsaw and Kraków, and he was interested in the work of the Polish "revisionists" such as Bronisław Baczko and Leszek Kołakowski).[265] It was in the Polish journal *Twórczość* that Lefebvre published his text "Marksizm i myśl francuska" (Marxism and French Thought, 1957)—the first open protest against the line of the PCF, which was written while Lefebvre was still its member and which coined a series of arguments to be spelled out in his books of the late 1950s.[266]

In "Marksizm i myśl francuska," Lefebvre opposed the Stalinization of the PCF and the assertion of the political authority of the Communist Party over ideological, cultural, and scientific activity, known as Zhdanovism, from the name Andrei

A. Zhdanov, secretary of the Central Committee of the Soviet Communist Party (1946–48).[267] Lefebvre argued that Zhdanovism led to the extreme polarization of the debates, and, as a consequence, the discussions on the French Left became impossible: dialectical thought was abandoned, and dogmatic schemes replaced specific and historical analyses of situations and problems.[268] The political criterion became transformed into a moral one—faithfulness to the party—which was crowned by the cult of Stalin. With all theoretical thinking subsumed under the foreign policy of the Soviet Union, Marxism became state ideology. This put an end to any development of science and philosophy (a "Marxist philosopher" was frowned upon as a "Communist with doubts," wrote Lefebvre), which were paralyzed by the division between "proletarian" and "bourgeois" science,[269] leading to the condemnation of Mendelian genetics, psychoanalysis, and cybernetics. In his text Lefebvre took responsibility, half-heartedly, for his earlier support of Stalinism (he confessed being "ashamed" for not protesting other than "by means of a persistent silence" against the "absurd ideological fight in the sphere of culture"), and yet he assured his support of Marxism, understood as "taking positions and taking the position of the party." What he questioned was not the party discipline but "the brutal, authoritarian, and undemocratic character of this discipline, and the brutal simplification of theoretical problems in the name of the party."[270]

The exchanges with Marxist dissidents from Central and Eastern Europe intensified after Lefebvre's break from the PCF, and they included his involvement with the group of Yugoslav Marxist "heretics" to whose journal *Praxis* he contributed.[271] Lefebvre was a member of the journal's advisory board, and he participated in several of the Korčula Summer Schools organized by the group: a meeting place for critical Marxist philosophers and sociologists from the whole world.[272] In his eyes Yugoslavia was a "political laboratory" that "achieved a political authority far superior to its economic and military importance" because of its "resistance to fascism, Stalinism, and etatist technocracy—by practical courage and theoretical energy."[273] Like for many on the New Left and in the *Arguments* group, Lefebvre hoped to discover in Yugoslavia the possibility of a "democratic planning" in opposition to the Soviet and French planning institutions, and he considered the experience of self-management as an alternative to the bureaucracy in the West and East.[274]

But state socialism posed not only a political and ideological problem but also a theoretical and scientific one: the question about the possibility of understanding the social dynamics behind the Iron Curtain by means of Marxist concepts. Since the 1960s Lefebvre described the post-Stalinist socialist states in the same way as he described capitalist states: as bureaucratic regimes of controlled consumption, oriented toward economic growth, and differing from the individualist Western model in their emphasis on collective consumption. This argument was accomplished in *De l'État,* in which Lefebvre characterized both socialist and capitalist states with the same concept: the "state mode of production" *(le mode de production étatique),*[275] driven by the logics of economic productivity and the reproduction of the social relations of production. Yet by using the same concept for countries on both sides of the Iron Curtain, Lefebvre tacitly admitted that the concept of mode of production is unhelpful for distinguishing between the two camps of countries, a conclusion shared by several sociologists working in state socialist countries at that time.[276]

In the paper "Sur quelques critères du développement social et du socialisme" (On Some Criteria of Social Development and of Socialism, 1965), published in the international edition of *Praxis,* Lefebvre suggested that the development of the socialist states and the various paths they took in the transition from capitalism can be used as criteria for the explanatory potential of Marxism. He argued that the work of Marx is "necessary to understand the modern world and to act in it, but this work is not sufficient." This is because of the specificity of twentieth-century capitalism characterized by an end of the social form embodied by the traditional European city and the crystallization of a new level of social practice: that of everyday life.[277] Both were generalized into the question of urban space; in *The Production of Space* Lefebvre asked, "What do we find when we apply the yardstick of space—or, more precisely, the yardstick of spatial practice—to societies with a 'socialist' mode of production?"[278]

Lefebvre never answered this question in an empirical manner, but it was addressed in the book *Społeczne wytwarzanie przestrzeni* (The Social Production of Space, 1988), by the Polish geographer Bohdan Jałowiecki, who visited France in the 1970s and was in touch with the ISU at the time when Lefebvre had already left it.[279] Jałowiecki's book was based theoretically on the discussions in French Marxist urban sociology and developed Lefebvre's arguments into a critique of the production of space in state socialism.

Jałowiecki opened his book with an essentially Lefebvrean statement: "The space we are living in is not a natural creation but a fully human work, produced by people in a way that is conditioned by natural, social, and cultural factors."[280] Referring to Lefebvre's essay "L'espace" (Space, 1972), Jałowiecki argued that space can be defined in four ways: as an abstract form; as a product of social practices in feudalism; as an intermediary, tool, instrument, milieu, and medium of social practices in competitive capitalism; and, finally, as the tool of reproduction of the social relations of production in monopoly capitalism and in "the early phase of the socialist formation," which, one year after the publication of his book, was revealed to have been its very late phase.[281] In Jałowiecki's view, with the shift from one mode of production to another, one definition of space spelled out in "L'espace" is not abandoned but rather included and extended by a new definition. Not unlike as described in Lefebvre's account of the Pyrenees, space produced in one mode of production is never fully surpassed with the change of this mode, being constantly filled, regrouped, or actively forgotten.[282]

The most innovative part of his book is Jałowiecki's investigation of the "political space" of the socialist People's Republic of Poland. The basis for the economic and political conditions of the urbanization of the country was the program of enforced industrialization, emerging from postwar economic and political conditions (the economic backdrop, war destruction, the change in property relations, the decision to enforce the proletariat as the driving force behind the new system, and the Cold War doctrine of self-defense and economic autarky, as well as, finally, the influence of the Soviet solutions). Developed with these constraints, the space of the People's Republic is described as "political space," because "the fundamental factors determining the social production of space are political decisions."[283] The main actors assigned with the task of spatial planning were political authorities (the central planning committee and the territorial planning agencies and planning offices of the various industry branches, coordinated by agencies of spatial planning), which planned economic and social development and worked out master plans.[284]

In reality, however, the planning decisions were made under the pressure of competing state enterprises and representatives of branches of industry. What was at stake in this competition, in the conditions of planned economy and the lack of a competitive market? While the issues of production costs and quality of commodities were paid lip-service by the authorities, the enterprises struggled for the maximalization of assets, which would allow them to sustain or even raise their productive output and their distributive capacities and thus to secure their political influence in relation to the local and central authorities. This was the inner drive of enterprises not only in Poland but in socialist countries in general, which, in contrast to capitalist firms, aimed at an accumulation of means of production rather than of profit.[285] Among these means, space was one of the most important. Accordingly, in Jałowiecki's account, late socialism is presented as a competition for space among enterprises, which, increasingly emancipated from the control of state power, aim at securing constant growth, not only in the production plant itself, but also in its reproductive facilities (housing for staff, transportation systems, and holiday villages). This hoarding of space was possible because of the restrictions imposed on the land market, yet without a complete nationalization of land; Jałowiecki writes that although these restrictions "provided favorable conditions for rational planning," the elimination of land rent resulted in the unlimited growth of industrial enterprises (which were not paying for the land) and the squandering of space in the center of cities.[286]

This analysis of socialist Poland accounts for both of the suggestions for revising Marxism that Lefebvre made in "Sur quelques critères du développement social et du socialisme." On the one hand, *Społeczne wytwarzanie przestrzeni* returns to the question of the relationship between the processes of industrialization and urbanization, whose interaction was seen by Lefebvre as putting an end to the traditional European city. Discussing the "industrial regions," Jałowiecki shows how industrialization hinders urbanization by subordinating all investments in space: transportation, housing, and social infrastructure.[287] This can be generalized into a characteristic of the production of urban space in late socialist Poland as it was subsumed by the logics of industrial enterprises. The industry became the main, if not the sole, factor in the construction of cities, while other functions not directly related to production, such as commerce, research, and tourism, were underfunded and underdeveloped. Consequently, state-owned industry impinged on the production of housing, spaces of consumption and leisure, and transportation, leading to spatial segregation, loss of urbanity, and ecological damage.[288]

On the other hand, the concept of the everyday suggests an understanding of state socialism as an urban revolution that did not keep its promises. In the first volume of his *Critique of Everyday Life,* Lefebvre wrote that "socialism (the new society, the new life) can only be defined *concretely* on the level of everyday life, as a system of changes in what can be called lived experience," and in *The Production of Space* he added, "A social transformation, to be truly revolutionary in character, must manifest a creative capacity in its effects on daily life, on language and on space."[289] This criterion—the critique of space in the perspective of everyday life *(critique quotidienniste)*[290]—was used by Jałowiecki, who argued, "The primacy of production over simple and extended reproduction of labor power meant, in fact, a loss of the fundamental aim of social economy, which is the rise of the conditions of life for the whole society."[291] Jałowiecki's investigation shows that this failure stemmed not just from planning fallacies but also from the political economy of space in Polish socialism—an account that, in many ways, intersects with Katherine Verdery's analysis of the "etatization of time" in Ceaușescu's Romania, resulting in an everyday marked by an arrhythmia of now-frenetic, now-idle work and a flattening of time in an experience of endless waiting.[292] As a result, the socialist state produced spatial disorder instead of a rational efficacy expected from the planned economy, subjecting everyday life to a series of spatial constraints rather than liberating it. On top of that, state socialism led to new forms of urban segregation instead of a classless society and, more generally, to massive inequalities in redistribution as a structural feature of the system and its condition of reproduction.[293] These conclusions tied in with Lefebvre's support of the strikes and protests in Poland in the early 1980s; he saw them as reclaiming self-management of everyday life and argued that the movement of the "Solidarność" trade union demonstrates that "the left critique of the state is closely akin to the critique of everyday life."[294] Complementing the study of the rural communities, industrial towns, and suburbanites in 1960s France, this critique of the production of space in state socialism suggests that what was at stake in Lefebvre's critical rethinking of Marxism in relation to the concepts of space and everyday life was both a revision of its explanatory value and a renewal of the work of Marx as a thinker of the possible.[295]

Lefebvre and the Institutionalization of Critique

Following the conviction that urban space replaces the factory as the privileged site of social conflict, empirical urban studies over the course of the 1960s and 1970s became leverage to revise and rethink Marxism for much of French Marxist urban sociology. Stirred by studies commissioned by the state to support the restructuring of French planning and urbanism, this research was particularly intense between 1968 and the mid-1970s, ending in the late 1970s with funding cuts in the wake of the economic crisis and with Marxist sociology running out of steam after the 1978 elections were lost by the Left, which also was followed by the end of the "Common Program"—the alliance between the PCF and the Socialist Party (PS).[296] What appears as a paradoxical renewal of sociology by the state's stabilizing the employment of its most critical political opponents is to be seen as a particularly intense moment within a more general process specific to the modern state: that of the institutionalization of critique within the processes of urban planning.

The empirical studies supervised by Lefebvre contributed to this process, which must be accounted for as one of the key conditions for his theory of space. Did the questions and themes of the state-funded research projects influence Lefebvre's theory, explicitly defined as "conceived against the state"?[297] What was the impact on the epistemic value of his theory by its instrumentalization within the planning discourses and operations? To what extent was this theory superseded by the production of new urban spaces for which it became an operative tool?

Sociologists within and against the State

Michel Amiot, in his book *Contre l'État, les sociologues* (Sociologists against the State, 1986), reconstructed French urban sociology between 1900 and 1980 by looking at its relationship of dependence and conflict with two other producers of knowledge: the state and the academic economy. This relationship was particularly complex in the postwar context, with the state redefined by means of a certain concept of the economy and transformed into the planning state (*État planificateur*)—an apparatus of informed intervention in all sectors of the society, including that of scientific research and thus also of social sciences.[298]

In his discussion about "democratic planning," Lefebvre defined planning as "a program of rational organization of production (industrial and agricultural) that secures harmonious development and growth without crises of productive forces."[299] This concept of planning originated in France from a conjuncture of several movements constituted in the 1930s, of which two were the most important: the groups uniting members of the administration and industry, such as the Groupe X-Crise; and the so-called nonconformist Catholic intellectuals gathered around the journal *Esprit,* supporting personalist humanism. Rarely interlinked before the Second World War, they encountered each other both in the Vichy institutions and in the Resistance and guided the development of planning ideas after the war. They were actively involved in the nationalizations of some sectors of the French economy and the foundation, under the directorship of Jean Monnet, of the Commissariat général du plan (1946), the central institution responsible for economic planning in postwar France. Opposed both to liberal capitalism and to state collectivism and skeptical about parliamentary democracy, they endorsed "economic humanism": the foundation of society on meritocracy, scientific knowledge, and state planning of the essential sectors of economy.[300] Since the 1960s, French sociologists tried to clarify this osmosis between the state and the private sectors—a condition called "monopolist capitalism of the state" by Marxists, who accused the state of serving big companies.[301]

This concept of planning necessitated a global and dynamic knowledge of society, based on an understanding of every element of the given situation and the anticipation of the situation in the long run. Dependent on interdisciplinary research, the planning state founded an unprecedented number of institutions of information gathering, coordination, and knowledge production. During the first Five Year Plan (1947–52) launched by the *commissariat,* with industrial development as its primary goal, the appeal went to economic sciences, which included, for example, the introduction of the theories of Keynes to academia. But already during the Second Plan (1954–57), which aimed at translating economic growth into the prosperity of French citizens, housing was a special concern, with over one million housing units built, and the social sciences were entrusted with the tasks of understanding the transformations of society in the processes of modernization and suggesting the instruments of growth management (or, in the words of the director of the Institut national de la statistique et des études économiques, determining the "limits of growth" by comparing the processes of modernization and the "resistance of human nature").[302] While some of the researchers, such as Jean Stroetzel, the successor of Gurvitch as director of the CES, embraced this role of sociology in facilitating reforms in technological modernization and spatial planning, others not only defended different concepts of the discipline and different visions of society but also assumed the role of spokespeople for weaker social classes.[303]

The criticism of the housing estates met the self-criticism of the planning agencies of the state as early as the 1950s—thus paralleling the most intense period of the construction of the *grands ensembles*—but until the mid-1960s this self-criticism was confined to internal memoranda, at least where the masterplans were concerned.[304] Notable precedents of the introduction of measures of critique into architectural design included the "apartment referendum" of 1959, organized by de Gaulle's first constriction minister, Pierre Sudreau, and his chief consultant, a Catholic activist, Jeanne Aubert-Picard. Aubert-Picard and her team consulted three hundred families living in state-subsidized housing, home-economic organizations, and family associations before elaborating, together with the architect Marcel Roux, a design of a model apartment, which was submitted to public scrutiny at the Salon des arts ménagers in 1959, redesigned after consideration of some of the criticism, and increasingly implemented in several large-scale housing estates from the early 1960s on.[305]

But it was not until the late 1960s that the general rejection of mass-housing schemes challenged the official discourse of the scientific rationality of planning, accompanied by a demand for more flexible and comprehensive regulations regarding land use, a wider participation of citizens in decision-making processes, and a social and political approach to urbanism as a means of social integration. This created a demand for a new type of studies—critical studies based on qualitative methods—and necessitated new ways of recruiting researchers, addressing not only big public and private research institutes, as was the case before, but also universities and small research groups without academic affiliation, such as the ISU. Open calls for contributions were used as main instruments to recruit researchers; formulated in a general way and encouraging the applicants to specify research topics in their submissions, these calls introduced procedures for negotiating research topics between researchers and commissioners.[306]

In the course of these negotiations, Marxist sociologists, such as Lefebvre and his team, were given the opportunity to reformulate research themes at the price of turning to a scientific field that was already claimed by three institutions pretending to scientific authority: the planning state, academia, and the PCF, with its doctrine of "scientific socialism." In the course of these negotiations, concepts began to take on different meanings, starting with that of the city, which, rather than being understood as a microeconomic model, was reinterpreted, on the one hand, as a process of capital accumulation and, on the other, as a system of signs, as influenced by structuralist linguistics and anthropology. Rather than furnishing the planners with new operative instruments, the sociologists aimed at turning the practice of planning and the institutions of the state themselves into objects of investigation; similarly, the demand of listing new needs of the consumers was reinterpreted into an analysis of urban struggles over collective consumption.[307]

These discussions permeate Lefebvre's books on space from the late 1960s and 1970s, which directly intervened in debates on urbanism and politics in order to challenge and redefine the concepts employed and to oppose their depoliticization, abstraction, and normalization. Lefebvre was particularly passionate in his critique of the discourse of urbanism, which came to the fore in the 1967 debate with Jean Balladur, the designer of the celebrated Mediterranean resort La Grande Motte, and Michel Ecochard, a CIAM member who elaborated urban plans in the French Protectorate in Morocco and, during the 1950s, in Iran, Syria, and Pakistan. During the debate Lefebvre criticized the misuses of the most discussed concepts of that time. He urged caution when postulating "multidisciplinary cooperation," which often slips into a struggle among disciplines for preponderance; he pointed out that "decentralization" becomes fictitious when operationalized by the centralized state; and he debunked the misuses of the procedures of "participation."[308] In another talk, he argued that procedures of participation as employed in the course of the 1960s during the design of the project of Toulouse Le Mirail by Candilis–Josic–Woods were a "mystification of a pseudo-democracy."[309] Participation as a tool of legitimization of an enforced consensus was also a target of his books, as were the concepts of the "environment of life" (*cadre de vie*), seen by Lefebvre as detaching urban questions from those of society and politics; "human scale," which easily takes a retrograde and formalist meaning; and "inhabitants" and "users," concepts replete in the discourse of urbanism since the 1950s.[310] The last was commented on retrospectively in a lecture in 1979, in which Lefebvre argued that the concept of the "user," once permeated with progressive claims for "use value" as opposed to "exchange value," has been increasingly exposed to the danger of depoliticization (with the "user" replacing the "citizen"), functionalization (by reducing "use" to services), and normalization (with the "users" increasingly defined according to an average within preconceived collective subjectivities).[311] All these concepts were appropriated by virtually all political actors, from the government to the far Left, and such slogans as "change life, change the city" (*changer la vie, changer la ville*) could have been found anywhere on the political spectrum.[312] Among the most contested concepts was the "way of life" (*mode de vie*), introduced to differentiate among factions of urban populations—a concept central to the work of the ISU, which was careful to distinguish its own use of this concept from other positions.[313]

The concepts coined by Lefebvre were themselves at stake in these debates, including his vision of the appropriation of space, the "right to the city," and the "urban revolution." They infiltrated the debates within the PCF, and the concern for the "right to the city" was very much present among the participants of the 1974 conference on urban matters, "Pour un urbanisme ..." (For an Urbanism ...), organized in Grenoble by the party's intellectual monthly *La nouvelle critique*, which gathered mayors, architects and planners, and social scientists, including members of the ISU, while direct references to Lefebvre were avoided.[314] The discourse and program of the PSU (Parti socialiste unifié) were even more directly influenced by Lefebvre's ideas, this party moving over the course of the 1960s from the problem of housing toward that of the alienated everyday life, campaigns for the environment of life, and the right to the city.[315] On the other hand, Lefebvre witnessed the incorporation of his wordings into the discourse of French planning, which took place within the "new urban policy" of the Valéry Giscard d'Estaing administration (1974–81), permeated by a conservative critique of the postwar rapid urbanization, which, according to Giscard, "after having arrived too late, arrived too fast."[316] But this incorporation had already begun during the final years of the presidency of Georges Pompidou (1969–74) and included the postulate of a new quality of urban everyday life; the redefinition of the city as a place of appropriation, festival, game, and interpersonal exchange; the support of the right to the city; the renewed interest in the centrality of streets and squares; and the attempt to reintroduce the collective dimension into urban space.[317] These ideas were expressed in the directive of Minister Olivier Guichard (1973), who condemned the *grands ensembles* and social segregation through habitat in the name of "human scale" *(mesure humaine)* and the improvement of the quality of "environment of life" *(cadre de vie).*[318]

In response, Lefebvre's writings are full of irony about "the parades, masquerades, balls, and folklore festivals authorized by a power structure [that] caricaturizes the appropriation and reappropriation of space" and warnings about centrality becoming a tool of social regulation, "elitist at best, military and policed at worst."[319] In the third volume of the *Critique of Everyday Life,* he noticed that "an idea or a project regarded as irredeemably revolutionary or subversive—that is to say, on the point of introducing a discontinuity—is normalized, reintegrated into the existing order, and even revives it."[320] This does not mean, he continued, that this project was not potentially active for a period of time; rather, its cooptation means that the opponents of the dominant order were unable to seize the opportunity and to carry out the project.[321]

At the same time, Lefebvre argued that the introduction of critical concepts into broad public discourse does not necessarily dismantle their critical potential but can be used to broaden the discussion and advance political goals. Lefebvre had already argued this in his mid-1950s article in *Twórczość,* in which he reflected on Marxism and Marxist dialectics becoming an intellectual fashion in France, gaining the upper hand over the individualist rationalism that dominated the prewar philosophical discussions. With "every Frenchman becoming a dialectician," what is being sold as "dialectical oppositions" resembles "an anthology of macabre jokes" and "parodic songs from Montmartre"—a spectacle of pure sophistry that is carried on in the misuse of other Marxist concepts, including alienation.[322] In this condition, wrote Lefebvre, a Marxist could be filled with indignation; protest against the "forgers, intellectual criminals, parasitic individuals, and rogues" who deprived the working class of the concept of dialectics—its main intellectual weapon; and call for a renouncement of concepts "misused in bourgeois thought."[323] This was the position of the Stalinist PCF and its ecclesiastic mode of the production of its doctrine.[324] Yet in contrast to the discourse of the PCF, which prevented the possibility of a discussion with political opponents, Lefebvre argued that Marxists should acknowledge that such concepts as alienation, after having entered almost everyday language, "became a place of meeting and discussion."[325] By "becoming worldly," a concept stakes out a field of political discussion in which this concept can be critically fathomed: the very method used by Marx, who picked up economic, political, and philosophical concepts from his predecessors as symptoms of specific historical conjunctures and developed them in a critical way.[326]

A similar strategy was used by Lefebvre himself, who mastered the co-optation of concepts from political opponents in order to shift demarcation lines and reformulate questions. This includes those concepts that became inextricably linked to his name, such as the right to the city, in which reverberate the 1930s discussions of "urban rights," suggested by Jean Giraudoux, who was a conservative thinker, in the first years of the Second World War close to the Vichy regime, and who introduced the Athens Charter to the French readers in 1943 as a possible remedy for the "destruction of the national soul."[327] Similarly, Lefebvre's *Urban Revolution* was not the first book published in France with this title, being preceded by the 1946 publication of the architect and urbanist Pierre Lauga, who called on architecture and urbanism to "rescue" political economy, as the subtitle of his book went, and postulated constructing new towns according to functional and economic principles. The same strategy was used by Lefebvre in his academic position; as a professor of Nanterre, he used the new authority of sociology to teach Marxism: "What I have taught under the cover of sociology was simply Marxist thought," not, however, identified by the writings of Marx, but developed to account for the transformations of the modern world, industrialization, and urbanization.[328] This suggests that research that would critically question the originality of Lefebvre's work in general and his writings on space specifically—the very questioning avoided by most of the research on his theory—must account not only for the complicated genealogy of his concepts but also for the engaged, contextual, appropriative, and performative character of his writings, which cannot be fully captured by the logics of originality.

The Crisis of a Superseded Theory?

Lefebvre's theory is to be seen as formulated in a conjuncture of two interrelated processes at the end of the late 1960s and in the early 1970s: the politicization of French urban sociology on the one hand, and the introduction of the questions of the city and urbanization into French politics on the other.[329] In this context, the incorporation of Lefebvre's concepts into state planning discourse was conditioned by a systematic erasure of the name of their author; as it was put by Jean-Pierre Garnier, the more Lefebvre was plagiarized, the less was he quoted.[330] In the 1978 book *La comédie urbaine ou la cité sans classes* (The Urban Comedy or a City without Classes), Garnier and Denis Goldschmidt argued that the co-optation of Lefebvre's discourse by state planning institutions was an attempt to conceal the withdrawal of the state from its social obligations vis-à-vis the suburbs by reducing the social problems faced in the city (unemployment, discrimination) to merely problems of urban design. Accordingly, the city was presented as autonomous and independent of social relationships; Lefebvre's concept of the right to the city was used as a substitute for other, more fundamental rights, in particular for the right to housing.

According to Garnier, this co-optation continued after the elections of 1981, won by the Socialist candidate François Mitterrand. Identifying socialism with the "civilization of the city" in his introductory address, Mitterrand promoted such concepts as urbanity, centrality, and the city as a work of art *(oeuvre),* which became part of the discourse of the political class. This was manifested in an interview with Michel Delebarre, the first "minister of the city" *(ministre d'État à la ville),* who pointed at a copy of *Le droit à la ville* as the supposed theoretical foundation of the new urban policy, and the integration of Lefebvre's ideas into the program Banlieues 89, launched by Roland Castro and Michel Cantal-Dupart in 1983.[331] These interventions, paralleled by Mitterrand's *grands travaux,* meant to promote the capital's centrality as an oeuvre, were undertaken to cover up the redirection of the public effort away from the problem areas, the unwillingness of the state to construct social housing and the widening gap between the center of agglomerations and the pauperized suburbs. "They demand work? Give them monuments! They want equality? Give them urbanity!" write Garnier and Goldschmidt.[332]

In the language of Luc Boltanski and Eve Chiapello, Lefebvre's theory appears emptied of "social" critique of capitalism and becomes reduced to its "artistic" critique. These two were distinguished in *The New Spirit of Capitalism* (1999), with the artistic critique targeting disenchantment and inauthenticity of the capitalist sphere in the name of autonomy and the possibility of self-realization, and the "social" critique opposing exploitation with demands of security and social justice.[333] *The New Spirit of Capitalism* tells the story of the artistic critique preparing the shifts in capitalism of the 1970s and 1980s by contributing to the valorization of flexibility, creativity, affective affinity, passion, and individualism, paralleled by transformations of the organization of labor on the morphological level (relocation and subcontracting) as well as organizational (reduction of hierarchical management structures) and legal transformations (flexibilization of contracts). These shifts were carried out by a new elite of experts, planners, consultants, and researchers, many of whom participated in the events of May '68 and whose influence was strengthened after the Left's accession to power in the 1980s. By responding to the demands of artistic critique and by incorporating the values in whose name postwar capitalism was criticized, a "new spirit of capitalism" was produced, providing new criteria of justice; facilitating their formalization and institutionalization; and giving new reasons for an involvement of the members of the society in the procedures of capitalism.[334]

For Boltanski and Chiapello, the artistic and social critiques are "not directly compatible," owing to their different ideological and emotional sources and various genealogies: the Bohemian lifestyle of the nineteenth century on the one hand and the history of the working class on the other. Because of this incompatibility, the associations between the two types of critique are bound to fall apart.[335] But this fatalism testifies, first of all, to the historical condition of which the book was a part, and *The New Spirit of Capitalism* can be read as an account of the emergence of a specific framework of perception within French society in the last forty years, in which the split between the artistic and the social critique appears unavoidable. This includes the crisis of the PCF overidentified during the postwar years with social revindication—a crisis to which the leftist anticommunist parties responded by developing a different critical discourse; the drying up of unitary narrations about the society, such as socialism or Catholicism; the deunionization of the French working class; and the restructuring of the class composition of France.[336]

Garnier, for his part, would add to this the emergence, since the late 1960s, of the *petite bourgeoisie intellectuelle,* which he perceives as a new class assigned with the role of mediation between the lower echelons of the population (workers, teachers, lower officials), from which it issued, and the technocratic elites, to which it aspired.[337] In this reading, the discourse of preservation, consolidation, and restoration of "social bonds" never engaged with Lefebvre's project of transformation of everyday life, and the questions of exclusion and inequality were framed as problems of urban design rather than consequences of contemporary capitalism. While Lefebvre pronounced that an idea is not responsible for its abuses, he was held responsible by some of his friends and acquaintances, including Claude Schnaidt, who argued that he should have stayed away from the concept of the right to the city, by which "he has given moral credit to a retrograde urban policy" and "got stuck in an anachronistic vision of urban centrality."[338]

What is at stake here is not just the question of misuse and legitimization but also the operationalization of Lefebvre's concepts within what Michel Foucault has called apparatuses of security. In his lectures at the Collège de France (1977–79), Foucault examined the origins of liberalism and analyzed the emergence of biopolitical techniques of governability in city planning in the late eighteenth century, which took advantage of the given logics of the situation in order to manage the circulation of air, people, commodities, and "crime" by maximizing what is considered positive and by minimizing what is considered negative. Such understood apparatuses of security aim at a management of open series (flows of specific elements, successions of events, and sequences of buildings) that are controlled according to a calculation of probability; the very idea of a state coordination of individual actors continued in the French postwar planning.[339]

In other words, Lefebvre's work on space needs to be accounted for within the transformations of the liberal modes of governability—a perspective that was implied by the book *Actualité de la pensée d'Henri Lefebvre: La question de la centralité* (Actuality of Henri Lefebvre's Thought: The Question of Centrality, 1998), by Laurent Devisme. Looking back at the past thirty years of French urbanism, Devisme's book aims at relativizing the scope of the co-optation of Lefebvre's theory in general and his concept of centrality in particular in a range of planning practices in France, including urban regeneration projects in historical neighborhoods, new business and commercial centers, and postwar new towns. Returning to Lefebvre's description of centrality, Devisme points out that it can be produced neither by marketing campaigns nor by any particular kind of urban morphology, because it is overdetermined by a variety of factors: urban design, functional programming, practices of everyday life, legal regulations, mental maps, tourist campaigns, and scientific and mass media representations, including the representation of centrality itself. In this sense, centrality cannot be fully controlled by any particular agent of power: the urban planner, the developer, or state authority.

However, the empirical part of Devisme's book shifts the discussion from the question of controlling centrality to that of centrality becoming an instrument of control. The author proposes a typology of centralities and distinguishes among the centrality of "sedimented centers," exemplified by the square Capitole in Toulouse and the square Plumereau in Tours; the "centers of decisions" described on the basis of the Parisian La Défense; and the "centers in the periphery," such as the new town of Hérouville. The analysis of these centralities focuses on practices of administrative and economic powers that take into account what is "there" (historical city, new business district, postwar new town) in order to purify it and transform it into a fixed norm: the image of a traditional European city, the vision of modernity, or the myth of a community. In Devisme's analysis, centralities appear as apparatuses of security: produced by administrative and economic powers, not by imposing an external norm, but by optimalizing what is found in situ. The possibility of dissent is thus not erased but rather reduced to a statistical error or marginal abnormality: centralities become regulators of urban reality and multivalent and flexible frameworks for a series of events consistent with an average found in reality itself. Yet this normativity of centralities that is attributed to three types of urban fabric cannot be taken for granted; thus, what is missing in Devisme's book is an analysis of the struggles that lie behind the production of these centralities and the spatial-social contradictions that propel these struggles; in short, what is needed is an examination of space as a stake of struggles.

With centrality becoming an operative concept, Lefebvre's theory appears superseded—a condition that might explain its current minor status within French urban research and the replacement of his general perspective on space by a more specific focus on citizens, users, or inhabitants constructing their narratives and their agency.[340] In other words, Lefebvre's theory seems to share the fate of Marxism, which Étienne Balibar, writing in the late 1980s, saw as "party to the superseding of its own future prospects."[341] Balibar argued that if Marxism is "superseded" (that is to say, if its revolutionary program cannot be realized as formulated on the basis of capitalism as Marx knew it), it is because contemporary capitalism has moved beyond the conditions that Marx knew. But this development of capitalism was partly a response to the Soviet revolution, which was an offspring of Marxism, or was considered to be one. At the same time, Balibar noticed that Marxism paradoxically preserved its explanatory value after its alleged realization in socialist countries: as a theory of social conflicts, it "appears to be *in advance* of its own 'completion.'" While the normativity of a "classless society," or at least a society "without class struggle," passed into actual institutions in these states, they were not politically static; on the contrary, state socialism was characterized by a struggle of workers against the monopolistic party–state, thus by a class struggle "of the most classical sort," which was the core of Marxist theory.[342]

The same is the case with Lefebvre's theory: the instrumentalization of the concept of centrality in the dominant practices of the production of space does not erase the struggles around centrality, even if the character of these struggles has been transformed since the time Lefebvre theorized them. On top of that, the introduction of concepts into official discourse offers an entrance point not only into "meeting and discussion," as Lefebvre wrote in *Twórczość*, but also into a revindicative struggle. The analogy with socialist Central Europe can be taken further: just as the workers in socialist Poland demanded influence on the decisions made in their name in the "workers country," so does the institutionalization of such concepts as centrality, and even more so the right to the city, open up the possibility of struggle for the excluded to be heard. Accordingly, beyond the context of the 1960s French welfare state, the right to the city becomes less a set of legal entitlements and more a claim that undermines other "rights" on which exclusion from the city is perpetuated—first of all, the absolute right to private property of space. This reveals the limits of the institutionalization of Lefebvre's theory: with the withdrawal of the republican penal state from Mitterrand's urban policy beginning in the 1990s,[343] the right to the city, which, first included in the 1991 *Loi d'orientation pour la ville,* was soon declared of "no normative nature," not the least in order to prevent derivative claims raised by the "experts," including Étienne Balibar himself, who pointed out the contradictions this new "right" triggered within the French legal system.[344]

These discussions have been contextualized by the worldwide rise of interest in Lefebvre's work beginning in the late 1980s, rediscovered in Anglo-American geography, sociology, and cultural and political studies and, since then, reflected in France itself. The titles of books by Edward Soja, David Harvey, and Fredric Jameson that paved the way to this discussion—*Postmodern Geographies* (1989), *The Condition of Postmodernity* (1990), *Postmodernism, or the Cultural Logic of Late Capitalism* (1991), respectively—complemented by the work of Derek Gregory and Michael Dear, reveal that this rediscovery took place within the debates on the "postmodern" condition, particularly sensitive to such themes in Lefebvre's writings as difference, the critique of modernity, the rejection of binary logics, and space.[345] While these readings were essential for putting Lefebvre's theory of space back on the intellectual map, for stimulating further research on it, and for clarifying some of its concepts, they have equally contributed to the worldwide introduction of his slogans into a discourse about the city that in many ways could not be further from his arguments. Is it possible to sustain Lefebvre's discourse about the ludic city after it becomes the rallying cry in architecture and urbanism of the experience economies?[346] What is the relevance of Lefebvre's call to go beyond functionalist separations of time and space in circumstances in which spatiotemporal flexibility becomes an essential part of the neoliberal urban reality?[347] What can be retrieved from the project of the empowerment of inhabitants in circumstances in which participation becomes an essential component of governability?[348] How can one celebrate the urban everyday, with the numerous gentrification projects carried out in its name? What is left of Lefebvre's embrace of the unforeseen when the event turns out to be the domi-nant paradigm for architectural practice?[349] How can his call for difference avoid identity politics reduced to a management of reified identities that are themselves products of oppressive structures and more often than not prevent an articula-tion of class interests?[350]

Clearly, the doubts underlying these questions cannot simply be rejected as misuses or misreadings of Lefebvre's theory; neither can they be explained away by a hermeneutics of his texts—an endeavor impossible to accomplish without accounting for their polemical character, written against the normalization of critical concepts. Rather, these questions suggest a close relationship between the credibility of Lefebvre's theory today and his project of a possible space—an entanglement that requires a closer look at his engagements with the practices of architecture and urbanism. This question about the possibility of the architectural imagination reaching beyond the immediate conditions of its instrumentalization was specifically what was at stake in the 1960s and 1970s architectural debates in which Lefebvre was immersed, and, as I will argue in the following chapters, this is why architecture became for him a privileged practice for investigating the conditions of critical thinking within the ongoing processes of its institutionalization.

The Experience of Critique

By addressing the crisis of Marxism and the institutionalization of critique in modern capitalism and by the modern state, which at the same time oppress their critics and hire them,[351] Lefebvre shaped a range of concepts that set orientation points for urban research and design today, such as the everyday, difference, scale, production of space, and the right to the city. Yet equally important in his work is what can be experienced only in direct contact with his texts, which constantly redefine the concepts, fine-tune the arguments, and adjust them in response to the arguments of his opponents: an experience of critical thinking from within an ongoing debate. This way of writing was reflected in Lefebvre's disciplinary and institutional nomadism and in his attempt not to be assigned a fixed place, to be "unclassifiable," as he described himself in a 1970 interview. "This means that I am not a part of the social division of labor; . . . of course, I am a professor, a teacher; I have a job, but I am not institutionalized by the society. I am not a specialist. . . . This allows the refusal of a premature solution."[352] For many, including some of his students at Nanterre, this statement was proof of his naivety if not his cynicism: Lefebvre might have believed that his theory is irreducible to the instrumental logics of the institutions within which it was developed—whether a research institute, a university, or the Communist Party—but at the same time he himself admitted that "everything is recuperable."

Cynicism seems to be thus a correct diagnosis here, provided that it is not understood as a moral flaw but rather, following Peter Sloterdijk, as the involvement of modern critique with the mechanisms of power.[353] This is why an external position is impossible: asked by an interviewer whether he considered himself living in exile, Lefebvre said that if this was the case, it was only in the sense of a voluntary exile, "within and outside society." But, he added, he would rather describe himself as peripheral, that is to say, positioned in relationship to centers of wealth and power but not included in them.[354] A critique without a fixed place, no doubt, but also a critique from within the given and constantly transforming conjuncture: this was the figure Lefebvre developed, sometimes more successfully, sometimes less, in his political and philosophical writings as much as in his multiple engagements with concrete research on space. Did his negotiation of the research topics with the planning state not prefigure his contribution to the emerging institutional analysis, theorized in the work of René Lourau as an analysis of an institution by producing a crisis from inside?[355] Did his attacks on poststructuralism—which he considered an illusion of the possibility of producing a rupture from within the text by means of the textual strategies of reading and writing—not stem from his disenchantment with the PCF and his attempt to "fight its dogmatism from within"?[356] In the following chapters, I aim at a reading of Lefebvre's work as an experience of a critical thinking from within a historical conjuncture that, as the double challenge to his theory demonstrated, is in many ways still ours.

Research
From Practices of Dwelling to the
Production of Space

N O CONCEPT IS MORE ATTACHED to the name "Henri Lefebvre" than that of "the production of space." The understanding of space as produced in social practices that, in turn, appropriate space as their tool, medium, and milieu was developed in Lefebvre's writings from *The Right to the City* (1968) to *The Production of Space* (1974). But this understanding was prepared by many research projects, discussions, seminars, and political engagements from the late 1950s on, and their review will allow tracking the origins and the stakes of Lefebvre's work.

Before turning to such sources of the concept of the production of space as the German idealist philosophy, the Marxist critique of the state, and the architectural debates of the 1960s and 1970s, I will focus on Lefebvre's engagements with the work of the Institut de sociologie urbaine and its studies of the practices of dwelling (*habitation*) carried out in the 1960s and early 1970s. In what follows, Lefebvre's theory will be shown as a development from within his rethinking of ISU's research on dwelling, which included his formulation of the three "moments" of space that form the core of his theory of the production of space: the triad of perceived, conceived, and lived space, as well as the "translation" of this triad into "spatial terms," resulting in the second triad of spatial practices, representations of space, and spaces of representation.[1]

While all researchers working with Lefebvre's theory agree that both triads have a transcultural and transhistorical character,[2] the wording used in *The Production of Space* to introduce the triads points at a highly specific cultural and historical context. Spatial practices were "defined" by the "extreme but significant case . . . [of] the daily life of a tenant in a government-subsidized high-rise housing project"; representations of space were understood as its conceptualizations by "scientists, planners, urbanists, technocratic subdividers and social engineers, as of a certain type of artists with a scientific bend"; and the spaces of representation were explained as space "directly *lived* through its associated images and symbols, and hence the space of 'inhabitants' and 'users,' but also of some artists and perhaps of those, such as a few writers and philosophers, who *describe* and aspire to do no more than describe."[3] In these explanations the discussions in French urban sociology, architecture, and urbanism from the 1950s to the 1970s reverberate, and in this chapter I will relate Lefebvre's theorizing of space to the research carried out by him and his collaborators in the 1960s and early 1970s, including his account of the practices of architects and his critiques of the modes of representation they employ, his exposure of urbanism as overdetermined by the state and the emerging society of consumption, and his exchanges with philosophers and artists addressing space. In particular, the ISU studies on dwelling in a detached house (*pavillon*) and in collective estates (*grands ensembles*) were what provided orientation points for Lefebvre's understanding of the production of space as not limited to the domain of bureaucrats, administrators, and planners but taking place in everyday activities of "'inhabitants' and 'users'"—qualified by Lefebvre with quotation marks in order to signal his distance from the planning and sociological discourse.[4]

The research of the ISU and in particular the study *L'habitat pavillonnaire* (1966), by Nicole Haumont, Antoine Haumont, Henri Raymond, and Marie-Geneviève Raymond, were carried out in several French cities, with special attention to the region of Paris.[5] The study defined the *pavillon* as "an individual urban or suburban house with a garden, as opposed to the collective estate and the rural house,"[6] an opposition particularly pertinent in the "paradoxical space" of the Parisian periphery, as Lefebvre put it.[7] This opposition between individual and collective housing shaped the French sociological discussions from the 1950s to the 1970s, with the stigmatization of the *pavillon* as anti-modern, individualistic, and petit-bourgeois—associations related to the debates on the housing question in France since the mid-nineteenth century, investigated within the ISU by Marie-Geneviève Raymond.[8] In the postwar discussions, this critique of the individual house was shared by a wide range of thinkers on the political spectrum.[9] For the technocratic proponents of modernization, the alleged individualism of the *pavillonnaires* (the inhabitants of the pavillon) and their supposed desire for isolation contrasted with the visions of a modern French society facilitated by collective housing and characterized by social mobility, the diminishment of class differences, and the emancipation of women. The social Catholics, including Chombart, were critical of the *grands ensembles* constructed in France since the mid-1950s but considered them in most cases the only possible choice in view of the great costs of individual housing. For Chombart they were potential places where the "social structures of tomorrow . . . are produced," "a new civilization tends to express itself," and a new cohesion among social classes can be established.[10] The political Left and the PCF specifically argued a homology among the working class, the public construction industry, rented accommodation, and collective housing, and they mocked the individual house as an alienated way of life resulting from the ideology of the petit bourgeois.[11]

In spite of these condemnations, the *pavillon* was an object of aspiration for 82 percent of the French population in the mid-1960s[12]—a fact that was the starting point of *L'habitat pavillonnaire*. The ISU argued that even if the daily speech of the *pavillonnaires* is permeated by conservative discourse grounded in decades of French debates around the housing question, the widespread preference for the *pavillon* cannot be explained as a projection of these debates on everyday life; rather, the preference stems from the *pavillon* lending itself to a set of practices that were not supported by the rigid layout of the collective housing estates as built until the mid-1960s. This conclusion led to a direct confrontation with architectural practices; in a retrospective account, Antoine Haumont and his colleagues wrote that *L'habitat pavillonnaire* had aimed at contributing to a concept of architecture that allows for the inhabitants' "mastery" of the habitat.[13] This concept was based on Lefebvre's distinction between *habiter* (to inhabit) ("an activity, a situation") and *habitat* (a "morphological description")[14] but free from his polemics against *habitat* ("a caricatural pseudoconcept . . . , a simplified function which limited the 'human being' to a handful of basic acts: eating, sleeping, and reproducing").[15]

The focus on dwelling as a set of practices led to a critique of the concepts of "need" and "function" associated by the researchers and Lefebvre himself with modern architecture, functionalist urbanism, and the Athens Charter. If this critique, which will be one of the returning themes of this chapter, reads as reductive today, it is because it identifies the modern movement and functionalist urbanism with French state urbanism of the late 1950s and 1960s, without accounting for the discussions in postwar architectural culture at that time, which shared many concerns of Lefebvre's writings on space. These discussions included, in particular, the development of the postwar Congrès internationaux d'architecture moderne (International Congresses of Modern Architecture, CIAM) and their critique of the Athens Charter in the name of "habitat" as encompassing the everyday practices of dwelling. Already at the seventh congress in Bergamo (in 1949), Le Corbusier urged the replacement of the Athens Charter by the "Charter of Habitat." The work on the replacement charter, while never completed, advanced in the 1952 meetings in Paris and Sigtuna, during which the French architect André Wogenscky suggested discussing "dwelling" (*habitation*) rather than habitat and redefining dwelling as a set of everyday practices that are not limited to a single apartment but extend to commercial, health, educational, social, and administrative services.[16] During the ninth CIAM meeting in Aix-en-

Provence (1953), organized under the title "Charter of Habitat," Alison and Peter Smithson challenged the Athens Charter and urged its replacement by a "hierarchy of human associations," and Wogenscky suggested that the meeting should study, instead of the four functions, "LIVING and everything that man plans and constructs."[17] As Shadrach Woods underscored, it was in Aix that the main concerns of Team 10 were developed, including the interrelationship among four functions of the Athens Charter (living, working, recreation, transportation) and the focus on change, growth, mobility, and identity: all themes that were extensively discussed during the last CIAM meeting in Dubrovnik (1956), prepared by Team 10.[18] In the 1954 Doorn Manifesto (originally called the Statement on Habitat), which is considered to be foundational for Team 10, the Athens Charter was presented as a response to the chaos in the nineteenth-century city, to be replaced by new criteria for planning that would account for the everyday in the postwar society.[19] Among the French members of Team 10, the concept of habitat became particularly prominent in the discourse of the architects Georges Candilis and Shadrach Woods, who, together with Alexis Josic, founded an office in 1955 and practiced in France and its North African colonies. In the writings of the partners, habitat was redefined as an ecological concept encompassing both the individual practices of dwelling and the collective dwelling culture, with the aim of mediating between the contradictions coming to the fore in the rapid processes of modernization: between the urban and the rural, the spiritual and the material, the modern and the traditional ways of living.[20]

These discussions, however, were restricted to architectural culture and did not influence large-scale French housing production until the end of the 1960s.[21] The inspiration for the ISU came rather from French anthropology (Marcel Mauss, Claude Lévi-Strauss, and Jean-Pierre Lebeuf), and in this vein, the *institut* focused on heterogeneous practices of dwelling, understood as procedures that modify the everyday spaces and their objects by giving them meaning.[22] This was followed by a double research method: the examination of the arrangement of the *pavillon* as a system of significations, on the one hand, and interviews with the inhabitants as a way to account for the meaning the *pavillonnaires* attached to the practices of dwelling, on the other.[23] In this method, dwelling was examined as a set of practices that produce the space of the *pavillon;* in the words of the ISU, "Space tends to be produced (*fabriqué*) according to rules that assign to spaces significations that are a function of a certain vision of social relationships."[24]

These practices were analyzed on three levels. First, the researchers focused on operations of marking, limiting, and arranging space, becoming familiar with it, and transforming it by manipulation of objects. Marking a space (by building a fence or taking care of a house) introduces distinctions between open and closed, clean and dirty, empty and full, seen and hidden, seeing and being seen— practices that, in the course of the 1960s, the ISU increasingly referred to with the general term *appropriation* of space.[25] The "marked" distinctions are always already socialized, in other words translated into such oppositions as public and private, female and male, work and leisure, which structure social groups in a given society (family, friends, acquaintances, neighbors, visitors). The second level of analysis accounts for practices of the socialization of space, that is to say, practices that introduce these distinctions into the domestic space. The researchers of the ISU define the socially accepted relationships between these oppositions by means of the concept of a "cultural model" defined in reference to the work of Georges Gurvitch and, in the course of the 1970s, approximated to Pierre Bourdieu's concept of "habitus": a system of durable, transposable dispositions that function as principles generating and structuring practices and representations that conform to socially determined rules without being understood as consciously presupposing them.[26] One of the main arguments of the research of the ISU was that inhabitants transform spaces in order to comply with their cultural model: a sense of what is and what is not appropriate to do in specific spaces in the *pavillon*.[27] This, for example, requires the introduction of boundaries, thresholds, and spaces of transition into areas expected to be associated with different levels of privacy, from the front garden, the entrance, the dining and living rooms, the kitchen, the children's bedrooms, to the master bedroom as the most private place, connoted by nudity and sexuality.[28] Contrary to what was assumed by Henri Raymond and his colleagues at the beginning of the research, the relationships defined by a cultural model cannot be attributed to a particular class. Accordingly, the inhabitants of the *pavillon* do not form a homogeneous sociocultural group, just as there is no specific "practice of the *pavillon*" but a practice of dwelling, that is to say, of organizing spaces according to the cultural model of the given society.[29] In the words of Raymond: "When we launched the research, we thought that the *pavillonnaires* have a particular way of life, but in reality what the research has shown is that everybody would like to share this way of life."[30] This is why this way of life cannot be reduced to an "ideology of the *pavillon*" and the political discourse about it—the third level on which dwelling is examined by the ISU.

This research influenced Lefebvre's theory of space in many ways, which does not mean that his reading of *L'habitat pavillonnaire* followed the intentions of its authors. Already in his introduction to this study, his descriptions of the practices of dwelling differed from the wording chosen by the ISU. Lefebvre did not write about "marking" but about the "appropriation of space," and instead of "socialization" of space he discussed the "utopia of the *pavillon*," in which the "inhabitants consume signs."[31] The most direct translation of such understood practices of dwelling in Lefebvre's theorizing of space was suggested in his paper "Besoins profonds, besoins nouveaux de la civilisation urbaine" (Deep Needs, New Needs of Urban Civilization, 1966). After introducing the concepts of appropriation, social imaginary, and ideology, Lefebvre showed the ways they can be applied to a study of the city. First, the city is to be studied as a dialectics of constraints and "appropriation, more or less successful, of space and time," which allows a differentiation among places appropriated by inhabitants and passersby. Second, there is an imaginary level of the city conveyed by the monuments that refer to something beyond their immediate presence: to the historical past or to the global scale. Finally, there is a dimension of ideology, including the state ideology conveyed by grand empty spaces.[32]

The research of the city by means of concepts initially employed to analyze the domestic interior was facilitated by rethinking dwelling in a broader perspective, both scalar and historical. Already in the introduction to *L'habitat pavillonnaire*, Lefebvre related dwelling to scales larger than the apartment or a building and qualified the practices of habitation by various societies and modes of production, in spite of a transhistorical persistence of some of their features.[33] By relating the specific research procedures applied in the *pavillon* study—the examination of words and objects—to a broad "anthropological" understanding of dwelling ("the earth is the dwelling of men"),[34] he redefined dwelling as consisting of practices that relate to multiple scales of social processes rather than being confined to an individual dwelling.[35]

Such a reading of the study was contested by its authors; Henri Raymond was convinced that Lefebvre's statements had nothing to do with their book, and he doubted whether Lefebvre had even read the manuscript.[36] While Raymond's doubts cannot be confirmed on a biographical level (friends of Lefebvre visiting his house in Navarrenx in the mid-1960s witnessed many discussions about the study on the *pavillon*),[37] they reveal an increasing dissociation between Lefebvre's research and that of the ISU by the end of the decade. Rather than following the ISU's interests in codifying a sociology of habitat, Lefebvre introduced the discussions of the practices of dwelling into a broad spectrum of debates, which included his critique of technocracy, the hypothesis of the "new working class," the polemics against structuralist linguistics, and his readings of German phenomenology. In other words, the attempts of the ISU, dependent on state research contracts, to develop an empirical methodology that would comply with the increasingly institutionalized criteria of scientific rigor, contrasted with Lefebvre's critique of methods of quantitative sociology as unsuitable for researching the practices of dwelling.[38] While the *institut* aimed at sharpening, specifying, focusing, and narrowing its concepts, Lefebvre historicized the concept of dwelling and opened it up to speculation about the possibility of moving beyond the industrial society. On this path, his rethinking of dwelling aimed at securing the open-ended character of this concept ("the dwelling is an open place").[39] Lefebvre warned of fixing the concept of dwelling according to its current norms and modalities. Dwelling does not have to be thought of as rooted in the earth; it might also be conceived as a global peregrination, a modern nomadism, as theorized since the mid-1960s by his friend Georges-Hubert de Radkowski at the Institut d'urbanisme de l'Université de Paris and as discovered by René Schérer in the "nomadic utopias" of Charles Fourier.[40] This is why Lefebvre's reading of *L'habitat pavillonnaire* opens up the possibility of a concept of dwelling that responds to the requirements of modernity without disposing of the symbolic dimension of space.[41] This reveals the programmatic facet of this concept coined not only to analyze the everyday in an emerging society of consumption but also to account for a presentiment of an alternative production of space.

Dwelling as Appropriation of Time and Space

Lefebvre's concept of the appropriation of space is the closest approximation of his understanding of dwelling:

> For an individual, for a group, to inhabit is to appropriate something. Not in the sense of possessing it, but as making it an oeuvre, making it one's own, marking it, modeling it, shaping it. This is the case with individuals and with small groups like families, and it is also true for big social groups that inhabit a city or a region. To inhabit is to appropriate space, in the midst of constraints, that is to say, to be in a conflict—often acute—between the constraining powers and the forces of appropriation.[42]

Appropriation of space covers a wide range of practices, whether individual or collective, that modify, reshape, adapt, adjust, or alter space on various scales, from a nook in a *pavillon* to an urban territory. This broad understanding is specified by opposing appropriated space to "dominated space," which is "the realization of a master's project," "transformed by technology," and "closed, sterilized, emptied out."[43] In the preface to *L'habitat pavillonnaire*, Lefebvre wrote that domination ravages nature, while appropriation "transforms it—the body and biological life provided, and the time and space—into human property"; it is thus "the goal, the direction, the purpose of social life": economic and technical growth is possible without it, but not social development.[44] This polemical opposition between domination and appropriation—as a social, spontaneous, and open-ended practice—was founded on the ISU's contrasting descriptions of the practices of dwelling in the *pavillon* and the *grands ensembles*.

Dwelling and Appropriation

Introducing the study on the *pavillon,* Lefebvre calls for a concept of dwelling going beyond two positions that, in his view, marked the postwar discussion in the wake of the housing crisis: on the one hand, the "scientific" methodologies aiming at an "accumulation" of facts "in such a way as to permit rapid implementation" and, on the other, the philosophical theorizing of dwelling as a "poetical" practice and a fundamental characteristic of the human condition.[45] In line with Françoise Choay's opposition between "culturalist" and "progressivist" urbanism in her celebrated anthology *L'urbanisme: Utopies et réalités* (Urbanism: Utopias and Realities, 1965), Lefebvre refers the first tendency to the discourse of Le Corbusier and the functionalist urbanism of French state planning institutions, while relating the second to such texts as Heidegger's Darmstadt lecture, "Building Dwelling Thinking" (1951), and Bachelard's *Poetics of Space* (1957).[46]

The writings of both thinkers were negative references for Lefebvre's argument. Although attracted to Hölderlin's concept of poetical dwelling, referred to in "Building Dwelling Thinking," he read Heidegger as evading the contemporary problems of urbanization, just as Bachelard's eulogy of a "traditional" and "patriarchal" house did.[47] While both authors are not "operative" in view of the housing crisis, they reveal this crisis to be about not just a shortage of accommodation but also an existential condition to which the *grands ensembles*—a result of a willingly reductive, "operative" urbanism propped up by quantitative, "positivist" sociology—cannot provide an answer either.[48] This reading of Bachelard is one-sided and does not take into account his epistemological work on space,[49] and the confinement of Heidegger to a conservative reading in this passage is reductive.[50] Yet Lefebvre's aim is not to provide a close reading of both thinkers but rather to sketch a concept of dwelling that, in the conditions of postwar urbanization, preserves the possibility of poetic dwelling understood by means of the Greek term *poiēsis,* that is to say, as a human creation.[51] Such a "new concept of dwelling" should address "the technical demands and modern agglomerations, yet without sacrificing the qualities, differences, and spatiotemporal appropriation."[52]

This concept of dwelling defined by a possibility of the appropriation of space links Lefebvre's reading of the work of Bachelard and Heidegger to the ISU study of the *pavillon.* In his preface to the study, Lefebvre noticed, "The concept of appropriation has become blurred and degraded."[53] In the conditions of excessive urban growth, planning failed to penetrate "the secret of qualitative appropriation of time–space."[54] In this situation, the concept of appropriation can be "clarified" only by means of "a critical study of space," as he claims in *The Production of Space,*[55] a statement that most probably refers to the study of the *pavillon:*

The contrast between "the *pavillon* habitat" and housing estates is strik-ing. Let us spell out some aspects of this contrast. In a detached house (no doubt in a small-minded way) modern man "dwells poetically." By that we understand that his "inhabiting" is in some way his creative work. The space in which he is able to organize it according to his own tastes and patterns is somewhat malleable. It lends itself to rearrange-ment. This is not so with the space provided for tenants or co-owners on an estate; that space is rigid, inflexible. It is difficult, often impossible (and almost always prohibited) to convert it. Space in a detached house allows the family group and its individual members to appropriate to some extent the conditions of their own existence.[56]

"What seemed insignificant or trivial revealed a meaning":[57] while earlier stud-ies of Chombart discussed the lack of possibility of the appropriation of space in the *grands ensembles,*[58] *L'habitat pavillonnaire* identified the general preference of the population for the *pavillon* by its lending itself to appropriation. For Lefeb-vre, this concept became a way to grasp dwelling as a poetic practice, a possibility of shaping space as an individual work (*oeuvre*)[59] within the overarching cultural and social reality.

The Model and Its Appropriation

Two contributions to architectural debate became for Lefebvre a subtext for this thinking: the 1969 study *House Form and Culture,* by Amos Rapoport, and *Pes-sac de Le Corbusier,* by Philippe Boudon, from the same year, the latter originat-ing from Boudon's diploma at the Institut d'urbanisme de l'Université de Paris, defended in front of the committee presided over by Lefebvre.[60] Despite the apparently disjointed themes (while Rapoport analyzes vernacular architecture, Boudon investigates the changes of the Pessac neighborhood introduced by its inhabitants), both books convey the concept of dwelling as a set of practices in which space is modified within a given social and cultural framework: inherited from the tradition or conceived by an architect.

In his book Rapoport described vernacular architecture as a set of socially accepted models that are adjusted, modified, and differentiated according to the needs of the inhabitants and the characteristics of the site.[61] He argued that one single factor—the climate, need for shelter, building materials, construction tech-nology, characteristics of the site, requirements of security, economics, or reli-gion—cannot determine the form of the vernacular house, which "is not simply the result of physical forces or any single causal factor, but is the consequence of a whole range of socio-cultural factors seen in their broadest terms."[62] The sociocultural forces are of primary importance to the form of the house, while the climatic conditions and the construction methods are modifying forces.[63]

While critical of much of Rapaport's work, Lefebvre's theorizing of appropriation is characterized by a similar dynamics of a modification of a given model, in the course of which an oeuvre, both collective and individual, is produced.[64] His understanding of the appropriation of space in the *pavillon* as "the socialization of individual space and the simultaneous individualization of social space"[65] coincides with Rapoport's account of the production of space by an individual modification of socially inherited models and the concomitant process of endowing such produced spaces with social meaning. The concept of appropriation as an expressive activity develops Rapoport's analysis of architectural forms not in terms of determinations but in terms of possibilities and constraints—and thus as meaningful choices.

Rapoport's characteristics of the practices of the vernacular builders resemble the activities of the inhabitants of Le Corbusier's neighborhood of Pessac, analyzed by Boudon.[66] This neighborhood, commissioned in 1924 by the Bordeaux industrialist Henri Frugès, designed by Le Corbusier and Pierre Jeanneret, and realized in 1926, was famously praised in Sigfried Giedion's *Bauen in Frankreich* (Building in France, 1928), not only as an artistic achievement to be compared with cubist and de Stijl paintings, but also as an answer to the postulates of the modern movement concerning standardization and mass production, with the related requirements of modular design and the minimalization of costs.[67]

When Boudon's study was carried out, forty years after the construction of the neighborhood, most of its plastic, architectural, and urbanistic qualities admired by Giedion were not perceivable as a result of the massive changes introduced by the inhabitants. In order to investigate the character of those modifications, Boudon focused on the relationship among three variables: the alterations introduced by the inhabitants or the owner of the house; the architectural disposition of the house; and its location in the district. Rather than perceiving the high occurrence of alterations as a symptom of failure of Corbusier's architecture, Boudon argued that the capacity to accommodate, facilitate, and even encourage these changes is a fundamental feature of the design of Pessac. This capacity stems from the spatial generosity of the houses and also from their architectural and technical characteristics: the open plan, the modular system, and the lack of definite functional distributions, of which the inhabitants took advantage. Boudon concluded, "The conversions would seem to have been effected, not—as I had assumed—in order to personalize the standardized appearance of the houses, but in order to bring out or enhance the personal qualities that they already possessed"; the more distinctive the house already was, the more it was altered.[68]

Photographs from Boudon, *Pessac de Le Corbusier,* comparing newly completed buildings and the same structures later transformed by inhabitants. Courtesy of Philippe Boudon.

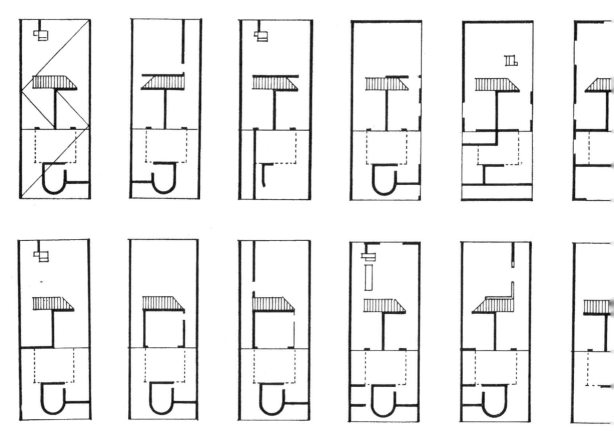

Study by Philippe Boudon about the Pessac neighborhood by Le Corbusier as an "open work," showing transformations of the houses. Published in Boudon, *Pessac de Le Corbusier,* 106. Courtesy of Philippe Boudon.

Not unlike Rapoport's analysis, Boudon's is governed by the dynamics between the constraints and possibilities: a similarity that surfaced in Boudon's claim that the houses in Pessac, by readily lending themselves to simple alterations, resemble the traditional lean-to house of the Bordeaux region.[69]

These conclusions were embraced by Lefebvre in his preface to Boudon's book:

> And what did the occupants do? Instead of installing themselves in their containers, instead of adapting to them and living in them "passively," they decided that as far as possible they were going to live "actively." In doing so they showed what living in a house really is: an activity. They took what had been offered to them and worked on it, converted it, added to it.[70]

The concept of the appropriation of space as a modification of a given model was developed by Lefebvre's students who investigated the neighborhood of

Pessac two years after Boudon, but in their account the model is understood as cultural rather than architectural. Jean-Charles Depaule, Laurent Bony, and Patrick Pincemaille contested Boudon's argument that it was the open and modular plan that facilitated the modifications introduced by the inhabitants. Rather, they claimed, the interventions of the inhabitants should be understood as an attempt to bring "order" into space or to "reappropriate" it, that is to say, to introduce the differentiation between private and public parts. This claim was based on a comparison between the houses that were designed as alternately turned "upside down": while the houses with the dining room in front were almost unchanged, those with the dining room in the back were transformed in order to screen such parts of the house as the kitchen.[71] Thus, referring to the ISU study of the *pavillon,* the authors argued that appropriation is dependent on the cultural model—the socially valid distinction between private and public—rather than on architectural means, such as the modular open plan.

Lefebvre's position differed from both studies. While Boudon, in his pursuit of specifically architectural research developed in the years to come, tried to explain the practices of the appropriation of space by their conditions of departure (the plan as facilitator of the changes introduced by the inhabitants), and the sociologists of Nanterre defined them by their socially determined aim (the cultural model to which space was to be conformed), Lefebvre aimed at formulating a dialectical concept of the appropriation of space as a creative and expressive negotiation between the spatial affordances and the cultural significations.[72] In a broader perspective, dwelling became inscribed into the dialectics of expression and alienation taken from the German idealist philosophy of the early nineteenth century: while men produce themselves within the community only by means of their own products, these, when fixed, acknowledged, socialized, or institutionalized, become alienating, that is to say, obstacles to further development.[73]

The Furttal Review

The ISU research on dwelling was contextualized by the increasing critique of the French state urbanism of the 1950s and early 1960s and its "architecture of growth," a critique that only recently began to be questioned by historians of architecture, pointing at the richness of programs, concepts, and technologies that prepared new ideas surfacing in French architecture after 1968.[74] This was the context in which Lefebvre published "Utopie expérimentale: Pour un nouvel urbanisme" (1961), a review of the project of a new city in the Furttal Valley, near Zurich, presented in the book *Die neue Stadt* (The New City, 1961), by Ernst Egli, Werner Aebli, Eduard Brühlmann, Rico Christ, and Ernst Winkler.[75] The project was launched in 1957 and was developed during several years by an

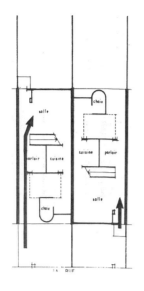

Transformations of a *petit maison* in Pessac, investigated by Lefebvre's doctoral students in response to *Pessac de Le Corbusier,* by Boudon. From Depaule et al., "Pessac," 6. Courtesy of Charles Depaule.

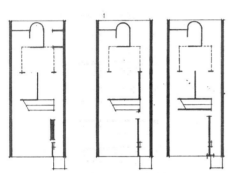
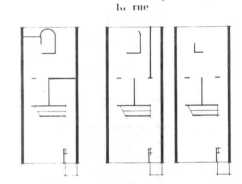

interdisciplinary team around Egli, professor of urbanism at the ETH Zurich. Lefebvre's close reading of Egli's project was an important source for his critique of functionalism and explains some of its idiosyncrasies: the project, while it programmatically distanced itself from the Athens Charter, was not representative of its more fundamental critique within the CIAM in the course of the 1950s and did not reflect the urbanistic discussions within the organization at that time.

The Furttal project was envisaged as a paradigmatic solution for the problems of congestion, traffic, housing, and the inscription of modern architecture into the Swiss landscape. This programmatic orientation stemmed from the genesis of the project, being an answer to the pamphlet *Achtung: Die Schweiz* (1955), by Lucius Burckhardt, Max Frisch, and Markus Kutter, who proposed the construction of a new model city as a contribution to the forthcoming Swiss Federal Exhibition.[76] The project was aimed not at a political utopia but rather at an optimization of social and economic relationships based on professional know-how.[77]

The city for thirty thousand inhabitants was designed near Otelfingen, a village in the Furttal Valley, north of Zurich. The project was based on a matrix of seven levels of "human organization" combined with a list of twelve basic needs.[78] Ernst Egli defined the role of sociology in the design by claiming that the urbanist "would be grateful if the sociologist could provide him, sociologically speaking, with a useful, spatial net of relationships in the city."[79] Following this homage, the hierarchy of social groups was identified in the design as the framework of spatial differentiation. Lefebvre summarized this approach in the following way:

> A sociological scheme underlies at the same time the technical project, the practical program, and the implicit ideology. This scheme is simple and clear. The city, conceived as a community, incorporates a hierarchy of levels or degrees. These levels or degrees lend themselves easily to an integration, since they are already elements constitutive of a social totality: the individual . . . , the family . . . , a neighborhood . . . , a group of neighborhoods . . . , a small district . . . , a district . . . , a city.[80]

In accordance with contemporary psychological theories, including Maslow's "hierarchy of needs" (1954), which suggests that the satisfaction of basic needs leads to an emergence of more refined aspirations, the authors extended the list of needs defined in the Athens Charter.[81] Their list of twelve needs included nutrition, hygiene, recreation, nursing, religion, science, art, protection, welfare, politics, administration, and upbringing.[82] These needs were combined with the levels of social groups (shown as a diagram and reproduced in Lefebvre's review), and the resulting matrix prescribed the answer to every need on each level of social organization.[83]

Such stipulated needs were attributed to urban facilities, designed according to three principles: the hierarchic organization of the city, the discernability of every part of the city, and the creation of cores.[84] These principles determined the spatial and social organization of the city: its hierarchic organization pertained not just to spaces but also to the structuralization of the social groups; the principle of discernability was related not only to the legibility of the architectural relationships in the city but also to a postulated transparency of social structures, which were lost in the industrial society; finally, the creation of cores was meant to relate the perceived urban reality to the social reality.[85]

This attempt to equate spatial and social organization made it necessary for the designers to take issue with the principle of the division of functions as stipulated in the Athens Charter. Rejecting this principle, the authors argued that functions "must be taken into account at every level of the community and its organization" and thus be "realized in a more ramified and interconnected form."[86] Yet in

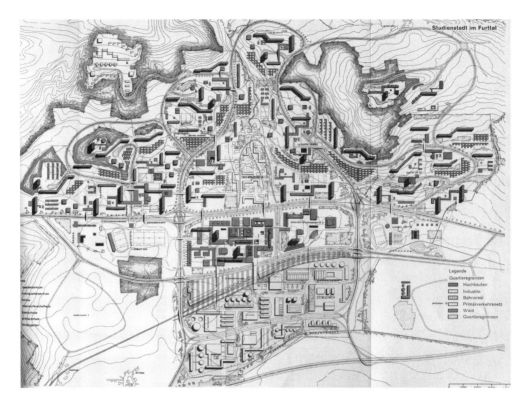

Study of the city in Furttal, general plan. From Egli and Fachgruppe Bauplanung der Studiengruppe "Neue Stadt," "Projekt einer Studienstadt im Raume Otelfingen im Furttal, Kt. Zuerich,"
n.p. Courtesy of Werner Aebli, Monika Weber-Egli, and Marcel Weber.

spite of these arguments, the city was designed in a functionalist manner, with
divisions: a housing area, administration, cultural and main shopping areas, and
an industrial district, all linked by a crossroads-free traffic system. The introduction of the "civic center" followed the debates about monumentality and community that had been perpetrated by the CIAM since the late 1940s.[87] In the Furttal
project, the center of the housing district consisted of lower structures that were
interwoven with the historical buildings of Otelfingen, surrounded by higher,
orthogonally composed slabs and enclosed in a semicircle of nine-story "backdrop buildings," punctuated by twenty-four-story towers, which were also used
to "crown" some of the hills:[88] a cubist composition responding to topography.

Lefebvre acknowledged the professional skills of the designers—an acknowledgment that, together with the appreciative hints to Le Corbusier, earned him
some angry remarks in the sixth issue of the *Internationale situationniste*[89]—but
he ended the review with a critique that would be developed in his subsequent
writings into a fundamental argument against postwar urbanism. He noticed that

Model of the new city in the Furttal Valley, general view. From Egli and Fachgruppe Bauplanung der Studiengruppe "Neue Stadt," "Projekt einer Studienstadt," n.p. Courtesy of Werner Aebli, Monika Weber-Egli, and Marcel Weber.

the project assumed isomorphism between social and spatial entities: "One composes the community with families like the functions of the city, with the elementary needs attributed to various levels."[90] The additive and analytical principle of their combination did not pay attention to a dialectical understanding of the city, which, rather than being a self-sufficient whole, should open itself up to the global dimension of the industrial society. Founded on the family as the basic social and spatial element,[91] the project not only endorsed paternalism and the reign of moral order, argued Lefebvre, but also was unable to assess the requirements concerning collective facilities that must take into account differences among social and professional groups.[92] Lefebvre wrote that this approach was concomitant with a "simplified theory of needs and functions" made operative in the project, which programmatically declared that a "precise and dispassionate research of the psychological and physical needs of the people" is a source of modern urbanism that "can dispassionately mobilize technology in order to satisfy [these needs]."[93]

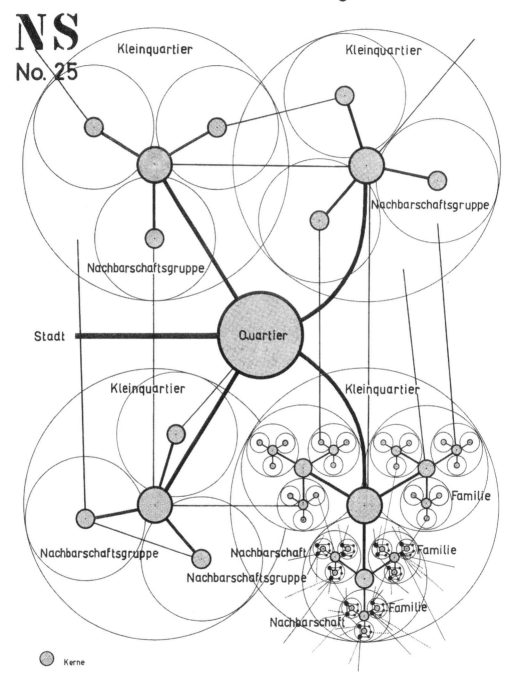

"Diagram of Human Relationships in the City," reproduced in Lefebvre's review of the project in *Revue française de sociologie*. From Egli and Fachgruppe Bauplanung der Studiengruppe "Neue Stadt," "Projekt einer Studienstadt," n.p. Courtesy of Werner Aebli, Monika Weber-Egli, and Marcel Weber.

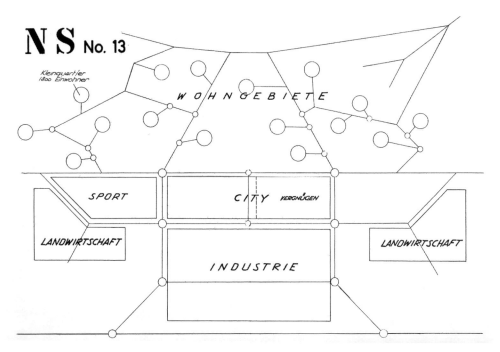

"Zones of housing and work as the basis for traffic": division of functions in the city in Furttal Valley. In Egli and Fachgruppe Bauplanung der Studiengruppe "Neue Stadt," "Projekt einer Studienstadt," n.p. Courtesy of Werner Aebli, Monika Weber-Egli, and Marcel Weber.

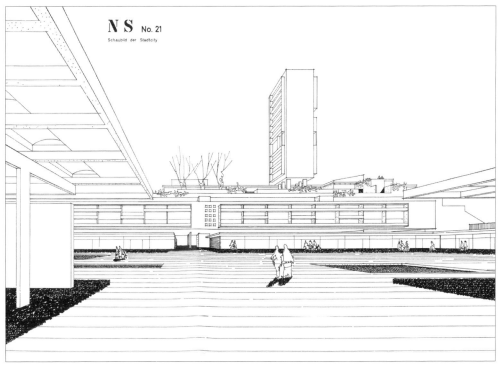

"Image of the city center" of the city in Furttal Valley. From Egli and Fachgruppe Bauplanung der Studiengruppe "Neue Stadt," "Projekt einer Studienstadt," n.p. Courtesy of Werner Aebli, Monika Weber-Egli, and Marcel Weber.

The Critique of the Concept of Need

The concept of need was a target of Lefebvre since the first volume of *Critique of Everyday Life* was published in its original French version (1947).[94] Dwelling on Marx's comments about the historical character of needs and their role within the cycle of capitalist production and consumption ("there is no production without a need, but consumption re-creates the need" wrote Marx in the *Grundrisse*),[95] Lefebvre postulated a Marxist critique of everyday life that includes the critique of needs.[96] This line of research coincided with the work of other Marxist theorists, including Herbert Marcuse, vividly received in 1960s France, who in the book *One-Dimensional Man* (1964) argued that the reproduction of capitalist relations of production requires a creation of "false needs" in consumers.[97] On the top of it, several years after the publication of Lefebvre's Furttal review, Jean Baudrillard theorized "the ideological genesis of needs" in an essay of that title (1969), concluding that needs are productive forces of capitalism, and thus "there are only needs because the system needs them."[98]

In the course of the 1960s the concept of need became increasingly challenged in architectural debates, and applying the procedure exercised in the Furttal project and expanding the list of needs became less and less credible.[99] This is because the position of architecture in the society of consumption changed, as it was reflected upon by numerous theorists, including Abraham Moles. In the paper "Theory of Complexity and Technical Civilization" (1965), Moles argued that either the concept of need can explain how objects are designed in response to specific situations, or, conversely, it can define situations in response to objects.[100] While the former characterized the context in which functionalism emerged at the beginning of the twentieth century, Moles acknowledged that in the 1960s the latter was taking place: "Products today are less developed out of needs, but moreover they themselves create the needs."[101] In spite of his attempts to formulate an answer to this condition, in a text published two years later Moles admitted that "functionalism is in crisis," because its principle of economy and rational application of existing means for clearly defined purposes contradict the contemporary "affluent society which is forced to produce and sell relentlessly."[102]

Within French urban sociology, the research of Paul-Henry Chombart de Lauwe, developed since the 1950s within the Groupe d'ethnologie sociale (GES) and the Centre d'étude des groupes sociaux, belonged to the essential contributions to the advancement and subsequent questioning of the concept of need and, in particular, the "need of housing." Chombart's ambiguous position—between academia and the planning state, between fundamental and applied research—was conveyed in his complex understanding of needs: critical and operative, speculative and empirical. In the introduction to the study *Famille et habitation* (Family and Dwelling, 1959), which reflects also on the earlier work of the GES,

Chombart urged the study of dwelling-related needs in their whole complexity: physiological, psychological, and cultural. He argued that researchers in the social sciences should study needs in cooperation with architects, administrators, and social services, so that families can "blossom" in their new accommodation, "freed" not only from their old housing but also from their old habits.[103] Much in the vein of functionalism as it was criticized by Lefebvre, Chombart asserted that studying these multiple needs allows the definition of how each aspect of accommodation can be satisfied by specific types of facilities.[104] From this position he formulated quantitative recommendations for urbanism (which included, for example, surface norms) and thus contributed to the ongoing normalization of housing units and legitimized their homogeneous and standardized character.[105] Yet, at the same time, he argued that universal norms are impossible, since physiological needs vary according to region, physical type, and profession, and psychological and cultural needs are even more differentiated. This means a call not only for specific and comparative research but also for an extension of the concept of need that would include, among other things, the need of space and its appropriation; the need of independence of each member of a group; the need to rest and to relax; the need of comfort and liberation from material constraints; the need of intimacy of the family; the need of social relations outside the family; and the need of separation of functions.[106] In this highly differentiated list, the concept of need loses its contours, and in the course of his subsequent work Chombart suggested superimposing on the scheme of "need, function, ensemble of functions" a series of other schemes, such as "situations—behaviors," "functions—social structures," and "behaviors—needs—aspirations."[107] The aspirations, so Chombart said, refer to silence, beauty, rest, familiarity, and dignity, and thus imply an emphasis on the singularity of each individual in opposition to what is generally shared, conveyed by the concept of need.[108]

Lefebvre's work in the course of the 1960s followed some of these lines, and he experimented with the concept of social needs that reflect the social and cultural development of individuals and groups.[109] He argued that such conceived social needs can be satisfied neither within an economic unit (as in the "Soviet model" as he saw it) nor within the family (as in the "bourgeois model"), but by conceiving a nexus of productive activities, dwelling, and leisure.[110] What was specific to his theorizing was the emphasis on the dialectical character of social needs as specific to groups and irreducible to the sum of the needs of its members; his list includes such pairs as security and the unforeseen, information and surprise, and the need for intimacy in the multiplication of social contacts.[111]

The concept of need was the main focus of the seminar at the Centre de recherche d'architecture, d'urbanisme et de construction (CRAUC) organized by Lefebvre, Paul Sivadon, and Michel Dameron (1968–70). In the final report and in the seminar discussions, the critique of the functionalist concept of need was omnipresent: Le Corbusier's dictum that "all men have the same needs" was criticized by Dameron, who preferred to speak about "comfort," which differs according to age, gender, social role, and personal experience.[112] Dameron opposed the doctrine of the division of functions, and he argued that needs cannot be diffracted into isolated components; he contested the possibility of a scientific determination of social needs as well, stressing that architectures of dwelling cannot be conceived by means of a purely scientific scheme and thus require "a decision that is developed according to cultural and political choices."[113] In other words, the problematization of the concept of need reintroduces politics into architecture, addressed by Lefebvre's postulate of an analysis of architecture by means of the dialectics of "demand" and "command" rather than that of needs and their satisfaction.[114]

Practices versus Needs

Lefebvre's contributions to the discussion about the concept of need were characterized by a long process of experimentation, critique, and an impatient search for counterproposals.[115] One such proposal was a project of a cultural center for a neighborhood of three hundred to four hundred flats, reviewed by Lefebvre in the paper "Bistrot-club: Noyau de vie sociale" (Bistro-Club: Kernel of Social Life, 1962). The center was designed with the aim of fighting social segregation and dispersion and of facilitating the integration of people, functions, and experiences in the new urban environment. The design was shown at the Salon des arts ménagers, organized in 1961 by the Syndicat des architectes de la Seine in the Palais de la Défense. According to the journal *Techniques et architectures,* the project aimed at creating "a node of attraction for stimulating social relationships in a new housing neighborhood," much like the role played by the cafés and the commercial streets in historical cities and towns.[116] The orthogonal structure (28 × 18 × 4 meters) was divided into six areas. Around the fixed core, constituted by the café as the place of encounter, the flexible arrangement and movable walls were expected to facilitate the emergence of various activities, like do-it-yourself (bricolage) and theater groups or the gathering of amateurs of photography, cinema, sport, and dancing. The project aimed not only at functional but also visual openness: the glass walls were designed with the intent to "let the street enter into the club" and to cast light toward the street.

All this was given credit in Lefebvre's text, which appreciated the project for its recognition of the club as "a nucleus of social life; a kernel of multiple activities; friendly encounters; various games, information and communication," and thus "the first effort to overcome analytical functionalism, which separates and projects on the ground all functions of urban life by dividing them."[117] Lefebvre's praise of transparency, the suggestion that a particular set of functions can integrate society, and his approving comment that in the club only nonalcoholic drinks were served (tuned in to the anti-alcohol campaigns of that time) were all rejected in the sarcastic response in the seventh issue of *Internationale situationniste* in 1962. Rather than seeing "a new phase of thinking of modern builders and urbanists," the *IS* saw the project as a manifestation of "the latest reformist theory."[118] The project's intended social integration, celebrated in *Le Monde*,[119] was equated with surveillance, and the club was considered a "means of supplementary control on the way to that *total surveillance* of production and consumption that actually constitutes the famous integration they aim at."[120] The aesthetic of the transparent walls was one more expression of the society of spectacle: the "totally reified man has his place in the show-window as a desirable image of reification."[121] The *IS* recognized that the bistro-club would not fulfill the hopes of overcoming "analytical functionalism," precisely because it was operating within the functionalist concept of need, which, once divided, were now reassembled in one architectural vessel.

The analysis of dwelling as an ensemble of practices rather than a set of isolated needs in *L'habitat pavillonnaire* can be read as a more convincing alternative to functionalist discourse.[122] In Lefebvre's words, it is not a matter of *"localizing* in a preexisting space a need or a function but, on the contrary, of *spatializing* a social activity, tied to a practice as a whole, by *producing* an appropriated space."[123] Accordingly, in *L'habitat pavillonnaire* the practices of closing and limiting space and of cleaning and storing were analyzed as meaningful interventions in space aimed at marking it and organizing it for appropriation.[124] For example, taking care of the house can be seen not as an activity stemming from hygienic necessity but rather as a practice of allocating clean and dirty spaces according to the culturally accepted relationships between them and the role models of consumption distributed in the mass media. While the inhabitants of the *pavillon* and those of the collective estates subscribe to similar models, the ISU argued that the latter have no margins of decision about the distribution of clean spaces, since the distinction between clean and dirty is immediately "functionalized"—that is to say, understood in terms of delineated needs—and thus "made incomprehensible."[125]

In this perspective, Henri Raymond argued that the role of the architect is not to answer predefined needs but to interpret possible practices.[126] This means furnishing the inhabitants with spaces that they can appropriate, that is to say, spaces they can modify according to the adopted models of sexuality, male and female roles, and relations with neighbors.[127] In *Habitat et pratique de l'espace*, Nicole Haumont and Henri Raymond stressed the richness of possibilities of the expression of cultural models and promoted an architectural thinking about them, urging architects to "think 'spaces' and less 'functions.'"[128] The authors argued that the architect should be aware of certain "sociological constraints"

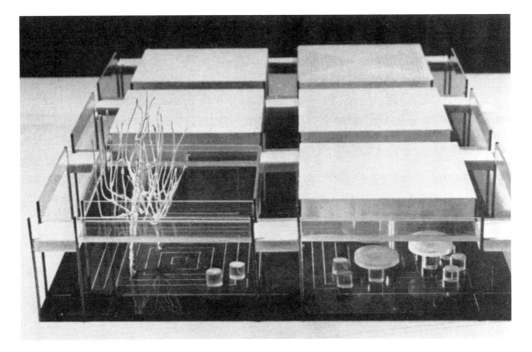

The model of the project for a bistro-club discussed by Lefebvre as "the first effort to overcome analytical functionalism," in his paper "Bistrot-club" (1962). Photograph by Étienne Hubert, published in *Techniques et architectures* 1 (1961): 39.

in order to offer to all inhabitants a minimum of sociological characteristics that embrace their cultural models.[129] Thus, Haumont and Raymond did not give specific advice to the designers but pointed out that the apartment should consist of a space of transition between the outside and the inside, open to the living room, closed to the kitchen and the bedrooms: "We ask the architect not to create a mode of life but to form spaces in which the models of habitat and the modes of life can manifest themselves."[130] Or, in the words of Bernard Huet reflecting on the consequences of the ISU studies for the design practices: "We don't want to design houses that materialize the cultural models, but ones that are capable of accommodating them."[131]

Against the Urbanism of Equilibrium

The concept of appropriation is thus defined within a broad family of concepts employed by Lefebvre in the course of the 1960s in opposition to those of need and function: cultural models, aspirations, comfort, social needs, demand and command, practices of dwelling. According to Lefebvre, this critique of needs should be developed into a more fundamental attack on the operations, premises, and imaginary of functionalist urbanism, associated with French state-led planning. This attack was directed against the principle of equilibrium and the procedure of balancing the set of identified needs with the set of planned functions.

While in the Furttal review Lefebvre seemed to have embraced a vision of a city as "an equilibrium, at the same time stable and vivid, a sort of self-regulation,"[132] in subsequent writings this concept became one of his main targets: in the text "Humanisme et urbanisme" (Humanism and Urbanism, 1968) he argued that it is deceptive to envisage a perfect equilibrium between architectural concepts, and in *The Urban Revolution* (1970) he claimed that the concept of an equilibrium, which regulates the movements and activities of people, is even a greater risk for a city than chaos.[133] In the study "Ville, urbanisme et urbanisation," written by Lefebvre with Monique Coornaert, the authors contrasted two planning approaches represented by the master plans of postwar English new towns and by economic planning, including North American land-use models. While the former aimed at achieving a static balance between a fixed number of inhabitants and working places and thus failed to conceive the growth of the city within a larger whole, the latter understood the growth of the city as the function of a series of demographic and economic data, but in this perspective the city loses any intrinsic characteristics.[134] Neither approach gives an account of preference, choice, experience, and imagination, and both fail to relate the city to larger levels of urbanization, according to Lefebvre and Coornaert's argument, which focused on themes that had been very much at stake since the 1950s in the discussions of Team 10.[135]

The concept of equilibrium is fallacious, Lefebvre argued, because it does not allow a grasp of what the phenomenology of the urban experience identifies as its essential feature: the unforeseeable, the surprise, the spontaneous. Spontaneity here is understood not psychologically but rather as the possibility of an appropriation of space facilitated by its "formal features," which were, according to Lefebvre, addressed by Christopher Alexander's essay "A City Is Not a Tree" (1967).[136] Alexander's account of functionalist cities as "trees"—mathematical structures in which no element of a unit is ever connected to other elements, except though the medium of that unit as a whole[137]—applied to the city design in the Furttal Valley. In this city every spatial entity located at a particular "level of human organization" was planned to be exhaustively contained in a higher entity (and only one) that refers to the next such "level." Influenced by "A City Is Not a Tree," Lefebvre repeated several times that a city with a tree structure leads to social segregation.[138] For Lefebvre, as for Alexander, the reductionism of functionalist urbanism stems not from a scientific analysis but rather from the tendency of the designers to give up the more complex structures of traditional cities, characterized by the experience of overlap, ambiguity, multiplicity.[139] In line with the postwar fascination with social functions of games, initiated in the

1930s by Johan Huizinga and developed by Roger Caillois, Lefebvre tried to capture this experience by means of the concept of the game—and contrasted it with the "boredom" of the functionalist urbanism, which, as it was put by Debord, "renders alienation tactile."[140]

Mourenx: Spontaneity and Self-Organization

Much of this condemnation of the "boredom" of the new housing estates stemmed from Lefebvre's ideological hostility toward state-led urbanism—and often contrasted with the feelings of the newcomers themselves, particularly those arriving from precarious living conditions, which included the popular neighborhoods of Paris that for an external eye looked so "lively," "spontaneous," and full of social contacts. But it is also possible to read Lefebvre's theorizing of boredom and spontaneity in a directly political way, as questioning the inhabitants' capacity for self-organization. This became a guiding line for Lefebvre's analysis of the industrial town of Mourenx in the Département des Pyrénées Atlantiques.[141] Lefebvre examined the city between the late 1950s and the late 1960s, and he often visited it with his friends, including Guy Debord and Michelle Bernstein on his way to and from Navarrenx.[142] The numerous accounts of these visits ranged from the paper "Les nouveaux ensembles urbains" (1960), which presents the results of the empirical study carried out at the end of the 1950s in the framework of his research in Centre d'études sociologiques, to a note in the photo album *15 jours en France . . .* (15 Days in France . . . , 1965) and a section in his tourist guide to the Pyrenees (1965).[143]

 The construction of the city followed the discovery of a gas deposit in Lacq in 1951.[144] Near the deposit, a natural gas processing plant was built, followed by the industrial complex, including an aluminum factory and several chemical factories.[145] This rapidly growing industry created a demand for four thousand dwellings. Of three proposals considered, both that of the integration of new neighborhoods into the two nearest larger cities, Pau and Orthez, and the integration of several neighborhoods into villages next to the deposits were rejected because of problems in obtaining the necessary land, the insufficiency of infrastructure, distance to the factory, and the lack of support of existing communities afraid of proletarian, thus presumably "Communist," inhabitants.[146] Consequently, the decision was made to build a new town of fifteen thousand inhabitants near

(opposite page) Mourenx and the industrial complex of Lacq: the object of Lefebvre's first urban study. Published in Bruneton-Governatori and Peaucelle, *Bâtiment A, rue des Pionniers.* Courtesy of Lacq Odyssée.

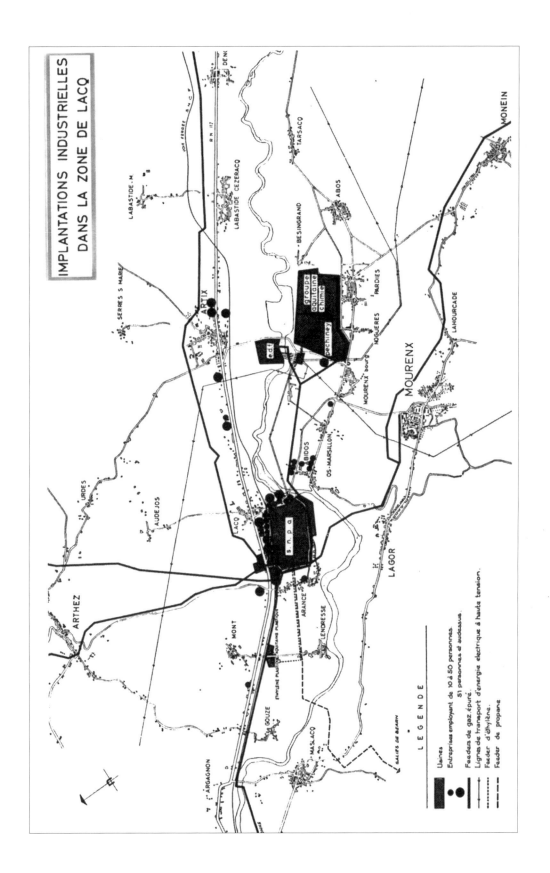

IMPLANTATIONS INDUSTRIELLES DANS LA ZONE DE LACQ

LEGENDE

Usines

Entreprises employant de 10 à 50 personnes.
51 personnes et au-dessus.

Feeders de gaz épuré.
Lignes de transport d'énergie électrique à haute tension.
Feeder d'éthylène.
Feeder de propane

Nikita Khrushchev visits Mourenx, 26 March 1960. Published in Bruneton-Governatori and Peaucelle, *Bâtiment A, rue des Pionniers.* Courtesy of Lacq Odyssée.

the old village of Mourenx. The architects and urbanists Coulon, Douillet, and Maneval were given this commission, and the construction of the new Mourenx started in 1957, with the first eight hundred flats occupied in 1958.

The plan of Mourenx consisted of a central area of facilities, surrounded by three groups of collective housing and three neighborhoods of single-family housing, some of substantial architectural qualities. (The housing scheme of the architects Novarina and Jaubert reflects the fascination of French postwar architecture with Scandinavian "humanized" functionalism.) Yet Lefebvre failed to mention them, and in his words this urban plan was a "projection on the grounds of the technical structure (hierarchical, professional) of the concerned companies." The city applied the structure of the factory to the area, segregating the inhabitants according to socioprofessional categories; workers lived in blocks of flats, supervisors in towers, management personnel in villas.[147] Or as it was put by one inhabitant, "In Mourenx everybody is considered according to the organization chart of the factory"[148]—a principle that, in the first years of the city, left professions unrelated to the structure of the factory (teachers, policemen) outside the system of assigned flats.[149] The absence of teenagers and old people in a city consisting mainly of young families with small children contributed to the lack of "turbulence, the unforeseen, the game."[150] (Only in a text of 1965 Lefebvre did notice that the presence of the French refugees from Algeria broke the social homogeneity of the town.)[151]

In Mourenx, buildings were reduced to signs: signs of their own functions and signs referring to other signs within a "formalized system."[152] This was conveyed by the photographs by Jean Dieuzaide in *15 jours en France . . .* , in which the differentiated series of cars in the parking lot is juxtaposed to the apparently self-referential system of openings in the pristine façades, whose sharp reflection is repeated in the window opened by a female figure, herself mirrored only as a shadow in the wet glass. But in Dieuzaide's photograph of the market, the rhythms of white walls and dark openings accommodate various social practices: shopping, bargaining, chatter, and strolling. It is this contrast between the immaculate façades of Mourenx and the potential for spontaneous everyday life that is the conclusion of Lefebvre's text, which ends by reinterpreting spontaneity as the capacity for socialization and political self-organization by the searched-for "new working class."

Like the theorists of the "new working class"—Serge Mallet, Pierre Belleville, and Alain Touraine—who stressed the contradiction between the advanced roles of the workers in the process of production and the antiquated structure of management in the factory, Lefebvre noticed the gap between the principle of separation, fundamental to the design of Mourenx, and the unitary flow of production processes. And yet, just as the intellectual capacities of the new working class were supposed to trigger a recognition of the outdated organization of the factories,

The new town of Mourenx: a combination of collective estates and neighborhoods of detached houses. Photograph by Claude Roux published in *Urbanisme* 75–76 (1962): 163.

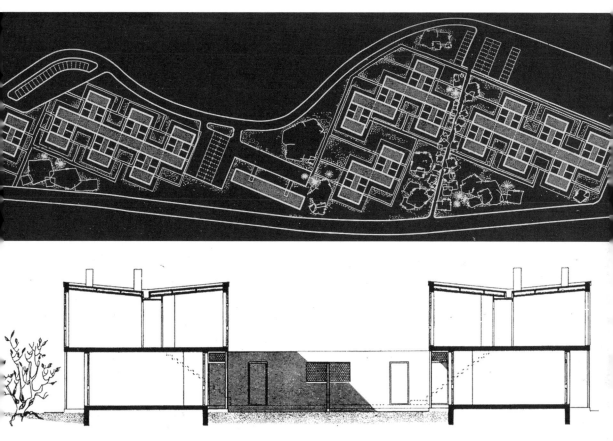

(top) Neighborhood of individual houses in Mourenx. Published in *Interbuild* 5 (1962): 21.

(bottom) Individual houses in Mourenx, section. Published in *Interbuild* 5 (1962): 21.

thus opening a possibility to challenge them, the projection of these patterns on the city facilitated, so Lefebvre claimed, a formation of new coalitions of inhabitants, united in their demands focused on the urban everyday. This is how he interpreted the formulation of a common list during municipal elections, which included trade unionists; farmers defending their interests against the state; and teachers of the new college, all of whom demanded autonomy concerning the municipal budget, use of public places, and organization of market places and who challenged the monopoly of the local supermarket.[153] These attempts at a collective appropriation of urban space and of the conditions of everyday life in the city were successful: as a result of a strike in 1962, the demands concerning the regulation of the positions of TV antennas, the drying of clothes, the use of greenery, and the utilization of dustbins and parking lots were fulfilled.[154] In a later text about Mourenx, Lefebvre wrote that the inhabitants were able to "express themselves, sometimes to impose their will" by operating in the "cracks" between

(*top*) Inhabitants of Mourenx protest against Société civile immobilière de la caisse de dépôts et consignations (SCIC), November 1962. Published in Bruneton-Governatori and Peaucelle, *Bâtiment A, rue des Pionniers.* Courtesy of Lacq Odyssée.

(*opposite page*) Mourenx, night view with industrial zone in background. Photograph by Jean Dieuzaide, published in *15 jours en France . . .* , 209. Courtesy of Archives Jean Dieuzaide, Toulouse.

Mourenx, window view of housing estates. Photograph by Jean Dieuzaide, in *15 jours en France . . . ,* 219. Courtesy of Archives Jean Dieuzaide.

Mourenx, street view of market. Photograph by Jean Dieuzaide, in *15 jours en France . . .*, 216. Courtesy of Archives Jean Dieuzaide, Toulouse.

the different powers ("economic and political, both regional and national").[155] He saw this as an attempt at democracy in urban life and as the principle of self-management imposing itself on the state and bureaucracy: while the new processes of automation in the factory have impoverished the social relationships among the workers, new social bonds have been searched for beyond the processes of production, that is to say, in relations among inhabitants and in cultural creation.[156]

Appropriation of Time and Space

When interviewed by Lefebvre, one inhabitant said about Mourenx: "Ce n'est pas une ville, c'est une cité": rather than referring to the urban practices that inspired Lefebvre to theorize the right to the city *(droit à la ville)*, the inhabitant seemed to define Mourenx by constraints and closures, the connotations that reverberate in the old French word *cité*, a term used until today in a variety of contexts, also in reference to the collective estates in the suburbs.[157]

This similarity between such estates and Mourenx was noticed by Pierre Merlin in the 1969 book *Les villes nouvelles* (The New Towns), who described the city as displaying "the characteristics that one reproaches in the *grands ensembles*": monotony of architecture and of the master plan, insufficient facilities, absence of urban life, geographic separation between the residential quarters and the activity zones.[158] This was not accidental: parallel to the construction of the new city, the SCIC (the developer of Mourenx) was responsible for the first *grands ensembles* of the Parisian region (including Sarcelles, Vernouillet, and Epinay).[159] Addressing a joke about Mourenx ("a socialist city in a feudal society"), Lefebvre argued that it was a paradigmatic example of postwar French capitalism, with all its actors present on the spot: the productive enterprises, the financial sector, big monopolist companies, and the state.[160]

The foundation of Mourenx was part of a national policy of the development of the *grands ensembles*, launched in spite of the preferences of the population for individual housing.[161] The decision to pursue this policy came after a period of intense discussion in the earliest postwar years, involving the supporters of "humanist" urbanism, such as Gaston Bardet and Robert Auzelle, and the adherents of the modern movement, such as Le Corbusier and André Lurçat. It was a discussion that focused less on the alternative between individual and collective housing and searched more for an optimal urban composition reconciling both types, as was the case in Mourenx.[162] The state support for collective housing projects was as much a choice in urban design as an attempt to improve social conditions, to put an end to the shantytowns and the housing crisis, and to stimulate economic development, including the rationalization of the building industry in the framework of the modernization of the French economy.[163] The rapid production of the *grands ensembles* in the 1960s (three hundred thousand new apartments per year for thirty years were deemed necessary in 1951) was characterized by the refinement of technical, financial, and administrative instruments of their planning, paralleled by almost simultaneously raised concerns about the rigid plans, the lack of social equilibrium, and the insufficient facilities in the *ensembles*. While the desires concerning the apartments (eat-in kitchens, private bedrooms, large bathrooms, big closets) were revealed in the research on public preferences, such as the 1947 study of the Institut national d'études démographiques and the 1959 "apartment referendum," and were addressed in new housing typologies adapted by some French construction companies since the early 1960s,[164] the criticism on the level of urbanism was more fundamental. The dullness of certain locations, the orthogonal monotony of some plans, the insufficient social infrastructure and public transportation, the incomplete construction of many apartments, and the uniformity of the social milieu had already all been raised in ministerial reports since the beginning of the 1960s, not to mention in several "personal notes" of the minister of construction Pierre Sudreau written to his collaborators at that time, which demonstrate a disapproval of "the lack of imagination and research" evident in some of the very *ensembles* authorized by his administration.[165] This self-critical discourse of the government was also a response to local resistance: in the years immediately following the war, the local authorities had accepted any measures to palliate the housing crisis, but in the course of the 1960s they demanded participation in architectural decisions.[166]

Beginning in the mid-1960s the dissatisfaction of the inhabitants, witnessed by Lefebvre in Mourenx, made itself heard elsewhere. In 1963, eight years after the first houses in Sarcelles were built, the tenants of this Parisian grand ensemble protested against the public developer, targeting the lack of urban facilities, insufficient public transportation, long hours of travel between work and home, and the decrease in the extension and richness of social networks and human interaction in comparison to their former experience.[167] Sarcelles had become the mass-media image of the dissatisfaction with postwar urbanism; it was called "an immense field of cement stippled with human beings," "a factory of young criminals and a school of violence," "one of the worst plagues that our society has ever invented," "a universe of concentration camps," "a silo for people."[168] This exalted rhetoric was a symptom of an anxiety about the future of the industrial society, for which the city was the only conceivable "horizon," as Françoise Choay put it in the preface to her anthology.[169]

In these conditions, it became clear to Lefebvre that the appropriation of space cannot be thought of as limited to an individual home or private apartment but must address the urban scale. He argued that with the new dimension of the city, familiar ways of appropriation of space disappear, replaced by reflective rationality and modern urbanism unable to penetrate "the secret of the qualitative appropriation of time–space."[170] This is why, in concluding his introduction to *L'habitat pavillonnaire,* he wrote that this study revealed a desire for an appropriated space, "on the level of private life as well as in public life, agglomeration, and landscape."[171]

In this perspective, appropriation needs to be thought of not only as multiscalar but also as straddling a multiplicity of times. In an interview, an inhabitant said that Mourenx could not be called a city because it lacked a church, a cemetery, and a promenade.[172] Devoid of the symbolic value of a cemetery, which would express the historical continuity of the community, and without a promenade, which would allow for "useless and unforeseen encounters," Mourenx was characterized by an absence of a "suprafunctional" element, once embodied in monuments.[173] Lefebvre noticed that in contrast to the clear, legible, comprehensive, and impoverished "text" of Mourenx, monuments convey symbols that have an "objective content, emotional effectiveness, archaic origins."[174] They gather references to nature, body, and childhood and dwell on the "most profound vital rhythms, such as day and night, the presence of the mother and the father, hunger, and sexuality."[175] In his "Psycho-sociologie de la vie quotidienne" (Psychosociology of Everyday Life, 1960), Lefebvre argued that monuments and symbols "introduce a depth to everyday life: presence of the past, individual or collective acts and dramas, poorly specified possibilities, and the more striking, beauty and grandeur."[176] This makes them media of the appropriation of space, which takes place in a way that is "affective and symbolic."[177] Lefebvre wrote that appropriation "ought to be symbolizable—ought, that is, to give rise to symbols that *present* it, that render it present."[178] By mobilizing symbols, the appropriation of space can relate to "tendencies and elemental, almost biological drives," which furnish appropriation with a "concrete" (singular, individual, experiential, practical) character.[179] In that sense, as a site of appropriation, housing becomes "a substitute for the monumentality of the ancient world" in the conditions of the postwar capitalist society, which "no longer totalizes its elements, nor seeks to achieve such a total integration through monuments."[180]

Consumption of Space: Words and Objects of the *Pavillon*

When Lefebvre revisited Mourenx in the mid-1960s, the city was not the same. "What changed in ten or fifteen years? The objects, obviously: the TV set, the fridge, the vacuum cleaner, present in Mourenx in a number of rooms. More subtly, the rhythms commanded by the objects. The family gathers in front of the TV."[181] If in the late 1950s Lefebvre saw Mourenx as a product of French state urbanism, in the 1960s he augmented this account by addressing the emerging consumer society of the *trente glorieuses* and what he considered this society's theoretical counterpart: structuralism.

Functionalism and Structuralism

The argument that links functionalism and structuralism, at first glance disparate, started with Lefebvre's critique of functionalist planning. In *Introduction à la modernité,* he argued that this planning operates by reducing the buildings and spaces to mere representations of their own functions: the city conceived as a system of functions becomes transformed into a system of signals commanding the behavior of their readers and into a system of signs referring to other signs within a closed system, "a global and complete vision of the city."[182] Conceiving the city as a closed system results not only in omitting those of its elements that cannot be included in a functional grid (the unforeseen being one of them, a monument or a multifunctional street another) but also in determining the functions by their relationship to one another rather than by a reference to the demands they were designed to answer. This was, according to Lefebvre, the case with the Furttal design, characterized by autonomization of segregated functions, which the designers aimed at balancing against one another, thus detaching them from the changing everyday life of the inhabitants.[183]

That particular elements of a system become detached from their references and transform into signs that have meaning only in relationship to other signs was, famously, a fundamental claim of structuralist linguistics. With structuralism rising to its peak in the French humanities and social sciences in the late 1960s, the analogy between functionalism and structuralism (and the latter's model of language) is a constant theme of Lefebvre, who describes both as operational strategies for the reorganization of postwar France. In the article "Claude Lévi-Strauss ou le nouvel éléatisme" (Claude Lévi-Strauss or the New Eleaticism, 1966), Lefebvre claimed that by developing the analytical procedures of classification and division, structuralism was both a symptom and a tool of the bureaucratic reorganization of the society that requires a new means of information processing and management.[184] The structuralist aspiration to depict societies as stable, self-regulating systems, according to Lefebvre, supported the tendency of bureaucracy to control and balance all realms of society.[185] Modern urbanism shares these fascinations with the equilibrium and the grid as operative matrices by which it "controls the consumption of space and of habitat" and facilitates the "colonization of everyday life"[186] (This explains, so said Lefebvre, the appearance of Sarcelles and Mourenx as "reminiscent of colonial or semicolonial towns," where everyday life is organized, subdivided, and squeezed into timetables.)[187]

Lefebvre concluded that although structuralist discourse considers itself to be a "discourse about the social"—the discourse that theorizes the social—it is in fact a "discourse of society," that is, society's ideological expression: "The tendencies to organize, to maintain, and to assert structures of equilibrium manifest themselves in a form of discourse and, first of all, in a discourse about form, coherence, equilibrium, and the system."[188] Lefebvre's account of structuralism as the ideology of immobility is highly polemical: structuralism is called a "justification of the state of affairs and the affairs of the state," and this is why Lefebvre described structuralism as the "new Eleaticism," alluding both to the claim of the impossibility of change in the thought of Parmenides and to the preoccupation with language in the paradoxes of Zeno.[189]

In other words, the segregation of needs and their transformation into a self-contained system of functions, the search for an equilibrium and the banishment of the spontaneous, the privileging of signs and signals and the rejection of symbols—all features of functionalist urbanism discussed by Lefebvre in his account of Mourenx—were not just accidental mistakes but rather symptoms of a greater reorganization of all realms of social reality in France of the 1950s and '60s. In order to grasp this shift, which involved technological, social, aesthetic, and political changes, Lefebvre coined the concept of a "bureaucratic society of controlled consumption" as opposed to concepts of an "industrial," "technological," "affluent," "leisure," or "consumer society," all of which he considered reductive in their focus on only one aspect of modern society.[190] Referring to Adorno and Horkheimer's critique of instrumentalized rationality, the concept of a bureaucratic society of controlled consumption garnered three claims: the role of bureaucracy becoming central as the ruling rationality and surpassing the rationality of the industrial society; the growing significance of consumption in relation to production, in the realm of both the economy and the construction of subjectivity; and the replacement of the public sphere with privatized everyday life as the place of socialization mediated by consumption.[191]

The Society of Consumption

It is precisely the correspondence among elements of a closed system that was made operative in the analyses of consumption by Roland Barthes, Jean Baudrillard, and Pierre Bourdieu in the course of the 1960s. Inspired by Lévi-Strauss's work on preliterate societies, these authors examined the society of consumption, itself perceived as distanced from writing and increasingly dependent on signs and images as means of communication. In the essay "The Ideological Genesis of Needs" (1969), Baudrillard wrote that if an instrument is defined by use value, a commodity by exchange value, a symbol by symbolic exchange, then an object of consumption is a sign that obtains its meaning within a system of signs, that is to say, by differentiating from other signs: in a system of differences.[192] In other words, "only when objects are autonomized as differential signs and thereby rendered systematizable can one speak of consumption and of objects of consumption."[193] Consumption is ruled by the logic of differentiation on two planes: the persons involved in the act of exchange are differentiated into trade partners, and the exchanged material is differentiated into distinct, thus significant, elements; by possessing these distinct goods, one achieves personal distinction.[194] Thus, Baudrillard concludes:

> Consumption does not arise from an objective need of the consumer, a final intention of the subject towards the object; rather, there is social production, in a system of exchange, of a material of differences, a code of significations and invidious values. The functionality of goods and individual needs only follows on this, adjusting to, rationalizing, and in the same stroke repressing these fundamental structural mechanisms.[195]

That functionalist urbanism and the society of consumption share the structuralist logics of differentiation reveals, in Lefebvre's view, a compliancy between them rather than a contradiction.[196] Commenting on the texts by Roland Barthes, Umberto Eco, and Françoise Choay, Lefebvre noticed in *The Production of Space* that structuralism becomes an attempt at a reformist functionalism. While in the introduction to her anthology Choay argued that linguistics reveals the inability of functionalist architecture to recognize the significations of a socialized object, in the English translation of "Sémiologie et urbanisme" ("Urbanism and Semiology," 1969) she pronounced "a rehabilitation of functionalism but on a less naïve grounds, getting rid of humanistic rationalizations."[197] A similar conclusion can be found in the essay "Function and Sign: The Semiotics of Architecture," by Eco (commented on by Lefebvre as displaying an "almost charming ideological naivety"), in which Eco argued that the semiotic approach gives a better account of functions, and thus "the principle that *form follows function* might be restated: *the form of the object must, besides making the function possible, denote that function clearly enough to make it practicable as well as desirable.*"[198]

This compliancy between functionalism and structuralism is a recurring theme in Baudrillard's *The System of Objects* (1968), an analysis of the postwar world of consumption, which originated with his dissertation, supervised by Lefebvre (1966). In this book Baudrillard redefined the understanding of "functionality" not as an adaptation to the goal but as an adaptation to an order or a system: "Functionality is the ability to become integrated into an overall scheme."[199] Thus, the structuralist methodology, the modern taste, and the technological requirements converge. Just as structuralism explains social relationships from

La maison à un étage

Nous présentons aujourd'hui à nos lecteurs un pavillon composé d'un rez-de-chaussée, et d'un étage, offrant l'avantage de pouvoir être interprété en plusieurs style différents moyennant les quelques modifications de toiture et de murs extérieurs représentées sur les croquis ci-joints.

De forme rectangulaire classique n'offrant donc aucune difficulté de construction quant à la toiture, la disposition intérieure du rez-de-chaussée est assez originale puisque la pièce de réception s'étend en forme d' « U » encadrant la cuisine et peut être aménagée suivant les goûts de chacun en réservant une partie à la réception proprement dite, l'autre étant consacrée à la prise des repas.

La cuisine comporte deux accès sans pour cela nuire à sa facilité d'emploi étant donné ses dimensions agréables.

L'escalier qui permet de parvenir au premier étage est intentionnellement central et donne un motif de décoration grâce aux deux piliers venant le soutenir.

Du point de vue commodité, la réception comporte une double porte vitrée servant d'accès par la terrasse et réservée aux visiteurs, une seconde porte simple située sur la façade opposée permet les allées et venues des intimes sans passer par la partie réservée aux invités.

Au premier étage, la distribution des pièces se fait rationnellement autour d'un palier sur lequel ouvrent cinq portes dont quatre chambres et une salle de bains.

Les chambres sont très légèrement mansardées, ce qui permet une économie de matériaux non négligeable sans pour cela gêner l'occupant, la hauteur libre minimum étant prévue à deux mètres. En outre, on pourrait faire disparaître la partie inclinée du plafond en réduisant légèrement la profondeur des pièces par l'installation de placards au droit de cette partie mansardée.

En ce qui concerne ses interprétations différentes quant à la façade, le type néo-moderne que nous indiquons en premier lieu comporte une couverture en tuiles mécaniques, les murs seraient revêtus d'un enduit ou crépis d'une couleur vive qui ne peut être précisée que suivant le lieu où serait édifiée la maison.

L'interprétation en style Normand s'explique elle-même : murs en pans de bois, toiture en tuiles plates.

Quant à la version Basque, c'est encore la toiture moins inclinée que dans les précédentes et couverte en tuiles rondes qui, alliées à l'arc en plein cintre, couronnant la porte d'accès, vient lui donner son caractère.

Nous ne saurions trop conseiller à nos lecteurs de ne pas s'écarter du style régional de leur contrée, et sommes à leur disposition pour étudier toutes modifications dans cet ordre d'idées suivant la région où ils envisageraient la construction de ce pavillon.

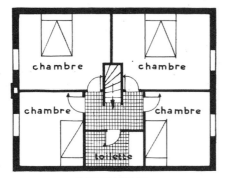

PLAN DE L'ÉTAGE

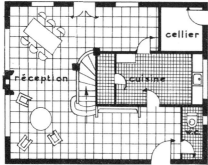

PLAN DU REZ-DE-CHAUSSÉE

NÉO-MODERNE

NORMAND

BASQUE

Ces plans à l'échelle de 2 cm. pour 1 m. sont mis à la disposition de nos lecteurs contre la somme de 2.000 fr. à verser à notre CCP 4402-20 ou en un mandat aux Éditions du Croissant, 16, rue du Croissant, PARIS-2e.

Design of houses in "neomodern," "Norman," and "Basque" styles, all sharing the same plan and structure. Published in *Votre maison* 12 (1950): 39.

the communication of women according to the rules of kinship and marriage, the communication of goods and services according to the rules of economy, and the communication of messages according to the rules discovered by linguistics,[200] Baudrillard wrote that the objects gathered in the modern interior "communicate." That is to say, they are characterized by "an overall coherence attained by virtue of their simplification as components of a code and the way their relationships are calculated."[201] The mass-produced objects become mass media;[202] in other words, in the modern interior "everything communicates"—the phrase exclaimed by Mme Arpel, the protagonist of *Mon Oncle,* by Jacques Tati (1958), while showing off her *pavillon* as a self-sufficient system of objects, contrasted in the movie with the picturesque house of flats of M. Hulot, which required constant micronegotiations among its inhabitants.[203]

The project of prewar architectural avant-gardes is thus realized: functionalism is a question not of style but of production. Lefebvre writes, "The same suppliers sell these goods, these objects, these houses in the 'Normandy,' 'Basque' or 'modern' style."[204] This statement alludes to catalogues of prefabricated houses and popular magazines, such as the journal *Votre maison,* which, in a 1950 issue, presented a design of houses in three styles: "Norman," "Basque," and "neo-modern." The placement of the openings in the façades was identical in every model, which were all based on the same plan and differed only in the shape of the entrance, the form of the door, and the division of windows according to the distillation of a few "characteristic" features of a traditional architecture.[205] This is why the differences among them are perceivable only when the houses are shown together, as they were published in *Votre maison:* in one strip.

The *Pavillon* as a System of Signs

In his preface to the study on the *pavillon,* Lefebvre wrote: "In the pavillon the resident consumes significations," then added, "The consumer of a detached house is intensely absorbed, not by things, but by signs."[206] Consumption is thus to be seen as one of the practices of dwelling:

> In the "world of the *pavillon*" more than elsewhere, every object is an element in a system. The object is not only loaded with symbols, it is a sign. Rather than being functionally adapted for use, it is caught in the system of signs.[207]

While appropriation mobilizes symbols that obtain meaning from their relation to body, nature, and time, consumption mobilizes signs that, as elements of a system—"an autonomous entity of internal dependencies"[208]—have meaning only in reference to the elements within the system. In the words of Roland Barthes, "The *depth* of a sign adds nothing to its determination; it is the breadth which counts; . . . every sign takes its being from its surroundings, not from its roots."[209]

This structuralist approach influenced *L'habitat pavillonnaire* and its focus on the interrelations among rooms, pieces of furniture, clothes, words, and images, ordered according to binary oppositions believed to reveal the deep structure of social reality. An example of this approach was the analysis of the impact of the TV set on the shifting relationships among the rooms in the *pavillon* examined as a "system of objects."[210] The arrival of the TV set changed the relationships among the rooms, analyzed according to the opposition between private and public areas and such distinctions as the practical and the aesthetic or work and leisure.[211] As an expensive piece of furniture, the TV set was placed in the dining room, since "it belongs to other pieces of furniture, in a place where the risk of damage is smallest."[212] Under this influence, the dining room was transformed into a living room: from a public area, used for nothing but reception, to a more frequent and common usage as a private place of leisure. This influenced the role of the kitchen, which changed from a multifunctional space to a room devoted to domestic work. With the shift in the use of the rooms, the requirements of the dimensions changed as well: while the size of the kitchen could be reduced, the living room had to be big enough for the whole family to watch the TV programs.[213]

In the preface to the study, Lefebvre wrote that the TV set is a privileged object that "governs the little world of objects and relations within the group."[214] (One of the interviewees expressed the desire for the furniture to be made in teak, "like my TV.")[215] With the arrival of the TV set, not only the use of spaces in the *pavillon* was changed but also the way these spaces were thought about: the authors underscore the expression of one of the inhabitants: "One lives among one's pieces of furniture."[216] This is "a revolution of habitat" that parallels the emergence of the society of consumption: the lived space of the *pavillon* is defined by the relationships among the pieces of furniture rather than by the delineation of rooms with assigned specific functions endowed with symbolic meaning.[217] This "revolution" modified gender relationships at the level of the family: the authors argue that the TV enhanced the opportunities for men's and women's equal access to information, a situation that contrasts with the gendered division of roles, which appears in the interviews reproduced in their book.[218]

This analysis reveals the processes of the "socialization of space," that is to say, the ways in which, "by means of significations attributed by the user to various parts of the *pavillon,* a practice and a representation of social relations are worked out."[219] Haumont and his colleagues scale down the meaning of Lefebvre's phrase about the "projection on the grounds of certain social relationships" from urbanism to dwelling.[220] In the Furttal review and the Mourenx study this phrase refers to urban space constructed according to the divisions of labor in the postwar society, whereas in *L'habitat pavillonnaire* the research focuses on the differentiation of space in the *pavillon* as a matrix of social relationships. This investigation reveals how, through the use of space, inhabitants gain consciousness and become capable of expressing the dominant cultural model: the relationships between what is public and what is private, what is female and what is male. By getting acquainted with the basic oppositions in the space of the *pavillon* (such as clean/dirty, shown/hidden), the child learns a matrix of signification that, in subsequent personal development, is identified with social distinctions.[221] This projection is a practice of dwelling itself; space is produced according to "rules, assigning significations to spaces, significations that are a function of a certain vision of social relationships."[222] In other words, the choice to eat in the kitchen or in the dining room is related not to particular features of these rooms as they facilitate a fulfillment of the expected "function" but rather to the relationship between the two rooms interpreted according to the valid cultural model.[223]

The Open Systems of the *Pavillon*

Lefebvre's reading of structuralism leads to an epistemological paradox: on the one hand he calls for resistance to structuralism as an extrapolation of the logics of the bureaucratic society of controlled consumption on the realm of the social sciences, but on the other hand this critique already assumes that structuralism captures these very logics and thus lends itself as an instrument of research on postwar French society.[224] The issue is thus less that of distinguishing "ideology" from "knowledge" in structuralism and more that of turning structuralism's instruments against structuralism itself.

This procedure was initiated in Lefebvre's essay about Lévi-Strauss with a reference to research on the *pavillon:* "To construct a model of dwelling (for instance, a dwelling in the *pavillon [l'habiter pavillonnaire]*), it is necessary to confront words and things within the field of practical reality."[225] Yet contrary to the structuralist-inspired argument about the merger of mass-produced objects of consumption with the speech of the *pavillon*'s inhabitants dominated by the advertisements, Lefebvre insisted that the objects in the *pavillon* ("houses, movable and immovable property, clothing, faces, and behavior") and the discourse of the inhabitants do not decode each other but rather form two partial systems, interconnected and distinct:[226]

> There are always gaps, discrepancies, even hiatuses between these
> two systems, which prevent our seeing them as two aspects of a single

system. They do not develop according to the same law or to one that is internal to each of them.[227]

The hiatus between the discourse of the inhabitants and their daily practices occurred to the authors of *L'habitat pavillonnaire* in an interview in Choisy-le-Roi, where an interviewee complained that she could not "hang up laundry to dry it in the courtyard because all would go black," just to add shortly later, "We are in the countryside here, we have good air."[228] This discrepancy led to the identification of discourse as a distinct level of analysis, linked by Marie-Geneviève Raymond, in her book *La politique pavillonnaire* (1966), to the French political debates around the politics of housing. Rather than searching for a general scheme that would clarify the causal relationships among words, objects, and practices in the *pavillon*,[229] Haumont and his colleagues focused on specific objects as mediators between words and daily practices. For example, the fence, when analyzed at the level of the appropriation of space, was considered a symbolic closure; on the level of signs and the socialization of space, it defines the relationships among the family, their neighbors, and society; finally, the fence is a means to protect the property, an attribute of the owner—the hero of the ideology of the *pavillon*.[230]

This understanding of the everyday in the *pavillon* as a series of levels "separated by cracks, gaps and lacunae" was embraced by Lefebvre.[231] He explained that the aim of the book *Everyday Life in the Modern World* was to demonstrate that "a system of everyday life does not exist."[232] This argument concluded his discussion of Barthes's *The Fashion System* (1967), which analyzed fashion as a self-contained system without any references to actual bodies, real garments, or specific practices, including the reading of *Elle* and *Le jardin des modes,* the journals examined by Barthes.[233] In his review Lefebvre urged an inquiry into the conditions this system requires to exist and to function: "In what sort of society does it take root, this closed system that has no value or meaning outside itself and that appropriates every meaning for its own personal use?"[234] Not unlike Bourdieu, who lambasted Barthes for failing to examine the structures of production and the modes of reception of mass media,[235] Lefebvre concluded that "Fashion"—that is to say, fashion as a closed system—requires an overarching set of conditions, consisting of activities, texts, organizations, and institutions. He argued that the main condition for Fashion is a society that combines self-repression with the illusion of freedom brought about by the world of consumption: the bureaucratic society of controlled consumption. In this society, fashion needs to be accounted for as one among many partial, or "open," systems of everyday life, which also include tourism, culture, technology, sexuality, the motor car, and youthfulness, separated by gaps, intervals, and cracks.[236]

The distinction between a closed and an open system fed into Lefebvre's life-long interest in "open totalities": consistent wholes that are not predetermined but allow for an open-ended social practice. His insistence on open totality expressed the "abhorrence of premature closure" characteristic of the proponents of postwar French Marxism under pressure resulting from the polemical identification of totality with totalitarism by Albert Camus or Emmanuel Levinas.[237] Already in *Le matérialisme dialectique (Dialectical Materialism,* 1939), Lefebvre theorized a possibility of a totality that is open to the future; this was advanced in *Sociologie de Marx (Sociology of Marx,* 1966), in which he tried to think reality as a "broken-up totality, fragments of which confront one another and sometimes separate when they do not enter into conflict."[238] The methodological consequences of this position were spelled out in the essay "La notion de totalité dans les sciences sociales" (The Notion of Totality in the Social Sciences, 1955), in which he not only contrasted closed totality with an open one, containing other (partial) totalities, but also proposed open totality as a fundamental concept for sociological research.[239] Lefebvre called for an exploration of the interstices and gaps between these partial systems, and his valorization of disequilibria, troubles, oversights, gaps, excesses, and defects of consciousness was an attempt to identify sites of novelty: possible strategic locations of political projects.[240]

The Utopia of the *Pavillon*

This analysis of French postwar society in a process of structuralization, restructuring, and destructuring that produces unfinished and open systems, rather than closed ones, was Lefebvre's first attempt at mobilizing structuralism without subscribing to the closure it implied.[241] The second was his argument built around the lived experience of the *pavillon.*

Not unlike Barthes in his analysis of fashion and Baudrillard in his account of the domestic interior, Lefebvre analyzed the words and objects of the *pavillon* as external to the conditions of their production: "Work (and creativity), material production and its relations (and the activity that produces created works) are put into suspension, put aside."[242] Space consumed in the *pavillon* assumes the half-real, half-imaginary existence of commodities, appearing cut off from the practices that produced them. But contrary to the structuralist accounts of consumption, Lefebvre's stressed that the *pavillon* is experienced not only beyond but also *against* the world of labor, and it is by taking the world of labor as a negative reference that the practices of dwelling in the *pavillon* are assigned their proper meaning.

This negative reference distinguishes the experience of the individual house from that of the collective estates. While the former erases the traces of work, the latter introduces an "unfortunate symmetry between work and housing," which appears as a continuation of the world of labor by other means.[243] The discourse on nature is symptomatic in this respect: while the garden of the *pavillon* evokes primordial nature, the functionalization of needs in the collective estates results in the reduction of nature to abstract "green spaces." Even though the *pavillon* is an urban phenomenon, the *pavillonnaire* thinks about it as outside the artificial, morbid, and enslaving city.[244] The garden becomes a mixture of reality and illusion that refers to nature untouched by the human hand. Lefebvre writes, "In 'naturality' we find, recreating themselves in an odd sort of waking dream, 'lived' happiness and the consciousness that lives it, the illusion and the real."[245]

The everyday in the *pavillon* is meaningful precisely through its own erasure: that which is most everyday imagines itself beyond the everyday, and the everyday becomes meaningful only by its transformation into the not everyday and the extraordinary.[246] In the world of the *pavillon* "everything is real and everything is utopian, without a clear difference; everything is nearby and everything is far away."[247] This is how Lefebvre understood utopia: as a place of what has no place or no longer has one: of "happiness, safety and rootedness, personality and naturality."[248] In other words, the lived of the *pavillon* is not a sign among others: this came to the fore in a discussion during the CRAUC seminar, when Lefebvre opposed Baudrillard's argument that "what is lived as comfortable signifies prestige."[249] But neither can the lived be understood by means of a reference to authenticity, creativity, or presence shining through the commodified everyday. Rather, the lived is an experience of "an 'elsewhere' inherent to places, to acts, to situations."[250] In Lefebvre's reading of *L'habitat pavillonnaire,* the modern everyday shared by everybody is paralleled by the collective dream about surpassing this very same everyday, that is to say, an experience of a possibility of a difference, without prescribing what this difference should be. It is consumption of space that conveys a hunch of an everyday beyond the society of consumption.

Dwelling as the Production of Space

Launching the discussion in *The Production of Space,* Lefebvre wrote, "A conceptual triad has now emerged from our discussion, a triad to which we shall be returning over and over again."[251] A glance at his earlier writings, and in particular at the studies of the ISU, suggests that this "discussion" is not restricted to the previous thirty pages of the book but rather relates to the thirty years of Lefebvre's research that preceded it.[252]

The conceptual triad referred to is that of the perceived, conceived, and lived space and its "translation into spatial terms": spatial practice, representations of space, and spaces of representation.[253] This double triad reflects two perspectives of Lefebvre's theory of space within the overarching Marxist theoretical framework: the semiology of the urban and the phenomenological description of urban life.[254] They were developed in the research of the ISU: the Marxist critique of alienation, of ideologies, and of everyday life; the semiological analysis of various ways of production of meaning; and the phenomenological account of the experience of space.

The double triad is accepted as the core of Lefebvre's theory by scholars investigating his work, including Rob Shields, Stuart Elden, Andy Merrifield, and Christian Schmid.[255] In spite of differences among them, which to a large extent stem from their accentuating various, often incongruent, formulations of Lefebvre, these authors agree not only about the specific understanding of each moment of space but also about the correspondence between the two triads. In the first book about Lefebvre's theory to be published in English, Rob Shields defined Lefebvre's spatial practices as "space perceived (*perçu*) in a commonsensical mode"; the representations of space as "discourses *on* space" or "the discursive regimes of analysis, spatial and planning professions and expert knowledges that conceive of space (*l'espace conçu*)"; and, finally, the spaces of representation as "discourses *of* space," "space *as it might be,* fully lived space (*l'espace vécu*)": the spaces of representation form the social imaginary.[256] Stuart Elden confirmed this reading and explained that, according to Lefebvre, the perceived space is physical space; the conceived space is a mental construct and an imagined space; and the lived space is that which is modified in everyday life—and this distinction is the basis for the conceptual triad of spatial practice, representations of space, and spaces of representation.[257] The analysis of Andy Merrifield was developed along similar lines: while spatial practices "secrete" society's space and have "close affinities with *perceived* space," the representations of space are described as conceptualizations, or "conceived" space, and spaces of representation are the lived spaces of everyday life.[258]

The most advanced discussion about the triads of space can be found in the book *Stadt, Raum und Gesellschaft: Henri Lefebvre und die Theorie der Produktion des Raumes,* by Christian Schmid, which begins with identifying three "fields" distinguished by Lefebvre: the physical field of nature and materiality, delineated in a practical and sensual way; the mental field of logics and formal abstractions, defined by mathematics and philosophy; and the social field, "the field of projects and projections, of symbols and utopias, of the *imaginaire* and . . . the *désir*."[259] They intersect in the processes of the production of space: the material production, or the spatial practice, which "produces the perceived aspect of space"; the production of knowledge, and thus representations of space and conceived space; and the production of meaning, "which is related to spaces of representation and which produces an experienced, or lived, space."[260] Social space in its broad meaning includes the perceived, conceived, and lived space, while in its narrow sense it is opposed to the critically understood mental and physical–material space.[261]

Toward a General Theory of Production of Space

Christian Schmid pointed out that what makes Lefebvre's theory productive in urban research is its general character, which allows integrating such categories as "city" and "space" into an overarching social theory and facilitates an investigation of spatial processes and phenomena from the private to the global levels.[262] The foregoing account of Lefebvre as a "thinker of 'dwelling'"[263] traces this general character of his theory back to a generalization of the research of the ISU and his own engagements with discussions in architecture and urbanism. His theorizing of space as socially produced and productive not only followed the dialectical relationship between the practices of everyday life and the spaces of the domicile investigated by the ISU but also involved a broadening of the research on the practices of dwelling themselves, which included a double operation: rescaling them beyond the domestic interior, and widening their historical scope beyond 1960s France.

The historicization of the processes of the production of space is evident in the wordings chosen by Lefebvre in order to describe spatial practices: "empirically observable" and "readable and visible" practices of material transformation of space that mobilize productive forces within a given economic and social system.[264] These wordings reveal the historical conditioning of spatial practices. When Lefebvre writes that spatial practice "secrets" (secrète) society's space,[265] he refers to the production of space by a living body, inspired by the book *Symmetry,* by Hermann Weyl, and by Marx's question of whether the spider can be said to be "working." (Lefebvre writes that even if the spider does not work, it "produces, . . . secretes and occupies a space.")[266] This comparison was also alluded to when contrasting Mourenx to the nearby *bastide* of Navarrenx: the development of the old town is compared to that of a seashell and opposed to the postwar spatial practices as a "projection onto a (spatial) field of all aspects, elements, and moments of social practice."[267] In this wording (une projection)[268] reverberate Lefebvre's reviews of functionalist urbanism as a "projection on the ground" of a "program of action and a program of life."[269] Urbanism was also the target when Lefebvre wrote that spatial practice "embraces" (englobe) production and reproduction,[270] coordinating all realms of the modern society: it not only plays a role in the economic processes of production, consumption, and distribution but also is essential in the reproduction of capitalist social relationships ("spatial practice in its entirety . . . has saved capitalism from extinction").[271]

Qualified by time, spatial practices are also differentiated by scales. Lefebvre calls for their theorizing as operating on the level of architecture, urbanism, and spatial planning.[272] It is by referring these scales to one another that spatial practices become essential regulators of everyday life: they link together "daily reality (daily routine) and urban reality (the routes and networks which link up the places set aside for work, 'private' life and leisure)."[273]

Spatial practices encompass a variety of scales by mobilizing the practices of representing space, the practices themselves "tied to the relations of production and to the 'order' which those relations impose."[274] Among representations of space—"conceived," or "mental," spaces—Lefebvre counts scientific theories of space, techniques of its control, architectonic and urbanistic conventions of design, cartographic procedures, and normative discourses on space.[275] What defines representations of space is a mixture of ideology and knowledge,[276] an account that not only dwells on Lefebvre's critique of urbanism from the 1960s but also reflects the climate of opinion around 1968 in France, characterized by an almost unanimous hostility toward any form of representation, whether in the mass media or in politics (parties and trade unions). In this context Guy Debord's condemnation of the society of spectacle became a common cause with the anti-institutional and self-management discourse of May 1968, radicalized in the post-'68 era, with Michel Foucault's Groupe d'information sur les prisons aimed at "giving the speech" to the prisoners and their families and with Gilles Deleuze's proclamation of an end of a theorizing intellectual as a "representing or representative consciousness."[277] In spite of these tendencies, Lefebvre decided to include representations in the triad of space as indispensable for its theorizing—a decision that might have been inspired by his exchanges with architects and by the discussions about the practice of design as a constant to-and-fro between representations and lived space.[278]

In this emphasis on the difference between the "mental" space of the planners and "lived space" reverberates the valorization of the space of dwelling, appropriated by the *pavillonnaires*. In *The Production of Space* the practice of appropriation defines the space of representation as a space that "the imagination seeks to change and appropriate."[279] While mental space is systematic and coherent ("subordinated to a logic"), lived spaces of representation "need obey no rules of consistency or cohesiveness."[280] Rather than being a system of interrelated signs, spaces of representation receive meaning from symbolic objects, attendant imaginary, and mythic narratives, themselves "elementary forms of appropriation of nature."[281] "Embodying complex symbolisms," spaces of representation relate the individual to the community by producing a bond grounded in experience and in history.[282] In other words, these spaces relate lived time to the past: individual past (by the reference to childhood); collective history (exemplified by the graveyard in the study about Mourenx); and imaginary origin: the primordial nature.

This theorizing of the spatial triad in *The Production of Space* broadens the investigation not only beyond the work of the ISU but also beyond the discourse of sociology: while the concept of perceived space gathers spatial practices at various scales, from appropriation of the *pavillon* to state planning, Lefebvre's theorizing of conceived space reflects its operative representations, disciplinary, institutional, or ideological; and his understanding of lived space widens the account of the imaginary experience of the *pavillon* lived beyond its conditions of production, that is to say, as a "space of representation." In formulating a concept of space that addresses society as a whole, the discourse of philosophy becomes indispensable.[283] But sociology is not a ladder to be disposed of after reaching higher levels of abstraction; rather, it offers a criterion that will guide Lefebvre in his research on space—that of developing the general account of the production of space from within an understanding of specific, historical, and localized social practices. In *The Production of Space* Lefebvre warned readers, "The perceived–conceived–lived triad (in spatial terms: spatial practice, representations of space, spaces of representation) loses all its force if it is treated as an abstract model."[284] Evidently, abstraction is necessary, but it must be a "scientific abstraction" that "aims at something concrete":[285] a "concrete abstraction," the main philosophical category by which Lefebvre's multifaceted research of social space was gathered into a theory.

Critique
Space as Concrete Abstraction

I N AN INTERVIEW IN 1970 Lefebvre recalled a 1943 conversation in Aix-de-Provence with Léon Brunschvicg, his former professor of philosophy at the Sorbonne. Commenting on the news of the German offensive on the Eastern Front, Brunschvicg conceived the battle of Stalingrad as a series of singular events in which a German soldier encounters a Soviet soldier and one kills the other one. This was consistent, argued Lefebvre, with Brunschvicg's understanding of thinking as being about judgments, thus about singular things, rather than about universal concepts. Clearly, Brunschvicg's view of the battle was not totally wrong, according to Lefebvre, who continued laughing, but he completely missed the level of strategy and the masses that make history something other than a chain of individual events.[1]

This conversation was not just about history but also about thinking in general, and it revealed Lefebvre's persistent conviction about the necessity of universal concepts for the understanding of social reality, including the concept of space, which he took as the privileged perspective for an account of the "modern world."[2] How is this universality of space to be understood? Since space is itself socially produced and has historical conditions of existence, its universality can be conceived neither as a Platonic idea nor as a Kantian transcendental form of sensibility. Rather, Lefebvre argues that space is one of the universal forms of social practice, as commodity and labor are in the analysis of Marx.[3] Like commodity and labor, space has a paradoxical quality of being at the same time, and in many ways, both "abstract" and "concrete": space appears to be a general means, medium, and milieu of all social practices, and yet it allows accounting for their specificity within the society as a whole. This relationship between abstract and concrete cannot be reduced to the familiar scheme of a concept and its exemplification: the universality of space is not simply a result of a conceptual abstraction that, following the Latin etymology of *abstrahere,* draws away or removes what is inessential, accidental, and contingent.[4] Rather, space—just like commodity and labor—is a "social," "real," "actual," or "concrete" abstraction; that is to say, its universality is produced by processes of an abstraction attributed to a range of social practices and reflected in the specific "abstract" experience of modern space.

Lefebvre's argument that space is a universal form of social practice belongs to the most fruitful parts of his theory, at the same time revealing its most fundamental tensions, which reflect those in the writings of Marx, his main guide in this argument. In particular, what comes to the fore in Lefebvre's theory of concrete abstraction is the oscillation in Marx's work between an attempt to deduce history from a single principle of social development and a retrospective analysis of historical conjunctions, overdetermined by a range of social practices. While the former perspective bears the mark of Hegel's idealism, the latter defines a materialist approach: two currents that Louis Althusser and Étienne Balibar distinguished in the work of Marx. For Lefebvre, these two currents can be bridged, and the concept of concrete abstraction is the main theoretical leverage in this attempt. While neither fully successful nor fully conclusive, this research program allowed him not only to develop a historical account of the space of capitalism but also to formulate the core concepts of his theory and his approach to spatial analysis.[5]

These philosophical references should not suggest that this chapter exchanges a conceptual speculation for the previously reconstructed understanding of the production of space and its triads from within Lefebvre's rethinking of the research on dwelling. What I am aiming at here is less a philosophical genealogy of his work and more an interrogation of the position of empirical research within his general theory of space. In other—disciplinary—terms, I discuss Lefebvre's attempt at a transdisciplinary theory of space, which is in excess over every specialized discipline but for which the theoretical, historical, and empirical studies developed within specific disciplinary fields and methodologies are indispensable.[6] Such theory would not subscribe to a positivistic project of a synthesis of partial knowledges, but would aim at a production of the concept of space as an object of research by drawing from various disciplines and relating their results to one another and, through this, reconfiguring their specific object matters and methodologies but also restructuring the place they occupy in the social division of labor and in social conflicts.

Such are the postulates of a general, transdisciplinary, "unitary" theory of space, which Lefebvre argued accounts for "all possible spaces, whether abstract or 'real,' mental or social."[7] He wrote that such theory would "discover or construct a theoretical unity between 'fields' which are apprehended separately," at the same time disclosing differences among them; these fields include "the *physical*—nature, the Cosmos; secondly, the *mental,* including logical and formal abstractions; and thirdly, the *social.*"[8] In Lefebvre's words, "This approach aims both to reconnect elements that have been separated and to replace confusion by clear distinctions; to rejoin the severed and reanalyze the commingled."[9] Since these "fields" are related to the realms of the perceived, conceived, and lived,[10] the aim of the unitary theory of space is to "discover or construct" a unity among the moments of space as neither indistinguishable nor disconnected.[11]

Transdisciplinary Theory of Space

This discussion is embedded in Lefebvre's reading of the accounts on space in postwar philosophy, sciences, and architectural theory. He questioned the inability of the French philosophy of the 1960s and early 1970s to produce something other than "either mere descriptions which never achieve analytical, much less theoretical, status, or else fragments and cross-sections of space"[12]—a theoretical weakness that contrasted with the intensity of the debates about space at that time and with new concepts of space formulated by phenomenology (Bachelard) and psychoanalysis (Lacan), spatial conceptions of ideology (Baudrillard, Debord), power (Foucault, Deleuze and Guattari), and text (Derrida, Kristeva, Barthes).[13] Lefebvre wrote that the relationships among these multiple "spaces" are not theorized: while structuralism assumes their identity, post-structuralist writers dramatize the splits between them.[14]

A similar dynamic can be discovered in scientific disciplines: while each of them "constitutes its own particular space, mental and abstract," the attempts at constructing a unity of these spaces result either in unsuccessful "interdisciplinary or multidisciplinary montages" or in syntheses based on illegitimate extrapolations of partial conclusions.[15] This is because the concepts underlying these disciplines might be incongruent: Abraham Moles argued that geography (together with architecture and urbanism) departs from a Cartesian space understood by means of the category of extension, while psychology (and, for instance, interior design) embraces a phenomenological perspective that "starts with my body, here and now, taken for the center."[16] Lefebvre, on his part, asserted

> an indefinite multitude of spaces, each one piled upon, or perhaps contained within, the next: geographical, economic, demographic, sociological, ecological, political, commercial, national, continental, global. Not to mention nature's (physical) space, the space of (energy) flows, and so on.[17]

The same inability to grasp space in its multiplicity characterizes, according to Lefebvre, the postwar architectural discourse, which he analyzed by reviewing the phenomenological work of Christian Norberg-Schulz and the contributions to the "organic history of architecture" by Bruno Zevi. For Norberg-Schulz the "primitive," total experience of space and its concept elaborated by ancient philosophers was split into several aspects covered by specific constructs, including the "pragmatic space" of physical action; the perceptual space; the "existential space," which forms man's stable image of his environment; the "cognitive space" of the physical world; the "abstract space" of pure logical relations; and the "expressive space," including "architectural space" and described by means of an "aesthetic space."[18] Norberg-Schulz's book *Existence, Space and Architecture* (1971) shares with Lefebvre the ambition to account for this multiplicity of spaces and to offer space "the central position it ought to have in architectural theory."[19] And yet, Lefebvre argued, this book either evokes the moments of space as indistinguishable or suggests rifts among the conceived, the perceived, and the directly lived space. "The true theoretical problem, however, is to relate these spheres to one another, and to uncover the mediations between them," he adds.[20]

A reading of Bruno Zevi's *Architecture as Space* (1948) leads to similar conclusions. Zevi lists multiple "interpretations" of a building: political, philosophical, religious, scientific, economic, social, materialist, technical, physio-psychological, and formalist. All of them are valid to the extent that they deal with architecture, that is to say, with space, because architecture consists in "the enclosed space in which man lives and moves."[21] In this account the "content" of architecture is "the men who live in architectural space. . . . The content of architecture is its social content"; in Lefebvre's words, "Zevi holds that a geometrical space is animated by the gestures and actions of those who inhabit it."[22] For Zevi, this interpretation of space is the point of departure for an integrated, comprehensive vision of architecture and its "organic unity" with men.[23] However, Lefebvre notices that in Zevi's book space is understood as primarily visual, in spite of its emphasis on bodily lived experience. Consequently, rather than recognizing that politics, economy, society, and culture are inherently spatial, Zevi tends to reduce them to factors that, to a greater or lesser extent, condition architectural space.

Not confined to theoretical discussions, the question about the unity and multiplicity of space arrived at the center of French debates in architecture and urbanism at the end of the 1960s and the beginning of the 1970s. What at first glance appeared to be very far from practical concerns eventually boiled down to a question about the possibility of an interdisciplinary cooperation among architects, urbanists, geographers, and sociologists in education, research, and design work. The concept of space—urban space, social space, or space *tout court*—developed since the 1950s by Chombart, Ledrut, and Lefebvre, was invested with the capacity to become a meeting point among these disciplines. This, however, required a redefinition of this concept to account for the multiple aspects of "space"—or the multiple "spaces"—these disciplines are concerned with.

This task was the focus of all the interdisciplinary seminars Lefebvre and his collaborators organized and participated in during his professorships in Strasbourg and Nanterre. These included the Royaumont colloquium (1968), at which Lefebvre chaired the session "Interdisciplinary Research and Urban Sociology," organized with the aim of overcoming incongruities among languages, concepts, and expectations, for which overspecialized education was blamed.[24] This ambition was also the core interest of the seminars in Port-Grimaud (1968), Oliva (1968), and Cogolin (1970) and, in particular, in the research project "Les besoins fonctionnels de l'homme" (1968–70). The minutes of this project reveal the recurrent question: How is it possible to relate the multiplicity of the aspects of space examined within the various disciplines, perspectives, and methodologies: "architectural space," "gestural space," the "space of inhabitants," "lived space"?[25] This discussion revealed a new sensitivity to social, cultural, and political differences in the city, which challenge the belief that a given functional program can result in one optimal spatial organization.[26] But what relates the spaces differentiated by gender, age, class, memory, and desire to one another? This is the political stake of Lefebvre's unitary theory of space, which is today more relevant than ever before: to think of space as a whole means to keep it open to everybody.

The Concrete Universality of Production of Space

The postulate of theorizing space within "the present mode of production," whether capitalist or socialist, by means of Marx's concept of concrete abstraction is expressed already at the beginning of *The Production of Space*. After asserting that "(social) space is a (social) product," Lefebvre claims that the mode of existence of space is that of money and commodities, which are, together with labor, theorized by Marx as concrete abstractions:

> Space has taken on, within the present mode of production, within society as it actually is, a sort of reality of its own, a reality clearly distinct from, yet much like, those assumed in the same global process by commodities, money and capital. . . .
>
> Is this space an abstract one? Yes, but it is also "real" in the sense in which concrete abstractions such as commodities and money are real. Is it then concrete? Yes, though not in the sense that an object or product is concrete.[27]

The Concrete Universal and Its Three Moments

Before discussing Marx we must go back to the philosophy of Hegel and his understanding of the distinction between the abstract and the concrete as well as the concomitant concept of a concrete universal. This distinction was announced in Hegel's article "Wer denkt abstrakt?" (Who Thinks Abstractly? written in 1807). Hegel argued that "common people" think abstractly, for example, a saleswoman who considers the convicted criminal only a murderer, that is, according to one isolated feature:

> This is abstract thinking: to see nothing in the murderer except the abstract fact that he is a murderer and to annul all other human essence in him with this simple quality.[28]

This is the basis for the critique of abstraction as conceptual domination, to be found in many philosophers since Hegel: abstract domination is a practical effect of conceptual one-sidedness.[29] By contrast, the "knower of man" thinks concretely, by considering the crime a result of the conditions of the life of the criminal, that is, his poor education, family relationships, or the possible injustice he suffered.

This distinction between the concrete as embedded in a variety of relations and the abstract as the impoverished, one-sided, and isolated can be applied to describe the features of things, phenomena, thoughts, and experiences. A concrete thing is related to other things in multiple ways, while a concrete thought consists of several definitions and descriptions that link it to other propositions and theories: each of these definitions reflects only a part or an aspect of the concrete reality, and thus each of them is abstract if taken by itself, separately from other definitions.[30] Hegel's understanding of the abstract and the concrete suggests that thinking about reality is always an ascent of the abstract to the concrete, that is to say, a synthesis of partial definitions into a comprehensive theory.

In Hegel's philosophical writings the distinction between the concrete and the abstract was applied to distinguish between concrete and abstract universals. An abstract universal is an isolated feature shared by a collection of objects, while a concrete universal (*das konkrete Allgemeine*) refers to an essence of a thing considered as embedded in the world of related and interacting things.[31]

In Hegel, a "notion" (*Vorstellung*) expresses abstract universals, while the "concept" (*Begriff*) expresses concrete universals. This difference was underscored by Hegel in his lectures on aesthetics:

> Now, as regards the nature of the Concept as such, it is not in itself an abstract unity at all over against the differences of reality; as Concept

it is already the unity of specific differences and therefore a concrete totality.[32]

Michael Inwood explained the difference between these two types of universals by contrasting "redness" and "life." Redness is a feature shared by all things red; this feature does not significantly influence the relationships of one red thing with other red things; thus, it is an abstract universal. By contrast, life, as a concrete universal, "constitutes, in part, an essence of living things, directing their internal articulations, and living things are essentially related to each other in virtue of their life: different species feed off, and occasionally support, each other, and species reproduce themselves."[33] This understanding of the concrete universal—as the internal principle of development or a driving force of an examined thing—will be crucial for Marx's advancement of this concept.

In *The Production of Space* Lefebvre follows Hegel and explains the concrete universal as constituted by the three "moments" of universality (or generality), particularity, and singularity.[34] They are called "moments" by Hegel in order to underscore that universality, particularity, and singularity cannot be sharply distinguished and to stress their tight logical, ontological, and epistemological bond[35]—a principle of reciprocal entailment and inseparability that is reflected in Lefebvre's theorizing of moments of space.

According to Hegel, the universal moment is the general principle of the development of things of a certain type. The particular moment is determined by the universal moment, but at the same time it is a differentiation from the universal moment and thus, in Hegel's words, its negation. The singular moment is an individual thing that is *concrete;* that is to say, it exists in a determinate embeddedness in the world. The singular is thus the final step of differentiation of the universal moment and, simultaneously, its realization. That is why Hegel writes that the "concrete" is the universal in all of its determinations and thus contains its other in itself.[36]

In *The Production of Space* Lefebvre experiments with the idea of an application of the moments of universality (generality), particularity, and singularity to space. He distinguishes the "level of singularities" as that on which space is experienced sensually by the body and attributed with rudimentary meanings, such as masculine or feminine. The "level of generalities" is related to the control and distribution of bodies in space as exercised by dominant powers, often by mobilizing symbolic attributes. Finally, the "level of particularities" is linked to smaller social groups, such as families, and to spaces "which are defined as permitted or forbidden."[37] In another attempt, Lefebvre divides space into "logical and mathematical generalities" (thus, representations of space elaborated by these disciplines), particular "descriptions," and singular places "in their merely physical and sensory reality."[38]

Even if these hypotheses are just sketched in *The Production of Space,* the thinking behind them reveals Lefebvre's attempt to theorize space as a dynamic relationship among its bodily experience, symbolic meaning, social organizations, and scientific representations. Thus, the reference to the Hegelian concept of the concrete universal is less an attempt to identify the moments of space with the moments of a concrete universal than an attempt to theorize the production of space as a dynamic exchange among its three moments.

This Hegelian source of the concept of production, and specifically of the production of space, was stressed by Lefebvre, who wrote, "By and large, the concept of production is still that same 'concrete universal' which Marx described on the basis of Hegel's thinking, although it has since been somewhat obscured and watered down."[39] Elsewhere, he adds:

> Does what Hegel called the concrete universal still have any meaning? One shall show this. What can be said without further ado is that the concepts of *production* and of the *act of producing* reveal a concrete universality.[40]

Production as a Concrete Universal

The concept of production applied in *The Production of Space* refers both to the narrow (economic) meaning and to its wide meaning, originating in the writings of Hegel and Marx. *Production* in the narrow sense refers to the fabrication of commodities by labor executed by repetitive gestures. A product understood in this sense, as associated with industrialization, is opposed to a "work" (*oeuvre*): "A *work* has something irreplaceable and unique about it, a *product* can be reproduced exactly."[41] In the wide sense, *production* refers to the concept of social practice defined as the material and "spiritual production" simultaneously, the production of means, objectives, instruments, goods, and needs.[42] In this perspective production is a creative activity, and its understanding comes back to the tradition of German idealism.[43] When Lefebvre writes that "(social) space is a (social) product," he refers to the wide concept of production; when he claims that "social space *per se* is at once *work* and *product,*" he refers to its narrow sense.[44]

Beyond production there is nothing human, adds Lefebvre in *La pensée marxiste et la ville* (1972),[45] where production is employed in order to characterize the city and urban space:

> The city covers the double sense of the term "produce." A work *[oeuvre]* itself, it is the place of production of various works, including that which

decides about the sense of production: needs and bliss *[jouissances]*. It is also the place where goods are produced and exchanged and where they are consumed. It gathers these realities, these modalities of "production," some of them immediate, others mediated (indirect).[46]

Following Hegel, Lefebvre understands production as a concrete universal, unfolding from the universal moment, through the particular, to the singular moment: "The (absolute) Idea produces the world; next, nature produces the human being; and the human being in turn, by dint of struggle and labour, produces at once history, knowledge and self-consciousness."[47] In this perspective the process of production is characterized by a rationality that transcends the rationality of particular agents involved with it.

Theorizing this immanent rationality of production while purging it of any reference to a preexisting causality or teleological guidance was seen by Lefebvre as a major achievement of Marx, which allowed him to understand the rationality of production by means of its internal conditions.[48] But in this reinterpretation the concept of production changes fundamentally and leaves behind not only Hegel's idealist concept of production as "a vehicle of reason's actualization of itself in the world" but also Marx's own early understanding of social practice.[49] Rather, production understood in a materialist way is conceived as a multiplicity of social activities that transform both nature and human "nature," that is to say, that produce means of existence and subjectivities. In that sense, this concept "transcends the philosophical opposition between the 'object' and 'subject'"[50] and defines humanity as transindividual, that is to say, as produced by multiple interactions among individuals who cannot be conceived in isolation from these interactions.[51]

The rationality immanent to production unfolds in a sequence of actions that order bodies, materials, techniques, skills, and social systems of organization. This is also how Lefebvre proposed investigating the relationship among the moments of space: as components of "the unity of a productive process."[52] This suggests an answer to the question about the conditions of the possibility of the transdisciplinary research on space: what links spaces investigated by various disciplines, together with the imaginary spaces and those experienced in the everyday life, is that they are socially produced "in accordance with certain schemas developed by some particular groups within the general framework of a society" and within its specific mode of production.[53] In other words, the moments of space are related by means of the process of their social production and characterized by a unity and contradictions of this process within a given society. This unity allows the theorization of space as simultaneously a product of social practices and their facilitator: space is "both produced and productive."[54] Lefebvre writes that being "an outcome of past actions, social space is what permits fresh actions to occur, while suggesting others and prohibiting yet others."[55] In this sense, space is simultaneously an instrument and a goal, a means and an end, a process and a product: "Production process and product present themselves as two inseparable aspects, not as two separable ideas."[56] Rejoining material production (the production of goods), production informed by knowledge, and the "production" of meaning, space "is at once result and cause, product and producer."[57]

From Concrete Practices of Dwelling to Abstract Space

The Hegelian distinction between the concrete (the embedded in the world) and the abstract (the isolated and one-sided) announces Lefebvre's concept of abstract space—the space of postwar capitalism—as characterized by an isolation of functions, practices, and ideas. According to *L'habitat pavillonnaire,* such an analytical approach, applied to distinguish and to discern needs, to divide them into isolated and homogeneous ("abstract") functions, and to assign them to available space, is the basis for the functionalist rationality of the collective housing estates: the intellectual requirement of clarity is thus extrapolated into the aesthetic postulate of transparency. This results in a division of space and time into specialized ("unifunctional") units that are supposed to answer delineated needs.[58] The matrix of the Furttal project is paradigmatic of such thinking, and in several texts Lefebvre writes that the *grands ensembles* are an outcome of analytical thinking, connected to the division of labor and the application of the analytical method.[59]

Lefebvre wrote that spaces considered in isolation are "mere abstractions," whereas they "attain 'real' existence by virtue of networks and pathways, by virtue of bunches or clusters of relationships."[60] As early as the Mourenx study he noticed that this abstract rationality expressed in functionalist urbanism lags behind the general development of technology, and it was precisely in the late 1950s and the 1960s that the distinction between abstract and concrete was employed in order to account for the recent changes in technology, society, and culture. This included Gilbert Simondon's *Du mode d'existence des objets techniques* (On the Mode of Existence of Technical Objects, 1958), built on the opposition between the "abstract" machines of the nineteenth century and "concrete" machines, where "the specificity of component parts gave way to their relational convergence, a synthesis of distinct functions in polyvalent objects and ensembles;" and in the Hegelian *Le nouvel age,* by Henri van Lier (The New Era, 1962), the "concrete machines" were understood as abandoning technical and functional individuality for a functional positioning within the network of an ensemble of machines.[61]

The "abstract rationality" of the actors of the postwar production of space (the state authority, the developer, the planner) is contrasted by Lefebvre with the "concrete rationality" of the practices of dwelling, embedded in and interrelated with the multiple levels of social reality. In the preface to Boudon's study on Pessac, Lefebvre defined this concrete rationality of the appropriation of space by its users to be "much more impressive and more complex than the abstract rationality."[62] Similarly, in the study "L'architecture sauvage," presented during the CRAUC seminar, Jean-Charles Depaule, Lefebvre's doctoral student at Nanterre, opposed the "abstract logics" of an architect, mobilizing institutionalized representations of space, and the "concrete logics" of the practices of appropriating space by the inhabitants who express themselves in space. According to Depaule the "concrete logics" reveals the true "logics of space": its determination, hierarchization, orientation, and meaning.[63] Elaborating on this opposition in *L'habitat pavillonnaire,* Haumont and his colleagues contrasted the collective estates and the *pavillon* as expressions of "two rationalities" that "appear to each other as irrational."[64] What the urbanists claim to be a clear division of functions in collective housing appears to the *pavillonnaires* as obscure in comparison with the world of the detached house, which gains coherence from the meanings assigned to it in the daily practices of dwelling.

In a similar way, Lefebvre's preface to Boudon's *Pessac de Le Corbusier* follows Hegel's descriptions of the concrete universal unfolding from the universal to the singular by means of a sequence of differentiations. This is also how Lefebvre described the production of space in Pessac as a process in which the abstract theory ("ideology") of modernist architecture became transformed into the project of the neighborhood on account of the conditions of the site and requirements of the client and then, after construction, appropriated by the inhabitants, who *"produced* differences in an undifferentiated space" by adapting it to their way of life.[65] In this process the rationality of the production of space cannot be identified with the rationality of any particular agent—the architect, the inhabitant, or the theorist—because, as Lefebvre adds in *The Production of Space,* even the most technologically developed system "cannot produce a space with a perfectly clear understanding of cause and effect, motive and implication."[66] Thus, when he envisages the emergence of an alternative—"differential"—space, it is described in Hegelian terms: "The road of the 'concrete' leads via active theoretical and practical negation, via counter-projects or counter-plans."[67]

Space as a Practical Abstraction

The tension between the materialist and the idealist understanding of production reappears in two perspectives on the concept of concrete abstraction that are developed in Lefebvre's theorizing of space: on the one hand, a retrospective analysis of specific practices of the production of space (a history of the emergence of capitalist space or a "history" of the appropriation of a house in Pessac); and, on the other hand, an attempt at capturing the dynamics of the production of space in one universal scheme. The relationship between these two perspectives is far from being settled down in Lefebvre's work, amplifying the tensions from Marx's *Grundrisse* (written in 1857–58) and *Capital* (first volume published in 1867).

Abstract Labor and Abstract Space

It was Marx's theorizing of labor in *Grundrisse* that directly influenced Lefebvre's understanding of concrete abstraction as an abstraction that "concretizes and realizes itself socially, in the social practice."[68] In this perspective, a concrete abstraction is a "social abstraction" that implies "a mode of existence distinct from a mental one, even if there is a connection between them; it has a *real* existence, that is to say, practical and not conventional, in the social relationships linked to practices."[69]

These statements closely follow the discussions of labor in *Grundrisse* as an "abstraction that became true" in the practice of capitalism. The discovery of the abstract character of labor—as a wealth-creating activity regardless of its further specifications—was attributed by Marx to Adam Smith:

> It was an immense step forward for Adam Smith to throw out every limiting specification of wealth-creating activity—not only manufacturing, or commercial or agricultural labour, but one as well as the others, labour in general.[70]

Marx claimed that labor could have been conceptualized only when the general features conveyed by this concept became decisive in social practices, most important, in economy. Thus, Smith's discovery was in fact a recognition of the social and economic reality of his time: it was in eighteenth-century England where industry for the first time required labor to be reduced to its elementary features and stripped of the personality of the worker. It was this type of labor—malleable, quantifiable, divisible, and measurable by time—that was compatible with the newly introduced machines and thus most efficient in the economic conditions of early industralization. Marx wrote that under such conditions "the abstraction of the category 'labor,' 'labor as such,' labor pure and simple becomes true in practice" (*praktisch wahr*).[71]

Marx saw labor as consisting of two aspects: the specific labor of a particular worker (in *Capital* it is called "concrete labor") and unspecific "abstract labor."[72] Thus, he wrote, "the concrete is concrete because it is the concentration of many determinations, hence unity of the diverse," whereas the abstract is "one-sided."[73]

In other words, the expenditure of labor power—the human capacity to work—in a particular form and with a definitive aim is called concrete labor, while the expenditure of labor power in a physiological sense is abstract labor. This abstraction is "made every day in the social process of production," as Marx wrote in the *Contribution to the Critique of Political Economy* (1859):

> The conversion of all commodities into labour–time is no greater an abstraction, and is no less real, than the resolution of all organic bodies into air. Labour, thus measured by time, does not seem, indeed, to be the labour of different persons, but on the contrary the different working individuals seem to be mere organs of this labour.[74]

This distinction reverberates in Lefebvre's differentiation between abstract and concrete space. Abstract space is the measurable space "occupied by separate objects"; it is the isomorphic space without any privileged orientation or direction (such as front or back, high or low); any linkage among objects in this space is neither impossible nor necessary. This is the space of the postwar urbanism that Lefebvre interpreted as a system relating isolated functions according to the differences among them, which contrasts with the concrete, "practical" space of everyday activities.[75]

When Marx wrote that labor is an abstraction that becomes "true in practice," he did not mean that something that is abstract becomes, suddenly, concrete; rather, labor is always already both concrete (as in the work of individuals) and abstract (as in a wealth-creating activity). What changed in the conditions of early industrialization—and what made the discovery of Adam Smith possible—was that the abstract character of labor gained the upper hand over the concrete one and became manifested in a range of social practices.

Similarly, one hundred years after Marx, when Lefebvre claimed that abstract space is becoming "true in practice," he did not argue that concrete space vanishes but rather registered a preponderance of abstract space in economic, social, and everyday life practices, analyzed already in the Mourenx study. In that sense, abstract and concrete spaces are facets of one phenomenon rather than mutually exclusive, as was the case with the contradiction between the abstract rationality of urbanism and the concrete rationality of the practices of dwelling. While Marx claimed that theoretical thought was able to formulate the concept of labor only after that concept had been realized in social practice, Lefebvre wrote that abstract space and its production could be theorized only after becoming relevant in social practices. In other words, although people have always worked, and things and practices have always been spatial, the emergence of the concepts of labor as well as those of space and its production was historical fact, overdetermined by specific intellectual, technological, political, social, and cultural conjunctures.

Modern Architecture and Modern Capitalism

Paralleling Marx's hypothesis that the moment of emergence of the concept of labor is a symptom of its accomplished instrumentalization in social practice, Lefebvre asks about the "moment of emergence of an awareness of space and its production."[76]

In Lefebvre's 1956 book about the painter Édouard Pignon (1905–93), this question was linked to the development of French painting from Cézanne to Picasso, a line in which Lefebvre situates the work of Pignon. Much of this book was devoted to the descriptions of the pictorial space as constructed in the active perception of the spectator. For example, the spectator of Cézanne's series of Mont Sainte-Victoire is described as a producer of a pictorial space who brings together the contradictory movements of forms on the canvas; this space combines continuity and discontinuity, local correspondences and ruptures[77]—the very characteristics that, in the late 1960s, Lefebvre will assign to the space of capitalism. In this account, pictorial space has the features that he will later attribute to social space in general: it is actively produced by relating what is "seen," "known," and "conceived," as Lefebvre wrote about the preceptions of Picasso's analytical cubist canvases;[78] and it is historical, reflecting the historicity of sense-perception, which stems from "the practical and social history of the eye and the gaze."[79] But if these paintings show what is invisible in vision—that is to say, the historical conditions of visibility—then their pictorial space allows for a "close, concrete perception of real objects."[80] In other words, they lend themselves as instruments of cognition of social space: the theoretical step to accomplish is to discover this space as itself produced.

Writing in the 1970s, Lefebvre argued that this step was made by the artists and architects of the Bauhaus, the Soviet constructivists and suprematists, and such individuals as Le Corbusier, Wright, Kandinsky, and Klee. Lefebvre claimed the work of the artistic and architectural avant-gardes of the early twentieth century demonstrated that objects in space cannot be produced in an isolated manner following the judgment of taste; rather, all objects at all scales (from furniture to a monument and, one may add, the city) should be grasped as related to one another by the same perceived, conceived, and produced space.[81]

That this understanding of space as a medium of relationships among objects leads to the "crisis" of the traditional concept of an architectural object was argued by Manfredo Tafuri. In his *Theories and History of Architecture* (1968), Tafuri supported this thesis with a range of examples: from Sant' Elia's diagnosis of the changing and contingent urban space as cause and consequence of the death of the architectural object, through Mondrian's account about the dissolution of architecture in the modern city, to the neoplasticist concept of utilitarian objects merging and neutralizing one another.[82] Tafuri's privileged example was Ludwig Hilberseimer, who postulated relating all processes and locations within the urban reality in one project. "The architecture of the metropolis is essentially dependent on two factors: the single cell of space and the organism of the city as a whole," wrote Hilberseimer, and this space as a constitutive element of an urban block becomes the main design factor for the whole city, at the same time being itself conditioned by the general plan.[83]

Clearly, the concept of space as a continuous medium of relationships, which can be linked to Le Corbusier's *plan libre*, Gropius's *fliessendes Raumkontinuum*, and El Lissitzky's isotropic space, by no means exhausts the multiplicity of conceptualizations of space tested by the architectural avant-gardes of the early twentieth century. In their discussions, at least two other distinctively different concepts of space were developed: the understanding of space as enclosure, influenced by Gottfried Semper, rethought by Hendrik Petrus Berlage and Peter Behrens, and incorporated into Adolf Loos's *Raumplan;* and the concept of space as an extension of the body, introduced in August Schmarsow's lectures on the history of architecture.[84] Moreover, it is virtually impossible to address the introduction of the concept of space into architectural discourse without taking into account the German discussions beginning in the 1880s in aesthetics, art history, and the psychology of perception, in the course of which a consensus about space as the "essence of architecture" was reached and later became commonplace in architectural culture between the world wars in Germany and beyond.[85] Lacking historiographic accounts of these debates, Lefebvre's rather speculative narration focused on the dependencies between architectural practices and the overarching social processes at the beginning of the twentieth century, including new technical inventions, new modes of perception, and new social and economic conditions: "For the Bauhaus did more than locate space in its real context or supply a new perspective on it: it developed a new conception, a global concept, of space." He continued that around 1920, in advanced countries, theoretical thought, industrial practice, and architectural and urbanistic research discovered a link "which had already been dealt with on the practical plane but which had not yet been rationally articulated: that between industrialization and urbanization, between workplaces and dwelling-places."[86]

Lefebvre realized that the definition of architecture by means of space, when combined with the understanding of space as overdetermined by a range of social actors, among which architects tend to have the least influence, reduces architecture to a facilitator of processes whose objectives and conditions are defined outside it, rather than staking out a field of architecture's specific disciplinary competence. This argument was developed by him in an account of the instrumentality of modern architecture in the capitalist reorganization of Europe:

> If there is such a thing as the history of space, . . . then there is such
> a thing as a space characteristic of capitalism. . . . It is certainly argu-
> able that the writings and works of the Bauhaus, of Mies van der Rohe
> among others, outlined, formulated and helped realize that particular
> space—the fact that the Bauhaus sought to be and proclaimed itself to
> be revolutionary notwithstanding.[87]

Or, as Tafuri wrote in his account on Hilberseimer, "Once the true unity of the
production cycle has been identified in the city, the only task the architect can
have is to *organize* that cycle."[88]

While during the CRAUC seminar in 1969 Lefebvre had opposed Bernard
Huet's critique of the Bauhaus as "reactionary" ("every position can be hijacked
to a certain extent"),[89] in the following years, he developed the argument about
the instrumentalization of the modern movement in the capitalist reorganization of economy and society. He argued that new planning procedures and new
systems of representing space introduced by the architectural avant-gardes were
essential for the development of capitalism. This was not different in state socialism, which shared with postwar capitalism the logics of bureaucracy and productivity. In his words, "The Bauhaus, just like Le Corbusier, expressed (formulated
and met) the architectural requirements of state capitalism; these differed little,
in point of fact, from requirements of state socialism as identified during the same
period by the Russian constructivists."[90]

Lefebvre and Tafuri contended that the unity of abstract space—recognized,
postulated, and instrumentalized by the modern movement—in fact accompanies
and facilitates the unity of the processes of production, distribution, and consumption in developed capitalism. While Adam Smith demonstrated that different professions are facets of labor in general, architects, artists, and theorists of
the modern movement showed that different places are interrelated in the processes of production, consumption, and distribution, located in one space. Thus,
abstract labor, defined by Marx as "an abstraction which became true in practice," and abstract space, described by Lefebvre as an "abstraction in action" or
"active abstraction"—are intrinsically related as conditions of developed capitalism.[91] Abstract space corresponds "to *abstract labour* . . . and hence general form
of commodity," wrote Lefebvre in *The Production of Space*.[92]

While, as I will show in the next chapter, Lefebvre rejected Tafuri's extrapolation of this experience of the modern movement into a general condition of
architecture as necessarily unable to think itself beyond the conditions of its
production, he was convinced until the end of his life about the essential link
between modern architecture and the project of capitalist modernization. For
example, writing in 1984, he argued that the Athens Charter provided an ideology, a code, and a model for innovative capitalism, scooping out new forces from

crises and wars.[93] This argument led to disagreements with his friends, such as Anatole Kopp and Claude Schnaidt, both defenders of the social program of the modern movement—Kopp, in 1980, condemning those "who make the young believe . . . that modern architecture and urbanism are creations of capitalism and that they have as their function the production of an environment favorable to repression, alienation, and the exploitation of workers"; and Schnaidt opposing the critique of the architectural avant-garde as technocratic and regretting that he had been one of the first to encourage Lefebvre to come to grips with the urban question.[94]

Space as Lived Abstraction

A juxtaposition of Lefebvre's theory of space and Marx's analysis of labor allows a second perspective on the genealogy of the triads of space, complementing their previously reconstructed formulation with the ISU studies on dwelling. Describing space as the "example and evidence" of the concept of concrete abstraction in *De l'État* (1977), Lefebvre argued that "physical, observed, and lived" space becomes worked on by means of representations of space, and thus space is produced not only by material and economic practices but also on the level of conceptual, aesthetic, symbolic, and phantasmic appropriation.[95]

Lefebvre's distinctions among the three moments of space rather closely follow Marx's comments from the *Grundrisse* about the importance of lived experience to the emergence of abstract labor. Marx argued that the economic, social, political, and technological developments that make abstract labor "true in practice" involve a shift on an emotional and personal level, and he described the worker's feeling of "indifference" to a specific type of work, which cannot provide him with personal identity anymore and "has ceased to be organically linked with particular individuals in any specific form."[96] In other words, abstract labor finds its counterpart in the "economic" subjects: sellers and buyers, if only of their own labor power.[97]

An even more direct inspiration for Lefebvre's work on space came from Friedrich Engels's *The Condition of the Working Class in England* (1845). Describing Manchester, Engels analyzed its morphology as structurally determined by socioeconomic causes and aims: the old center is dissolved, and the city is divided into dilapidated workers' districts, factories, and villa neighborhoods. Lefebvre read Engels's account of Manchester as a double movement of disclosure and concealment: while the misery of the workers' districts was shrouded from the view of the upper class, the spatial segregation manifested in the social relations of the city—above all the contradiction between the proletariat and the bourgeoisie. Examining the city as a social phenomenon—a manifestation of the hidden structures of the society—Engels understood it as a revolutionary place, allowing the workers to reflect on their situation.[98] Not unlike Marx in describing the emergence of abstract labor in economic practices, theoretical reflection, and the lived experience of the worker, Engels read the city at the same time as a material artifact, a manifestation of the deep structure of the society, and a vehicle of revolutionary experience.[99]

The writings of Marx and Engels, but also the arguments of the Annales School that social change involves economy and ideology as much as everyday experience, resonate in Lefebvre's examination of the new experience of space perceived, conceived, and lived. Examples of this experience include the reductive perception of space by a driver on a highway and the impoverished use of space in functionalist housing estates.[100] What the architects and the artists of the architectural avant-garde discovered as one continuous space expressed the collective spatial experience facilitated by technology. The media of this experience multiplied beginning in the second half of the nineteenth century: high-speed means of transportation, which produced modes of perception that inspired futurist paintings; new technologies of representation, such as aerial photography, which allowed the wide public to perceive the metropolis in its wholly new scale; the generational experience of the trenches of the First World War—"the cubist war"—which revealed a new type of landscape transformed by human action; and the unprecedented level of stimulation in the metropolis, depicted in Fernand Léger's *The City* (1919)[101] and described by Georg Simmel as the source of a new type of blasé subjectivity ruled by the logics of monetary economy: calculation, reason, and interest.

This new experience of space was paralleled not only by an abstraction of architectural representations—such as isometry, preferred by the avant-garde over perspective—but also by the abstraction of architectural and urbanistic discourse in response to the enlargement of the scale of the urbanization processes. This is particularly evident in the French debates in which Lefebvre was immersed. With the discussions about the redevelopment of the fortifications of Paris in the first decades of the twentieth century,[102] the introduction of a new scale of thinking in the housing question within the expanding metropolis, and the institutionalization of urbanism in France as an autonomous discipline, such generic terms as *free spaces (espaces libres)* became a way to describe vast areas left between the buildings in the peripheries of the city. While the definition of these spaces in terms of hygienic concerns stemmed from the nineteenth-century debates about the courtyard and the street, their other roles debated before 1900, such as in security, socialization, and aesthetics, became increasingly erased from the discussions of the first decades of the next century.[103] This increasing irrelevance reverberates in Lefebvre's general argument that the doctrine of the division of functions disentangled the complex assemblages of uses established, in the course of historical development, at every level of urban reality, from the apartment to the city as a whole.[104] But this increasing abstraction of the architectural vocabulary was not restricted to the discourse of the "progressive" architects; for example, it was reflected in new techniques of the calculation of *green spaces (espaces verts)* introduced in the 1920s in the French garden cities, independently of the formal directions of specific designs.[105] In other words, the abstraction of space was not a question of individual invention or design ideology but a result of an overarching social process. This makes clear that the experience of abstract space is not a manifestation of an alienated, inauthentic modern individual unable to reach the "real life," which is "elsewhere." Rather, with the concept of abstract space, the division between "reality" and "illusion" is left behind, and what is addressed is the real-and-illusory experience of space, which was analyzed already in the study on the *pavillon:* an "intimate" and "objective" mixture of the phenomenal and the essential,[106] a sensuous–suprasensuous reality that characterizes the ghostly existence of commodities.

Space as a Commodity

What characterizes abstract space in Lefebvre's view is not only that it facilitates capitalist production, distribution, and consumption but also that it is itself transformed into a commodity: produced, distributed, and consumed. In analogy to Marx, who argued that the abstract character of labor stems from its commodification, Lefebvre investigates the conditions and consequences of turning space into a commodity.

Just like every commodity, space reflects the duality of the abstract and the concrete aspects of labor by which it is produced. In *Capital,* Marx theorizes this dual character of a commodity as a concrete abstraction described as a "sensuous–suprasensuous thing" (*sinnlich–übersinnliches Ding*).[107] Concrete ("useful") labor produces use value, while the amount of abstract labor socially necessary for the production of use value determines the exchange value of the product. Lefebvre commented that use value is related to the need, the expectation, the wish, while exchange value stems from the relationship of a commodity to other commodities, indeed to all things in the world of commodities. In Marx's words, "As use values, commodities are, above all, of different qualities, but as exchange values they are merely different quantities, and consequently do not contain an atom of use value."[108]

In *The Production of Space,* Lefebvre sketches a narrative of the emergence of the commodity economy as conditioned by an (often violent) introduction of standard measurements of length, weight, distance, and durability, as well as by the technical, legal, political, and social consequences of these introductions.

These systems of representation dominate not only specialized practices but also the practices of everyday life: in the conditions of modern capitalism, the commodification of labor–time structures not only the spatiotemporal conditions of work but also the whole daily routine, with its lunch breaks, commuting time, rush hours, and so on. Accordingly, in order to become a commodity, space must be subjected to systems of representation and procedures that allow it to be quantified: divided, measured, and compared.[109] In the words of the Marxist philosopher Alfred Sohn-Rethel:

> The exchange abstraction excludes everything that makes up history, human and even natural history. . . . Time and space thereby assume that character of absolute historical timelessness and universality which must mark the exchange abstraction as a whole and each of its features.[110]

As in Marx's example of abstract labor measured by time, the historical process of the commodification of space required the implementation of a system of representation that would depict different "pieces of space" as distinct and endowed with comparable features. Represented by this system, a piece of space must radically differ from a "place" traditionally characterized by blurred borders and qualitatively defined by identity, natural peculiarities, topography, authority, religion, tradition, and history. An early symptom of this transition "from nature to abstraction" is the evolution of systems of measurement, which proceeded from measuring space with parts of the body to universal, quantitative, and homogeneous standards.[111] Lefebvre relates these requirements to Cartesian analytical geometry.[112] He does not argue that the concept of a homogeneous space was developed within capitalism, let alone that it was a "superstructural" reflection of the capitalist mode of production: the concept of an isotropic, boundless, singular, and irreplaceable space stems from late antiquity and thus predates the ascension of capitalism.[113] Rather, Lefebvre argues that the Cartesian system of representation became "practically true" in capitalism: it became instrumentalized in the social practices of capitalist societies.

Lefebvre noticed that the space of capitalism is characterized not only by a tendency toward homogenization but also by a parallel tendency to fragment. This paradoxical simultaneity of two contradictory tendencies is in his view the most important characteristic of abstract space. Alluding to the empirical studies by the ISU and his study of Mourenx, in *The Production of Space* Lefebvre describes the everyday experience of postwar space as "homogenous yet at the same time broken up into fragments."[114] Abstract space is split into multiple spaces: housing, labor, leisure, sport, tourism, and others;[115] it is pulverized and sold off in parcels, fragmented into functions that represent "needs" as simple, purified, and fractured by boundaries. Yet at the same time this is a globally controlled space, generically designed, and dominated by the international real estate market. This experience of a simultaneous homogeneity and fragmentation is that of the post-war consumerist culture: in Georges Perec's *Things* (1965), Jérôme and Sylvie, a couple of market researchers, are confronted with a multiplicity of consumerist fantasies, "drift[ing] from marvel to marvel, from surprise to surprise," while having the impression that these visions formed "a coherent structure which they could at last grasp and decipher."[116] These tendencies to homogenize and fragment are interdependent: "space 'is' whole and broken, global and fractured, at one and the same time."[117] In abstract space, writes Lefebvre, things are, "paradoxically, united yet disunited, joined yet detached from one another, at once torn apart and squeezed together."[118]

This simultaneity of homogeneity and fragmentation is, according to Lefebvre, intrinsic to its Cartesian model: homogeneity results in fragmentation, and fragmentation determines homogeneity. This system of representation is unable to account for any other features of pieces of space than their location expressed with the three coordinates of analytic geometry: areas or volumes differing in location differ in "everything," have "nothing in common." Thus, space appears as an aggregate of independent, distinct areas or volumes. At the same time this system of representation offers no immanent criteria for delineating these areas or volumes; by eliminating "existing differences or peculiarities,"[119] Cartesian geometry does not suggest any privileged line of division of the space in question. Like Lewis Mumford, Lefebvre stressed that the grid lends itself to any parceling required by land speculation—but also to functionalist zoning and social segregation.[120] Deprived of intrinsic differentiations, the entirety of space is endowed with a geometric homogeneity that means both a representation and a practical attitude toward the management of space.

The simultaneous tendencies toward fragmentation and homogenization are complemented by the hierarchization of space, which Lefebvre noticed in the processes of gentrification of the Marais and Quartier Les Halles.[121] These tendencies are overdetermined not only by economic factors but also by social, political, and cultural developments.[122] Among these developments, Lefebvre lists the world market, science, demographic pressures, and technology. The last is particularly important, because it allows an intervention on all levels of space—from the local, through the regional and the national, to worldwide.[123] While such "techniques of spatialization" as systems of irrigation, town planning, and canal and road building were developed throughout history, only when they were related to a broad set of conditions of modern society has their accumulation been reflected in the production of space through the increasing domination of conceived and perceived space over lived space.[124]

The agency of the state was essential in this process, and it was discussed in Lefebvre's *De l'État,* which draws on the ISU analysis of the segregation of social classes in the wake of the liberalization of the French real estate market in the

1960s.[125] In *De l'État,* Lefebvre argued that the state produces space as *national territory:* physical space, modified and transformed by networks, circuits, and flows, as well as the space of ideology and knowledge tied to power and social hierarchies.[126] It seems not accidental that these statements coincided with Michel Foucault's discussion of the state territory in his lectures at the Collège de France in the late 1970s: Foucault's account of the processes of individualization by means of disciplinary practices accompanying the biopolitical management of population as a whole pointed at a similar dynamic that Lefebvre addressed in his hypothesis of the simultaneous processes of fragmentation and homogenization of state-produced space.

The Flat Space of Modern Architecture

It is space conceived by the architectural avant-gardes of the early twentieth century that Lefebvre saw as a symptom of the simultaneous tendencies toward homogenization and fragmentation. In his essay "L'espace," Lefebvre described this space as being "at the same time abstract and concrete, homogenous and nonarticulated":

> The architectural and urbanistic space, as space, has this double character: disarticulated and yet broken up under the fictitious coherence of the gaze, a space of constraints and of dispersed norms. It has a paradoxical character that we try to define here: interrelated and disjointed.[127]

In his essay Lefebvre claimed that this disjointed space is maintained visually and technologically by means of the scheme as generator *(schéma générateur)* tied to a practice of the given society—a phrasing in which reverberates Le Corbusier's praise of the plan ("the plan is the generator") from *Toward an Architecture* (1923).[128]

And it is precisely this simultaneous homogenization and fragmentation, according to Lefebvre's collaborators Henri Raymond and Marion Segaud, that characterize Le Corbusier's buildings. In the study "Analyse de l'espace architectural" (Analysis of Architectural Space), presented at the CRAUC seminar, they interpreted Le Corbusier's architectural promenade as a universal medium, without a relationship to the site, punctuated by architectural events. This is a space, according to Raymond and Segaud, where the satisfaction of a need happens instantly in the assigned place, transforming the need into its own image.[129] Raymond and Segaud's rereading of Le Corbusier's architectural promenade as a sequence of punctual events suggests that in the midst of what was called the "new spatial culture" of the 1960s France,[130] the architectural discourse was haunted by a paradoxical *flat* space. This is the space that comes to the fore in multiple accounts of that time, including Tafuri's critiques of the avant-garde concept of space as a diagram linking the processes of production, consumption, and distribution; this space also permeated the structuralist readings of the post-war city as a generative tissue of meaning production and Lefebvre's own take on the modernist treatment of volumes as surfaces and plans.[131] This tendency to reduce space to two dimensions was called by Lefebvre the "geometric" formant of abstract space, which complements its two other formants: "optical"—the transformation of objects in space into images; and "phallic"—the fascination with verticality symbolizing male force, fertility, and violence.[132]

The Form of Space

Lefebvre argued that the commodification of space does not just pertain to abstract space as a whole but, more fundamentally, produces this space as a whole:

> Space thus understood is both *abstract* and *concrete* in character: abstract inasmuch as it has no existence save by virtue of the exchange-ability of all its component parts, and concrete inasmuch as it is socially real and as such localized.[133]

This description of an "exchangeability" of precisely "all" component parts of space refers to Marx's definition of the "form of exchange value." In *Capital*, after characterizing a commodity by use and exchange value, Marx writes that it "manifests itself as this twofold thing that it is, as soon as its value assumes an independent form—viz., the form of exchange value." This form is never assumed by an isolated commodity, "but only when placed in a value or exchange relation with another commodity of a different kind."[134] In *Capital*, Marx arrives at the definition of the "general form of value" *(allgemeine Wertform)*, which "expresses the values of the whole world of commodities in terms of a single commodity set apart for the purpose."[135] In other words, the exchange value of a commodity is not established alone in relation to *all* other commodities; it also becomes *manifested* only in comparison with all other commodities.

For Lefebvre, space of capitalism is not just commodified, but commodification becomes the operational logics of spatial practices.[136] Just as the exchange value of a commodity is defined by its relationship to all other commodities, every "piece" of space in abstract space is defined in relationship to *all* other such "pieces." This allows a distinction between concrete and abstract features of space: while the former are "absolute" (localized, situated, specific for particular places, and self-contained), the latter are relational, or "relative" (stemming from the connections among locations). Having in mind this relative character of abstract space, Lefebvre writes that capitalist space is "social" in the sense that it is "not a thing among other things nor a product among other products: rather, it subsumes things produced, and encompasses their interrelationships in their coexistence and simultaneity."[137] The relative character of abstract space that facilitates its instrumentalization in the processes of capitalist production does not replace its "absolute" features but rather gains preponderance in the majority of social practices: as a concrete abstraction, space is both absolute and relative.[138]

This ambition to provide a general definition of space led Lefebvre to speculate on the "form of space" that he called "centrality." While the form of commodity is the possibility of exchange independently of what is exchanged, the form of space is the possibility of gathering independently of what is gathered: objects and people, products and works, signs and symbols, acts, situations, practical relationships.[139] It is in the city and urban space where centrality is manifested: already the Greek polis made simultaneous what in the countryside was taking place and passing according to natural cycles and rhythms.[140] While the form of the commodity as the possibility of exchange independently of what is exchanged characterizes all commodities regardless of their specific features, centrality is the most general relationship among locations that can be attributed to each of them independently of its specific features.

Lefebvre stressed that every form has not only a mental (or "logical") existence but also a social existence: while the mental form describes logical relationships, social forms "regulate countless situations and activities."[141] Accordingly, he describes the urban form in its *mental* existence as simultaneity of events and perceptions, whereas its *social* existence is encounter and assembly, since every social space implies "actual or potential assembly at a single point, or around that point."[142] In this analysis, form detaches itself from content and becomes "pure and transparent: intelligible," but without a content it has no existence: like the form of exchange, "the form of social space has an affinity with logical forms: it calls for a content and cannot be conceived as having no content; but, thanks to abstraction, it is in fact conceived of, precisely, as independent of any specific content."[143] In other words, like every act of exchange, each specific centrality is socially produced.

The Dialectics of Centrality

Lefebvre writes that the practices that produce centralities are contradictory: centrality consists of "simultaneous inclusion and exclusion precipitated by a specific spatial factor." In this account, centrality is dialectical, and "the center gathers things together only to the extent that it pushes them away and disperses them."[144]

This dialectical understanding of centrality—defined by the opposite forces of dispersal and gathering, inclusion and exclusion—distinguishes Lefebvre's theory from earlier concepts of centrality: for instance, Engels's analysis of economic centralization of forces and means of production in the growth of industrial cities, and Walter Christaller's hexagonal scheme of central places designed in order to guarantee the most efficient consumption and distribution processes within the Fordist–Keynesian concept of spatial development.[145] In consequence, Lefebvre's centrality is conceived in a constant process of production:

> Any centrality, once established, is destined to suffer dispersal, to dissolve or to explode from the effects of saturation, attrition, outside aggressions, and so on. This means that the "real" can never become completely fixed, that it is constantly in a state of mobilization.[146]

The dialectics of centrality defines the relationship among the moments of space: their unity and the contradictions among them.[147] Such understanding of dialectics implies a revision of dialectics as conceived by Hegel, which reverberates in Marx's value theory. Lefebvre wrote that where Hegel sees two parts, there is always a third one that is in conflict with the others: a dialectical relationship requires three components, not two, because "relations between the two boil down to oppositions, contrasts and antagonisms."[148] Lefebvre adds that binary oppositions "freeze the dialectical movement" and thus cannot help understanding change, process, and life: the main focus of dialectics.[149]

By including a third term in theorizing dialectics (or "trialectics," as Edward Soja called it),[150] Lefebvre rethinks the dialectical contradiction as irreducible to the idealist contradiction between two terms that are removed, preserved, and raised to a higher level—the three meanings of the German term *Aufhebung*. This attempt to develop a different—materialist—understanding of contradiction has a lot in common with the work of Althusser, notwithstanding Lefebvre's attacks on this author of "Contradiction and Overdetermination": Lefebvre's discussion of the "unity and contradiction" among the three moments of space translates into the question of a contradiction that emerges on multiple levels and thus implies a possibility of thinking materialism as a theory of distributed, or overdetermined, causality.

This also means that the relationships among the three moments of space cannot be grasped in one deductive scheme and that they are contingent, unstable, and to be sustained by historically and geographically situated social practices. This is why, while describing the spaces of postwar capitalism as both fragmented and homogeneous, Lefebvre asked, how could "such properties, 'incompatible' from a logical point of view, be said to enter into association with one another and constitute a 'whole' which not only does not disintegrate but even aids in the development of strategies?" He replies that the answer cannot be found in specific features of space but only in social practice: "Only act can hold—and hold together—such fragments in a homogenous totality. Only action can prevent dispersion, like a fist clenched around sand."[151]

While Lefebvre's analysis of dwelling suggests that the production of space is governed by the dialectics of differentiation of a concrete universal, in his research on the production of space on larger scales this discussion shifts toward a theory of dialectical centrality. The relationship between these two schemes was never worked out in his theoretical writings, neither was the dialectical relationship among the three moments produced by specific social practices. These relationships can be studied only in concrete analyses of historical events. Lefebvre undertook two such investigations, which will be discussed in chapter 4: a study of the Paris Commune of 1871 and an examination of the Parisian May '68.

The History of Urban Space

The reading of Lefebvre's theorizing of space as a concrete abstraction reveals a polarization between an account of space as overdetermined by a multiplicity of social practices and research on the universal form of space unfolding in history. This polarization cannot be done away with by identifying its poles with two of Marx's definitions of concrete abstraction that Lefebvre worked with—as an "abstraction true in practice" and as a "sensuous–suprasensuous thing"—since this polarization is immanent to many of his concepts, including that of production, abstract space, and the dialectics of centrality. As a consequence, Lefebvre's research of space oscillates between two perspectives—empirical and retrospective on the one hand, and speculative and deductive on the other—which coincide with what Louis Althusser and Étienne Balibar argued to be a fundamental rupture in the work of Marx himself.[152]

Is it possible to bring these two perspectives together? The Soviet philosopher Evald Ilyenkov argued that their combination is not only possible but also necessarily implied by Marx's research on value as concrete abstraction. In his book *The Dialectics of the Abstract and the Concrete in Marx's Capital* (1960), Ilyenkov pointed out that value reflects the "universal and necessary element, a 'cell' of capital, constituting the universal and most abstract expression of the specific nature of capital," and, at the same time, it is "a concrete economic fact—direct exchange of a commodity for another commodity."[153] Accordingly, the analysis of value requires a double approach. On the one hand, it involves a philosophical investigation of the internal contradiction of value—between use and exchange value—which is considered the universal stimulus of the historical development of capitalism. But, on the other hand, this contradiction cannot be solved theoretically, and thus an empirical research is necessary to account for the specific social practices that produce mediators between the two sides of value. According to Ilyenkov, money is the most important of them, allowing a translation between use and exchange value; a second is labor power, a unique commodity whose use value consists precisely in the fact that in the course of its consumption it is transformed into its counterpart: exchange value.[154]

Ilyenkov's reconstruction, often sharpening and clarifying what in Marx's writings is open and ambiguous, does not solve the problem but rather makes it evident: in his reading of Marx's method, the empirical analysis is subordinated to a speculative perspective awaiting concrete application in historical research. In that sense Ilyenkov's argument reveals the core of what Balibar called "an almost unbearable tension" in Marx's schema of historical causality, which "both entirely *subordinates* the historical process to a preexistent teleology and yet *asserts* that the motor of transformation is nothing other than the 'scientifically observable' facts of material life."[155]

The Regressive-Progressive Method

Rather than starting with a single contradiction between use and exchange value, Lefebvre refers in the majority of his writings to the historical method of Marx and the procedure of employing concepts that express social relationships in the most advanced stage of social development to investigate the structure and the relations of production of previous social formations.[156] In this perspective, the concept of abstract space is applied to cast light on the historical development of space and to understand it as always already produced:

> The production of space, having attained the conceptual and linguistic level, acts retroactively upon the past, disclosing aspects and moments of it hitherto uncomprehended. The past appears in a different light, and hence the process whereby that past becomes the present also takes on another aspect.[157]

This approach was theorized by Lefebvre as the "regressive–progressive method," spelled out in his 1953 text "Perspectives de la sociologie rurale" (Perspectives of Rural Sociology), in which it was claimed to be indispensable for research on space.[158] The application of this method to rural sociology suggests that besides Marx, whom Lefebvre claimed to be its founder,[159] the tradition of French historians of the late nineteenth and early twentieth centuries might have been its second source. In particular, Marc Bloch employed the "regressive method" in his rural history of France and argued for "reading history backwards," because the later periods are better known than the earlier ones, and it is prudent to proceed from the known to the unknown.[160]

In his essay on rural sociology, Lefebvre describes the reality of the rural communities as characterized by a "horizontal" complexity, which concerns the differences among synchronous agrarian structures stemming from differences in technologies and social structures, and by a "vertical" complexity, which originates from the "coexistence of formations differing in age and date."[161] These two complexities—with which he was already dealing in the Pyrenees study—cross each other and influence each other, and thus the regressive–progressive method is applied to investigate their multifaceted relationships.

This method consists of three "moments." The first is the descriptive moment, which includes the "participatory observation on the ground."[162] Clearly, this observation is informed by a "general theory"; this was also the case in the Pyrenees study, which started with several questions formulated within Marxist discourse (about collective property or land rent) but without reducing the history of the valley to one overarching contradiction. According to Lefebvre, this descriptive moment is followed by an analytico-regressive one, which aims at an exact dating of the described reality. Finally, the task of the "historico-genetical" moment is to study the "modifications introduced to the previously *dated* structure by its subsequent development (internal and external) and by its subordination to wider structures"; thus, the general process of development of the structures in question is explained in the framework of the historical processes.[163]

A useful comment about the application of this method can be found in Lefebvre's article "What Is the Historical Past?" (1959), a review of the book *The Parisian Sans-culottes and the French Revolution,* by Albert Soboul (1958), his former colleague at Musée national des arts et traditions populaires. Lefebvre writes that the French Revolution made a certain number of events *possible;* thus, "each time one of these possibilities is realized, it *retroactively* sheds a new light on the initial event." That is why, he argues, "when historians take into account their own experience in their research into the past, they are profoundly right to do so." The possible is a concept that "has been adopted in all fields of the social sciences and therefore now has a very general methodological character." It allows for a "theory of a deeper objectivity which does not exclude a certain relativity," governed by the principle that *"the past becomes present (or is renewed) as a function of the realization of the possibilities objectively implied in this past."*[164]

This understanding of reality as a realized possibility was complemented, in *The Urban Revolution,* by an understanding of possibility as the virtual aim of the current tendencies. Accordingly, Lefebvre shifted the accents in the explanation of the two directions of his method, and the regressive movement was defined as one "from the virtual to the actual, the actual to the past," whereas the progressive research is developed "from the obsolete and completed to the movement that anticipates that completeness, that presages and brings into being something new."[165]

Historicizing the Capitalist City

Lefebvre's understanding of space as a concrete abstraction was applied in his regressive–progressive analysis of the city and urban space in capitalism. This research, fundamental for *The Production of Space,* was adumbrated in *The Right to the City* and spelled out in the 1972 book *La pensée marxiste et la ville,* which reconstructs Marx's and Engels's comments on the city, complements them, and questions the capacity of Marxism to account for the processes of urbanization by drawing conclusions from Lefebvre's research in rural sociology, the studies of the *pavillon,* and his critiques of urbanism.

Lefebvre begins with an account of the historical role of the city ("the subject of history") as the "place, tool, and scene" of the transformation from feudalism to capitalism:[166] a perspective that appears today rather limited, since this transformation cannot be understood without accounting for its other conditions, such as primitive accumulation and accumulation through colonial dispossession. In this account, the city is held responsible both for the destruction of the former social formations and for the early accumulation of capital and the creation of commerce and the market. The city is thus conceived as productive, replacing nature as the "laboratory" of social forces in which humans "produce" their social existence.[167] While for Marx space is a part of the forces of production, in *La pensée marxiste et la ville* Lefebvre argues that this statement particularly applies to the city and urban space.[168] Following the progressive–regressive method, Lefebvre conceives the city, urban space, and its relation to the countryside as explanatory categories for a reconstruction of Marx's analysis of the economic, political, technological, and social transformations that led to the emergence of capitalism.[169] At this point the theorizing of space becomes related to the examination of other concrete abstractions: abstract labor and capital; the city, according to Lefebvre, is the place where abstraction becomes "fulfilled in practice" by the power of money and the force of the division of labor.[170]

In *La pensée marxiste et la ville,* Lefebvre argues that Marxist theory is not complete. For instance, it does not explain why the class of real estate owners persisted in capitalism; neither does it properly theorize the question of land and land annuity. In particular, Lefebvre develops the argument about the city as a force of production by means of an analysis of the productive roles of urban space in the creation of surplus value (by labor); the realization of surplus value (i.e., the generation of capital through the sale of commodities and services); and the distribution of surplus value (by private institutions and those of the state).[171]

From the perspective of the creation of surplus value, the role of the city seems marginal at first glance: it is the production unit (an enterprise, a corporation, an industry branch, and an agricultural production unit) that is essential. Yet, as a force of production, the city facilitates the maintanence and perfection of the division of labor that is necessary for capitalism and gathers together the instruments and actors of the productive process.[172] Since Marx, Lefebvre argues, researchers have discovered the city as the place of concentration of people, markets, information, and decisions. But the city has an even more essential function: it furnishes capitalism with mechanisms of self-limitation, which condition its survival. While capitalist society has a tendency to dissociate its own conditions (dividing labor, separating the producers from the means of production and the process of production from that of sale, etc.), after reaching a certain level of growth, these divisions can be damaging for capitalism: the economic crisis consists of precisely the dissolution of the factors of production. Thus, Lefebvre claims that it is the city and urban framework *(le cadre urbain)* that act against the dislocation and dissociation of the conditions of the productive process: in the city the forces of cohesion and of dissociation act against each other.[173] This argument was developed in *The Production of Space,* in which Lefebvre discusses the postwar development of the capitalist city as a texture and medium of connections and thus a means of production that links together "various flows involved: flows of energy and labour, of commodities and capital."[174]

The second role of the city and urban space in capitalism, according to Lefebvre, is the facilitation of the realization of surplus value by means of the market and the credit system.[175] This includes the city's containment of both productive and nonproductive labor, the latter being necessary for the processes of production (providing services, maintenance, and administration) and for the processes of consumption (securing the demand for products). Lefebvre wrote that the city and society "merge":[176] since it is necessary for capitalism to secure the distribution of products (and thus the realization of the surplus value) by manipulation, protection, and control of the market, the reproduction of surplus value and that of the social relations of production cannot be separated.[177]

Finally, the role of the city in the distribution of surplus value relates to the satisfaction of needs of the population. Lefebvre notices that among "social needs," sketched already by Marx in his 1875 *Critique of the Gotha Programme,* a new need is emerging: "that of the urban life *[vie urbaine],* of the city," which can be satisfied neither by the market nor by state institutions.[178] As explained in *The Right to the City,* the need for urban life includes the need for places (and times) of simultaneity, encounter ("places where exchange would not pass through exchange value"); it is in these needs that "the right to the city" seeks its legitimization.[179]

Toward a Complete Urbanization

Lefebvre's account of the role of the city and urban space in the creation, realization, and distribution of surplus value links his readings of Marx with his research on the development tendencies of postwar capitalism. The hypothesis of the "merger" between society and the city as the increasingly dominant productive force in capitalist society, sketched in *La pensée marxiste et la ville,* feeds into what in *The Urban Revolution* he called the "complete urbanization of society." Not unlike the operaist argument about "the great shift of the frontline from the factory to the metropolis," as it was retrospectively put by Antonio Negri, Lefebvre sees the complete urbanization of society defining a new stage of the worldwide development of capitalism beyond postwar Fordism.[180]

Lefebvre characterizes this stage by the generalization of the production of space: "The productive forces, stimulated by the two world wars, have grown to such an extent that they *produce space.*"[181] He argues that the investments in space, both urban and rural, allow thwarting the law of the decrease of the average rate of profit;[182] thus capital has rushed into the production of space rather than limiting itself to classical forms of production.[183] This argument inspired other Marxist theorists, including David Harvey, who, however, sees this secondary circuit of capital not as becoming more influential than its primary (industrial) circuit but as a cyclical process of expansion and contraction synchronized with the pattern of capitalist growth and crisis.[184]

For Lefebvre, this analysis of political economy of space must be complemented by its critique, which accounts for the "self-preservation of space as the worldwide medium of the definite installation of capitalism."[185] Such critique addresses the expansion of capitalism into global space and a constitution of "new sectors" of production and reproduction, among which Lefebvre lists leisure, everyday life, knowledge *(connaissance)*, art, and urbanization.[186] These processes result in a gradual merger between the processes of production and reproduction and in a collapse of their respective spaces beyond their functionalist division into housing, work, and recreation.[187] But the complete urbanization of society means also a sharpening of the specifically urban dialectics between the center and the periphery at any scale of the society, from a metropolitan region to the global scale: the enhanced marginalization and control of large parts of urban populations are paralleled by a global tendency toward a strengthening of the limited number of sites of economic wealth, political power, cultural prestige, technological competence, and knowledge production.

The instrumentalization of space in economic development and in the reproduction of social relationships needs to be analyzed by focusing on its specific contradictions, argues Lefebvre, instead of looking for a coherence, for an "urban system" of structures and functions.[188] The simultaneity of the homogenization and fragmentation of space is one of them; others include the contradiction between the urbanization of the countryside and the ruralization of the city (that is to say, the subordination of urban space to the laws of agrarian economy and land annuity)[189] and the concomitant paradox of the dependence of capitalism on the exploitation of nature, which it destroys in the course of this exploitation. But for Lefebvre the most striking contradiction is conveyed by the concept of the "urban": at same time an "abstraction" and, "a utopia."[190] The emptiness of urban space is that of a form of commodity but also that of an empty signifier onto which the desire for difference is projected, including the desire for a different space and a different time expressed in the practices of habitation in the *pavillon*. In other words, the urban is as much an instrument of capitalist production and reproduction as it is a social resource for a different—"differential"—space.

Project
Urban Society and Its Architecture

I N JUNE 1972, the Groupe de sociologie urbaine Paris 10 and the Institut de recherches at the Unité pédagogique no. 8 organized a colloquium at the Mediterranean tourist new town of Port Grimaud under the topic of architecture and the social sciences with the ambitious aim "to constitute architectural space as an object of study."[1] Even though sociology was included in the title of the colloquium, it was linguistics that fascinated the two most prominent contributors, Henri Lefebvre and Manfredo Tafuri. Tafuri called for an analysis of structuralism as one of the ideologies of the capitalist city, representing the belief that a management of contradictions secures the permanent technological innovation and development of capitalism.[2] Lefebvre would agree with much of this, but during the discussion, when Tafuri referred to the operaist argument of workers' struggle as the engine of capitalism, Lefebvre's answer was ironic: "You put everything into your system." "Not mine, that of capitalism," responded Tafuri.[3]

The controversy between Tafuri and Lefebvre concerned not whether architecture is to be put on trial but rather what kind of critique should it be, how far should it go, and what should it aim at? In Port Grimaud, Lefebvre asked, "What is architecture? Is there something specifically architectural? Is it an art, a technique, a science?" He concluded, "I argue that architecture is a social practice."[4]

The analysis of architecture in this perspective starts with recognizing the practice of an architect as "a producer of space, but never the only one" who "operates within a specific space—the sheet of white paper."[5] This practice is defined by its external constraints imposed by other agents of the production of space (developers, bankers, planners, and "users") and its internal competencies and limitations set by its specific concepts, ideologies, and modes of representation, drawings, models, and abstractions.[6] Architecture thus becomes a sum of the aims, instruments, and regulations assigned to it; its field of possibilities is delineated by its dependencies and synergies with other practices, disciplines, and institutions.

In this perspective Lefebvre would agree with Tafuri's program, published three years earlier in the journal *Contropiano,* to disclose the origin, development, and end of modern architecture as a project "to resolve, on the level of an ideology all the more insidious because it lies entirely within concrete activities and real production cycles, the imbalances, contradictions and delays typical of the capitalist reorganization of the world market."[7] Developing this argument in *Architecture and Utopia* (1973), Tafuri identified the role of the modern movement in architecture as the final step in the Enlightenment's venture of the creative destruction of the feudal city, aimed at clearing the ground for the fully rational capitalist planning, accommodating the shock of everyday life in the modern metropolis, and launching a pedagogical endeavor to discipline the subjectivity of urban dwellers according to the daily cycle of production, consumption, and distribution.[8]

For Tafuri, architects' position within the social division of labor overdetermines all their operations, making it impossible to reflect with architectural means on the conditions of architectural production. In other words, the project and the critique must be kept apart: in *Theories and History of Architecture* (1968) Tafuri argued that any attempt at relating them to each other, either by introducing the methods of planning into criticism or by grafting critical tools into the practice of architecture, is bound to fail. This is because the project is always oriented toward novelty, while the critique is always historical and endowed with a demystificatory task, that of recovering "the original functions and ideologies that, in the course of time, define and delimit the role and meaning of architecture."[9]

Tafuri's position was contrasted to that of Lefebvre by Fredric Jameson, who linked them to two different lineages within Marxism. In his essay "Architecture and the Critique of Ideology" (1982), Jameson related Tafuri's writings from the late 1960s and early 1970s to Althusserian Marxism and the vision of capital's global domination colonizing the last pockets of resistance (the unconsciousness and the precapitalist agriculture of the Third World), paralleled by a sense of a complete blockage of alternative solutions. Jameson contrasted this reading of Marx's argument that no qualitative change can arrive until all possibilities of capitalism are exhausted to the positions of Antonio Gramsci and Lefebvre, which were guided by a different claim of Marx: that the conditions of new social relations necessarily mature within the very mode of production they are going to surpass.[10] The condition of possibility for these alternative projects is a critique of the uneven development of world history; in the case of Lefebvre this would include an analysis of the nonsynchronicities of capitalist societies from his *Critiques of Everyday Life.*

One consequence of this reading of Lefebvre's position could be, according to Jameson, a creation of "enclaves" of new social relationships within the current mode of production to be subsumed; one could think of the red bases (basi rosse), originating in Mao's revolutionary agitation in the 1920s and promoted by Italian operaists, as a means of the direct appropriation of commodities and autoreduction of services (transport, utilities).[11] A second consequence could be the call for "producing and keeping alive a certain alternate 'idea' of space, of urban, daily life," in order to develop the self-consciousness of the architectural profession and equip it for the new tasks whose materialization will become possible only after the political transition takes place.[12] Yet, for Lefebvre, what is at stake is neither to prepare an ideology for future architectural practice nor to produce exceptions to the capitalist mode of the production of space, but rather to theorize the consequences of the fact that the reproduction of this mode is based on its own exception; that is to say, the practice of dwelling, which, as his reading of the pavillon study demonstrates, reproduces relations of production only to the extent that it is lived as external to them.[13] This suggests that the general account of the practice of an architect within capitalist society is to be complemented by a research on architectures of dwelling, pertaining to the everyday practices of the production of space within and beyond the dominant structures of time and space in postwar capitalism.

This program comes close to what Lefebvre understood as a "project": neither a prediction nor a projection, but research on tendencies that emerge within the current society. Writing in a 1981 contribution to the urban planning competition regarding New Belgrade in Yugoslavia, in which he participated with Serge Renaudie and Pierre Guilbaud, Lefebvre stressed the multiplicity of these tendencies:

> If it is true that the city has been a place of civilization, its rupture may annihilate this role. Or the urban may well be a space of dissociation of the society and the social (in a chaos, in a mass agitated by diverse movements). Or it will be a space of reappropriation (of daily life, of the social). If there is no absolute determinism but always (in biological life and in human time) possibilities, which are often opposed, a choice more or less conscious is made. The urban today and tomorrow? A sheaf of possibilities, the best and the worst.[14]

Within this perspective, much of Lefebvre's work was devoted to examining a possibility for a "differential" space contrasted to the abstract space of postwar capitalism—research carried out by means of the very concepts that he introduced in order to account for postwar society: that of everyday life, but also that of the practice of appropriation, centrality, and difference. This suggests that this project is not a separate part of the theory of the production of space, distinguished from Lefebvre's studies on the processes of urbanization; rather, it is a set of postulates formulated from within these studies, their consequences generalized beyond the context of their formulation, theoretical preconditions that allow such generalizations, and textual strategies that make it possible to construct concepts at the same time precise and open-ended enough to grasp the multiplicity of urban futures. Addressing these issues will make it clear that rather than adding one more element to the ones discussed so far, this chapter will show Lefebvre's project as a specific orientation of his theorizing of space in general.

Lefebvre coined multiple concepts on this path. He urged the construction of "concrete utopias"—a concept that goes back to Ernst Bloch and refers to an investigation of possible futures from within the affordances and limitations of a given situation. Contrasted to "abstract utopias" extrapolating from the status quo, "concrete utopias" are "models" of possible development: operative ways of testing hypotheses that account for complex and aleatory reality and thus are never exhaustive and always require a confrontation with other models.[15] But Lefebvre's project was also developed by an attention to specific "moments" in which the possibility of a different everyday "reveals itself" but also "exhausts itself in the act of being lived."[16] This is why he defined a moment as "the attempt to achieve the total realization of a possibility."[17] What is specific for these concepts—moments, models, concrete utopias—is an operation called "transduction," after Gilbert Simondon's theory of individuation, a term that Lefebvre redefined as an operation of stabilizing a virtual object by proceeding "from the (given) real to the possible."[18]

While none of these concepts can be restricted to architecture, in what follows they will be related to architectural operations and linked to design practices examining possible solutions under given circumstances; to architectural research operating by means of models; and to accounts of experiences of architecture. This does not mean that the project of Lefebvre can be simply approximated with architectural designs. Such approximations would be already compromised by the variety of his references: his calls for a city based on game and spontaneity were claimed to be hardly distinguishable from those of situationists;[19] his fascination with "ephemeral cities" and "movable centralities" can be referred to the inflatable architectures of the Utopie group;[20] and his discussion of space was associated with the topological avant-garde of the 1960s, or the *urbanisme spatiale*.[21] Not to mention his fascination with the early designs of Ricardo Bofill, taken for many of Lefebvre's acquaintances as "the greatest mystificator of the whole history of architecture."[22] These affiliations could be complemented by his tentative praise of the functionalist design for the city of Furttal in the early 1960s and his enthusiasm for the critique of functionalism by Christopher Alexander, as well as for the spectacular architecture of the Montreal Expo in 1967 (with the geodesic dome by Buckminster Fuller, the Habitat '67 by Moshe Safdie, and the suspended structures by Frei Otto),[23] his personal contacts with Fernand Pouillon and Constant Nieuwenhuys, and his admiration for the architecture of Jean Renaudie in his late writings of the 1980s.

The necessity of coming to terms with what appears to be an opportunistic embrace of different architectural positions, formal languages, and ideologies prevents a recourse to familiar schemes of illustration or mutual legitimization. Taking some of these architectures as the guiding line for a reading of Lefebvre's project does not equate with an attempt to specify theoretical concepts by means of architecture, just as the role of the concepts is not that of finding a common denominator for architectural images. In this chapter, the choice of the discussed projects—Fourier's "unitary architecture," the campus of Nanterre, Bofill's City in Space, Constant's New Babylon, and the project for New Belgrade—does not stem from their alleged faithfulness to Lefebvre's texts, let alone from the auctorial commentaries relating these projects to his writings. Rather, what relates these designs to Lefebvre's project is the operation of transduction as the specifically architectural performance. Reading these architectures as going "from the real to the possible"—possible urban spaces envisaged by these projects, but also the potential of Lefebvre's concepts to understand the possibilities open for the social production of space—requires disposing of the clear-cut distinction between architecture as a producer of projects and philosophy as the producer of concepts.

From Unitary Architecture to Differential Space

If, according to Lefebvre, space is produced always already as perceived, conceived, and lived, then its project needs to relate new ways of conceptualizing the processes of urbanization to alternative spatial forms and to a vision of a different urban everyday life. In that sense, at the center of Lefebvre's project resides the question of the relationship between the moments of space: what was discussed before as an epistemological requirement of a unitary theory of space that would "reconnect elements that have been separated and . . . replace confusion by clear distinctions" becomes a postulate for an alternative to abstract space.[24]

If the counterpart of the failed theorization of space in the postwar debates was the fragmented and homogenized abstract space of functionalist urbanism, then the postulated unitary theory of space infers a "differential space." This last kind of space is envisaged by Lefebvre as restoring the unity of the moments of space, integrating the body shattered in abstract space, and distinguishing what became identified in abstract space (social relationships and family relationships, or sexual pleasure and social reproduction).[25] Such understood space would become a political stake, because, as Lefebvre wrote in the Yugoslav journal *Praxis* (1965), social progress must be defined by means of a refusal of the "dissociated, functionalized, structured" everydayness and by a radical transformation of everyday life. This would mean that the "everyday becomes political," not by its absorption into the political life, as in Stalinism, but by becoming a criterion for political practice that aims at restituting the unity of understanding and action.[26]

Collective Luxury: The City of Fourier

This postulate of a unification of the moments of space is what Lefebvre shared with the "unitary urbanism" of the Situationist International (IS) and its call to overcome functionalist city planning in order to construct a "unified milieu in dynamic relation with experiments in behavior."[27] According to Lefebvre, unitary urbanism, postulated by Guy Debord in the late 1950s, aimed at linking parts of the city that were separated spatially; this is how Lefebvre reported one of the *dérives* in Amsterdam, where walkie-talkies were used by participants in different neighborhoods to communicate their experiences with one another.[28] He saw these attempts as reacting against the fragmentation of the city: "That was the meaning of unitary urbanism: unify what has a certain unity, but a lost unity, a disappearing unity."[29] But this fragmentation was unavoidable, and, according to Lefebvre, unitary urbanism was caught in a longing for the unity of the historical European city—a symptom of which were the map clippings used in the celebrated *Naked City* collage (1957), all chosen from the central districts of Paris. Considering the IS unable to think the simultaneous explosion and implosion of the city, Lefebvre saw its radical contribution not in an alternative project but rather in the critique of postwar urbanism, characterized by Attila Kotányi and Raoul Vaneigem (1961) as a "blackmail of utility" and "the organization of participation in something in which it is impossible to participate."[30] This negative character of unitary urbanism was brought to a logical conclusion by the rejection of urbanism *tout court* by Debord in the course of the 1960s and its replacement by the critique of urbanistic ideologies.

Agreeing with this critique of totalizing instruments of urbanism, its procedures and criteria of judgment, Lefebvre speculated about an architecture that would open the possibility of the production of spaces both interrelated and differentiated: a "unitary architecture"—instead of "unitary urbanism"—developed by a reading of the socialist thinker Charles Fourier (1772–1837). Fourier's project of overcoming separations produced by capitalist modern society through an appeal to the irreducible differentiation of people and their desires offered a common denominator for two seemingly opposed ideas: that of "unitary architecture" and that of differential space.

For Lefebvre, the starting point of Fourier's project was the discovery that each social group has consistency only in its proper space and that to invent a group and a social relation is to invent, or produce, a space.[31] In that sense the concept of the production of space itself suggests the possibility of a society beyond alienation, that is to say, above all, beyond work in the modern sense[32]—all the more so because, as René Schérer stressed in his readings of Fourier, his concept of production is never an economic one but rather concerns the production of desire.[33] This discovery of the social production of space led Fourier, in Lefebvre's view, to envisage the phalanstery—a building for 1,620 inhabitants and a node for the society to come.[34] Although of all architects, Fourier admired most the baroque master Jules Hardouin-Mansart and the palaces designed by him, including the extension of Versailles,[35] Lefebvre stressed Fourier's fascination with the Parisian Palais-Royal: a place of theater, gallery, encounter, commerce, work, leisure, and luxury; a space of bad reputation despised by all moralists, both revolutionary and conservative.[36] Speaking in a 1972 TV interview, itself shot in the Palais-Royal, Lefebvre described it as a space leading the discourse, stimulating pleasures, and relating one pleasure to another so that they reinforce one another: such is the unitary architecture of a phalanstery in which differences come together and separations are overcome.[37]

The phalanstery is read by Lefebvre not as a singular building but as an integral part of the "Fourierist city." This take, developed in a 1972 text, which followed the colloquium "Actualité de Fourier," celebrating the bicentennial of Fourier's birth, allows the gap to be bridged between an architectural reading of the phalanstery, depicted by Fourier's "disciples" (including Victor Considerant) as an autonomous building in a rural landscape or a small industrial settlement,[38] and the contributions to the debates about the redevelopment of Paris in the 1830s and 1840s by architects such as César Daly and the urbanist known as Perreymond, both inspired by Fourier. This question about the relationship between architecture and the city, which underlies much of Lefebvre's architectural references of that time, was inscribed into the 1960s rejection of what was perceived as the submission of architecture to urbanism within the modern movement. In this context the rediscovery of Fourier sounds paradoxical at first glance, because his writings were an essential part of the self-constructed genealogy of the architectural avant-garde: in Tony Garnier's project of the industrial city, which refers to Fourier by mediation of Émile Zola's *Work* (1901); and in Siegfried Giedion's tracing of the ideas of decentralization in modern urbanism to Fourier.[39] This genealogy was developed by historians and theorists of architecture, from Peter Serenyi's linking the phalanstery, the monastery of Ema, and Le Corbusier's *unité d'habitation;* through Roger-Henri Guerrand's view of the phalanstery as a "machine for dwelling" and a predecessor of the social program of modern architecture; to Franziska Bollerey's and Anthony Vidler's persistent uncovering of the

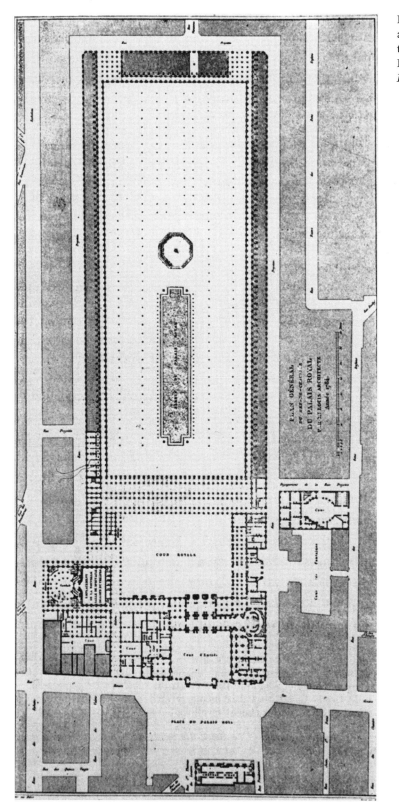

Palais-Royal (Paris) after the modification of 1784. From Fontaine, *Le Palais-Royal*.

multifaceted relationships between Fourier and the architectural avant-garde of the early twentieth century.[40]

This suggests that Lefebvre, at that time developing a critique of the avant-garde and of functionalist urbanism, embarked on a very different reading of Fourier from the one inscribed into the tradition of the architectural modern movement and its association, in the postwar Western European context, with the Keynesian welfare state. In this rereading Lefebvre was inspired by Roland Barthes's 1970 book *Sade, Fourier, Loyola,* which showed all three—the libertine, the socialist, and the founder of the Jesuit order—as logothetes, that is to say, as founders of language. Barthes noticed that what is specific to Fourier's style is that he withholds the decisive utterance of the doctrine, giving only its examples, seductions, "appetizers"; "the message of his book is the announcement of a forthcoming message."[41] Fourier is an author of procrastination; or, in the words of Walter Benjamin, "Fourier loves preambles, cisambles, transambles, postambles, introductions, extroductions, prologues, interludes, postludes, cismediants, mediants, transmediants, intermedes, notes, appendixes."[42]

The same is true of Fourier's architectural work, in which he was never tired of stressing that the described buildings are intermediary stages, which proliferate and multiply: the phalanstery is preceded by a *tourbillon* and a *tribustery* and an experimental, or testing, phalanstery. These buildings are associated with various stages of human development, including the sixth period *(garantisme),* which immediately follows the period contemporary to Fourier *(civilisation)* and which prepares the next periods.[43] Thus, *garantisme* is characterized by a series of institutions that secure solidarity and collaboration among the members of society, and Fourier writes that this period will realize the wishes and dreams of the *civilisation,* but it will not shed the kernel of evil—the unassociated family, which will be resolved only in the seventh period. In that sense, *garantisme* is a reformist period, and architecture belongs to its essential means: "A man of taste, a political architect, could transform *civilisation* by a mere reform of architectural practice."[44]

Fourier's contribution to this reform was the plan of an ideal city conceived in the 1820s and published in 1841 in a section of his *Théorie de l'unité universelle* (Theory of Universal Unity) and in 1849 in the pamphlet *Des modifications à introduire dans l'architecture des villes* (The Modifications to Be Introduced in the Architecture of Cities). The city was designed in four rings: the central part; the suburbs; the rural annexes; and the roads, distinguished by a gradation in ornamentation (which is aimed at collective pleasures) and by a differentiation in density and height: what appears as a mere "luxury or superfluity" is, according to Fourier, a "theory of higher politics that will contribute to the fundamental principle of social happiness: the germ of association."[45] This understanding of luxury for the collective—a "collective luxury," as it were—was essential for the project of the Fourierist city. Every house was required to have free ground around it in order to prevent speculation and secure the circulation of air; the more central the location of the house, the smaller the free area, which, nonetheless, had to be at least as large as the whole surface of the house. In that way, Fourier noted, only the wealthy could afford a small house that would require a big allotment in order to comply with the rules of isolation. For the bourgeoisie one would build large apartment blocks for twenty to thirty families, differing in wealth, which would be furnished with common services and meeting places connected by galleries inspired, according to Walter Benjamin, by the first Parisian arcades.

Many of these ideas were developed by the followers of Fourier: Victor Considerant, Perreymond, and César Daly in their contributions to the journal *Revue générale de l'architecture et des travaux publics,* founded in 1839 and edited by Daly. Like the Saint-Simonians, the Fourierists stressed the importance of the railway system, supported public works as a means of economic and social development, and argued for a foundation of a new type of financial institution necessary to finance urban development, in that sense preparing the ground for Haussmann's development of Paris under Napoleon III.

These ideas were present in Perreymond's project of the development of the center of Paris, published in 1842 and 1843 in Daly's *Revue générale.* The project conceives the city as a biopolitical regulator designed to facilitate the circulation of people, commodities, and capital according to an empirically identified statistical average. This design required such drastic decisions as uniting the Île de Cité and the Île Saint Louis into one administrative and cultural center, to be furnished with a façade to the new square created on the filled southern arm of the Seine; the introduction of six arteries to connect this center with other parts of the city, the national territory, and surrounding countries; and the construction of a new market.[46] One of the essential aims of the project was to tackle unemployment by stimulating economic development—a theme very much in the air in the 1840s Paris, which culminated in the February Revolution of 1848, whose socialist postulates included that of the "right to work." Writing in 1849, Perreymond argued that the first task of society is to organize the system of work and its spatial counterpart, the city: "Work is life, and life can exist only on the condition that it renew itself, that it propagate itself without ceasing, without ever stopping."[47]

This concept of work greatly differed from Fourier's, and it was this difference that determined the "actuality" of Fourier's concept, in Lefebvre's view. Fourier argued that work can be thought of as central for society only if its understanding is radically changed. That is to say, work should be conceived by means of the concept of passion, which is the foundation of Fourier's general theory of association: fascinated with Newton, Fourier saw passion as the force of attraction between subjects, just as gravitation is the force of attraction of material objects.

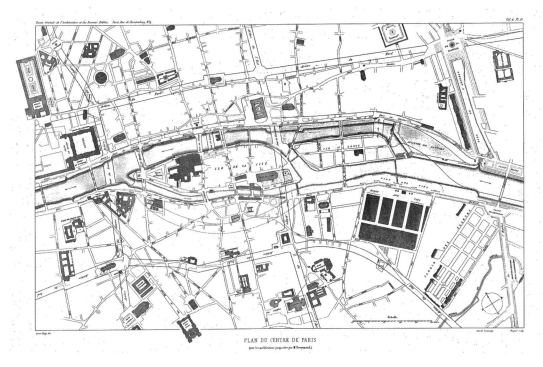

PLAN DU CENTRE DE PARIS
(pour les modifications proposées par M Perreymond.)

Proposal for the development of the center of Paris by the Fourierist urbanist known as Perrey-mond, who suggested filling in the southern arm of the Seine in order to unite Île de Cité and Île Saint Louis into an administrative and cultural center of the French capital. He also introduced six new arteries (only four visible in this drawing) and proposed constructing a new market. Published in *Revue générale de l'architecture et des travaux publics,* 1843. Courtesy of the Trésor, Delft University of Technology.

This concept reinterprets the character of work and bases it on passions and pleasure, thus challenging the difference between work and consumption.

The Saint-Simonians were criticized by Fourier precisely on these grounds: rather than a change in human nature, he argued, the only thing that can make men happy is to found social order on a system of combinations of man's passions and desires. "I am the only reformer who has rallied 'round human nature by accepting it as it is and devising the means of utilizing it with all the defects that are inseparable from man," he wrote to Victor Considerant in 1831. "All the sophists who pretend to change men are working *in denial of man,* and what is more, in denial of God since they want to change or stifle the passions which God has bestowed on us as our fundamental drives."[48] Fourier attacked civilization and capitalism as restraining the fulfillment of the passions of man and thus producing indigence, competition, boredom, deceit, and adultery. Rather, Fourier argued, social reforms must be based on the twelve passions of man, his fundamental instinctive drives: the luxurious passions (desires of the five senses); the four group passions (respect, friendship, love, and parenthood); and the three serial passions—the passion to make arrangements, concordant or compromise; the passion for intrigue; the passion for variety.[49]

The main principle for achieving pleasure was, in Fourier's view, to combine passions, and this conveys the main principle of his architecture: he writes that to isolate passions and operate separately with them will fail in respect to each of them.[50] Fourier argues that architects should not simply take care of the useful, because "one occupied only with the useful does achieve neither the useful nor the pleasant."[51] These statements coincided with Lefebvre's critique of functionalist urbanism: as conceiving the city in terms of the useful, the needed, and the necessary rather than on the basis of the pleasant and passionate, and classifying needs in order to satisfy them one after another rather than focusing on their associations.

Fourier argued that at the core of his "unitary architecture" was the productive relationship of all senses. He wrote, "Senses are thus reliable guides for social progress," and, consequently, one should think of progress as a product of sensual pleasures that are composed, collective, and integral.[52] For example, in describing common dinner rooms, he showed how the sense of taste is composed (combined with the spiritual pleasure of a conversation); collective (developed in the community of the group); and integral (embracing all fields and relationships).[53] The production of pleasure is thus the main aim of architecture, theorized as a technology of the association of senses, forms, bodies, and ideas.

This concept of an architecture of association is the engine of Fourier's vision of the phalanstery, designed on the basis of the 810 fundamental passionate combinations and represented by both sexes, whose combination resulted in 1,620 persons as the appropriate number of inhabitants. The phalanstery was conceived as an assemblage of dissimilar people, types, and ages that allows their novel combinations and thus realizes a multiplicity of relationships of love and labor.[54] Fourier's principle of combination was that of a formal and arbitrary correspondence; thus, an association is not a humanist principle (bringing together everyone with the same mania) but rather a principle of contrast; neither was his vision a liberal one, aimed at "understanding" or "admitting" passions, but it strived at exploiting them for the greatest pleasure of all and without hindrance to anyone.[55]

These comments make clear that, when read in the early 1970s by Barthes and Lefebvre, both authors tracing the emergence of the postwar society of consumption, Fourier's writings gained a new type of actuality exposing the prospective tendencies of social development. This is why Lefebvre's texts about Fourier end in a state of undecidability, hesitating over whether his work is topical as a "utopian" socialist or as a "dystopian" socialist, that is to say, whether he is an author of a project of the architecture of pleasure and spontaneity or rather a prophet of the society of consumption and the socialized worker. While for Benjamin the main metaphor of Fourier's understanding of society was the *machine,* for Barthes and Lefebvre this metaphor in Fourier's texts was, clearly, *information:* not only the paradigm for social development in 1960s Western societies, but also the dominant model for understanding consumption as differentiation within a system of signs. This parallel was confirmed by the fact that the main question of Fourier—and indeed one of the main reasons for his strategy of procrastination—was the problem essential to consumption: how to prevent boredom stemming from an excess of pleasures.

In that sense, Fourier's unitary architecture, which is based on systematic combinations of differences, comes close to the *pavillon* as described in Lefebvre's analysis of the consumption of space, but it also comes close to the research of Henri Raymond on the holiday village of the Club Méditerranée in Palinuro, in southern Italy.[56] Resembling Fourier's paroles, the villages of the Club Méd since its creation in 1950 were advertised as "antidotes to civilization," aimed at producing a rupture with the world of work, its hierarchies and social distinctions. This was achieved by instantiating welcome and farewell rituals, replacing cash with colored beads, and focusing on self-indulgent physical pleasure by the "members" of the club dressed in the Tahitian sarong, suggesting a "liberated" body.[57] Raymond called Palinuro "a concrete utopia"—"imaginary reality and yet lived practically"[58]—that displayed the representations of happiness in the emerging consumer society in France. Associated with "huge meals, idle bronzed bodies, abundance in the midst of underdeveloped countries, and a commitment to narcissistic, apolitical hedonism,"[59] the headquarters of the Club Méd in Paris became one of the targets for the students in May '68.

Beyond the specific case of Club Méd, Lefebvre would argue that to condemn spaces of leisure would be as uncritical as accepting their discourse of the "antidote of civilization." Surely, spaces of leisure epitomize the consumption of space; they are inherent components of the processes of reproduction of social relationships; and they caricature Marx's project of the society of nonwork—as Lefebvre was never tired of reminding his readers.[60] But just as the Atelier de Montrouge, Roland Simounet, Paul Chemetov, Jean Deroche, and many other French architects of the 1950s perceived the holiday villages as fields of experimentation with new combinations of materials and housing typologies for an emerging society of leisure, Lefebvre read spaces of leisure as pointing to a possibility of a different everyday life: the beach, for example, appeared to him as offering to the body moments of integrality beyond the fragmented and homogenized gestures, spaces, and times within the Fordist division of labor. This is why the true revolution of everyday life was for him the introduction of two weeks of paid holidays by the Front populaire in 1936, which allowed the masses to discover nature, the beach, and the sea.[61] In this context, his critique of the postwar processes of urbanization can be read as pointing at the missed dialectics of the social–democratic project

(*top*) Postcard from Club Méditerranée in Palinuro, 1979, described by Henri Raymond as "a concrete utopia" of the French consumer society.

(*bottom*) Picture of the beach from the collection of photographs from Norbert Guterman's visit to Navarrenx. Courtesy of Norbert Guterman Archive, Butler Library, Columbia University, dossier Henri Lefebvre, 1939–49.

of modernization, as conveyed by many among the architectural avant-gardes of the 1920s and 1930s, which required complementing the minimal housing (*Existenzminimum*) by means of social facilities, or "collective luxury," in Fourier's terms. At the same time, if spaces of leisure can be read as prefiguring a differential space, it is because "in and through the space of leisure, a pedagogy of space and time is beginning to take shape."[62] This pedagogy is not an institutionalized disciplinary practice but a formation of senses, like in *Physiologie du Goût* (1825), by Jean-Antheleme Brillat-Savarin, a contemporary of Fourier who postulated a pedagogy of the sense of taste. This sensual experience is not an instance of forgetting but rather a proposal of a different way of life that comes as a hunch in privileged moments at the beach, the park, or the garden of a *pavillon,* however commodified, ridiculous, or negligible they might appear within an orthodox Marxist analytical framework.

Nanterre as Differential Space

Lefebvre's reading of Fourier suggests the need to think of differences not as a system of complementary elements (what Lefebvre called "induced" differences) but rather as related to one another in a dialectics of unity and contradiction, "producing" a rupture of the system.[63] In other words, association and gathering, which Fourier envisaged as specific to "unitary architecture," are not sufficient criteria of the envisaged performance of a differential space, and the complementary processes of exclusion, repulsion, and dispersion must be accounted for. Precisely the simultaneity of these contradictory movements is what Lefebvre aimed at capturing in his concept of dialectical centrality as the universal form of social space, and an examination of specific historical centralities is what can advance his concept of differential space.

Of Lefebvre's historical writings, the book *L'irruption de Nanterre au sommet (The Explosion: Marxism and the French Revolution,* 1968)—a participatory observation of May '68, which he witnessed at the university in Nanterre —lends itself to a reading as an approximation of the performance of differential space, in particular when contextualized with the study *La proclamation de la Commune, 26 mars 1871* (1965), resulting from his archival research in the Feltrinelli Foundation in Milan.[64] For Lefebvre, March 1871 and May 1968 became occasions to examine moments of the production of centralities in a violent reclamation of the urban center by those who were excluded: "People who had come from the outlying areas into which they had been driven and where they had found nothing but a social void assembled and proceeded together toward the reconquest of the urban centers."[65] In both cases, centralities were produced as concatenations of violence and playfulness, celebration and struggle (Lefebvre reproduced in his book the poster of a public concert organized by the Communards): a dialectical relationship between "necessity and chance, determination and contingency, the anticipated and the unpredicted."[66]

The campus in Nanterre was laid out on the allotments previously belonging to the military, located behind the Défense, in the northwestern suburbs of Paris. In the early 1960s it was not accessible by the RER, as it is today, but only by the train from the Gare Saint-Lazare. (Rémi Hess recalled Lefebvre saying in one of his lectures in 1966, "When one commutes from Paris to Nanterre, when one sees what happens, one understands how the city rises, how it is being developed, and one becomes truly a philosopher.")[67] When he arrived on the spot, Lefebvre described it as "misery, shantytowns, excavations for an express subway line, low-income housing projects for workers, industrial enterprises."[68] This was not uncommon for the Parisian agglomeration, where in the mid-1960s one could still find 120 shantytowns with approximately fifty thousand inhabitants.[69] A photo essay by Alain Nogues, published in the fourth issue of the journal *Espaces et sociétés,* has shown the shantytown of Nanterre, and the faculty buildings can be seen in the long take from Godard's *La Chinoise.*[70]

The functionalist master plan by the architectural firm Chauliat was laid out for fifteen thousand students. The plan included the organization of three faculties (humanities, law, and political sciences), dormitories with fourteen hundred rooms, two canteens, and libraries around a "green" center with sport facilities. The flat buildings of the faculties were punctuated by slabs, and the dormitories and the libraries formed groups of freestanding slabs of differing heights. The first buildings were completed in 1964, and the Faculty of Humanities was opened in 1966. According to a presentation in the architectural journal *Techniques et architecture* (1968), the composition of the master plan and the buildings was aimed at ensuring the "rational functioning" of the faculty and the creation of "a harmony of the ensemble in variety sufficient to prevent monotony."[71] This language of functional rationality and abstract aesthetics was challenged by Lefebvre, who considered Nanterre a gathering of the contradictions of the late Gaullist era. In a speech presented during a conference in Strasbourg (1975), he introduced the concept of a "space of catastrophe": "One should always, when studying a space, specify its space of catastrophe, that is to say, the limits where this space explodes."[72] In that sense, Nanterre was the space of catastrophe for the *trente glorieuses.*

This focus on an amassment of contradictions that bring about social change, together with the attempt to develop a concept of distributed causality and a sensitivity to nonsynchronous contradictions, brings Lefebvre's analysis close to the concept of overdetermination addressed by Louis Althusser, and in particular to his assessment of the success of the 1917 revolution in Russia as stemming from the accumulation of historical contradictions specific to feudal, capitalist, imperialist,

Poster of a concert on 6 May 1871, organized during the Paris Commune, Institut Feltrinelli, Milan. Reproduced in Lefebvre, *La proclamation de la Commune.*

Shantytowns in Nanterre. Photograph by Alain Nogues, published in *Espaces et sociétés* 4 (1971). Courtesy of Alain Nogues.

(top) The campus of Nanterre shortly after its construction. From *La Chinoise,* directed by Jean-Luc Godard, 1967.

(bottom) View from a student room in Nanterre of the shantytown and former military area. Published in Duteuil, *Nanterre 1965–66–67–68,* 89. Courtesy of Jean-Pierre Duteuil.

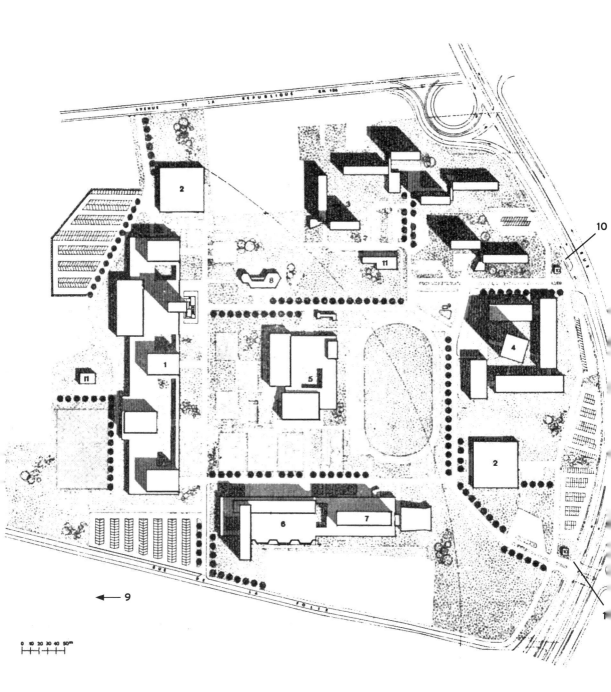

Master plan of Nanterre university. The campus consisted of the Faculty of Humanities (1), canteens (2), students' dorms (3), libraries (4), sport facilities (5), the Faculty of Law (6), the Institute
of Political Studies (7), a cultural center (8), a railway station (9), security posts (10), and boiler
rooms (11). Published in *Techniques et architecture* 1 (1968): 130.

Aerial view of Nanterre campus and the railway line to Paris. Published in *Techniques et architecture* 1 (1968): 131.

and colonial exploitation.[73] For Lefebvre, these processes can be accounted for only when space is introduced into the analysis: contradictions of society emerge *in space* and engender contradictions *of space*.[74] He writes, "The contradictions of space thus make the contradictions of social relations operative," and spatial contradictions "'express' conflicts between socio-political interest and forces; it is only *in* space that such conflicts come effectively into play, and in so doing they become contradictions *of* space."[75] Contradictions of space envelop, presuppose, and amplify historical contradictions and superimpose themselves upon those contradictions, and, by this, they produce a contradictory whole that "takes on a new meaning and comes to designate 'something else'—another mode of production."[76] This is the aim of Lefebvre's research on Nanterre: to account for a process in the course of which differential space becomes manifested from within the contradictions of abstract space.

Already the positioning of the campus, in relation to both the neighboring shan-tytowns and the center of Paris, pointed at a spatial and social conflict: "Functionalized by initial design, culture was transported to a ghetto of students and teachers situated in the midst of other ghettos filled with the 'abandoned,' subject to the compulsions of production, and driven into an extra-urban existence."[77] Lefebvre writes that Nanterre became a *heterotopia*—"the other place," "the place of the other, simultaneously excluded and interwoven," a place defined by differences.[78] Similarly to the Haussmannian reorganization of Paris, he considered Nanterre to be an expression and tool of the dominant social order. Like the new town of Mourenx, he saw the campus as a projection into space of an industrial rationality producing "mediocre intellectuals" and "junior executives."[79] According to Lefebvre, the late modernist architecture of the campus reflects the intended project: the attempt to reproduce the social relations of production.[80] In a TV interview, commenting on the students' protests from his office in Nanterre, he said, "In order to answer the question why it started here, one should look outside the window."[81] This was developed in *The Explosion:*

> The Faculty buildings were designed for the functions of education: vast amphitheaters, small "functional" rooms, drab halls, an administrative wing—the meaning of this morphology will soon become apparent. All this becomes the focus of political rebellion.[82]

Following the functionalist logics, the plan of the campus separated and antagonized differences among work, housing, and leisure, between private and public spheres, between male and female students, thus transforming them into lived contradictions. Lefebvre considered the twofold segregation in Nanterre—functional and social, industrial and urban—"an experience as well as a

Lefebvre interviewed on *Enquêtes sur les causes des manifestations:* "In order to answer the question why it [May '68] started here, one should look outside the window." 11 May 1968. Institut national de l'audiovisuel, Paris.

Henri Lefebvre among students in Nanterre. Published in Duteuil, *Nanterre 1965–66–67–68,* 92. Courtesy of Jean-Pierre Duteuil.

physical environment."[83] He noticed that this segregation brought about para-doxical effects: "The university community in which the 'function of living' becomes specialized and reduced to a bare minimum (the habitat)—while tra-ditional separations between boys and girls, and between work and leisure and privacy, are maintained—this community becomes the focus of sexual aspirations and rebellions."[84] These words refer to the "right to sexuality," demanded by the leaflets distributed by the anarchists in Nanterre, who organized several debates about this issue.[85] Thus, it is not by chance that in October 1968, shortly after the students' revolt, Lefebvre gave a speech on sexuality in which he sketched a spatial "semantics of desire" and called for urban spaces that would allow its "symbolic and practical" realization.[86]

These claims faithfully depict the mood in Nanterre, as a leaflet of one of the radical Left groups shows, sarcastically appreciating the "functional" campus, which is "better than Sarcelles" because everything is on one spot: the dorms are just three minutes from the faculty. Thus, as the leaflet goes, the campus introduces an "economy of pace, activity, and relations": discipline, morality, hygienic love, and a level of concentration on work that is impossible in the politicized and distracted chatter of the Latin Quarter; consequently, instead of "leftist intellectuals," Nanterre produces "apolitical intellectuals" in the service of the state: "In the end, our state has understood that the youth have a need: that of work, and, in order to work well, of a total rest: the political, cultural, and sexual preoccupations decrease our productivity."[87]

Yet according to Lefebvre, the social effects produced in this space were very different from the ones intended. The concentration of the perceived, conceived, and lived contradictions of space makes the campus a *social condenser,* that is to say, an architecture "which leads to crystallization, precipitation so to say, of social relations in a given society."[88] Coined by the Soviet architect Moisei Ginzburg, the concept of a social condenser was popularized among the French architects and planners in the 1960s by the eye-opening book *Town and Revolution* (1967), by Anatole Kopp, who explained it as an architecture designed to become a "mold" in which socialist society "was to be cast."[89] In the Soviet architecture of the late 1920s and early 1930s, social condensers were aimed at turning "the self-centered individual of capitalist society into a whole man, the informed militant of socialist society in which the interests of each merged with the interests of all."[90] This was the aim of workers' clubs, designed, among others, by Konstantin Melnikov and Ilja Golosov; the collective housing facilities, of which the Narkomfin in Moscow, designed by Ginzburg and Ignati Milinis, was the most famous; as well as industrial centers. During the CRAUC seminar, Kopp defined a social condenser as a building "voluntarily unadapted to the period in which it was constructed in view of a more remote period,"[91] and in Lefebvre's use of this concept, Kopp's definition takes a double meaning: on the one hand, the Fordist logics expressed in Nanterre was anachronistic in the face of the emerging processes of the deindustrialization of Paris; on the other hand, the social space of the campus conveyed a hunch of a different society.

However, the concept of a social condenser, with its suggestion of spatial determinism, might be misleading, and it is at odds with Lefebvre's emphasis on the lived experience of Nanterre, which was not predefined by the material layout of

L'ÉTUDIANT EN FRANCE EST APRÈS LE POLICIER ET LE PRÊTRE
L'ÊTRE LE PLUS UNIVERSELLEMENT MÉPRISÉ
QUAND ON NE LUI CHIE PAS DANS LA GUEULE ON LUI PISSE AU CUL

Nous ne remercierons jamais assez l'État de nous avoir offert une cité et une université si fonctionnelles...

Habiter à trois minutes de la faculté... pouvoir travailler sur place... c'est mieux qu'à Sarcelles...

Les étudiants sont enfin entre eux, et peuvent se préparer, dans le calme, l'ordre, à leur vie adulte, pour servir la France et la faire toujours progresser, par leur capital intellectuel, vers LA PAIX DANS LA PROSPÉRITÉ...

Économie de pas... Économie de relations... : au Quartier latin, on perdait son temps à draguer ou à discuter ; on était des «intellectuels de gauche». Economie d'activité : à Nanterre, on travaille, on ne se disperse pas dans la politique, on est bien au chaud, tout seuls, on est des «intellectuels apolitiques»...

A la cité, personne «n'embête» personne. Ceux qui n'en peuvent plus font l'amour de temps en temps, pour l'hygiène. Heureusement, le bâtiment des filles est interdit aux garçons, empêchant la cité de devenir un lieu de perdition...

Même quand quelqu'un a envie de se suicider, personne ne l'arrête. On est très calme. On travaille et on dort...

Enfin, NOTRE ÉTAT a compris de quoi la jeunesse avait besoin : du travail, et, pour bien travailler, du repos total : les préoccupations politiques, culturelles, sexuelles diminuent notre productivité... Il faut restreindre au minimum le besoin instinctif et destructeur des individus pour faire de la FRANCE UN PAYS SAIN ET VIGOUREUX...

Ceci est un hommage à la politique de NOTRE PAYS, et d'autres aussi heureusement.

Alors, en attendant les élections qui nous permettront d'exprimer notre plus belle confiance et notre plus belle abnégation envers l'Etat, MONTRONS-NOUS, DÈS AUJOURD'HUI, RECONNAISSANTS ENVERS TOUT CE QUE NOS DIRIGEANTS FONT POUR NOUS...

Sachant combien Missoffe cherche à établir un dialogue avec la jeunesse (cf. livre blanc), il nous semble fécond de renforcer cette collaboration en suggérant quelques-unes de nos idées. Elles visent à préparer les jeunes d'une façon concrète à leur future vie d'adulte...

1) LE PORT DE L'UNIFORME POUR TOUS LES JEUNES.
2) INTRODUCTION DE GRADES AUX PLUS MÉRITANTS ET DE BONNETS D'ANES A CEUX QUI PERSÉVÈRENT DANS LEUR ATTITUDE NÉGATIVE.
3) SANCTION CORPORELLE POUR TOUS CEUX QUI CONTINUENT A PROFANER L'AMOUR ET DONNENT LE SPECTACLE LE PLUS RÉPUGNANT A L'INTÉRIEUR MÊME DES LIEUX DE TRAVAIL...

Student leaflet in Nanterre, 1968: "The student is in France the most generally despised being, after the policeman and the priest." Published in Duteuil, *Nanterre 1965–66–67–68,* 73. Courtesy of Jean-Pierre Duteuil.

space. For Lefebvre, what happened on the campus was an experience of all the contradictions of 1960s French society: between the authorities and "the youth" (a new sociological category coined in the 1960s); between those privileged living in the city center and those deprived of the "right to the city"; between the state and its citizens; between the older and the younger generations; between institutions set up to steer the modernization of postwar society and those originating in past modes of production.[92] In this context, the very architectural plan that transforms differences into lived contradictions allows for new processes of differentiation: in Nanterre, those relegated to the periphery recognized themselves as constituting a new centrality that raised the claim to universality as a prefiguration of a society to come:

> This fragment of a broken, rejected, and marginal university regains a kind of universality. Among the students *all* tendencies manifest themselves, especially *all* those which oppose the established society.[93]

In Nanterre, "an original dialectic movement" began to emerge: "social marginality against centralization, *anomie* against norms, contestation against decisions."[94] For Lefebvre, the periphery and the center become inextricably linked: it was Nanterre's peripheral relation to Paris that made it the center of the outburst.[95] This dialectics of centrality manifested in the shifts of the movement from the suburbs to the Latin Quarter and the Sorbonne, which became a *utopian* place, transcending the "segregations and multiple dissociations which had been projected onto the terrain in the explosion of the city,"[96] a central and relevant place due to its sudden openness and inclusion of all social classes and unfettered speech, which started with the discussions at the Faculty of Sociology in Nanterre.[97] In this movement, the possibility of an alternative space as a horizon for social development was manifested:

> The interaction of center and periphery revealed the importance of a new social, political, and cultural sphere—*urban society* which brings with it a new set of problems. The centrality achieved and maintained by the movement sent this movement back to the margins of urban reality—to the suburbs, outlying areas, production and housing centers. The movement reverberated from these margins back toward the centers of decision-making.[98]

The centrality in Nanterre is thus conditioned by a reference to an absent "other" reality: the center is always a center of a utopia; it represents "what does not have a place, what is elsewhere, the nonplace."[99] In Nanterre this utopia was that of the city as the place where differences meet and acknowledge one another.

"The City—past, absent, future—assumes a *utopian* value for the boys and girls caught in a *heterotopia* which generates tensions and obsessive fantasies."[100] For the students—most of whom came from the wealthy western parts of Paris—"the absence of civilization is transformed into obsession."[101]

It was Lefebvre's research on the Commune that suggested to him the revolutionary potential of the image and imagination of the city. After having analyzed documents, proclamations, and leaflets from the period, he argued, "The Parisian insurrection of 1871 was a great attempt of the city to establish itself as a measurement and a norm of human reality."[102] Referring to statistics, sociological research, and novels, Lefebvre discusses the emergence of the image of the city as an ideology, utopia, and myth in the conditions of the Haussmannian cleansing of the lower classes from the center of Paris and their allocation in the peripheral quarters. Lefebvre quotes, for one, the exclamation of Jules Vallès from *Le cri du peuple,* one of the most successful journals of the Commune: "We are marching under the same flag: the steeple of Paris."[103] It is this image, and the medieval word *commune,* according to Lefebvre, that allowed the unification of a variety of social forces otherwise related neither by a political program nor by a social class.[104] This is why in his eyes "the Commune was, until now, the only attempt at a revolutionary urbanism": attacking the symbols of the ancien régime; recognizing the neighborhood as the site of socialization; defining social space in political terms; and challenging the belief in the innocence of monuments, with the demolition of the Vendôme column and the transformation of churches into clubs.[105] Thus, when Lefebvre writes that the image of the city was the trigger of May '68, he also means material images, perhaps photographs, perhaps even photographs of the Commune, which he reproduced in his book as testimonies of the first major political events fixed on light-sensitive film and a direct reference of the students.[106]

Multitemporal Centralities: Monuments for the Urban Society

Lefebvre's study of Nanterre defined differential space by its specific performance: that of gathering and dispersing differences within an urban whole. This dynamic was described by means of the concept of dialectics of centrality and employed in order to understand a specific historical conjuncture—an attempt that cannot be read without a sense of disappointment, since in *The Explosion* the social agency characterized by this dialectics was but hinted at by Lefebvre.[107] And yet the account of the shifting centralities of May '68 as a dynamic process linking the campus to the Latin Quarter, the suburbs of Paris, and its center opened up two paths for Lefebvre's research on centralities as differentiated by times on the one hand and by scales on the other. This research program was spelled out in *The*

Production of Space, which investigates centralities as historical, differing from the ancient city to the postwar urbanization and linking historical times together, and as established at various scales and mediating among them, from the scale of a single room to that of the planet. This research was contextualized in Lefebvre's contributions to discussions in the architectural culture of the late 1960s and early 1970s, including the rediscovery of the historical European city and its monuments (condensations of nonsynchronous times) and the debates about megastructures as mediators among a variety of scales within a metropolitan territory.

Architectonics of Space

The Nanterre study discusses the campus as an amassment of specific contradictions of postwar French society, a statement that is generalized in *The Production of Space,* in which Lefebvre argues, "Each period, each mode of production, each particular society has engendered (produced) its own centrality: religious, political, commercial, cultural, industrial, and so on."[108] This history of space does not simply reflect the sequence of modes of production but rather accounts for their contradictions, their nonsynchronicities, and the possibilities that emerge from the given situation—much in the vein of Lefebvre's analyses of the "sociological fossils" in the Pyrenees and Tuscany.[109]

The historical character of space contrasts with the production of space by a living body. Referring to research on forms produced by animals,[110] Lefebvre gives the example of a shell whose geometry "corresponds merely to the way in which energy, under specific conditions (on a specific scale, in a specific material environment, etc.), is deployed; the relationship between nature and space is *immediate* in the sense that it does not depend on the mediation of an external force, whether natural or divine."[111] This is the level on which basic geometric "laws of space"—symmetries, axes, planes, centers, and peripheries—are established.[112] They govern the deployment of energies of the living body, which, at the same time, creates its own space from within its internal rhythms—a hypothesis that opens up a possibility of a "rhythm analysis" focused on the "concrete reality of rhythms," their use, and appropriation.[113]

This analysis can be related to the human body only when any particular historical period is bracketed off. Since the production of space has been meaningful at every stage of human history and never purely practical or geometric, such an "anthropological" stage is ahistorical in the sense that it does not belong to a sequence of dated events.[114] Like language for Jacques Derrida, social space has no beginning: it has been always already produced, and thus a research perspective that would think of space as an empty stage on which the human agent arrives in order to socialize it is necessarily futile.[115] Thus, when Lefebvre writes, "The body serves both as point of departure and as destination," the implied itinerary is not that between the beginning and the end of history but rather that of the unfolding concrete universal, developing from the singular through the general to the particular.[116]

In *The Production of Space*, Lefebvre asks whether this hypothesis—that a living body produces space by deploying its energies—can be extended to social space. In other words, can the historical processes of the social production of space be understood as deployments of productive forces of the society in question? Yet while human societies cannot be conceived independently of the universe of nature, "there is no reason to assume an isomorphism between social energies and physical energies."[117] Accordingly, the history of space can be conceived neither as a "causal chain of 'historical' (i.e. dated) events" nor as a sequence, "whether teleological or not, of customs and laws, ideals and ideology, and socio-economic structures or institutions (superstructures)."[118]

This suggests that *The Production of Space* does not have to be read as an attempt to crack open the logics of historical development—a historicist narrative of which Lefebvre was often accused.[119] Rather, it can be understood as a problematization of the *immediate* relationship between society and the spaces it produces. Not unlike Lefebvre's procedure in the Pyrenees study, the book focuses on specific relationships among spatial practices, representations of space, and spaces of representation in determined historical conjunctures.[120] The history of space becomes a history of centralities—a history of socially produced relationships among the three moments of space, "their interconnections, distortions, displacements, mutual interactions, and their links with the spatial practice of the particular society or mode of production under consideration."[121]

Since centralities are historical in the sense that they are not only historically specific but also often gather what was produced in remote periods, such a program involves research on the nonsynchronicities of the moments of space. These nonsynchronicities were already addressed by Lefebvre in the differentiated temporalization of the moments of space: the dependence of the spatial practices on the economic and political structures; the tuning of representations of space according to the pace of the scientific discourses and techniques; and the negotiation among personal, collective, and imaginary temporalities in the spaces of representation. "Nothing disappears completely," claims Lefebvre, and he discusses the persistence of natural and historical residua, "stratification and interpenetration of social spaces," and accumulations and sedimentations of relicts, traces, and survivals of past spaces, described with metaphors borrowed from geometry, topology, physics, hydrodynamics, and embryology.[122]

The concept of centralities as both synchronous gatherings of moments of space and as diachronic nodes of temporalities refers to Ernst Bloch's theorizing of modernity as the "synchronicity of the nonsynchronous" in his book *Heritage of Our Times* (1935) and in particular in the essay "Non-Synchronism and the Obligation to Its Dialectics." It also reflects the concept of the multiplicity of social time, developed by Georges Gurvitch, the supervisor of Lefebvre's dissertation at the Sorbonne. In *La multiplicité de temps sociaux* (The Multiplicity of Social Times, 1958), Gurvitch claimed that every social class, group, and profession is characterized by its specific time, and thus society consists of a variety of often conflicting and colliding times, which can be unified and related only in social practice.[123]

Since "each new addition inherits and reorganizes what has gone before,"[124] each multitemporal centrality is in constant development:

> The process of condensation and the centralizing tendency may therefore be said also to affect pre-existing contradictions, which they duly concentrate, aggravating and modifying them in the process.[125]

In order to discern the rules that govern this dynamics, Lefebvre launches the project of spatial architectonics with this goal: "to describe, analyze and explain this persistence, which is often evoked in the metaphorical shorthand of strata, periods, sedimentary layers, and so on."[126] Since the aim of the architectonics of space is to reassemble and relate the discoveries of various disciplines (ethnology, human geography, anthropology, prehistory and history, sociology),[127] it can be seen as a part of his unitary theory of space.

The term *spatial architectonics* reveals architecture as the inspiration and model for the concept of centrality: understanding this term according to the philosophical tradition (Kant defined "architectonics" as the "art of constructing systems") would ignore Lefebvre's hostility to system building, and *The Production of Space* specifically ends with this reminder: "We are concerned with nothing that even remotely resembles a system."[128] It is architecture—or, more precisely, a monument—that lends itself as the privileged object to Lefebvre's research on synchronous and diachronic centralities:

> For millennia, *monumentality* took in all the aspects of *spatiality* that we have identified above: the perceived, the conceived, and the lived; representations of space and spaces of representation; the spaces proper to each faculty, from the sense of smell to speech; the gestural, and the symbolic.[129]

Consequently, *The Production of Space* discusses Greek temples, Roman public architecture, medieval cathedrals and monasteries, and public spaces of the Renaissance city.[130] These discussions are sketchy, and their historical accuracy is not rarely questionable,[131] and thus their relevance is, first at all, theoretical: Lefebvre considered the monuments as paradigmatic objects for the architectonics of space because of their archaeological structure; monuments "involve levels, layers and sedimentations of perception, representation, and spatial practice which presuppose one another, which proffer themselves to one another, and which are superimposed upon one another."[132]

Ambiguity of Monuments

Lefebvre's thinking about the monuments seems to have been impacted by the spatial redevelopments of Paris: the large-scale interventions of the 1960s (Maine Montparnasse, La Défense, Boulevard périphérique) followed by urban renewals (Les Halles, Marais, Place d'Italie). His interest in Parisian monuments was stressed by his friends: Maïté Clavel recalls many strolls with Lefebvre and Nicole Beaurain, his companion at that time: "Il était un marcher dans la ville," said Clavel.[133] These fascinations were shared with the situationists, reflected in their choice for the places of the *dérive:* the Place de Stalingrad with the Ledoux rotunda, Balthard's Halles, Square des Missions Étrangères, and the Gare Saint-Lazare. But this rediscovery of monuments also took place in the discourse of architecture and urbanism in late-1960s and early-1970s France, influenced by Italian architectural theory; the redefinition of the legal category of the monument; the rediscovery of Haussmannian Paris; and the first successes of Bofill's large-scale architecture.[134] Beyond the French context, this discussion was inscribed into a more general interest in monuments as gathering meaning, memory, and history, marked by *Architecture of the City,* by Aldo Rossi (1966); *Complexity and Contradiction in Architecture,* by Robert Venturi (1966); *Meaning in Architecture* (1969), edited by George Baird and Charles Jencks; *Existence, Space and Architecture,* by Christian Norberg-Schulz (1971); and *Architecture 2000,* by Jencks (1971)—to mention just the books commented on by Lefebvre.

For Lefebvre, monuments are essentially ambiguous. He sees a monument as "repressive": a seat of an institution, it organizes a "colonized" and "oppressive" space, and it mobilizes symbols for passive contemplation at a time when they have already lost their intimate meaning.[135] But, simultaneously, it is a place of collective social life. A monument can be confined neither to a functional description (it is transfunctional) nor to a specific culture (it is transcultural). This is why monuments have the capacity to inscribe an "elsewhere" into the space of the everyday: they not only refer to multiple historical times but also point beyond history. Relating to the mythical beginnings and to a utopian future, monuments "render present the past and the future": they are multitemporal centralities that exert control and yet inspire collective actions; they condense urban promises, potentials, and dangers; they proclaim "duty, power, knowledge, joy, hope."[136]

For Lefebvre, the source of this ambiguity is the dialectics of centrality: the capacity to attract, gather, and assemble is countered by the power to repel, exclude, and disperse: "A monument exercises an attraction only to the degree that it creates distance."[137] This dialectics is performed under the conditions of the current regime of knowledge and power, and yet the multitemporal character of monuments allows their given political and economic conditions to be historicized and thus relativizes them. In other words, monuments are untimely and irreconcilable with the postwar production of space. Associated with precapitalist social formations, they are, at the same time, paradigmatic examples of the dialectics of centrality that manifested in Nanterre in the possibility of a future urban society. Thus, the sense of loss of historical monuments expressed by Lefebvre is not a nostalgic gesture ("I do not wish a return of history")[138] but a desire for a different space.

Lefebvre's accounts of monuments for a future society are kept very general and are fundamentally negative: the monuments reveal breaking points of abstract space—everyday life, the urban sphere, the body—and they are defined as surpassing the contradictions that make them impossible in abstract space.[139] This is why, in Lefebvre's work, the monument, rather than a prospective vision, becomes an epistemic tool: a litmus test for postwar abstract space.

This analysis begins with his narration about the "victory" of the building over the monument—what could be called the bourgeois revolution in architecture—leading to a replacement of preindustrial oeuvres by products of capitalism. This replacement stands for the dominance of the repetitive, the standardized, and the generic over the singular, the unique, and the specific. Its symptom, which gained particular interest in France in the course of the 1960s, was architectures produced by nonarchitects, or what Jean-Charles Depaule called "private monuments," such as the house of Raymond Isidore in Chartres; the Palais idéal, by Facteur Cheval, in Hauterives; and the Watts Towers in Los Angeles, by Simon Rodilla. In a dissertation supervised by Lefebvre, Depaule analyzed this "wild," "primitive," or "fierce" architecture (*architecture sauvage*) as external neither to the modern division of labor, which it opposes, nor to the contemporary cultural models, which it appropriates.[140] These "palaces of dreams"[141] were read by Lefebvre as a protest against the sway of everydayness, which makes impossible what, ultimately, was at stake in the monuments: the experience of joy and death. In the period that disposed of both the seriousness and the serenity of the monastery or the cathedral, the longing for them comes back in the privatized, grotesque form of the *pavillon:* a parody of an aristocratic palace.[142]

The untimeliness of the monuments makes them inconceivable within the representations of abstract space expressed, in Lefebvre's view, by the structuralist interpretations of the city. Taking issue with Françoise Choay, Umberto Eco, and Roland Barthes, the last of whom argued, "The city is a discourse, and this discourse is actually a language," Lefebvre stressed that monuments do not have a "signified" meaning but rather a multiplicity of meanings that refer to the body and to power—references that semiology cannot grasp.[143] Monuments are not created for a "reader": visitors to the cathedral discovered its space by becoming aware of their footsteps, listening to the singing, and breathing the incense-laden air: "They will thus, on the basis of their own bodies, experience a total being in a total space."[144] The disenchantment of modern societies brought about not only a liberation from this world of "sin and redemption" but also an increasing impossibility for fragmented bodies to experience such "total being in a total space."[145] At the same time, this liberation allows a rethinking of the relationship between power and monuments, revealing that this relationship cannot be understood as a coded link between a signified and a signifier: power has no code, because power includes control of all codes.[146]

This is why the monument is, for Lefebvre, a counterexample of structuralist readings of architecture: rather than carriers of signs, monuments must be understood as vessels of symbols, alluding to nature, the body, and childhood, expressing a longing for an immediate and direct relationship between people and nature.[147] Theorizing monuments by means of structuralist models of language—which, for Lefebvre, were symptoms of the capitalist form of exchange—reduces the temporalities of monuments to an instant differentiation within a system of signs. By evading "history and practice," this theorizing manifests the ultimate victory of exchange value over use value, and it opens the way to the tourist consumption of historical urban spaces. Lefebvre added, "He who conceives the city and urban reality as a system of signs implicitly hands them over to consumption as integrally consumable: as exchange value in its pure state."[148] The path toward the postmodern city was open.

Scaling Centrality

The multitemporal dialectics of centrality in the Nanterre study pertained to a sequence of scales: from the building of the Sorbonne, through the campus on the outskirts of the city, to the whole metropolitan territory. This multiscalar character of centralities was stressed in *The Production of Space*:

> There is no "reality" without a concentration of energy, without a focus or core—nor, therefore, without the dialectic: centre–periphery, accretion–dissipation, condensation–radiation, glomeration–saturation, concentration–eruption, implosion–explosion. What is the "subject"? A momentary centre. The "object"? Likewise. The body? A focusing of active (productive) energies. The city? The urban sphere? Ditto.[149]

Centralities produced on various scales were called by Lefebvre "levels of social practice,"[150] and he wrote that human beings are "situated in a series of enveloping levels each of which implies the others, and the sequence of which accounts for social practice."[151] Thus, levels are not autonomous wholes; they cannot be completely disassociated from one another: "Wherever there is a level there are several levels, and consequently gaps, (relatively) sudden transitions, and imbalances or potential imbalances between those levels."[152]

The most general distinction Lefebvre introduces is that between micro and macro: two equally complex levels, mutually irreducible and interrelated in multiple ways.[153] When it comes specifically to social space, three levels can be distinguished: the global level; the mixed, mediating, intermediary level; and the level of dwelling that Lefebvre calls "private" in spite of his previous reservations about this term ("private life remains privation").[154] The global level is captured by the concept of concrete abstraction and its focus on the interdependencies among space, the global market, and the modern state, with its managerial strategies, distributive operations, and its overarching representation of space.[155] The production of space on this level can be investigated by examining roads, highways, and other traffic infrastructures, natural parks, new towns, and master plans but also large-scale projects and monuments (ministries, prefectures, cathedrals).[156] The intermediary level is "specifically urban," representing "the characteristic unity of the social 'real,' or group."[157] It is the level on which space is produced in the course of cooperation and competition among social groups. Relating the site and the immediate surroundings with the global condition, this level is described by Lefebvre as that of streets, squares, avenues, and public buildings such as city halls, parish churches, and schools. Finally, the level of dwelling refers to housing of all sorts, from large apartment buildings to shantytowns. It refers to a diversity of heterogeneous ways of living, urban types, patterns, cultural models, and values associated with modalities and modulations of everyday life.[158] In *The Production of Space* these three levels are linked to spatial planning, urbanism, and architecture, and thus the postulate of the unity and differentiation among levels of space is translated into the postulate of collaboration and distinction among these disciplines.[159]

This general scheme opened up two questions for Lefebvre's project of differential space. First, the dependence between the urban level and its specific social practices elicited the question of an appropriate urban scale that could provide material frameworks for those practices, accommodate them, or even facilitate them. Second, the vision of the processes of urbanization as produced at various levels of social practice provoked the question of the bond among those levels. Both controversies pointed at the intermediary level as the specific level on which the project of differential space is to be conceived: either as a centrality that corresponds to specific collective practices, or as a mediator among individuals, social groups, and society as a whole. These two perspectives coincided with two projects to which Lefebvre kept returning in his writings: the City in Space, by Ricardo Bofill, and Taller de Arquitectura, and New Babylon, by Constant Nieuwenhuys.

This discussion was inscribed into a longer debate in French architecture, urbanism, sociology, and geography about the possibility of a correspondence between urban morphologies and social morphologies.[160] Inspired by Fourier's idea of a social unity that would replace isolation and antagonism by solidarity and association, this discussion, since the late nineteenth century, moved from a focus on the communal spaces of buildings toward a focus on larger urban territories. This coincided both with the widening of the scale of design, management, perception, and experience of the metropolis, such as Paris, and with discussions in French sociology and geography about the community defined in opposition to the modern society, as addressed by Pierre Guillaume Frédéric Le Play, Paul Vidal de la Blache, Gustave Le Bon, and Émile Durkheim. Yet in the first decades of the twentieth century, the urbanists were who pushed forward the French discussions about urban communal morphologies, inspired by the English typology of a garden city and by the research on the neighborhood unit in the United States, both developed in the 1940s by Gaston Bardet in his nested hierarchy of "community levels."[161] After the Second World War, this typological research advanced with such concepts as that of the *îlot ouvert,* suggested by Robert Auzelle, who aimed at combining modern planning techniques with historical, sociological, and geographical insights inspired by Chombart, with whom Auzelle shared his progressive Catholicism.[162]

When in the early 1960s Lefebvre began theorizing the levels of social practice, similar themes were discussed internationally among architects, with Team 10 investigating the "hierarchy of human associations" and, at the end of the decade, with a worldwide interest in investigating megastructures as an attempt at a specific scale adequate to the sprawling metropolis. Both positions reveal a new tendency in the way scales were conceptualized, shifting from the effort to delineate a hierarchy of bounded spaces—with which Lefebvre took issue in his review of the Furttal project—to an interest in the realm of the in-between. This was researched by Aldo van Eyck, theorizing the doorstep during the Team 10 meetings, and also in the envisaged performance of megastructures mediating between the human scale and the scale of the city.[163] In the debates among French architects, urbanists, and sociologists, the rising awareness of the disappearance of the in-between realms in cities contributed to the increasing importance of the concept of space in the course of the 1960s, a concept considered able to capture these ambiguous realms, and to a proliferation of debates about "intermediary spaces," "spaces of transition," and "semipublic" and "semiprivate" spaces, complemented by the discourse about the "surroundings," the "extension of housing," "thresholds," and "passages."[164]

The Production of Centralities—from the Building to the District

The ISU studies on housing, with their attention to spaces of transition, such as entrance halls, windows, loggias, balconies, and terraces,[165] were among the main sources of these debates in the 1960s. The intentions of the researchers notwithstanding, their studies contributed to the tendency of the domestic interior to become a model for urban space in France beginning in the early 1970s, with the themes of individualization, privatization, complexity, diversity, and security. This theorizing of the realm of the in-between went hand in hand with the engagement of the ISU in debates about the relationship between social and spatial morphologies, discussions not always easily distinguishable from each other.[166] In the work of the ISU, the debate about the relationship between the two morphologies was translated into the question about the possibility of a collective appropriation of space at various scales: from a room and a building, through their ensemble, to a district within the Parisian agglomeration. In accordance with the study of the *pavillon,* to appropriate space meant to inhabit it, that is to say, to gather moments of space in the lived experience of individuals or social groups—in other words, to produce centralities.

In *The Production of Space,* Lefebvre wrote, "The lived, conceived and perceived realms should be interconnected, so that the 'subject,' the individual member of a given social group, may move from one to another without confusion—so much is a logical necessity." However, he added, "Whether they constitute a coherent whole is another matter. They probably do so only in favorable circumstances, when a common language, a consensus and a code can be established."[167]

The ISU study *La copropriété* (The Co-Ownership, 1971) can be read precisely as an analysis of the conditions "unfavorable" for a collective appropriation of space. This book, resulting from an investigation of co-owned housing estates in late 1960s France, was authored by Nicole Haumont, Henri Raymond, and Antoine Haumont and was prefaced by Lefebvre. Based on interviews carried out in several French cities and statistical analysis,[168] the study stressed the hiatus between the successful individual appropriation of private apartments and the lack of collective appropriation of shared spaces. While individual appropriation through "operations" of fitting out, do-it-yourself activities, or caretaking allows a division and marking of space according to cultural models, the collective spaces remain unappropriated, in spite of the mass-media publicity of co-ownership as a "community" that shares the same "way of life."[169] Accordingly, the study concludes, "The French inhabitant, who perfectly knows how to master a certain type of space, has not found the social means to master a collective space; neither did he find collective spaces that are capable of expressing his individuality."[170]

This impossibility of producing centralities by gathering the moments of space into stable wholes, not only on an individual level, but also on a collective one, was, according to the study, the result of the domination of national financial policies and developers' investment strategies in the processes of the production of space.[171] This discovery adds to Lefebvre's analysis of abstract space: the dominance of the exchange value of space results not only in its fragmentation into allotments but also in its pulverization into a myriad of aspects that cannot be related by the everyday practices of the community of inhabitants who are supposed to pick up the pieces.

The authors of *La copropriété* conclude that co-ownership, as a node of capital flows, refers to "juridical, economic, psychological, and social realities that are not necessarily coherent" and that do not constitute a level of social practice.[172] This failure of the collective appropriation of space is interrelated, according to the study, with the inability of architecture to express the community and, as a consequence, the impossibility of imagining the community by means of architectural scales such as the apartment house, the block, and the neighborhood. Rather than being an expression of a specific, differentiated community, the co-owned buildings impose on their inhabitants generic signs of social distinctions.[173] For Lefebvre, this leads to a "space that *classifies* in the service of a class": a strategy that distributes social strata and classes across the territory, "keeping them separate and prohibiting all contacts—these being replaced by the *signs* (or images) of contact."[174]

If the co-owned building failed to become a level of social practice, can such a level be found in the district, the traditional scale of socialization in the city? This was the question posed by the ISU study that resulted in the publication *Le quartier et la ville* (The District and the City, 1967), which interrogated the distribution of activities, facilities, and social groups in the district.[175] The authors asked whether a district is a relevant scale for contemporary social practices (an "embryo" or a "matrix" of the collective life).[176] Can it be considered a level of social practice that allows the inhabitant to become involved in collective life? Or, to phrase the questions in terms of planning: is the district a proper framework for collective facilities?[177]

To answer these questions, the study examined four suburban cities within the Parisian agglomeration: Argenteuil, Choisy-le-Roi, Suresnes, and Vitry-sur-Seine. The spatial entities under consideration were delineated not only by means of a morphological, social, and functional analysis but also by taking into account representations of space and ideologies. For example, a *pavillon* neighborhood was defined as consisting of material structures, the everyday practices of its inhabitants, and the "ideology of the *pavillon*"; similarly, an industrial zone was described as "the sum of the enterprises and the people whom they employ, *plus* the economic strategy of the firms that shaped this zone and that are still present there."[178] In that sense this study can be read through Lefebvre's theory as questioning whether the three moments of space are gathered on the level of district; in other words: can the district become a level of social practice? Or, is there a centrality of the district?

The study answers these questions negatively: the division between work and housing enabled by the rise in mobility weakens the links among the inhabitants of a district, and the institutions that influence the life of the inhabitants operate on a larger scale, namely, that of the municipality. In the wake of these processes the role of the local authorities is redefined and has shifted from the task of defending the common interests of the community toward the satisfaction of needs of individuals (accommodation and educational, cultural, and social facilities).[179] Even the Catholic and Communist organizations that have been traditionally related to the scale of the district (the parish, the committee of the district, the association of parents) need to articulate themselves on a more structured and more institutionalized level in order to be efficient and participate in the decision-making processes. Thus, the authors conclude that the material reality of the district, whether of fifty or of two thousand apartments, "does not offer a sufficient basis for the collective life" that would not be limited to the duality of housing and work.[180] Rather, they see the network of collective facilities as points of reference for the inhabitants that allow them to relate to one another: as a meeting place, a cultural club, or a sport center may substitute for the district.[181] The city, rather than being a fabric divided into specific parts, is to be conceived as a network organized around several formative elements: the traffic circulation and the big collective facilities.[182]

These conclusions were embraced by Lefebvre in his essay "Quartier et vie de quartier" (District and the Life of the District), which was included within the study. One of the main targets of this essay was Gaston Bardet, representing French culturalist urbanism. Writing in the 1940s, Bardet opposed both the traditional concentric city and the urbanism of Le Corbusier, instead defining six "levels" corresponding to six scales of community life, which were distinguished by their number of inhabitants, the specific social bond among them, and the spaces in which everyday life takes place.[183] Countering Bardet, who stressed the importance of smaller urban scales, Lefebvre argues that the district should not be considered an essential element of which cities are constituted, because collective practices in contemporary society are dependent on institutions of larger scale. This critique is not intended to dispose of the district but to reconsider its relationships with the urban totality and with architectural objects. Developing this argument in *The Production of Space,* Lefebvre proposes that architecture

LES ECHELONS COMMUNAUTAIRES
DANS LES AGGLOMERATIONS URBAINES [1]

Plus l'homme mesure le monde, de l'infiniment petit à l'infiniment grand, plus il se voit contraint d'ajouter des files de zéros aux chiffres dont il avait l'habitude de se servir, puis de créer de nouvelles unités : microns ou années-lumière, pour réduire l'allongement de ces files. Ces multiplications et ces divisions, ces puissances et ces racines, auxquelles s'est habitué l'homme moderne, l'amènent à concevoir, puis à manier, de pures abstractions qu'il ne peut plus imaginer visuellement.

Ne pouvant plus imaginer — c'est-à-dire construire avec des morceaux de réalité tangible — la plupart des hommes ont perdu l'intuition même de cette réalité. L'intellect pur — privé de points d'appui, vidé de substance concrète — conçoit une ronde d'éléments que mesure un nombre impressionnant de zéros et d'indices. Pris dans ce vaste mouvement hélicoïdal qui semble s'élever en tourbillonnant des électrons vers les nébuleuses, l'homme, saisi de vertige, semble oublier les échelons, les registres successifs que gravit à chaque pas cette hélice, échelons qui ne correspondent pas seulement à une simple amplification, à une simple multiplication, à une simple file nouvelle de zéros. Il oublie non seulement les échelons, autrement dit l'échelle des éléments, mais surtout leurs rapports avec sa propre échelle.

Et pourtant la leçon du monde est lumineuse. En ajoutant des zéros au chiffre qui mesure un élément, on obtient non pas cet élément agrandi, mais un élément d'une autre échelle, d'une autre espèce, un élément d'une autre nature, ayant une autre structure, régi par d'autres lois.

L'échelle de l'électron, c'est le milliardième de millimètre, l'échelle de l'atome c'est le dix millionième de millimètre, l'échelle de la cellule c'est le millième de millimètre, l'échelle de l'homme c'est le mètre... l'échelle de la nébuleuse c'est 100.000 années lumière... L'atome n'est pas un électron multiplié par 10^2, la cellule n'est pas un atome multiplié par 10^4, l'homme n'est pas une cellule multipliée par 10^6, et chaque système nouveau n'est pas un individu amplifié. Pour éviter toute erreur d'interprétation, disons : comme dans un agrandissement photographique, une projection conique où à chaque point en correspond un autre, deux échelons peuvent être *arithmétiquement* multiples l'un de l'autre, ils ne se correspondent pas *géométriquement*.

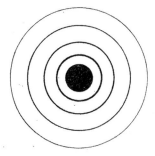

Fig. 222. — La ville telle qu'on la conçoit ordinairement : une cible, un agrandissement illimité d'une tache centrale.

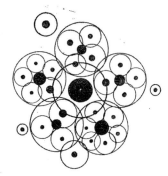

Fig. 223. — La ville telle qu'elle est : une grappe, une fédération de communautés.

(1) Rapport présenté à la première Session des Journées du Mont-Dore, paru dans le n° 8 de la revue *Economie et Humanisme*, puis repris dans les *Documents Economie et Humanisme*, Cahier Collectif : *Caractère de la Communauté*.

First page of Gaston Bardet's essay on the community levels in urban agglomerations. Bardet contrasts the historical concentric scheme of the city with the "city as a cluster" conceived according to community levels. Bardet, "Les échelons communautaires dans les agglomérations urbaines," 233.

be thought of not as text but as "texture": architecture as "archi-texture" would include strong points, nexuses or nodes in "the populated area and the associated networks in which it is set down, as part of a particular production of space."[184]

The City in Space and the Research of a New Spatial Unity

What scale does allow a collective appropriation of space if not a co-owned apartment block or a district? The answer to this question requires challenging the traditional scales of the production of space: that of architecture with the building confined within the laws of private property and that of urbanism claimed by the state as its level of competence.[185] Lefebvre argues that the dichotomy of architecture and urbanism prevents a collective appropriation of space and must be disposed of.

This argument is spelled out extensively in his text "Espace architectural, espace urbain" (Architectural Space, Urban Space, 1981), published in the catalogue of the exhibition Architectures en France: Modernité/Postmodernité (Architectures in France: Modernity/Postmodernity), held at the Centre Georges Pompidou, in Paris. The exhibition examined the period of revision and reinvention of French architecture from the 1960s through the 1970s and offered Lefebvre an occasion to recapitulate his understanding of architecture and urbanism of that time. In the text he refers to the opposition between the city and the architectural object in order to describe two poles that asymptotically stand for two tendencies within the production of homogeneous and fragmented abstract space. The first is that of urbanism dominating architecture, imposing a unified plan on the city in which it allocates architectural objects, as Lefebvre saw it in the plan of the new town of Evry. The opposite pole is that of an architectural object "liberated from all urbanistic constraints," which is added to the urban level of disjointed fragments, as in the housing in Marne-la-Vallée, by Ricardo Bofill, finished in 1982.[186]

Lefebvre's critique of Bofill's housing project in the 1980s contrasts with his admiration of the earlier work of this architect. In particular, in the course of the 1970s, Bofill's project La ciudad en el espacio (the City in Space) was considered by Lefebvre as a possible starting point for a production of the contemporary city.[187] Together with New Babylon, by Constant Nieuwenhuys, Bofill's project became the most important reference in Lefebvre's quest for a new type of a spatial unity that would be at the same time "macro-architectural" and "micro-urbanistic." In spite of all the differences between these designs, Lefebvre argued that the shared aim of both was a mediation between dwelling and traffic, private and public spaces, and a facilitation of mobility and encounter: "In their own way, both Ricardo Bofill, with his 'City in Space,' and Constant, with 'New Babylon,' aim at specifying a new unity that bridges architecture and urbanism and offers a scale on which one can work and produce."[188]

In this simultaneous reference to both designs reverberates the debate about the megastructures of the late 1960s and early 1970s, which questioned the role of architecture within the conditions of an unlimited urbanization. The designs of the City in Space and New Babylon comply with the criteria employed by Reyner Banham to identify megastructures in his 1976 book on this topic: the modular unity, the possibility of an unlimited extension, and the division between the long-lasting structural frame and the exchangeable elements.[189] And yet, in spite of Banham discussing New Babylon and mentioning the City in Space,[190] their performance was conceived in a different way, both aiming at a complete reconstruction of the postwar city rather than being an addition, however large, that would match the scale of the ongoing processes of urbanization.

This was the main objective of the City in Space: to leave behind disciplinary distinction between architecture and urbanism without losing the possibility of articulating scalar differences in the city. The project, developed in twenty-five volumes between 1968 and 1970, was based on the previous experiences of the Taller de arquitectura, with such projects as the La Manzanera (1962–63) and the Barrio Gaudi housing scheme in Reus (1964–68) and as continued by the Walden 7 housing block (1969–74).[191] The starting point of the City in Space was a critique of sprawling suburbs, bad zoning, and uniform blocks around the historical cities.[192] These processes became particularly acute in late-1960s Spain, characterized by massive migration from the countryside to the cities, in the face of which planning regulations often remained of no consequence.[193] For Lefebvre, this "explosion" of the city meant that the situationists' unitary urbanism, with its focus on historical cities, "lost any meaning." While "Guy Debord abandoned the problem of the city and of urbanism as an ideology," Lefebvre was convinced that "the explosion of the historic city was precisely the occasion for finding a larger theory of the city, and not a pretext for abandoning the problem."[194]

If this conviction was shared by the City in Space, it did not mean a renewed faith in urbanism. Prefacing the project, Bofill argued that urbanism is unable to address the contemporary urban condition: introduced in the nineteenth century in order to appease the exacerbation of class struggle in the rapidly growing cities, the operations of urbanism are torn between an ideology of social peace and the practice of segregation and speculation.[195] Thus, urbanism should be abandoned, and the city must be constructed by means of architecture alone, starting with the single housing unit. Consequently, even if in the later stages the project opposes functional zoning and postulates a mixture of functions, the discussion is developed not on the level of urbanism but on that of architecture, developing a matrix for accommodating these functions tailored for apartments.

This attempt at constructing a city by means of housing requires a complete rethinking of design methods. Thus, the project begins with a "deductive" approach to city planning, taking as its starting point a set of geometric elements and the rules of their association. This method, demonstrated in the first part of the project (Generic Project), is complemented by the second part (Experience 1), which introduces an "inductive" way of modifying the deduced model by confronting it with requirements and constraints stemming from the social reality of late Franco's Spain.[196]

The Generic Project is a "structural investigation," that is to say, an interrogation of "a purely architectural problem, which permits a grasp of the laws producing a form or a group of determined forms, laws that can be selected as most suitable for the realization of any project."[197] This procedure starts with one basic cell with the form of half of a cube; three of them are configured in an L shape, which becomes the atom of the city. With such elements added to one another, a "unitary internal structure" is developed by taking into account architectural criteria, such as the proportion between interior and exterior space; the disposition of the street and squares; the placement of vertical communication systems and infrastructure; light conditions; the required surface of the external façade; the number of entrances; and the dimensions, use, and orientation of apartments.[198] The cell is repeated and rotated in a way that suggests a spiral movement, in order to be clustered into larger, complex aggregations. This is a purely formal procedure, which can be applied to any design, whether a skyscraper or a linear city.[199] By repeating this operation several times, the resulting larger forms become, finally, grouped together into several urban types. The steps of this recurrent procedure—of generating urban forms by means of repetition and clustering of smaller aggregates—are legible in the structure organized as a sequence of consecutive scales.

This procedure arrives at a project of a continuous urban tissue that allows mixing activities, uses, and social groups: "an open flexible structure that would permit the growth and accommodation of new types of life and relationships."[200] This tissue is differentiated by its varying intensities and temporary activities rather than by an allocation of specific centralities or functional divisions. In the drawings produced by the Taller, the section and the plan look almost the same: the City in Space appears as a cluster of small housing units surrounding a sequence of larger spaces, filled with people and vegetation. The urbanity in this multilayered, "superconcentrated city" is explained as a maximalization of choices concerning work, modes of life, intimate relationships, and the employment of free time, but a condition of this individual freedom is a return to the collective character of the city and its public spaces in which differentiated ways of life become manifested. The authors call for an integral spectacle "in which all

5

ESQUEMA DE PERSPECTIVA ISOMETRICA DEL NUCLEO MAYOR.

City in Space, isometry of the geometric nucleus of the project. In Bofill and Taller de arquitectura, "Problemas de significado y estructurales." Courtesy of Ricardo Bofill.

mceg-2

MALLA O COMPLEJO URBANO.

MACROMODELO GENERADO POR YUXTAPOSICION DEL MCe G 1 CONSIDERADO COMO FIGURA ACABADA.

"Fabric or urban complex": the result of a multiplication of the basic element according to the "spatial chess." In Bofill and Taller de arquitectura, "Problemas estructurales." Courtesy of Ricardo Bofill.

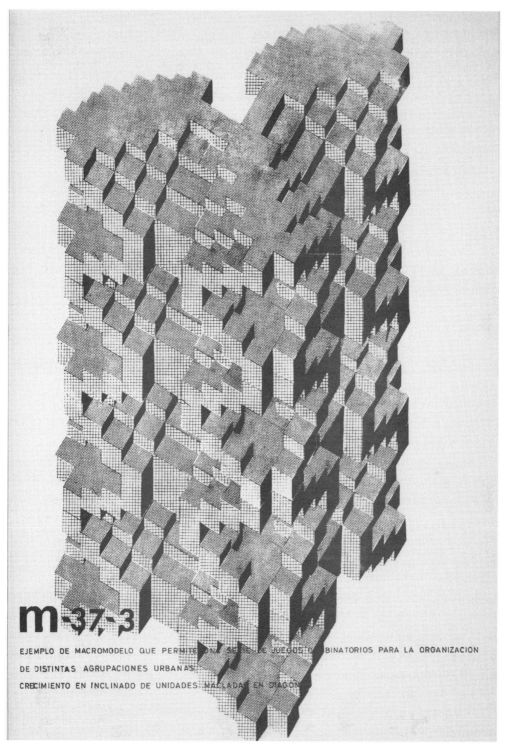

m 37-3

EJEMPLO DE MACROMODELO QUE PERMITE UNA SERIE DE JUEGOS COMBINATORIOS PARA LA ORGANIZACIÓN

DE DISTINTAS AGRUPACIONES URBANAS

CRECIMIENTO EN INCLINADO DE UNIDADES MALLADAS EN DIAGÓN

City in Space, isometry of a macromodel consisting of a combination of several elements. From Bofill and Taller de arquitectura, "Problemas estructurales." Courtesy of Ricardo Bofill.

inhabitants are actors and spectators"[201]—a spectacle that, in the City in Space, is not reduced to an imposed image, as will become the case with some of Bofill's historicist designs, but is produced by modern communication and advertising technologies, understood as means of education and mass culture, integrated into the urban fabric.[202] This is suggested by one of the collages, which juxtaposes a monochromatic photograph of the model with images of the activities of its inhabitants, cut from popular magazines and retouched. This demonstrates Bofill's design approach: the abstract "deductive" model is filled in and modified in an "inductive" way.

On the "inductive" stage of the design process, the social, economic, and technological conditions of late 1960s Spain are taken into account. Special attention is paid to innovative technologies of prefabrication, which would become Bofill's trademark in the years to come. In this phase the prospective client was expected to get involved in the design process and decide about the program, size, and form of the apartment. While in the deductive part the design was generated by means of a multiplication of a singular cell according to geometric laws of its transformation, in the inductive part the production of space is based on the decisions of individual owners mediated by the market: it is the prospective inhabitants who, by choosing the apartments, decide about the definitive form of the city. This was reflected in the legal part of the design, which regulated the ownership relationships between the individuals and the collectives.[203]

These are the three premises of the City in Space: the set of architectural operations that produce multiple spatial configurations open to individual desires, the mediating role of the market, and the innovative technology of construction. Bofill and the Taller argue that it is specifically by means of architectural innovations, in terms of construction and form, that architecture intervenes in the everyday and addresses social questions.[204] And precisely these three aspects—ways of life, financing, and construction—were what proved to be the most provocative in the project when it came to its realization. In 1968 the Taller obtained a site in Moratalaz, in the suburbs of Madrid, which was made available by the minister of housing, interested in prefabricated construction and impressed by the neighborhood in Reus. For Bofill this suburban location, on the edge of the city sprawling into the countryside, provided a possibility to test the ideas about new types of urbanity, speculated upon in the City in Space. At that time the Taller set up new departments, including a juridical and a sociological department, the latter cooperating with Lefebvre as a consultant.[205]

The project was launched with a big public event, an "urban festival" located on the site, with a jazz concert and the spectacle of invited mimes, whose performance is approximated in their later appearance in the movie *Esquizo*, directed by Bofill (1970). For fifteen hundred apartments the organizers received ten

City in Space, fragment of an urban unit for fifty thousand inhabitants. From Bofill and Taller de arquitectura, "Ejemplo de una agrupación urbana superior a los 50,000 habitantes." Courtesy of Ricardo Bofill.

The urban unit for fifty thousand inhabitants in City in Space consisted of a combination of previ-ously designed elements. In Bofill and Taller de arquitectura, "Ejemplo de una agrupación urbana superior a los 50,000 habitantes." Courtesy of Ricardo Bofill.

thousand offers from prospective buyers, attracted by the innovative plans, not laid out according to functional elements, but divided according to the practices of dwelling: into calm spaces, contemplative spaces, spaces for social contacts. The project offered spaces for various ways of life and types of relationships, including gay couples, households with more than two adult persons, and unmarried couples with children, according to Bofill's description. In his words, "We all came from bourgeois families, and we hated the bourgeois family."[206] The target of the project could not be stated more clearly: it aimed at accommodating the differentiated lifestyles of the middle class, rising in the quickly modernizing Spain.

Although included in the official plan of Moratalaz in January 1969, this "political, ideological, and architectural experience" ended abruptly in a violent confrontation with Carlos Arias Navarro, the mayor of Madrid and later the prime minister of Spain.[207] Under pressure from developers, who accused the project of illicit dumping, the construction permit was canceled; a second cause of its demise was, according to Bofill, its spirit of liberty and the openness in regard to different types of relationships among people, beyond the traditional bourgeois, Catholic family. This was also argued by Lefebvre: the City in Space was abandoned because the political regime was menaced by spaces of encounter at this scale.[208] Under the threat of the withdrawal of his license of architecture, Bofill retreated from the project.[209]

No doubt, the City in Space, with its ambition to "improve" the traditional urban way of life,[210] announced in many ways Bofill's postmodern schemes, in particular the Marne-la-Vallée project criticized by Lefebvre, with its return to the monumental typologies as models for urban life and the concept of the city as a stage for the "exalted" everyday life. (As Lefebvre wrote in the *Urban Revolution*, probably thinking about socialist realism, "The extension of monumental space to habiting is always catastrophic.")[211] But such a retrospective reading would neither fully do justice to the historical conditions of this project nor allow an understanding of the programmatic position of this "concrete utopia" beyond both a "realistic architecture" that fulfills the "demands and desires of the clientele," whatever its political position, and a "utopian architecture" that disagrees with current practice and creates images of a future city without breaking from the preconception of urbanism.[212]

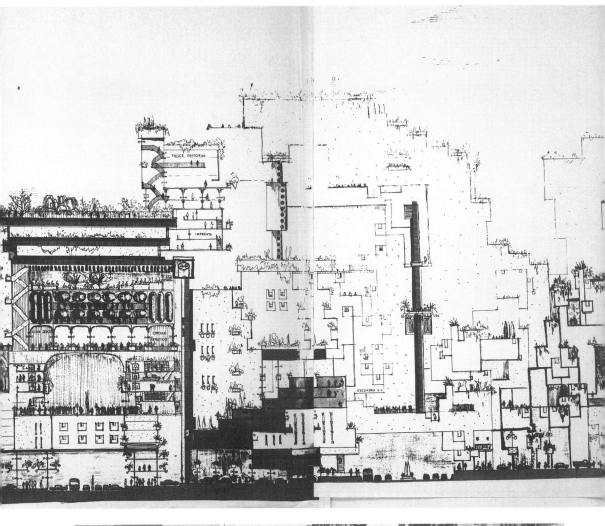

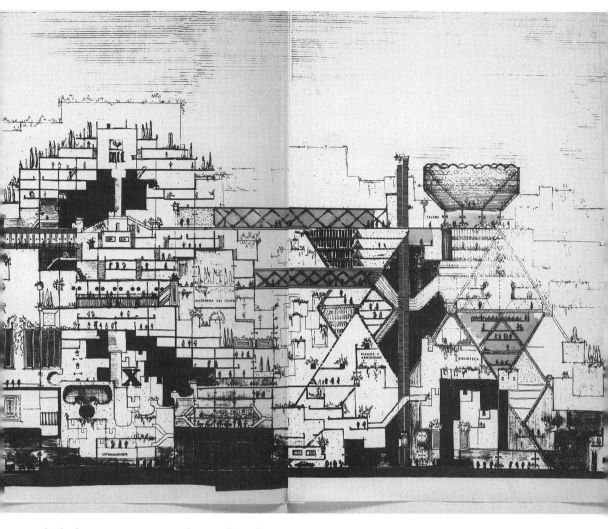

(*top*) The "superconcentrated city" allows for a maximum of choices concerning work, modes of life, personal relationships, and use of free time. From Bofill and Taller de arquitectura, "Visualización." Courtesy of Ricardo Bofill.

(*opposite page bottom*) In City in Space, inhabitants were to be "actors and spectators" of one comprehensive spectacle. In Bofill and Taller de arquitectura, "Towards a Formalization of the City in Space."

Construction principle of City in Space. In Bofill and Taller de arquitectura, "Experiencia 1." Courtesy of Ricardo Bofill.

PE 19

PERSPECTIVA ISOMETRICA DEL SISTEMA CONSTRUCTIVO, ESTRUCTURA, POSIBLES PANELES, ABERTURAS Y CIRCULACIONES DE UN NUCLEO.

Design of a unit from which City in Space was to be constructed. From Bofill and Taller de arquitectura, "Experiencia 1." Courtesy of Ricardo Bofill.

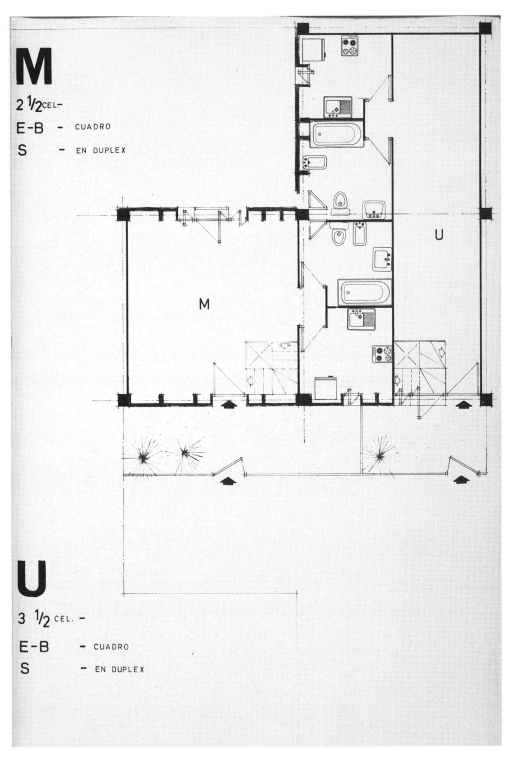

Plan of a housing unit in City in Space. In Bofill and Taller de arquitectura, "Plantas de las vivien-das, con situación de los bajantes en cuadro." Courtesy of Ricardo Bofill.

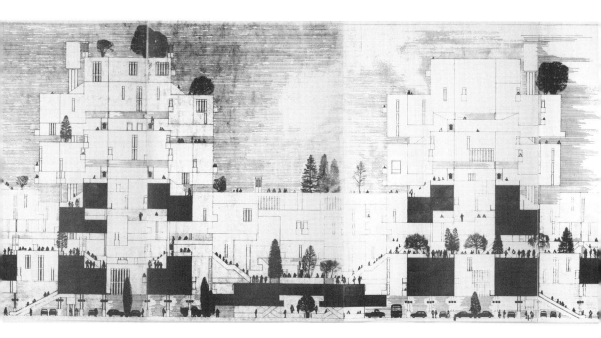

(*top*) Prototype of City in Space. In Bofill and Taller de arquitectura, "Prototipo y visualización de un ejemplo." Courtesy of Ricardo Bofill.

(*left*) City in Space aimed to combine the collective character of public spaces and the individualization of ways of life. In Bofill and Taller de arquitectura, "Prototipo y visualización de un ejemplo." Courtesy of Ricardo Bofill.

New Babylon: Architecture and the Politics of Scale

If the City in Space aimed at a scale beyond the traditional scalar regimes of architecture and urbanism, New Babylon—the other "concrete utopia" admired by Lefebvre—speculates on the possibility of mediation among scales of urban reality.

Such possibility was hinted at by Lefebvre in the essay "Quartier et vie de quartier": "The unity of the city, sprawling and spreading out, may be embodied, to say it like that, in a privileged fragment."[213] This fragment—a redefined district or an architectural ensemble that gathers various facilities—is absorbed by the totality of the city without renouncing its independent dynamics. It is envisaged as the "smallest difference among the multiple and diverse social spaces" of which the institutions and centers of larger scale are in charge, thus assuming the role of a transmitter positioned "between the geometric space and social space, a passage point from one to another."[214]

This postulate of a space of transmission is a persistent theme in Lefebvre's work,[215] leading to the concept of an architecture as a "social interchange," introduced during the CRAUC seminar to complement the concept of a "social condenser":

> In a sense almost parallel to that of a road interchange, this interchange would serve as a transition, as a bridge, a passage, between different structures and existing social institutions.[216]

Like the concept of the social condenser in the Nanterre study, the understanding of architecture as a social interchange brings about a mechanical image of architecture's production of social effects—much like the effigy of modern architecture constructed by Lefebvre as the target of his writings. Yet a reading of Constant's New Babylon by means of Lefebvre's concepts suggests that if the architecture of social interchange is a machine, it is a detoured machine, a machine whose uses are subjected to political decisions and open to a multiplicity of possible effects.

New Babylon—"a camp for nomads on a planetary scale," "a playtown of homo ludens," "a décor for new mass culture"[217]—was developed by Constant between the mid-1950s and the early 1970s. The project was conceived as a model of the urbanization of a society to come that, owing to the full automatization of production and collective ownership of land and means of production, leaves productive work behind and faces unlimited free time as its main stake and challenge. New Babylon wagers on the replacement of the capitalist "utilitarian" society by the "ludic" society, in which efficiency, production, competition, and individualism are to be replaced by appreciation for a sense of adventure, exploration, disorientation, cooperation, and mass creativity. The vast spaces of New

Babylon lend themselves to a constant transformation: while the imperative of production in the Fordist society resulted in a rigid division of the city into spaces and times of work, housing, and leisure, the everyday in the ludic society is characterized by an unending stroll through atmospheric spaces manipulated by New Babylonians.

This project can be read as drawing consequences from Lefebvre's dialectical theorizing of social space as socially produced and productive. "Spatiality is social," argued Constant, and thus "the city shapes its inhabitant every bit as much as the inhabitants shape their city."[218] This dialectics was addressed by Constant by means of two main techniques of unitary urbanism: the psychogeographic research on the influence of the environment on the behavior and emotions of individuals, and the construction of situations by "collective organization of a unitary ambience and a game of events."[219] Accordingly, Constant distinguished two aspects of unitary urbanism: "a transformation of our habits, or rather of our way of life or lifestyle," and "a profound change in the way our material environment is produced."[220] To relate them to each other meant a redefinition of psychogeography as a procedure of research and design that tries to identify and explain "the unconscious influences exerted by the urban atmosphere" and to use them as "a means of activating our environment."[221]

Specifying these programmatic statements, the dialectical connection between space and social practice was spelled out in Constant's letter to the students of the Institut d'urbanisme de l'Université de Paris (5 October 1969). The letter commented on the *dérive* performed by the students during one weekend (2–3 May 1969) in Amsterdam within the framework of a seminar by Hubert Tonka, Lefebvre's assistant at the *institut*. After being received by Constant in Amsterdam, on their return to Paris the students sent him the mappings, descriptions, and sketches that document the attempt to "address the city in a lived experience" and "from within a practice."[222] In his response, Constant took issue with the tourist paths chosen by the students (starting from the Dam Square in the center of the city) and criticized them for being guided by a preconceived image of the city and utilitarian objectives (such as being on time in a meeting place). Constant was disappointed by what he saw as their passivity, lack of creative response to the environment, and negative motivations in deciding about the route. He wrote, "An escape from disgust, a judgment of moral order, lassitude are difficult to combine with the will to creation that is at the origin of an experimental behavior" and thus, by definition, at the origin of the *dérive*. The students, according to Constant, did not grasp the dialectical relationship between space and social practices: when they describe a street as boring, they show a lack of interest in their own presence there, not seeing that their own presence changes this very street. Constant writes that one should "go with the wind, but not without intervention":

The *dérive* is not simply a mode of behavior; it is also a technique of the apprehension of urbanism, but a technique that is typical for a creative person. The *dérive* cannot be studied; it must be played, lived, re-created in every moment, in relationship to the present situation. If one calls the *dérive* a method, this method should, in the end, lead to a creation of an urban milieu that would be a synthesis between the décor and experimental behavior, that is to say, unitary urbanism.[223]

And yet Constant's own project manifests how difficult it is to grasp this dialectics between décor and experimental behavior. The series of models, drawings, and collages by means of which New Babylon was presented reveals two opposing poles within this dialectics: the three-dimensional infrastructure, which evokes a strong emotional impact, and the sequence of surfaces, which suggests an endless possibility of transformation. The relationship between this double character of New Babylon—a spatial framework and a generative surface—was far from being settled in the architectural modes of representation chosen by Constant in the 1950 and 1960s. This tension also characterizes his paintings from the 1970s, which juxtapose fragmentary perspectives with an atmospheric space of planes and shadows, thus continuing the themes of the sketches for New Babylon: abstractly drawn people in labyrinthine spaces, but also model-building techniques with the imprints of the same kind of perforated metal grids that were used for Constant's models or straight lines drawn with a ruler that emulate the gesture of cutting.

It was Constant's choice to employ architectural modes of representation that inevitably confronted him with the questions of scale. Lefebvre's take on New Babylon allows bypassing the two readings that had dominated the discussion about this project since the 1960s as either a utopia of a liberated future or a dystopian, consumerist, high-tech pleasure prison overshadowed by the trauma of the Second World War.[224] Beyond this dichotomy, Lefebvre's focus on scale and the practice of scaling allows addressing the transitional character of Constant's work as an attempt of a political engagement with the postwar processes of urbanization.

Not only was the discussion about scale important for Constant from the beginning of his work on New Babylon, but it was also what he argued, retrospectively, to have been his main difference from Debord, with whom he cut off contact in 1960, after three and half years of productive exchanges.[225] In a lecture to the students of the Delft University of Technology in 1980, Constant claimed that "unlike other situationists" he realized that unitary urbanism cannot be focused on only "micro-scales or 'ambiances,'" because they depend on the "macro-structure," so "the elaboration of the extremely sketchy idea of unitary urbanism was therefore inextricably bound up with a critique of city planning."[226]

The mapping of the *dérive* of students of the Institut d'urbanisme de Paris in Amsterdam (2 May 1969), commented on by Constant Nieuwenhuys in a letter of 5 October 1969. Rijksbureau voor Kunsthistorische Documentatie Den Haag, Constant Archive, box 319.

In particular after his withdrawal from the IS, Constant problematized the relationships among the scales of New Babylon and contested their seamless unity, as intended in Debord's proposal for a 1960 Amsterdam exhibition, conceived there as linking a micro-*dérive* in a labyrinthine interior and a *dérive* in the streets of the city.[227] This differentiation among the scales of the project was a consequence of rethinking its basic premises: Constant wrote that an urban plan that responds to an intensified social mobility implies a "rigorous organization on the macro level" combined with a "greater flexibility at the micro level, which is that of an infinite complexity."[228] Accordingly, New Babylon was developed into a "design of a worldwide macro-structure capable of guaranteeing freedom of time and freedom of place: the continuity of a network rather than the quantity of individual settlement."[229]

New Babylon operates with three scales, which are articulated by a series of thresholds. Constant's "microscale" is one of personal encounters, micro-atmospheres, and fleeting ambiences, suggested in the plan by discernible sets of various grids and patterns. These freely transformable arrangements are often drawn as overlapping and expanding beyond the borders of the sectors that represent the middle scale of the project. This suggests that the sectors are not simply containers of a certain number of microscales but are distinguished by means of a different performance, composition, construction, and appearance. The sectors are connected to each other, usually in a linear way, so that their network is perceived from within as a continuous space, and their ensemble constitutes the macroscale, itself to be considered as a provocation in the face of a functionalist society obsessed with efficiency.[230] The macroscale can be perceived only when measured against the landscape, and Constant's collages and photographs often juxtapose an external view of the seemingly endless chain of sectors with the unlimited landscape untouched by human hand or, by contrast, a landscape fully artificial and filled with fast traffic junctions, parks, agricultural production units, and automated factories. The juxtaposition between the vast and abstract landscape and the individual practices—a returning theme in Constant's work, including his holiday sketches—is dramatized by the appearance of minuscule figures and cars in the models of New Babylon.

The sharp distinctions among the scales of New Babylon, reinforced by the choice of their means of representation, is relativized in the actual perception of the models, today in the collection of the Gemeentemuseum in The Hague, models whose close-up photographs were shown in Constant's slideshows presenting the project in the early 1960s. When seen *as architectural models*—that is to say, when the body of the visitor to the museum bends down in order to adjust to the size of the model and to look at it as if from a horizon of passersby— what the visitor perceives are, precisely, the shifts among scales: from the large opening between the metal tubes on which the model rests; through the spaces

Constant Nieuwenhuys, *Theoretical Collage of New Babylon*, 1974, plate 1, showing three scales of the project: the sectors, their chains, and the landscape. Courtesy of Gemeentemuseum Den Haag.

between the mirroring horizontal surfaces made of Plexiglas; to the view from above, when the reflections on the Plexiglas give way to transparencies, revealing a superimposition of multiple plans etched in the color-tinted sheets.

Both in the drawings and in the models, the macroscale of New Babylon is never shown in its full extension; its representations are snapshots of a process of its incessant rearrangement. This process does not take place in a void: Constant perceives New Babylon as a mode of reconstruction of the postwar European city, characterized by the functionalist refraction of new districts and the destruction of old neighborhoods by freeways, as well as the commodification of historical cities by tourism.[231] This was also stressed by Debord: in order to "construct new ambiances that are simultaneously the product and the instrument of new modes of behavior," we must "employ in an empirical fashion, initially, the quotidian activities and the cultural forms that already exist at this moment, even as we deny them any inherent value."[232] More specifically, Debord and Gil

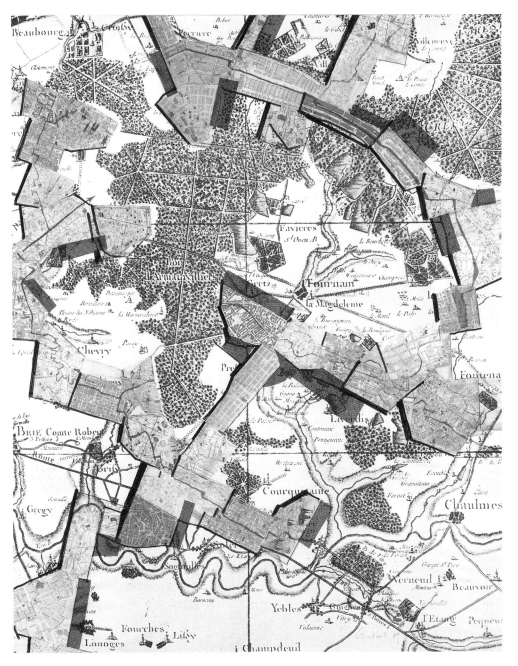

(*top*) Constant Nieuwenhuys, *Sectors around a Forest,* no date. In this collage the sectors are represented by clippings from historical and contemporary city maps. Courtesy of Gemeentemuseum Den Haag.

(*opposite page top*) Constant Nieuwenhyus, *Sectors in a Mountain Landscape,* 1967, model picture. Courtesy of Gemeentemuseum Den Haag.

(*opposite page bottom*) Constant Nieuwenhyus, *Sketch from a Journey: Summer 1965.* Courtesy of Gemeentemuseum Den Haag.

Wolman wrote in 1956, "The *architectural complex*—which we conceive as the construction of a dynamic environment related to styles of behavior—will probably detourn existing architectural forms, and in any case will make plastic and emotional use of all sorts of detourned objects."[233]

This strategy was at the center of a series of collages and drawings that insert New Babylon into the fabric of existing cities, such as Amsterdam, The Hague, Cologne, Munich, Barcelona, Antwerp, Rotterdam, and Paris. These drawings are accompanied by a narration about the sectors assembling collective functions and sociocultural attractors, which become slowly enlarged, augmented, and linked to one another while their activity becomes specialized and increasingly autonomous from the residential areas.[234] The sequence of sectors become zones of urban intensity, and this is why the grid is denser in highly populated areas, what can be observed in large-scale maps such as that of the Rhine region or of the Netherlands. These drawings evince that the scale produced by New Babylon is not limited to that of the interlined sectors but also includes that of the areas in between them: urban territories or parks and forests, as in the collage showing a forest surrounded by sectors represented by clippings of Dutch, Italian, English, Russian, and Czech historical cities. These collages demonstrate that New Babylon is not simply a rejection of the postwar city but rather its critique and the project of its reconstruction, of which the essential operation is that of rescaling.

Nowhere can this be seen better than in a series of collages that superimpose New Babylon on the map of Amsterdam and The Hague. The introduction of the network of sectors reacts to the given urban structures: roads, waterways, and monuments are appropriated and integrated into the project. The delineation of urban territories suggests the possibility of mixing parts of historical neighborhoods with chunks of port infrastructure or combining segments of wealthy districts with poorer ones. After these operations, New Babylon performs a complexification of the city across borders imposed by urban renewal, the tourist industry, and monument preservation. In the 1968 Amsterdam collage, the project is developed by the coloring of existing parts of the city, suggesting their delineation or their lifting into the air. In another composition, such monuments as the Royal Palace, Berlage's Stock Exchange, the Rijksmuseum, and the Zoological Museum are marked in the same way as hubs of intensity in their sectors, which, after this operation, appear as an intensification of the city by a massive concentration of monuments. Similarly, in the collage of The Hague, the sectors appear as an accumulation of the existing city, marked by grids much denser than that of the road system: this is most explicit in the "theoretical collage" of New Babylon, in which the sectors are collaged together as pieces of various cities aligned with one another in a landscape of existing villages and high-speed traffic lines.

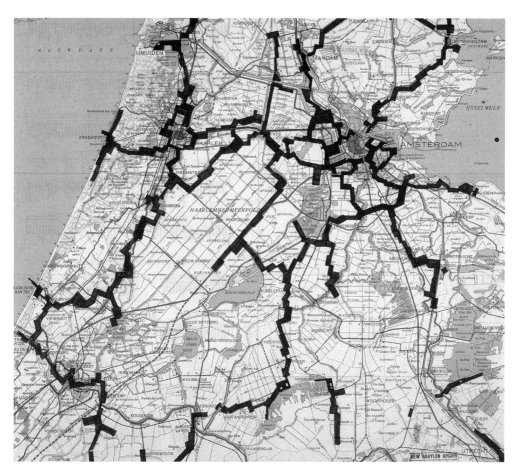

Constant Nieuwenhyus, *New Babylon: Holland,* 1963. Courtesy of Gemeentemuseum Den Haag.

This fragmentary reading of New Babylon, guided by Lefebvre's theorizing of an architecture of social interchange, opens up a possibility of a political understanding of Constant's project. New Babylon not only reorganizes the existing city structures, dividing homogeneous wholes and producing heterogeneous aggregates, but also disrupts the concentric relationship between center and periphery. Rather than being a utopian or a dystopian vision, it offers a conceptualization of centralities that are neither static nor hierarchical but are envisaged as linear zones of increased urban intensity, zones that reorganize the relationship among scales in urban society.

This reorganization of scales announces Lefebvre's theorizing of the "politics of scale," developed in the writings subsequent to *The Production of Space,* most importantly in *De l'État,* in which he argues that scales are not given but are socially produced and politically contested presuppositions, media, and outcomes of social relations.[235] In *De l'État,* Lefebvre registers the emergence of new

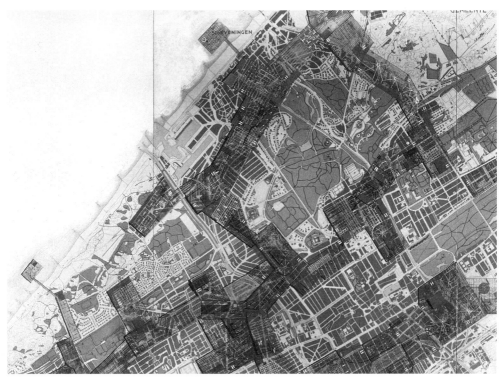

social movements that aim at a "new appropriation of space."[236] He writes that these movements "put emphasis on the relationships between the people (individuals, groups, classes) and space with its levels: neighborhood and the level of the immediate; the urban and the mediations; the region and the nation; and, finally, the global."[237]

Neil Brenner reads these statements in the context of the scale debate in sociology, geography, and political sciences, marked, since the 1990s, by the contributions of Bob Jessop, Neil Smith, Erik Swyngedouw, and Brenner himself.[238] Lefebvre's work on scale prefigured some of these discussions, in particular, the account of the crisis of the Fordist–Keynesian welfare state since the 1970s understood as a crisis of the national scale as the primary object of economic management, distribution of welfare, and definition of citizenship, profoundly shaken by the processes of globalization, the emergence of a new level of capital accumulation, and the transationalization of labor.[239] Reading Lefebvre in this context, Brenner considers his theory as opening up the possibility of a "dialectical approach to the *scaling processes*" and a "politics of scale" addressing struggles over "reorganization, reconfiguration and even transcendence" of scalar hierarchies: a politics focused not only upon supraurban spaces such as region, national states, and the world economy but also upon struggles to transform scalar hierarchies and interscalar relations themselves.[240]

The call for an architecture that would contribute to such politics of scale can be traced to much of Lefebvre's work, from his texts about Mourenx and the Bistrot-club to his writings of the 1980s, such as the essay "Constitutez vous en avant-garde" (Constitute Yourself into an Avant-Garde, 1984), written for the *Archivari,* the journal of the Sodédat.[241] In this essay, Lefebvre proposes three criteria of an "architectural invention," introducing three then-recently completed social housing neighborhoods: La Maladrerie in Aubervilliers (designed by Renée Gailhoustet and her colleagues in the framework of the Sodédat, 1975–86) and two projects of the Ateliers Jean Renaudie: in Givors (from 1976–81) and in Saint-Martin d'Hères (1974–82). First, Lefebvre postulates an architecture that does not isolate its object but opens itself up to the urban, to the city, to the social life and the urban society. This opening can be achieved by an architecture that, as the second criterion goes, "treats space as an articulation of several levels: the organization of territory, the biggest level, that of the site; the urbanistic plan, that

(*opposite page top*) Constant Nieuwenhyus, *New Babylon: Amsterdam,* 1963. The project suggests developing the city across the borders imposed by urban renewal, the tourist industry, and monument preservation. Courtesy of Gemeentemuseum Den Haag.

(*opposite page bottom*) Constant Nieuwenhyus, *New Babylon: The Hague,* 1964. Elements of the city are appropriated and integrated into the project, creating new connections and new urban intensities. Courtesy of Gemeentemuseum Den Haag.

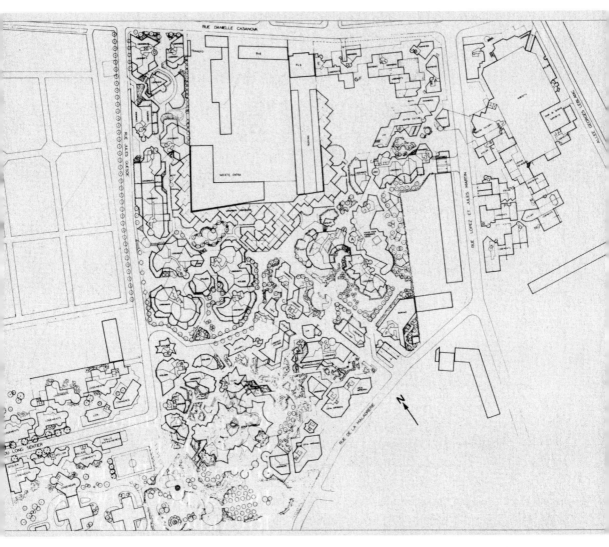

La Maladrerie in Aubervilliers, designed by Renée Gailhoustet, Magda Thomsen, Yves and Luc Euvremer, Vincent Fidon, Katherine Fiumani, and Gilles Jacquemot. Together with the project of Jean Renaudie in Givors, this building was discussed by Lefebvre in *Archivari,* the journal of Sodédat. Published in *Sodédat 93: Un laboratoire urbain,* supplement to *L'architecture d'aujourd'hui* 295 (1994): 52.

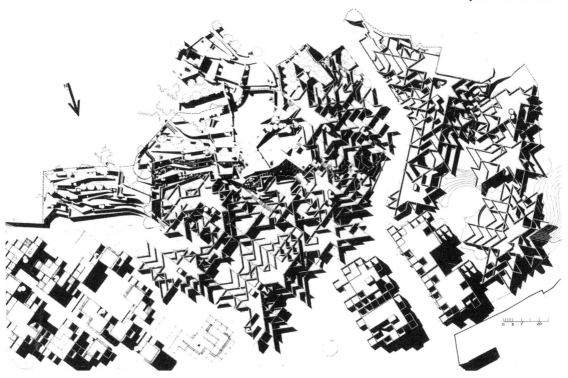

Jean Renaudie, renovation of the center of Givors, 1974–81. Published in *L'architecture d'aujourd'hui* 196 (1978): 9.

of the city; the architectural project, that of dwelling."[242] Essentially, and similarly to his article on the neighborhood seventeen years earlier, Lefebvre understands architecture as a mediator among the various scales. Read in the context of these two, the third criterion—the reminder that "poetically man dwells"—returns to the analysis of appropriation as a practice of dwelling in the *pavillon* and suggests that the "poetic way of dwelling" can be reinterpreted as mediation between individual and collective practices.[243]

New Belgrade: New Citizenship and Self-Management

Lefebvre's theorizing of the politics of scale addresses a possibility of differentiating the urban everyday according to multiple modes of belonging, of which none excludes the others. This vision was conveyed by the concept of new citizenship formulated by the Groupe de Navarrenx in the late 1980s.

The Groupe de Navarrenx, an interdisciplinary circle of philosophers, architects, and sociologists formed in August 1985 around Lefebvre, theorized the concept of new citizenship as an intersection of several themes: the possibility of conceiving difference *and* equality together, the registration of changes in the character of modern labor, the emergence of urban society on the global scale, and the theory of self-management.[244] Within the general perspective of the withering of the state, the group envisaged a project of new citizenship as a contract that would regulate the relationships among individuals, society, and the state. Yet new citizenship cannot be theorized without a conception of its "places," since, in the condition of the complete urbanization of the society, the citizen (*citoyen*) is to be thought of as a *citadin,* an urban dweller or a dweller in an urban society. Or, as it was put by a member of the group, the architect Serge Renaudie, new modes of communication and transport allow multiple possibilities of "being together" that are not restricted to local scales, such as the neighborhood, and include the global dimension.[245]

In his text "Du pacte social au contrat de citoyenneté" (From the Social Contract to a Contract of Citizenship), Lefebvre contrasted the rights conveyed by the new citizenship to human rights: while human rights refer to the human species as a whole, the citizens' rights stem from various modes of belonging in a given society. In the emerging urban society these modes of belonging cannot be restricted to inclusion in a family or a nation; rather, they are differentiated by collectives, professions, and various scalar regimes: village or city, region, state, continent, and the world.[246] Inspired by Rousseau's social contract, Lefebvre defines these rights in a contractual form: the "right to expression" goes with the obligation of debating the questions of the society and all its members; the "right to identity in difference (and equality)" includes the responsibility for the collective as a whole; and the "right to urban services" requires collective forms of living together, not prescribed juridically, but enacted in everyday life.[247] Other "rights" stipulated by Lefebvre, such as the right to culture and to information, are also related to an obligation. Many of these postulates reiterate what, in the late 1960s, he used to call the "right to the city": the "right to freedom, to individualization in socialization, to habitat and to inhabit"; "the right to the *oeuvre,* to participation and *appropriation*"; and the right to "urban life, transformed, renewed."[248] By seeing the right to the city as a right of the new citizen—and, as he put it elsewhere, "implying a revolutionary concept of citizenship"—Lefebvre underscores the imaginary character of the city as a mode of belonging and urges us to rethink the right to the city beyond the framework of human rights and away from its understanding as an entitlement.[249]

This requires "inventing urban culture in the domains and levels of the architectural, urbanistic, and territorial"—the very aim of the urban design project by Serge Renaudie, Pierre Guilbaud, and Lefebvre himself, submitted to the International Competition for the New Belgrade Urban Structure Improvement (1986).[250] The ideas behind the design are spelled out in its accompanying description, of which Lefebvre was responsible for the general introduction, leaving the main architectural and urban ideas to Serge Renaudie.[251] If the authors argued that the question of citizenship is one with which architects and urbanists find themselves inevitably confronted, it is because citizenship is understood not as something granted by authority but as a "dynamic possibility offered to individuals who inscribe themselves into the movement of collectivity, of 'vivre-ensemble' [living-together]: the City."[252] Such citizenship would come to define the "new urban culture," and it would acknowledge the multiplicity of spatial and temporal relationships among that culture's individuals and various social groups.[253] The competition entry embraces the complexity of the city, its richness, constant change, and multiplicity of relationships and modes of belonging:

> Each activity, function group or unit (for example, the individual in relation to the collectivity) must be able to preserve its personal identity; notably in its connection with other activities, otherwise the simple act of connection would prevail and dominate.[254]

The project argues for "encounter" rather than "connection" in response to the reality of the city defined by productivism, standardization, rationalism, and zoning.[255] New Belgrade was initially planned in 1946 as the center of the political community of Yugoslav nations, with housing entirely absent from the city, which was to be dominated by administrative buildings of the central government. After Tito's break with Soviet patronage in 1948, the new plan of New Belgrade reflected the introduction of self-management socialism and decentralization as an alternative to the Soviet model. Realized in the 1960s and 1970s according to the prewar CIAM concept of the functional city, the new plan of the New Belgrade Central Zone (1960) shows housing blocks of six thousand to ten thousand inhabitants each, complemented by schools and basic services, which form the urban structure of the central part of the new city.[256] In the study that prepared the 1986 competition rationale, Miloš Petrović produced a wholesale critique of New Belgrade as developed according to "imported" and "outmoded" models of Le Corbusier's Radiant City and Lucio Costas's Brasília, with the strict separation of the four functions of the Athens Charter; rigid axial organization; the isolation of the main administrative buildings; and the organization of residential zones according to the superblock principle. The design of the city by means of its envisaged ultimate form, rather than through processes of growth, and the large open areas and buildings, together with low population density, led to the "loss of human dimension" and the lack of urban vitality, variety, and attractiveness.[257] It was this layout that the competition rationale criticized, regarding its unfinished open plan as an economic, social, and physical void and an empty field of disjunction—an argument built on references to baroque and classicist urban

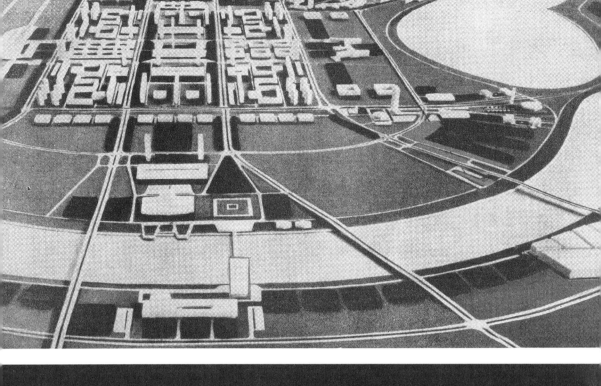
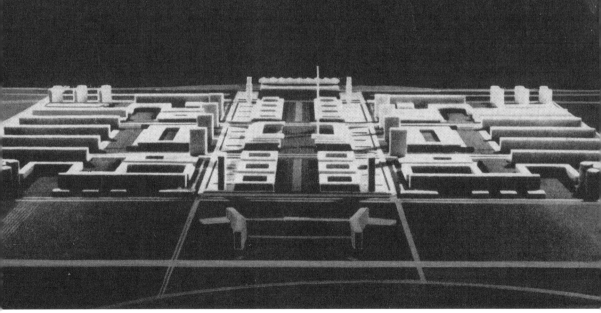

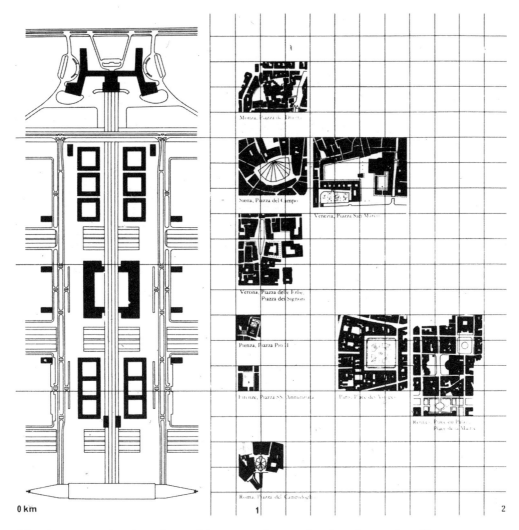

(above) "Comparative view of part of the center of New Belgrade and a number of important squares in the world": a critique of the design of New Belgrade published by Miloš Petrović in "A Study for the Restructuring of the Center of New Belgrade and the Sava Amphitheatre," which contributed to the theoretical basis for the rationale of the International Competition for the New Belgrade Urban Structure Improvement, 1986. Published in *Ekistics: The Problems and Science of Human Settlements* 52, no. 311 (1985): 223.

(opposite page top) Model of New Belgrade, 1960. Published in Siegel, "Novi Beograd," 140.

(opposite page bottom) Model of the New Belgrade Central Zone, 1960. From Siegel, "Novi Beograd," 141.

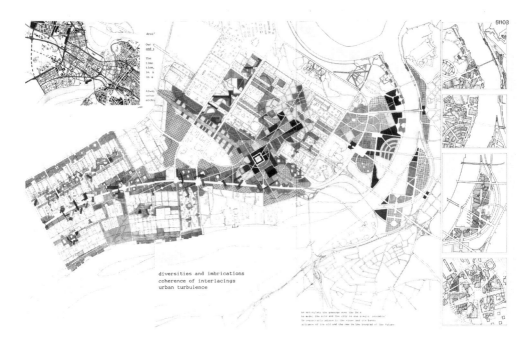

Pierre Guilbaud, Henri Lefebvre, and Serge Renaudie, entry in the International Competition for the New Belgrade Urban Structure Improvement, 1986. General master plan, traffic plan, and four exemplary situations of the urban design. Archive of Serge Renaudie. Courtesy of Serge Renaudie.

planning, without mention of the Yugoslavian sociopolitical context or the ambition to rethink the specificity of a socialist city.[258]

In contrast to the functionalist plan, but also in contrast to the increasingly dominant discourse of postmodern historicism, Guilbaud, Lefebvre, and Renaudie suggested joining New Belgrade with the old city center across the river Sava, linking its districts to one another, grouping and reassembling the neighborhoods, and creating nodes of urban intensity. The drawings submitted by the designers' team show an attempt to complicate the geometry of the orthogonal layout of the city by densifying the network of streets in one of the main axes of the urban ensemble and introducing new geometries (diagonal, circular, or curved). Patches of similar development were foreseen at the banks of the river, between New Belgrade and the old town.

These operations followed three design principles that expose an interference between Lefebvre's discourse and the research for urban complexity, increasingly prevalent in French urban planning since the mid-1970s. The first principle, diversity, aimed at a multiplication of possibilities of urban life and relationships between the individual and the community, stemming from the diversity and mixture of elements in the city: production units; management rules and urban practices; communication networks; activities, uses, rhythms, densities,

51103

droit à la ville

Our exploded cities must be deconstructed and reconstructed.

The city is a "combinatoire" open to time in which, at all levels of organisation, phenomena of communication, going in all directions, establish themselves in a complex structure.

Always more numerous possibilities of urban combinations permit unlimited architectural solutions.

Pierre Guilbaud, Henri Lefebvre, and Serge Renaudie, entry in the International Competition for the New Belgrade Urban Structure Improvement, 1986. The complex structure of the design aims to stimulate a multiplicity of urban phenomena. Archive of Serge Renaudie. Courtesy of Serge Renaudie.

and scales; modes of interaction and connection of elements; and dimensions of buildings. The second principle, that of overlap, involved combinations of different elements envisaged to stimulate interconnections, interactions, interferences, interpenetrations, encounters, coincidences, and conjunctions. The third principle, requiring "respect for specificities," returned to Lefebvre's critique of functionalist urbanism as a system of differences and stressed that the diversity of the city must be based on the specificity of its elements ("it is about encounter, not about connection"): each activity, function, group, and unit must be able to preserve its own identity. Aiming at a translation of these principles into an urban plan, the architects suggested introducing new types of buildings with complex programs mixing work and housing, covering selected traffic lines by extended bridges, implementing new modes of construction procedures involving public and private cooperatives, multiplying means of public transport, and reinforcing the existing centralities in each neighborhood rather than creating a new city center for New Belgrade.

These principles of diversity, overlap, and respect for specificities expressed the declared political goal of the project: it is through multiple urban experiences that a differentiated population reinforces its capacity of organization and self-management. However, this approach missed the tone of the competition rationale, which resulted in the project's exclusion in the first stage of the jury procedure; while Guilbaud, Lefebvre, and Renaudie agreed with the competition's critique of functionalist urbanism, the absence of political and social questions from its rationale contrasted with their embrace of "self-management," which makes Yugoslavia "one of the rare countries to be able to concretely pose the problematic of a *New Urban*."[259] As Ljiljana Blagojević noticed, the call for the "self-management of City, Space and Time," for the right to the city, and for urban citizenship that "presupposes a transformation of society according to a coherent project" was at odds with the apolitical stance of the competition outlines, which were based on the premise that "only the modern urban structure of New Belgrade needed improvement, and not the society."[260]

The political position of Guilbaud, Lefebvre, and Renaudie's contribution to the New Belgrade competition was inscribed into Lefebvre's long fascination with self-management understood as the possibility of the self-production of man within the community but beyond the state. This definition was modified in various moments of his intellectual career according to specific theoretical questions and political circumstances: in his fascination with Christian philosophy in the early 1930s; his anarchistic reading of Marx's theme of the withering of the state; and his persistent interest in historical precedents of communitary forms (the direct democracy of the Campan Valley and the Paris Commune). After he left the PCF, these interests continued in his engagement with the journal *Arguments,*

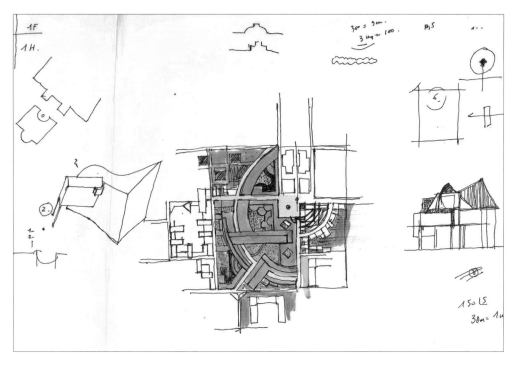

Serge Renaudie, sketch of new central area in New Belgrade, 1986. The new geometry is superimposed on the orthogonal grid of the city. Archive of Serge Renaudie. Courtesy of Serge Renaudie.

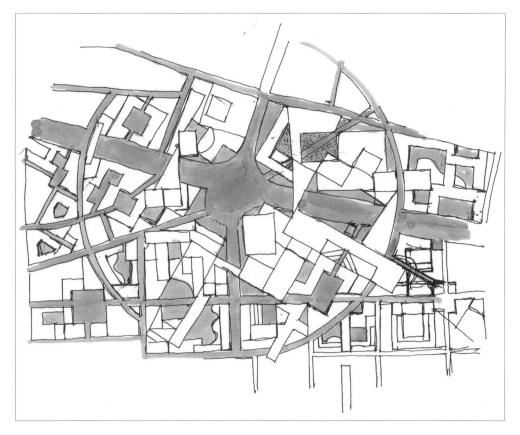

Serge Renaudie, sketch of the new central area in New Belgrade, 1986. Archive of Serge Renaudie. Courtesy of Serge Renaudie.

publishing on the Soviets, the workers' councils in socialist Hungary and Poland, and the self-organized students' syndicates; in his discussions of the Yugoslav experience; and in his theorizing of the rights of the citizen, in which he included the right to self-management.

French political debates between the 1960s and 1980s that questioned the possibility of radical democracy were a persistent context of Lefebvre's thinking of self-management: this term's embracement by the United Socialist Party (PSU) in the 1960s was followed by the embrace of the Socialist Party (PS) in the early 1970s, and the PCF tentatively adopted a politics of self-management in conjunction with its experiments with Eurocommunist ideology in the second half of the 1970s.[261] Lefebvre contributed to these discussions with his texts published in the journal *Autogestion* in the 1960s and during his rapprochement with the PCF in the 1980s. In a speech to its members (1982) he described the workers as exploited in three ways: as producers, as consumers, and as tenants; thus, the struggle for time and the struggle for space must imply a project that "unites the levels or dimensions too often separated: the architectural level . . . and the level of urbanism, that is to say, the organization of urban space; and, finally, the general organization of space, of transport; and the relations between centers and peripheries."[262] "Such a project necessarily has a political spirit," he added, calling for a direct democracy in the city linked to territorial self-management that would restructure the scalar relationships between the state and local decisions (committees of users, districts, and cities).[263]

In other words, the questions of space and the politics of scale were what allowed Lefebvre to specify his theory of self-management from the 1970s on. In an interview in 1976 he referred to the politicization of the production of space in France, Mexico, Yugoslavia, and Italy, claiming, "The problematics of self-management move more and more from the organization of enterprises to the organization of space."[264] Accordingly, in "Du pacte social au contrat de citoyenneté," he defined self-management as knowledge and control by a group—gathered in a company, a town, region, or country—over the conditions of its existence.[265] Consequently, if self-management is to be thought of as a political program rather than restricted to an exceptional and local intervention, we must take into account a variety of scales and think about the relationships among them. This conviction was expressed as early as 1966, in the paper "Henri Lefebvre ouvre le débat sur la théorie de l'autogestion" (Henri Lefebvre Opens the Debate on the Theory of Self-Management), in which he argued that, historically, the associations organized according to the principle of self-management were usually established in the "weak points" of the existing society. (In mid-1960s France, he speculated about these weak points as the university, the rural regions south of the Loire, the *grands ensembles,* and the public sector of the economy.)[266] But self-management as a political project requires an extension to other levels of social practice and an appropriation of the "strong points" of the society: the economic sphere and the state apparatus.[267] In light of this, self-management must be conceived as a struggle against both the state and the market, since an opposition to only one of them would give dominance to the other. On the one hand, the homogenizing centrality of the state cannot be exchanged for a series of dispersed units of individual producers, because this would imply the dominance of the market as the only possible medium of the relationship among these producers; on the other hand, the market cannot simply be rejected, because the sole power capable of such operation is the state itself.[268]

Self-management can be thus constituted only in a long-term process of overcoming both the state and the market. This is the role that Lefebvre envisaged for "democratic planning" operating on every scale of social reality, which he approximated with Yugoslavian planning in his writings from the 1960s. In the 1961 text "La planification démocratique" (Democratic Planning), he identified the main principles of such planning as decentralization, self-management, and a balance between the local plans and the general plan prescribing main decisions (the division of profit, investment policy, and trade relationships abroad). This text referred to the first phase of the Yugoslav system of workers' self-management and social self-government, institutionalized by the 1953 constitution, strengthened in the 1963 Economic Reform Constitution, and followed by a new understanding of planning as "a direct expression of production and socio-economic, as well as democratic relations of the self management socialist society."[269] Implemented since the mid-1950s, the self-managed planning process aimed at constant exchanges among institutions of the state, thus providing an analytical and technical background and suggesting broad social, economic, and environmental goals on the one hand and the negotiation of this planning by citizens assembled in organizations of associated labor and local communities on the other.[270] In these negotiations the self-managed enterprises and housing cooperatives became major actors, influential in the construction of New Belgrade but also decisive for the implementation of the 1961 Socialist General Plan of Zagreb, which aimed at integrating new cooperatives with the old city and the urban landscape and at reimagining the city as a network of interconnected urban nodes distributing housing, workplaces, shops, and social and cultural institutions.[271]

Yet it was already in this period that the contradictions within the Yugoslav system became apparent, including the ambiguous status of social ownership, which led to a conflict between holders of ownership rights and holders of management rights, and the dichotomy between formal participative decision-making processes and the informal hierarchical domination of the Communist Party.[272] Lefebvre was aware of these contradictions, having closely followed the changes in Yugoslavia over the course of the 1960s owing to his intense contacts with the Praxis philosophers. Since the mid-1960s the shift toward "market socialism" had included the acceptance of the allocative mechanisms of the market, an opening to Western commodities and financial markets, the decentralization of the banking system, and the deregulation of the prices of consumer goods.[273] Highly critical of these developments, Lefebvre doubted the possibility of the institutionalization of self-management, stressing that it "must continually be enacted."[274] Otherwise self-management is transformed into an instrument of the state and its attempt to appease contradictions, while *autogestion reveals contradictions in the State because it is the very trigger of those contradictions*," argued Lefebvre in the late 1970s.[275]

This long process of Lefebvre's fascination followed by his disenchantment with Yugoslav self-management suggests that what might have been at stake in the project submitted by him, Guilbaud, and Renaudie, at the time when the regime in Belgrade was steering away from the ideas of self-management, was something other than the naivety of an intellectual who still believed in Yugoslav socialism three years before the end of the Cold War. Declaring the failure of urbanism in both capitalist and socialist countries,[276] the text accompanying the project's competition entry was untimely but not anachronistic: it restored a utopian understanding of self-management. This utopian aspect comes to the fore in the text's suggestion, in the margin of the description of the design, that New Belgrade should be left behind as a ruin and started anew on the slopes of the nearby hills:

> The slabs and towers, increasingly abandoned, would become the ruins of another time, a museum in memory of a past era where individuals were not yet entitled to be citizens in full measure.[277]

This vision is strangely familiar today in view of the blocks in decay in New Belgrade, which, contrary to Lefebvre's hopes, was not relocated but displays phenomena specific to most postsocialist cities: segregation, gentrification, and the privatization of urban space.[278] In that sense, Lefebvre's call to leave New Belgrade behind can be read as a postsocialist "progressive nostalgia" that has the courage to address self-management not according to its historical reality but according to the ambitions and hopes it suscitated.[279] Such vision requires a return to Lefebvre's most general descriptions of self-management as "the effort of the people . . . to take initiative in the organization of everydayness, to appropriate their social life"[280]—wording that almost exactly repeats the definitions of many of his concepts, including that of socialism and new citizenship, and thus, as their common denominator, reveals the most persistent and universal understanding of Lefebvre's project.

Architecture and Universality

The account of Lefebvre's project reveals the highly ambiguous position architecture takes in his work. While in his readings of Fourier, Bofill, and Constant, architectures appear as epistemological objects facilitating research on the possibility of a differential space, the study on Nanterre seems to suggest that such space can be conceived only *in spite of* architecture: the production of a differential space was accounted for in this study as conditioned by a breakdown of the spatial organization of the campus. For many of those around Lefebvre, including his then-assistants Jean Baudrillard and Hubert Tonka, and an increasing number of French architects inspired by Manfredo Tafuri, such works as *The Explosion* confirm that society cannot be changed by means of architecture. "To imagine . . . that it is possible to act politically through urbanism, architecture, and the *détournement* of either is a dream," said Tonka in a 1971 interview.[281] This is why, commenting on the May '68 graffiti "objet, cache-toi" (object, hide yourself), at the staircase of the Sorbonne, the architect Jean Aubert, of the Utopie group, felt himself targeted as a producer of objects: "We were the object, obviously."[282] Contrary to Fourier's belief in changing society "by a mere reform of architectural practice," in the perspective of Tonka and others, architecture's reformism is necessarily oppressive: society can be changed only by a revolution, and revolution can happen only in spite of architecture.

Reform or revolution—this has been the dominant alternative dividing Left politics since the beginning of the last century, as suggested in Lenin's "What Is to Be Done?" (originally published 1902) and in the title of Rosa Luxemburg's pamphlet (1900), in which Fourier was mocked for the idea of "changing, by means of a system of phalansteries, the water of all the seas into tasty lemonade."[283] Yet the argument that radical social change cannot be achieved by means of reform did not prevent Luxemburg from seeing reform as a means of bettering the living conditions of the workers and strengthening their abilities to self-organize, thus preparing them for the decisive struggle. Similarly, Claude Schnaidt noticed: "It is impossible to prove that reformist urban practices or limited improvements of living conditions are all necessarily co-opted by the capitalist system and that they, consequently, avert a revolutionary transformation of the society." Continuing, Schnaidt clarified the reason for this: "To the extent that they make repressed needs come to the fore and allow a partial possibility of their satisfaction, they facilitate an awareness of those needs and contribute to the formation of a will to radical change among the masses."[284] In contrast, for Tafuri and his followers, architecture's reformism is essentially the opposite of radical social change: since any attempt at a critique developed from within architecture serves as a stimulus to advance capitalist planning, it is necessary to "avoid in every way the danger of entering into 'progressive' dialogue with the techniques for rationalizing the contradictions of capital."[285] Consequently, Luxemburg's alternative is to be identified with the one of Le Corbusier's from *Toward an Architecture*—"architecture or revolution"—in concluding that architecture must be avoided.[286]

Lefebvre refused to accept this alternative. In spite of his appreciation of the "skillful and intelligent pragmatism of the people concerned with reforms" and his fascination with the "revolutionary will," he wrote that both neglect the central aim of the gradual abolition of the state and thus lead to variants of state socialism, which can be countered only by means of self-management.[287] This argument was laid out in "La planification démocratique," in which he debunked the contradiction between reform and revolution: "This alleged antinomy has confused many problems and blocked many solutions," hindering the reformists from completing their reforms and pushing the revolutionaries to inefficiency.[288] This is why, he continued, "revolution appears to us today as a sum, or rather as a totalization of reforms," provided it is accompanied by stripping power and ownership of the means of production from the bourgeoisie as a class.[289] This complex and contradictory historical process is based, according to Lefebvre, on the increasingly social character of productive labor and the multiplicity of the networks of exchange and communication.[290]

In other words, Lefebvre's rejection of the contradiction between reform and revolution was founded on his conviction that the possibility of changing society as a whole must be sought within this very society. This was the guiding line of his readings of the unitary architecture of Fourier and his suggestion of reforms that aimed at shattering the capitalist society by turning its most powerful desires against this society itself. (The publication of such a subversive project required bypassing censors of the Restoration, and with this objective in mind Fourier filled his books with ideas inspired by early nineteenth-century advertisements, including stories about copulating planets and seas of lemonade, a strategy that was more successful in diverting attention from the political significance of his writings than he might have hoped for.) Also, in the Nanterre study, the processes of gathering and dispersion—considered the specific performance of architecture within an urban whole—were examined as an explosive production of differential space that subverts the spatial scheme aimed at the reproduction of social relationships. A similar intuition was the common denominator of Lefebvre's reading of New Babylon, called by Constant "realizable from the technical perspective, . . . desirable from a human perspective, and . . . indispensable from a social perspective,"[291] and of the City in Space conveying Bofill's attempt at a "feasible" utopia, a path between "utopia and reality, dream and compromise."[292] While the disjunction between the paths of Constant and Bofill—the former withdrawing from architecture and the latter jumping on the bandwagon of French state urbanism—can be seen as symptomatic of the dichotomy between reform and revolution becoming dominant in architectural culture from the 1970s on, Lefebvre's persistence to pursue a different path stemmed from his research on the tendencies that emerge within postwar abstract space but that point to a different type of space: the socialization of labor; the reclamation of the new rights, such as new citizenship; and the generalization of the processes of the production of space.

In this sense, the concept of the production of space, which was discussed in the previous chapters of this book as a way to account for the practices of dwelling in the *pavillon;* a way to theorize the relationships among moments of space within its unitary theory; and a way to historicize the development of capitalism, is to be understood as a project. In a 1972 interview published in the journal *Actuel,* after repeating his argument that the architectural avant-gardes of the early twentieth century discovered the possibility of producing space rather than isolated objects in space, Lefebvre claimed, "It is necessary to rationalize this intuition and introduce the concept of the *production of space* as a fundamental concept."[293] Notwithstanding his critique of spaces produced by the avant-gardes as oculocentric and phallic, he stressed the progressive potential of their rediscovery of space—as opposed to land, land rent, and ownership structures inherited from history—symbolically expressed in a range of architectural forms, from Le Corbusier's houses on *pilotis* to Yona Friedman's cities in space. With the development of productive forces "men could come to terms with new forms of the production of space and control them rather than getting locked in the repetition of mass social housing and motorways."[294] This is why the dominant production of space does not conceal the possibility of a different development but reveals it:

> The possibilities are sketched by means of the dominant process: the overcoming of private and public, of the monument and the building, of the conflict between space and the society, this vision of a space conceived, perceived, and globally realized, linked to the lived and the universal.[295]

The project of Lefebvre is not to be limited to the interstices between the dominant social practices of producing space but rather becomes manifested in their universality. This aspiration to a universal dimension allows recognition of what is shared by particular struggles and singular events, which, in reverse, give specific meaning to universal claims. This figure was the guiding line of Lefebvre's reading of the everyday in the *pavillon* as conditioned by the collective dream of surpassing this very everyday but also the guiding line of his readings of architectural projects: New Babylon aiming at a global scale, City in Space projecting an endless urban tissue, the Fourierist city with its unlimited combinations of all possible differences, and even Nanterre, where differences are condensed and generalized. In these readings, the production of space at every scale of social reality becomes both the main challenge and the main promise of modernity: not yet an architectural project, but a condition of its possibility.

Afterword
Toward an Architecture of *Jouissance*

ONLY A FEW MONTHS before finishing this book, I found, in a private archive, Henri Lefebvre's unpublished manuscript with the title "Vers une architecture de la jouissance" (Toward an Architecture of *Jouissance*). The history of this 225-page manuscript requires additional study; what is clear by now is that it was commissioned and written within the framework of a larger research project in 1973, thus one year before the publication of *The Production of Space,* but never published, since the head of the project considered it unsuitable for the project's purpose.

The manuscript is divided into twelve chapters. It begins with identifying architecture as its main research object and proceeds to discuss a range of themes, with special focus on the relationships between buildings and monuments in the first chapter; the questions of power, revolution, and subversion in chapter 2; and the discussion of the body and the relationship among *jouissance,* pleasure, desire, and pain in chapter 3. At this point the focus of the manuscript extends from a specific investigation of architecture to a more general research on spaces of *jousissance,* and in chapter 4 Lefebvre refutes several possible objections to this change of perspective. Chapters 5 through 11 discuss the contribution of various disciplines to the research on the space of *jouissance,* among them architecture. Finally, in chapter 12, Lefebvre discusses architecture as a specific level of social practice, that of image, immediacy, and the irreducible, but also the level on which the possibilities of everyday life emerge, and thus the proper level on which new projects are conceived.

It is not possible here to provide a fair account of this rich text, full of architectural examples, discussions with authors that extend the set of references known from other works of Lefebvre, accounts of his personal memories, and links to the theory of the production of space and to the architectural discourse and practice of the early 1970s. The manuscript can be read as an initiation of research on architecture by means of Lefebvre's theory, and it suggests that such research should be developed according to five postulates: first, the assumption of the relative autonomy of architecture in respect to other social practices; and yet examined, second, as a social practice in relationship to others; third, a special attention to the practices of the body; fourth, an application of transdisciplinary concepts that, fifth and finally, allow for a contextualization of research in architecture within a broad transdisciplinary study of social space.

Only if we think of architecture within the general transformations of society, labor, and the everyday, but in relative autonomy from them, can the "forgotten, erased place of architectural work . . . be defined," writes Lefebvre.[1] Instead of condemning the architectural object as an effect and instrument of overwhelming social forces and "rather than repeating that nothing can be done because of capitalism, which commands and co-opts,"[2] he encourages us to think of architecture as irreducible to the mode of production, state, and social relations: Lefebvre suggests a dialectical understanding of the conflict between a specifically architectural imagination and the forces aimed at instrumentalizing it.

This dialectics reaffirms the double perspective in Lefebvre's research on architecture discussed in this book: architecture as a practice of the architect interacting with other actors within the general division of labor, and architecture as a means of addressing the practices of dwelling that mediate between the times and scales of urban society. Architecture as understood from these perspectives opens the way toward a concrete utopia that, in contrast to scenarios of unhindered growth, "is negative":

> It takes as a strategic hypothesis the negation of the everyday, of labor, of the economy of exchange, etc. It also negates the sphere of the state [*l'étatique*] and the primacy of the political. It takes *jouissance* as its starting point and aims at a concept of new space, one that can be based only on an architectural project.[3]

This project must depart from the body—the individual body and the social body—and counter its fragmentation in the division of labor and its identification with a spectacular image referring to other images. From within this negation Lefebvre envisages an architecture as a spatial "pedagogy" of the body and its rhythms: an architecture of *jouissance* understood as a formation of senses.

Jouissance is thus a transdisciplinary concept that cannot be confined to a particular discipline, but it requires a contribution from every one of them; in that sense it joins the family of concepts that have been discussed in this book, including those of production, dwelling, centrality, and space itself. Lefebvre argues for multidisciplinary research on the places of *jouissance,* which would include the contributions of philosophy, anthropology, history, psychology and psychoanalysis, semantics and semiology, and economy. Among these disciplines, architecture is endowed with the task of accounting for the historical experience of places of *jouissance,* from the Roman thermae, through the Gupta shrines and Renaissance urban spaces, to the designs by Ledoux and Fourier—a vision of architectural research that the forthcoming publication of "Vers une architecture de la jouissance" will bring into debate.

□□□ **Acknowledgments**

Writing this book involved a lot of talking, and I am grateful for all the conversations that this book occasioned and was sometimes a pretext for. I thank the former students, friends, collaborators, colleagues, and companions of Henri Lefebvre, including Nicole Beaurain, Ricardo Bofill, Philippe Boudon, Maïté Clavel, Monique Coornaert, Dan Ferrand-Beshmann, Jean-Pierre Frey, Mario Gaviria, Rémi Hess, Michèle Jolé, Jean-Pierre Lefebvre, Thierry Paquot, Anne Querrien, Henri Raymond, Catherine Régulier, and Serge Renaudie. I greatly benefited from interviews I was granted by them, their knowledge of Lefebvre's life and work, and access to private archives. This book owes a lot to conversations with Ljiljana Blagojević, M. Christine Boyer, Neil Brenner, Grègory Busquet, Jean-Louis Cohen, Laurent Devisme, Jean-Pierre Garnier, Michael Hays, Patrick Healy, Edward Soja, and Jean-Louis Violeau.

I particularly appreciate two people without whom this publication would have been impossible: Ákos Moravánszky and Christian Schmid, of the Swiss Federal Institute of Technology (ETH) in Zurich. Since my grant at the ETH in 2003–4, when the research resulting in this book was initiated, through the work on my dissertation, to my current research at the chair of architecture theory at ETH Zurich, I have been discussing my work with them and enjoying their persistent and invaluable support and encouragement.

This book was developed from my dissertation, defended at the Faculty of Architecture, Delft University of Technology, and supervised by Arie Graafland, whose comments, criticism, and endorsement were always helpful for my work.

I also thank the institutions that assisted me in this research during the past six years. My position at the Faculty of Architecture at the Delft University of Technology allowed me to develop my dissertation, and the travel grants I received from this university were indispensable for my research in Paris between 2005 and 2007. This work was initiated at ETH Zurich with the support of the Swiss National Science Foundation. My gratitude also goes to the Fonds voor beeldende kunsten, vormgeving en bouwkunst, which funded my research at the Institut d'Urbanisme de Paris in 2008, and to the scholars at the *institut,* including Laurent Coudroy de Lille, Thierry Paquot, Stéphane Tonnelat, and in particular Michèle Jolé, for their hospitality and assistance. Much of the research for this book was completed during my fellowship at the Jan van Eyck Academie in Maastricht (2008–9); my work greatly benefited from discussions at the *academie,* especially from the seminar "After 1968," headed by Katja Diefenbach.

Henri Lefebvre on Space is significantly indebted to two conferences focused on the work of Henri Lefebvre, urban research, and design—"Rethinking Theory, Space, and Production: Henri Lefebvre Today" (2008) and "Urban Research and Architecture: Beyond Henri Lefebvre" (2009)—which were organized by Ákos Moravánszky, Christian Schmid, and myself at ETH Zurich, the Delft University of Technology, and the Jan van Eyck Academie, with the support of these three institutions as well as that of the Swiss Federal Scientific Foundation and the Brupbacher Fonds. Some ideas in this publication were developed during seminars at the Berlage Institute in Rotterdam and sharpened in conversations with Pier-Vittorio Aureli, Vedran Mimica, Miguel Robles-Durán, and Roemer van Toorn.

My research on the theory of Henri Lefebvre was presented during seminars and conferences at various institutions, including the Amsterdam School for Cultural Analysis, Amsterdam University; Berlage Institute, Rotterdam; Center for Interdisciplinary Research, University of Bielefeld; Center for Metropolitan Studies, Berlin University of Technology; Central European University, Budapest; Delft University of Technology; École Normale Supérieure—Lettres et Sciences Humaines, Lyon; Fordham University, New York; Graduate School of Visual Art and Design, Utrecht; Institut d'Urbanisme de Paris; Jan van Eyck Academie, Maastricht; Massachusetts Institute of Technology, Cambridge, Massachusetts; Södertörn University College, Stockholm; Université Paris 8, Saint-Denis; Swiss Federal Institute of Technology, Zurich; and Warsaw Museum of Modern Art. I thank the participants of these events for their comments and criticism.

Elke Beyer, Neil Brenner, Katja Diefenbach, Michael Hays, Rémi Hess, Mark Jarzombek, Tahl Kaminer, Ákos Moravánszky, Christian Schmid, and Laurent Stalder read the manuscript or its parts at various stages, and I greatly benefited from their comments.

At the origins of this theoretical and historical book lies empirical research on the contemporary practices of architecture and urban space in Nowa Huta, a new town constructed since the late 1940s by the socialist regime in southeastern Poland. This earlier study allowed me to formulate many of the questions raised in this book, and I extend my thanks to scholars who assisted me during my research on Nowa Huta, including Ewa Kuryłowicz, Jadwiga Sławińska, and Piotr Winskowski, as well as the Collegium Invisibile, Warsaw, which granted me a research fellowship (2001–2).

□□□ Notes

INTRODUCTION

1. Chombart de Lauwe, *Un anthropologue dans le siècle,* 94–95; see also Violeau, *Situations construites,* 123. Unless otherwise noted, all English translations from foreign-language sources are my own.

2. Pflieger, *De la ville aux réseaux,* 71–72.

3. In his recent book, Pierre Macherey deplored Lefebvre's effort "to comprehend and to order, which never arrives at a full clarification of the confusion and which, with an eye on masking this incompletion, sails away and opens new territories of analysis, abandoning fields incompletely cultivated." Macherey, *Petits riens,* 287. For a philosophical reading of Lefebvre, see also Müller-Schöll, *Das System und der Rest*—or, rather, for a reading of a "philosophy in the course of its overcoming *(Aufhebung)*"; Müller-Schöll, *Das System und der Rest,* 8.

4. Blanchot, "Marx's Three Voices," in *Friendship,* 98–100.

5. Grawitz and Pinto, *Méthodes des sciences sociales,* 1:448.

6. Lefebvre, *The Production of Space* (1974). The focus on the relevance of Lefebvre's work for urban empirical research and urban design was at the center of two conferences: "Rethinking Theory, Space and Production: Henri Lefebvre Today" (Delft University of Technology, 11–13 November 2008); and "Urban Research and Architecture: Beyond Henri Lefebvre" (ETH Zurich, 24–26 November 2009); www.henrilefebvre.org.

7. See Foucault, *Security, Territory, Population;* Foucault, *The Birth of Biopolitics.*

8. Tafuri, *Architecture and Utopia.*

9. Avermaete, *Another Modern;* Mumford, *The CIAM Discourse on Urbanism;* Woud, ed., *Het nieuwe bouwen internationaal.*

10. See the "CIAM grid" published in *Programme du 7ième congrès CIAM;* Avermaete, *Another Modern,* 63ff.; and Mumford, *The CIAM Discourse on Urbanism.*

11. Avermaete, *Another Modern;* Heuvel and Risselada, eds., *Team 10, 1953–81;* St. John Wilson, *The Other Tradition of Modern Architecture.* See also Solà-Morales, "Another Modern Tradition."

12. Lefebvre, "Evolution or Revolution," 249. See also Elders, *Internationaal Filosofen-projekt;* and the Dutch documentary *Het Internationaal Filosofen Projekt: Arne Naess, Leszek Kołakowski, Henri Lefebvre, Freddy Ayer,* directed by Louis van Gasteren (1971), NOS.

13. Prigge, "Urbi et Orbi—zur Epistemologie des Städtischen"; Diener et al., *Switzerland.*

14. Kipfer et al., "On the Production of Henri Lefebvre"; Kipfer et al., "Globalizing Lefebvre?"; Brenner and Elden, "Introduction: State, Space, World."

15. Lefebvre, *Critique of Everyday Life,* 2:118. When quoting from any published English translation, I have adopted that version of the work rather than presenting my own translation of the original, unless otherwise stated.

16. Kipfer et al., "Globalizing Lefebvre?"

17. See the prefaces by Michel Trebitsch to Henri Lefebvre's *Critique of Everyday Life* and to reprints of Lefebvre's books, including *Le nationalisme contre les nations;* and *Frédéric Nietzsche.*

18. See also Gottdiener, *The Social Production of Urban Space;* Gregory, *Geographical Imaginations;* Hess, *Henri Lefebvre et la pensée du possible;* Kipfer and Milgrom, "Henri Lefebvre"; Kleinspehn, *Der verdrängte Alltag;* Meyer, *Henri Lefebvre;* Meyer, *Von der Stadt zur urbanen Gesellschaft;* Prigge, "Urbi et Orbi"; Prigge, *Peripherie ist überall;* and Prigge, "Die Revolution der Städte lesen."

19. Kipfer et al., "On the Production of Henri Lefebvre." See also Harvey, *Social Justice and the City;* Harvey, *The Urbanization of Capital;* Harvey, *The Urban Experience;* Soja, *Postmodern Geographies;* Soja, *Thirdspace;* Soja, *Postmetropolis.* See also Elden, "Politics, Philosophy, Geography"; Schmid, *Stadt, Raum und Gesellschaft.*

20. What is particularly missing is an account of the readings of Lefebvre's work in Latin America, especially in Brazil, where Lefebvre's theory was introduced by the sociologist José de Souza Martins. For many years Martins taught a seminar at the Faculty of Philosophy and Humanities at the University of São Paulo that focused on the methodological questions in Marx and Lefebvre; the papers of some contributors were published in Martins, ed., *Henri Lefebvre e o retorno da dialética.* Together with his lectures on the sociology of everyday life, this seminar influenced a range of empirical studies with special attention to São Paulo. Complementing the empirical work of Martins himself, these studies included books by Ana Cristina Arantes Nasser, Ana Fani Alessandri Carlos, Amelia Luisa Damiani, Odette Carvalho de Lima Seabra, Marilia Pontes Sposito, and Fraya Frehse. Martins himself published several books influenced by the theory of Lefebvre, in particular three books on the suburb of São Paulo: *Subúrbio; A sociabilidade do homem simples;* and *A aparição do demônio na fábrica.* I would like to thank Fraya Frehse and José de Souza Martins for making this information available to me. For the application of Lefebvre's theory to an analysis of processes of urbanization in Latin America, Southeast Asia, and the Middle East, see also the contributions to the

conferences "Rethinking Theory, Space and Production: Henri Lefebvre Today" and "Urban Research and Architecture: Beyond Henri Lefebvre" (see n. 6).

1. HENRI LEFEBVRE

1. Bidet and Kouvelakis, eds., *Critical Companion to Contemporary Marxism.*

2. See Rafatdjou and Sangla, "Henri Lefebvre," 26. This issue of *Société française* is devoted to the work of Lefebvre.

3. Combes and Latour, *Conversation avec Henri Lefebvre.*

4. Boltanski and Chiapello, *The New Spirit of Capitalism,* 326.

5. Garnier, "La vision urbaine de Henri Lefebvre," 131.

6. See Lane, *Pierre Bourdieu,* 35.

7. Busquet, "Idéologie urbaine et pensée politique dans la France de la période 1958–1981," 103.

8. See Brenner and Elden, "Introduction: State, Space, World," 31ff.

9. Hess, *Henri Lefebvre et l'aventure du siècle ;* Shields, *Lefebvre, Love and Struggle;* Ganas, *Henri Lefebvre (1901–1991).*

10. See Burkhard, *French Marxism between the Wars;* Marx, "Travail et propriété privée"; Marx, "Notes sur les besoins, la production et la division du travail"; Marx, *Morceaux choisis;* Elden, *Understanding Henri Lefebvre,* 15ff.; Tosel, "Henri Lefebvre ou le philosophe vigilant (1936–1946)."

11. See Hess, *Henri Lefebvre,* 51ff.

12. Ibid., 85. Hess writes that Lefebvre, unable to find a publisher in France, sent these investigations to the Soviet Union, and only later did he find them published— without the name of the author—in *Pravda* (ibid.). See also Lefebvre, *Henri Lefebvre: La ville/À voix nue.*

13. The trade union was the Communist-dominated Confédération générale du travail unitaire; see Lefebvre, "La structure sociale de l'Ardèche"; and Lethierry, *Penser avec Henri Lefebvre,* 114; see also Pierre, *La Drôme et l'Ardèche entre deux guerres 1920–1939,* 132. On the period in Privas, see the interview with Lefebvre, *Henri Lefebvre, philosophe.*

14. Lefebvre, "La structure sociale de l'Ardèche," 8–9.

15. Lethierry, *Penser avec Henri Lefebvre,* 115.

16. Henri Lefebvre, "Curriculum Vitae," October 1943, dossier: Henri Lefebvre, archives of the Musée des arts et traditions populaires (MNATP, Paris).

17. See Ockman, "Lessons from Objects"; and Lebovics, *True France.*

18. Albert Soboul to Henri Lefebvre, 9 December 1943, dossier: Henri Lefebvre, archives MNATP.

19. Lefebvre, "Curriculum Vitae," archives MNATP; see also Hess, *Henri Lefebvre,* 114–16.

20. Lebovics, *True France,* 177; Rivière, "Recherches et Musées d'ethnographie française depuis 1939"; Rivière, "Le chantier 1425." See also Boëll et al., eds., *Du folklore à l'ethnologie.*

21. Lebovics, *True France,* 177–78; see also dossier: chantier 1810, archives MNATP.

22. Henri Lefebvre to Georges-Henri Rivière, 11 May 1944, dossier: Henri Lefebvre, archives MNATP.

23. Ibid.

24. See Bidart et al., *Pays aquitains.*

25. Georges-Henri Rivière was engaged in this debate in many ways, lecturing and publishing on rural architecture. For example, he discussed the concept of a "rural museum" at the 1937 CIAM Logis et loisirs congress; he organized the International Congress of Folklore at which architecture was extensively discussed; he attended at least two meetings of ASCORAL (Assemblée de constructeurs pour une rénovation architecturale); and he defended the theory of the necessity of a renewal of rural architecture by means of rationalization, standardization, and scientific planning. See Rivière, "Musée rural—musée de terroir"; Rivière, "Formes"; and Ockman, "Lessons from Objects," 168–69.

26. Henri Lefebvre to Georges-Henri Rivière, 23 January 1944, dossier: Henri Lefebvre, archives MNATP.

27. Henri Lefebvre, "Première thèse: Plan: Campan: Historie d'une communauté pastorale pyrénéenne," received on 15 May 1944, dossier: Henri Lefebvre, archives MNATP.

28. Henri Lefebvre, "Rapport d'activité (juillet–août 1945)," dossier: Henri Lefebvre, archives MNATP.

29. Henri Lefebvre, "Centre 1810: Travaux effectués par M. H. Lefebvre," October 1945, dossier: Henri Lefebvre, archives MNATP.

30. Henri Lefebvre to Georges-Henri Rivière, 2 July 1946, dossier: Henri Lefebvre, archives MNATP.

31. Trebitsch, "Preface: The Moment of Radical Critique," xiiff.

32. Lefebvre, "Les communautés paysannes pyrénéennes," 484.

33. Ibid.; Lefebvre, "Une république pastorale"; Lefebvre, *La vallée de Campan.* Some of the ideas are included in Lefebvre's book *Pyrénées;* for a reading of the two later publications, see Berdoulay and Entrikin, "The Pyrenees as Place."

34. See Treanton, "Les premières années du Centre d'études sociologiques (1946–1955)."

35. Trebitsch, preface in Lefebvre, *Critique of Everyday Life,* xxv–xxvi; Gauchet, "Changement de paradigme dans les sciences sociales."

36. Treanton, "Les premières années du Centre d'études sociologiques."

37. Chombart de Lauwe, *Paris et l'agglomération parisienne;* Chombart de Lauwe, *La vie quotidienne des familles ouvrières;* Chombart de Lauwe, *Famille et habitation;* Chombart de Lauwe, *Paris, essais de sociologie 1952–1964.*

38. They included Bordeaux, Maubeuge, Paris, Rouen, and Saint-Etienne. See Cupers, "Concerning the User."

39. Chombart de Lauwe, *Famille et habitation,* 1:16; Chombart de Lauwe, *Des hommes et des villes.*

40. See Chombart de Lauwe, *Un anthropologue dans le siècle,* 94–95.

41. See Gombin, "French Leftism"; and Delannoi, "Arguments, 1956–1962, ou la parenthèse de l'ouverture."

42. See Trebitsch, preface in Lefebvre, *Critique of Everyday Life,* vol. 1; and Treanton, "Les premières années du Centre d'études sociologiques." For a discussion about the influence of the thesis of the production of space on French geography, see Claval, *Histoire de la géographie française de 1870 à nos jours.*

43. Lefebvre, "Marxisme et sociologie."

44. Lefebvre invited to the Group of Rural Sociology the best specialists in that discipline in France, including Daniel Halévy, Michel Cépède, Louis Chevalier, and René Dumont; see Trebitsch, "Preface: The Moment of Radical Critique," xiii.

45. See the annual programs of the CES, dossier no. 0019780305, Archives nationales.

46. Hess, *Henri Lefebvre et l'aventure du siècle,* 166; Lefebvre, *Le temps des méprises,* 221; Lefebvre, "An Interview with Henri Lefebvre," 32; "Table et index pour l'année 1950"; dossier no. 0019780305, Archives nationales.

47. Henri Lefebvre to Norbert Guterman, 2 December, year unidentified, box: Henri Lefebvre 1939–49, Norbert Guterman Archive, Butler Library, Columbia University New York.

48. Hess, *Henri Lefebvre et l'aventure du siècle,* 169.

49. See Gurvitch, ed., *Industrialisation et technocratie;* Friedmann, ed., *Villes et campagnes;* and *Sociologie comparée de la famille contemporaine.*

50. See the materials on the activities of the CES in the late 1940s and 1950s, dossier no. 0019780305, Archives nationales.

51. Lefebvre, *Le temps des méprises,* 218–19.

52. On Lefebvre's research in rural sociology, see Lefebvre, "Théorie de la rente foncière et sociologie rurale," in *Du rural à l'urbain,* 79–87; on Halbwachs concept, see Jaisson, "Temps et espace chez Maurice Halbwachs (1925–1945)."

53. Lefebvre, "Henri Lefebvre ou le fil du siècle."

54. See Roberts, "Philosophizing the Everyday."

55. Lefebvre, *Critique of Everyday Life,* 3:18–19.

56. For an account of Lefebvre's critique of everyday life, see Gardiner, *Critiques of Everyday Life;* Highmore, *Everyday Life and Cultural Theory;* and Sheringham, *Everyday Life.*

57. Macherey, *Petits riens,* 295.

58. Lefebvre, "Entretien avec Henri Lefebvre," 6.

59. Lefebvre, *Le temps des méprises,* 222.

60. Henri Raymond, interview with the author, Paris, autumn 2007; see Lefebvre, "Les nouveaux ensembles urbains."

61. See the program of the Centre d'études sociologiques for the academic year 1957–58, dossier no. 0019780305, Archives nationales.

62. Lefebvre, *Du rural à l'urbain*.

63. Among other notable seminars was one focused on "urban growth, spontaneous phenomena, and problems of planning," organized by the Association des travailleurs scientifiques, in which Lefebvre took part together with about sixty other participants, including sociologists, geographers, urbanists, historians, statisticians, and demographers; see P. G., "Formes de croissance des villes."

64. See Raymond, "Urbanisation et changement social"; Friedmann, ed., *Villes et campagnes;* Lefebvre, discussion, "Structures familiales comparées." See also Lefebvre, "La communauté villageoise."

65. Clavel, *Sociologie de l'urbain,* 14; Chombart de Lauwe, *Paris et l'agglomération parisienne;* Chombart de Lauwe, *Paris, essais de sociologie 1952–1964;* Chevalier, "Le problème de la sociologie des villes."

66. Laude, "Le Centre d'études sociologiques en 1959," 407.

67. Debord's talk in the group was published in *Internationale situationniste* 6 (1961); see Debord, "Perspectives for Conscious Changes in Everyday Life"; see also Lefebvre, *Le temps des méprises,* 109–10.

68. Bellos, *Georges Perec,* 254–56.

69. Hess, *Lefebvre et l'aventure du siècle,* 177.

70. See Editors of *Fortune* magazine, eds., *The Exploding Metropolis;* and Jacobs, *The Death and Life of Great American Cities.* For the French discussions, see the conversation between Roger Vailland and Shadrach Woods published as Vailland and Woods, "Retour à la sauvagerie," which voiced many concerns developed in Lefebvre's 1968 *The Right to the City,* including the blurring of the city and the countryside, the crisis of the city center and of monuments, and the isolation, atomization, and privatization of urban everyday life under the influence of the car and new communication technologies. See Lefebvre, *The Right to the City.* See also Schmid, *Stadt, Raum und Gesellschaft,* 125ff.

71. Raymond et al., *Architecture, urbanistique et société,* 27. See also Frey and Raymond, *Paroles d'un sociologue,* 81; and Institut de sociologie urbaine, "Organisation urbaine et comportements sociaux."

72. See Hirsch, *Oublier Cergy . . . ,* 32, 289. In particular, Coornaert recalls a meeting between Lefebvre and Michel Picard, the collaborator of Paul Delouvrier—the head of the district de la Région de Paris (interview with Monique Coornaert, Paris, autumn 2007).

73. This double focus on the material structures and the ways of life was expressed in the title of one research report sent to the district: Institut de sociologie urbaine, "Organisation urbaine et comportements sociaux"; see also Institut de sociologie urbaine, *Choisy-le-Roi.* The studies by Coornaert resulted in a series of unpublished

research reports (including "Études sur la mobilité" written with A. Antunes, 1965); an article, "Ville et quartier"; and the ISU study *Le quartier et la ville,* which focused on four suburbs of Paris: Argenteuil, Choisy-le-Roi, Suresnes, and Vitry-sur-Seine; see Coornaert et al., *Le quartier et la ville.*

74. Monique Coornaert to Łukasz Stanek, letter from 2 November 2007. Initially, Lefebvre was appointed as the president of the ISU, Coornaert was the vice-president, Nicole Haumont was the treasurer, and Antoine Haumont and Henri Raymond were the members (interview with Monique Coornaert); see also letter from Henri Lefebvre to the members of the ISU, 29 January 1964, private archive of Monique Coornaert, Paris.

75. See also Paquot, *Un anthropologue dans le siècle,* 195.

76. See Coquery, "L'urbanisation française."

77. Lefebvre, *Critique of Everyday Life,* 1:42 ff.

78. Frey and Raymond, *Paroles d'un sociologue,* 86–87.

79. Interview with Henri Raymond, Paris, autumn 2007.

80. See Raymond, *Une méthode de dépouillement et d'analyse de contenu appliquée aux entretiens non directifs;* Raymond, "Analyse de contenu et entretien non directif"; and Raymond, *Paroles d'habitants.*

81. Frey and Raymond, *Paroles d'un sociologue,* 88; Jolé, "Henri Lefebvre à Strasbourg," 42.

82. The last credit is contentious: Raymond claimed that the book was authored by the whole team, and Nicole Haumont signed it in order to support her thesis, defended at that time (Frey and Raymond, *Paroles d'un sociologue,* 88).

83. Frey and Raymond, *Paroles d'un sociologue,* 88; interview with Henri Raymond; interview with Maïté Clavel, Paris, summer 2007. See also Clavel, "Henri Lefebvre."

84. Jolé, "Henri Lefebvre à Strasbourg," 40; interview with Nicole Beaurain, Paris, autumn 2007.

85. Interview with Rémi Hess, Paris, autumn 2007.

86. Jolé, "Henri Lefebvre à Strasbourg," 40. In Ulm, Moles taught courses in cybernetics, "social dynamics of culture," and "development of concepts"; see "Entwicklung des Lehrprogramms der Hochschule für Gestaltung."

87. Interview with Nicole Beaurain. In his interview with me, Henri Raymond emphasized the importance of the conversations with Abraham Moles to Lefebvre, an influence that reverberates in several of his books from the mid-1960s, including *Le langage et la societé* and *Position.* Moles attempted to apply to social analysis the concepts derived from electronics, telecommunication, system theory, and cybernetics, combining them with the phenomenology of Heidegger and Bachelard, for example, in Moles and Rohmer, *Psychologie de l'espace.* Raymond said that Moles and Lefebvre shared not only the ambition to develop a multidisciplinary research on space but also a general intellectual attitude: "People like Abraham Moles and Lefebvre do not belong to an institution. OK, the institution accommodates them, but it's not their thing. . . . The institution is not their problem. What they were concerned with was something very

different; it was about living with ideas, about having a good time with ideas, to live with a certain fantasy. . . . Everything in their lives was entirely orientated towards encounters, towards strokes of luck; and Lefebvre experienced this very well when he met the situationists" (interview with Henri Raymond, Paris, autumn 2007).

88. See Jolé, "La sociologie urbaine à Strasbourg avec Henri Lefebvre"; Ross, "Henri Lefebvre on the Situationist International"; and "Hans Ulrich Obrist in Conversation with Raoul Vaneigem."

89. Interview with Maïté Clavel; see also Lefebvre, *Le temps des méprises,* 243–44.

90. Lefebvre, "Entretien avec Henri Lefebvre," 7.

91. Jolé, "Henri Lefebvre à Strasbourg," 40–41.

92. Ibid. See also Lefebvre, "Bistrot-club."

93. Jolé, "Henri Lefebvre à Strasbourg," 41–42.

94. See Clerc, ed., *Grands ensembles, banlieues nouvelles.*

95. Quoted in Jolé, "Henri Lefebvre à Strasbourg," 43. See Dissard and Trystram, eds., *Sociologie et urbanisme,* vol. 1: *Essai de synthèse et notes de sociologie,* and vol. 2: *Méthodologie et bibliographie;* and Trystram, ed., *Sociologie et développement urbain,* vol. 1: *Introduction, Aix-en-Provence, Le Havre, Toulouse,* and vol. 2: *Bordeaux, Lille, Rennes, Strasbourg;* the latter includes the contribution of Lefebvre's team on Strasbourg (409–58). See also issue no. 93 of the journal *Urbanisme* (1966), with the articles of Dissard and Trystram and contributions on Aix-en-Provence, Le Havre, and Toulouse.

96. Jolé, "Henri Lefebvre à Strasbourg"; Jolé, "La sociologie urbaine"; see also Ledrut, *L'éspace social de la ville;* Ledrut, "The Social Space of a Town"; and Duvignaud, "Ledrut, l'espace, la ville."

97. Interview with Michèle Jolé, Paris, summer 2008.

98. See Raymond, "Habitat, modèles culturels et architecture."

99. Trystram, ed., *Fondation Royaumont pour le progrès des sciences de l'homme.*

100. Chevalier, *Sociologie critique de la politique de la ville,* 66 ff.

101. Thoenig, *L'ère des technocrates.*

102. Lefebvre, "An interview with Henri Lefebvre," 28–29. See Bodiguel, "La DATAR." See also Desportes and Picon, *De l'espace au territoire.*

103. Chevalier, *Sociologie critique,* 71.

104. Ibid., 80 ff. Among the attempts of this reorientation of French planning was the program "métropole d'équilibre," launched by DATAR. In order to accommodate the migration of the rural population and to slow down the growth of Paris, eight cities were selected in 1964 as the future "balanced metropolises": Lyon, Marseille, Lille, Toulouse, Bordeaux, Strasbourg, Nancy, and Nantes. Between 1966 and 1972 seven research offices of spatial planning (OREAMs, Organisations d'études d'aménagement des aires métropolitaines) were created in these metropolises (without Toulouse). The OREAMs worked out the masterplans, which proposed quantitative perspectives of urban growth (population, employment, traffic) and gave a general orientation for the regional spatial planning policy, as Merlin explains in his *L'aménagement du territoire.* Although the

program was set aside in the course of the 1970s, when the oil crisis made quantitative estimations of the masterplans obsolete (Merlin, *L'aménagement du territoire,* 184 ff.), the work in the OREAMs became the first professional experience in the career of several of Lefebvre's students and young collaborators.

105. Lefebvre, *The Urban Revolution,* 78; see also Merrifield, *Henri Lefebvre: A Critical Introduction,* 88.

106. Amiot, *Contre l'État, les sociologues,* 133.

107. Violeau, *Les architectes et mai 68,* 351 ff.

108. Busquet, "Idéologie urbaine et pensée politique dans la France de la période 1958–1981."

109. Vaneigem, "Comments against Urbanism."

110. Busquet, "Idéologie urbaine et pensée politique dans la France de la période 1958–1981."

111. Pflieger, *De la ville aux réseaux,* 23.

112. See Baudrillard, "Le système des objets"; Lourau, "L'analyse institutionnelle."

113. See Bobroff, "Politique urbaine et traitement des quartiers anciens (le cas de Montauban)"; Rame, "Étude des obstacles a la diffusion culturelle au Havre et ses prolongents"; Sag, "Contribution à l'étude des formes et techniques de la participation dramatique à la résidence universitaire d'Antony"; Abassi, "Introduction à la sociologie urbaine de la ville de Téhéran"; Scovazzi, "Esquisses sur le développement urbain de l'Amérique du sud de colonisation espagnole et de l'Argentine"; Tolan, "Problématique de l'urbanisation en Turquie"; Bernard-Simonet, "Le problème des régions rurales dans les pays industrialises"; and Dembelle, "Sociologie politique des paysans du Mali."

114. Coit, "Silences et révoltes des usagers (une comparaison des mouvements sociaux urbains aux États-Unis, en France, en Grande-Bretagne et en Italie)"; Depaule, "Les sauvages de l'architecture"; Bauhain, "L'image de l'espace"; Burlen, "Pratique idéologique et discours des architectes"; Segaud, "Le Corbusier, mythe et idéologie de l'espace."

115. Clavel, "L'aménagement étatique de l'espace"; Granger, "Ecosystème socio-culturel et planification intégrale."

116. Raymond, "L'architecture." Other dissertations supervised by Lefebvre and related to urbanism and architecture included Deshays, "Urbanisme et terrorisme"; and Cossalter, "D'un espace l'autre."

117. Interview with Monique Coornaert. See also Tonka, "Pratique urbaine de l'urbanisme"; and the anonymous article "L'Institut d'urbanisme en autogestion." For a historcial account about the IUUP, see Coudroy de Lille et al., *Un ancien institut.*

118. Orville, "Paris XX arrondissement, les incidences de certains types d'habitation sur la délinquance juvénile."

119. Cattiau, "Histoire générale des festivals et essai d'une phénoménologie des festivals français," i ff.

120. Solinas, "Essai d'organisation touristique à Castel Sardo [Sardaigne], Italie."

121. Ibid., 5.

122. Ibid., 140.

123. Boudon, "Étude socio-architecturale des quartiers modernes Frugès construites à Pessac par Le Corbusier"; see also Boudon, *Lived-in Architecture.*

124. Parts of the book were published in *AMC: Architecture mouvement continuité,* special issue on May '68 and supplement to issue 167 of the *Bulletin de la Société des architectes* (1968): 3–7. Lefebvre's book was extensively discussed in the architectural press after its publication, and it became a catchword of the period; see, for example, Emmerich, review of Henri Lefebvre's *Le droit à la ville, L'architecture d'aujourd'hui* 144 (1968): xxxvi–vii; and the discussion of French architecture of the 1960s in *AMC: Architecture mouvement continuité* 11 (1986), in particular the entry "La droit à la ville," 58–59. Similarly, Jean-Pierre Garnier recalled in a radio interview, *Profils perdus: Le temps des mépris,* broadcast on France Culture on 10 March 1994, that in the 1970s *The Right to the City,* together with *The Urban Revolution,* was at the top of the reading list in several architectural schools in Paris.

125. Lefebvre, "Propositions de recherches sur la vie urbaine," 151ff., quote from 153. The text was signed by Lefebvre as the director of the *institut.*

126. Ibid., 161–66. See also Lefebvre's comments, in Carporzen, ed., *Marquage et appropriation de l'espace,* 5. See also the minutes of the discussion in Sturge-Moore, ed., "Architecture—mythe—idéologie," 107.

127. Haumont et al., *La copropriété;* Haumont and Raymond, *Habitat et pratique de l'espace;* Boucheret et al., *L'espace du travail dans la ville;* Haumont, *Les locataires;* Haumont, "Paris." See also Institut de sociologie urbaine, *Les modes de vie;* Boucheret et al., *Les equipements dans la région parisienne;* Raymond, *La gare dans le mode de vie et l'espace suburbain;* and Bauhain et al., *Espace urbain et image de la ville.*

128. Interview with Mario Gaviria, Zaragossa, summer 2008. The results of this study were published in Gaviria's book *España a go-go,* which lists Lefebvre as a consultant.

129. See Gurvitch, *La vocation actuelle de la sociologie.*

130. Lefebvre and Coornaert, "Ville, urbanisme et urbanisation," 89.

131. Lefebvre and Coornaert's "Ville, urbanisme et urbanisation" reviews contemporary American scholarship, including articles from the *Journal of American Institute of Planners* and *Town Planning Institute Journal,* and refers to many French sociological, urbanistic, and philosophical publications, such as Coornaert's own sociological research, carried out outside the ISU in 1966 on the ZUP Montreynaud in Saint-Etienne (interview with Monique Coornaert).

132. Lefebvre and Coornaert, "Ville, urbanisme et urbanisation," 85, 104.

133. See Moley, *Les abords du chez-soi,* 8.

134. Lefebvre presided over group no. 1 of the commission, which addressed the question of the humanities taught to architectural students; he also participated in group no. 2, "Architecture and Urbanism." Many architects and urbanists took part in these two groups, including Robert Auzelle, Georges Candilis, Antoine Grumbach, Bernard Huet, Jacques Kalisz, and Yonel Schein; see Lengereau, *L'État et l'architecture,* 94.

135. For the program of the *unités pédagogiques,* see "Unités pédagogiques d'architecture—France."

136. See lecture notes by Henri Raymond, today at the Centre de recherche sur l'habitat, Paris: "Les variations saisonnières chez les eskimos," n.d.; "Le grand panopticum de l'espace," n.d.; "Espace et société chinoise" (1971).

137. Pawley and Tschumi, "The Beaux Arts since 1968."

138. Violeau, *Les architectes et mai 68,* 267.

139. Dan Ferrand-Bechmann, discussion at the conference "Henri Lefebvre: Penser le possible . . . ," Université Paris 8–Saint Denis, Paris, 29 June 2006; see also Ferrand-Bechmann, "À propos de Henri Lefebvre et Henri Raymond"; and Frey and Raymond, *Paroles d'un sociologue,* 123.

140. Interview with Henri Raymond; interview with Maïté Clavel; see also Violeau, *Les architectes et mai 68,* 219.

141. Lucan, *France,* 98–117.

142. Interview with Henri Raymond. This impact was, for example, revealed during the seminar "Modèles culturels habitat," held at Nanterre on 4 February 1976, during which many contributions revolved around the relevance of the study of the *pavillon* for architectural and urbanistic practices; see Institut de l'environnement, ed., *Modèles culturels habitat,* in particular the contributions by Huet ("Modèles culturels et architecture"); Raymond ("Modèles culturels"); and Jean-Charles Depaule ("Quelques remarques sur l'usage de 'L'habitat pavillonnaire' dans le projet"). See also the lecture notes of Henri Raymond, "Étude critique de l'habitat néo-paysan," 1971, Centre de recherche sur l'habitat, Paris.

143. Lucan, *France,* 17.

144. See Scott-Brown and Venturi, "Levittown et après."

145. See Depaule, "Quelques remarques sur l'usage de 'L'habitat pavillonnaire' dans le projet," 129.

146. See Huet, "Modèles culturels et architecture"; Cohen, "Transalpine Architektur"; and Cohen, "La coupure entre architectes et intellectuels"; see also Cohen, "Infortune transalpine: Aldo Rossi en France"; and Castex et al., *Formes urbaines.*

147. Francastel, *Art and Technology in the Nineteenth and Twentieth Centuries,* 52; Chombart de Lauwe, *Paris, essais de sociologie 1952–1964.*

148. Lefebvre, "Utopie expérimentale."

149. Busbea, *Topologies;* Avermaete, *Another Modern;* Blain, ed., *L'Atelier de Montrouge;* Blin, *L'AUA;* Lucan, *France.*

150. Haumont and Raymond, *Habitat et pratique de l'espace.*

151. See Lucan, *France,* 67; and Moley, *Les abords du chez-soi;* see also "Village-Expo."

152. Lucan, *France,* 118.

153. Monnier, "La croissance et l'innovation typologique," 282; Moulin, "Avons-nous encore besoin d'architectes?"

154. Lefebvre, *The Production of Space,* 221.

155. Interview with Ricardo Bofill, Barcelona, autumn 2008; e-mail exchange with Serge Renaudie, spring 2009.

156. The seminars included: (1) "Santé physique et santé mentale," 17–18 March 1968; (1a) "Système nerveux—organes sensoriels—perception—fonctions symboliques—sommeil," 6 October 1968; (2) "Marquage et appropriation de l'espace," 14–15 December 1968; and (3) "Architecture—mythe—idéologie," 8–9 February 1969; they were followed by the symposium "Image du corps et structure de l'espace," 26 October 1969. See Bedos et al., eds., *Les besoins fonctionnels de l'homme.*

The research projects included Raymond and Segaud, "Analyse de l'espace architectural: Le Corbusier"; Leroy et al., "Représentation et appropriation de l'espace (Plan de l'Institut Marcel Rivière)"; Leroy et al., "Appropriation de l'espace par les objects (Chambres de l'Institut Marcel Rivière)"; Depaule, "L'architecture sauvage"; Depaule et al., "Pessac"; Burlen, "La réalisation spatiale du désir et l'image spatialisée du besoin"; and the (confidential) project "Salle à geometrie variable," by Bernard Duprey.

157. Lefebvre, "La sexualité"; Lefebvre, "Espace et ideologie"; Lefebvre, "Les deux niveaux de la sociologie."

158. Bedos et al., eds., *Les besoins fonctionnels de l'homme,* 1.

159. Genzling quoted in Sturge-Moore, ed., "Architecture—mythe—idéologie," 7.

160. Lefebvre quoted in Carporzen, ed., *Marquage et appropriation de l'espace,* 56.

161. Huet quoted in Sturge-Moore, ed., "Architecture—mythe—idéologie," 65.

162. Pingusson, ibid., 66.

163. Bedos et al., eds., *Les besoins fonctionnels de l'homme,* 5.

164. See Lefebvre, "Réflexions sur la politique de l'espace"; Lefebvre, "La ville et l'urbain"; Lefebvre, "Engels et l'utopie"; Lefebvre, "Le mondial et le planetaire"; and Lefebvre, "Les autres Paris" (the three first articles were published in *Espace et politique*). Besides Lefebvre and Kopp, the board of editors between 1970 and 1974 included: Bernard Archer, Manuel Castells, Michel Coquery, Jean-Louis Destandau, Colette Durand, Gérard Heliot, Serge Jonas, Bernard Kayser, Raymond Ledrut, Michel Marie, Alain Medam, Jean Pronteau, Edmond Preteceille, Jean Pronteau, Henri Provisor, Pierre Riboulet, Christian Topalov, and Paul Vielle (although not everybody in this list collaborated on every issue). The journal published contributions from foreign authors, including Marco de Michelis and Marco Venturi, who, for example, discussed the communist urban policy in Bologna; see de Michelis and Venturi, "Le centre de direction de Bologne."

165. Castells, "La rénovation urbaine aux Etats-Unis"; Lefebvre, "Les autres Paris"; Castells, "Lutte de classes et contradictions urbaines."

166. Alquier, "Contribution à l'étude de la rente foncière sur les terrains urbains"; Lojkine, "Y a-t-il une rente foncière urbaine?"; Ascher, "Quelques critique de 'l'économie urbaine'"; Ascher, "Contribution à l'analyse de la production du cadre bâti."

167. See, for example, Castells, "L'urbanisation dépendante en Amérique latine."

168. With articles by Raymond Ledrut, Richard Fauque, and Marion Segaud.

169. Rieffel, *La tribu des clercs,* 12.

170. See, among others, *Un nouvel humanisme* (Chaîne nationale, 10 September 1949); *Royaumont: Tricentenaire du mémorial de Pascal* (Chaîne nationale, 11 December 1954); *Le matérialisme dialectique* (France 3 nationale, 7 May 1958); *Dialectique et sociologie* (Chaîne nationale, May 25, 1962); *La république des égaux et le scepticisme historique* (Chaîne nationale, 26 January 1963); *La philosophie de Karl Marx* (Chaîne nationale, 16 February 1963); *L'homme, le public et la connaissance* (France Culture, 16 May 1964); *Dix ans de création philosophique* (France Culture, 28 January 1967); *La beauté: Pour-quoi la mode?* (France Culture, 7 February 1967); *La fête et les sociétés industrielles* (France Culture, 20 February 1974); *Mode—effet—tournure* (France Culture, 1 Febru-ary 1970); *Le travail et le jeu* (France Culture, May 1974); *Le repos du 7ème jour* (France Culture, 1 June 1975); *La pornographie et le cinéma* (France Inter, 17 September 1975); *Tristan Tzara* (France Culture, 24 September 1975); *Les surréalistes, mêmes* (France Culture, 6 August 1989). For TV interviews, see: *Esquisse pour un portrait—Roger Vail-land* (26 February 1968); *Enquêtes sur les causes des manifestations* (Canal 1, 11 May 1968); *L'invasion de la sexualité dans la vie quotidienne* (25 January 1971); and *Paul Nizan* (France 3, 3 January 1996). Lefebvre gave many interviews, both on the radio and on television, specifically about his own work, including *Entretien avec Henri Lefebvre* (France Culture, 11 July 1975); *Henri Lefebvre: L'homme en question* (Canal 3, 17 April 1977); *La conscience mystifiée* (France Culture, 30 September 1979); *Entretien avec Henri Lefebvre* (France Inter, 2 October 1975); *Océaniques des idees: Henri Lefeb-vre ou le fil du siècle* (Canal 3, 27 June 1988); and *Henri Lefebvre, philosophe* (France Culture, 20 August 1991); see also twelve discussions with Gilbert Maurice Duprez, *Entretiens avec Henri Lefebvre,* broadcast between 7 and 19 December 1970 on France Culture. In the late 1960s and early 1970s Lefebvre was also a frequent guest on the programs *Les idées et l'historie, Récréation, Culture française, Notre temps,* and *Les après midi de France Culture* on France Culture; and *Inter-actualités* on France Inter. For international appearances, see *Het Internationaal Filosofen Project: Arne Naess, Leszek Kołakowski, Henri Lefebvre, Freddy Ayer,* directed by Louis van Gasteren (1971), NOS; and *Urbanose 15—Entretien avec Henri Lefebvre,* directed by Michel Régnier (1972), Office National du Film du Canada.

171. See the series *Aménagement de la cité* (or *Aménagement dans la cité*), broadcast on France 3, including *La vie nocturne de la ville* (19 March 1963); *Les problèmes et les modalités du week-end* (29 August 1963); *La vie quotidienne des grands ensembles* (3 October 1963); and *Débat sur les grands ensembles* (France 3, 31 October 1963). See also *Oratorio reportage: Claude-Nicolas Ledoux ou la ville idéale* (France 2, 21 November 1969); *Les futurs perdus* (15 May 1970); *Fables pour le futur* (19 June 1970); *Ricardo Bofill invité d'Inter-Actualités* (France Inter, 10 May 1975); *Un certain regard: Charles Fou-rier* (Canal 1, 6 September 1972); and *Paris Paris où le temps d'une génération 1936–1957* (Antenne 2, 4 and 11 September 1983).

172. See the texts by Lefebvre, including the preface to *Matériau/technologie/forme;* "Autour des deux dates 1937–1957"; "Habiter"; and "Espace architectural, espace urbain."

173. Lévy, "Paul-Henry Chombart de Lauwe, un sociologue à la télévision 1957–1960."

174. Including, for example, "Journées nationales d'études sur les parcs naturels régionaux," 25–30 September 1966, in Lurs-en-Provence; and the Grand Prix International d'urbanisme et d'achitecture in Cannes (1970); see Antoine et al., eds., *Les journées nationales d'études sur les parcs naturels régionaux;* and *Villes nouvelles, recherches pour une ville future.*

175. See *Architectural Design* 9–10 (1980): 18–21, 48–49, 53, 56, 79; see also Lefebvre, "An Interview with Henri Lefebvre," 36; and Lengereau, *L'État et l'architecture,* 435.

176. Violeau, *Les architectes et mai 68,* 234, 209.

177. Interview with Nicole Beaurain.

178. Ibid., see also J.-P. Lefebvre, "Sur 'L'unique et l'homogène dans la production de l'espace,'" 15.

179. Interview with Maïté Clavel; see De Carlo, "Editoriale: La testata, i contenutie gli assunti, la struttura della rivista."

180. Interview with Mario Gaviria.

181. Ibid.; interview with Nicole Beaurain.

182. Interview with Jean-Pierre Lefebvre, summer 2007.

183. Including the AUA, Jean Renaudie, Renée Gailhoustet, Ricardo Porro, Lucien Kroll, Massimiliano Fuksas, Team Zoo, Herman Hertzberger, Zvi Hecker, Roland Simounet, Jacques Bardet, Jean Deroche, Georges Maurios, Serge and Lipa Goldstein, Bernard Kohn, Henri Gaudin, Michel Corajoud, Christian Devillers, Léna Pérot, and Patrick Bazaud; see Violeau, *Les architectes et mai 68;* and *Sodédat 93, un laboratoire urbain,* supplement to *L'architecture d'aujourd'hui* 295 (1994).

184. Lefebvre, "Sur 'L'unique et l'homogène dans la production de l'espace,'" 15.

185. In the interview Jean-Pierre Lefebvre recalled a colloquium about urbanity in 1984, when Henri coined the concept of "anti-city" ("antiville"), developed later by Jean-Pierre.

186. J.-P. Lefebvre, *Quel altermonde?;* J.-P. Lefebvre, "Quotidienneté et production de l'espace chez Henri Lefebvre," manuscript, 2007 (in Lefebvre's possession); see also Kofman and Lebas, "Lost in Transposition—Time, Space and the City," 9. Andy Merrifield specified that in 1983 and 1984, at the invitation of Fredric Jameson, Lefebvre spent a semester in the History of Consciousness Program at the University of California, Santa Cruz, and he took numerous trips to Los Angeles, together with Jameson and Edward Soja (Merrifield, *Henri Lefebvre,* 73–74). Lefebvre participated in the conference "A City: A Conference on Urban Ideologies and Culture," organized in his honor at the University of California in March 1983. These experiences invigorated Lefebvre's previous interests in the relationships among architecture, urbanism, and cybernetics; see Lefebvre, "Informatique et urbanisation en Californie"; and Yann Couvidat, "L'exemple de la baie de San Francisco." See also Lefebvre, "Il modello californiano, gli Stati Uniti e il nuovo ordine mondiale"; and Lefebvre, "La technologie, le communication."

187. Interview with Jean-Pierre Lefebvre; see also J.-P. Lefebvre, *Une expérience d'écologie urbaine,* 140.

188. J.-P. Lefebvre, *Quel altermonde?* 9; interview with Jean-Pierre Lefebvre; Lefebvre, "Quotidienneté et production de l'espace chez Henri Lefebvre," 296 (manuscript in Lefebvre's possession).

189. Lefebvre, "Constituez vous en avant-garde"; see also Lefebvre, "La splendeur de la ville."

190. Quotation from "Manifest pour le création d'un mensuel," ETH Zurich, Archive of the Institute of Theory and History of Architecture (GTA), Claude Schnaidt files, letters: Henri Lefebvre.

191. See Lefebvre and the Groupe de Navarrenx, *Du contrat de citoyenneté,* 372.

192. Interview with Catherine Régulier, Navarrenx, summer 2009. See also Chemetov, "Henri Lefebvre nous parle . . . des villes méditerranéennes."

193. Interview with Catherine Régulier.

194. Maurice Blanchot, "Slow Obsequies," in *Friendship,* 85.

195. For Marxism as "*constitutively* . . . crisis theory," see Kouvelakis, "The Crisis of Marxism," 25.

196. Lefebvre, "Marxisme," 4–5.

197. See Tosel, "Henri Lefebvre ou le philosophe vigilant (1936-1946)."

198. Jessop, *State Power,* 140–41.

199. Lane, *Pierre Bourdieu,* 35ff.

200. Lichtheim, *Marxism in Modern France;* Balibar, *The Philosophy of Marx,* 3; Stalin, *Dialectical and Historical Materialism.*

201. Lefebvre, *The Production of Space,* 102–3.

202. Castells, *The Urban Question,* 86, 94.

203. Ibid., 94, 73.

204. Schmid, *Stadt, Raum und Gesellschaft,* 36.

205. Castells, *The Urban Question,* 80, 86.

206. Ibid., 89–90.

207. Ibid., 93.

208. Ibid., 87.

209. Schmid, *Stadt, Raum und Gesellschaft.*

210. For a discussion about Castells's critique, see ibid., 35ff.; but also Soja *Thirdspace,* 43; Shields, *Lefebvre, Love and Struggle,* 145; Elden, *Understanding Henri Lefebvre,* 142; and Merrifield, *Henri Lefebvre,* 101ff. For a bibliography, see Elden *Understanding Henri Lefebvre,* 163–64.

211. Röhr and Röhr, "Urbane Revolution und städtischer Raum"; for a discussion of Castells's *The Urban Question* by the same authors, see their paper "Die kapitalistische Stadt." For the reception of Lefebvre's ideas in West Germany, see Treusch-Dieter, "Revolution der Städte?" For an overview, see Ronneberger, "Contours and Convolutions of Everydayness," and, more recently, Belina and Michel, "Raumproduktionen."

212. Röhr and Röhr, "Urbane Revolution und städtischer Raum," 755.

213. Ibid., 756.

214. Ibid., 756–57.

215. See Trebitsch, "Preface: The Moment of Radical Critique," xviii; see also Lethierry, *Penser avec Henri Lefebvre,* 136 ff.; and Bykhovskii, "'Itog i ostatok' ili balans renegata."

216. Castells quoted in Pflieger, *De la ville aux réseaux,* 71.

217. Henri Lefebvre, "Plan d'une étude sur la communauté rurale (pastorale) dans les Pyrénées," attached to the letter of Henri Lefebvre to Georges-Henri Rivière, 23 January 1944, dossier: Henri Lefebvre, archives MNATP; Henri Lefebvre, "Première thèse: Plan: Campan: Historie d'une communauté pastorale pyrénéenne," and "Deuxième thèse: Campan: Le présent," last two documents received by the archives on 15 May 1944, dossier: Henri Lefebvre, archives MNATP.

218. Lefebvre referred to Bloch's *French Rural History;* and his "La lutte pour l'individualisme agraire dans la France du XVIIIe siècle," three parts of which were published in *Annales d'histoire économique et sociale;* and his *Feudal Society.* Lefebvre referred also to Braudel's *The Mediterranean and the Mediterranean World in the Age of Philip II.*

219. Braudel and Febvre had participated in the 1951 colloquium "Villes et campagnes," in which Lefebvre presented his research on the Pyrenean family; see Friedmann, ed., *Villes et campagnes.*

220. Burke, *The French Historical Revolution,* 14, 24, 46–47.

221. Lefebvre, "Problèmes de sociologie rurale."

222. Lefebvre, "Les communautés paysannes pyrénéennes," 61.

223. See ibid., 30, 49 ff., 54 ff.

224. Ibid., 3.

225. Ibid., 4–6.

226. See also Lefebvre's comment on liberalism in his preface to the book by Vachet, *L'idéologie libérale,* xi–xiv.

227. Lefebvre, "Les communautés paysannes pyrénéennes," 7.

228. Ibid., 66–67.

229. Ibid., 455.

230. See Bloch, *Feudal Society;* Febvre, *The Problem of Unbelief in the Sixteenth Century;* and Braudel, *The Mediterranean and the Mediterranean World in the Age of Philip II;* for a discussion, see Burke, *The French Historical Revolution.*

231. Lefebvre, "Les communautés paysannes pyrénéennes," 478.

232. Ibid.

233. Lefebvre, *La vallée de Campan,* 83.

234. Lefebvre, "Les communautés paysannes pyrénéennes," 56.

235. Lefebvre, "Première thèse: Plan: Campan: Historie d'une communauté pastorale pyrénéenne," 3, archives MNATP.

236. See Schmid, *Stadt, Raum und Gesellschaft,* 34, 294ff.

237. This had been Lefebvre's first extensive contribution to the theorizing of the territory, to which, as Brenner and Elden argued, he returned in *De l'État.* See Brenner and Elden, "Henri Lefebvre on State, Space, Territory."

238. Lefebvre, "Une république pastorale."

239. See Lefebvre, "Les communautés paysannes pyrénéennes," 48ff.

240. On the medieval and early modern city, see Arnade, Howell, and Simons, eds., "Productivity of Urban Space in Northern Europe"; on the historicity of space, see Arnade, Howell, and Simons, "Fertile Spaces," 515–48.

241. Ibid.

242. Lefebvre, "Théorie de la rente foncière et sociologie rurale," 80.

243. Hess, *Henri Lefebvre et l'aventure du siècle,* 175.

244. Lefebvre, discussion in *La dépolitisation, mythe ou réalité?*

245. Lefebvre, *Le temps des méprises,* 219ff.

246. Lefebvre, "Les classes sociales dans les campagnes."

247. Class was addressed not only by Lefebvre but also in the lectures of Charles Bettelheim, Chombart de Lauwe, and Touraine and during the discussions of the study group on "sociology of social classes"; see the materials on the program of the CES in the late 1940s and 1950s in Archives nationales, dossier no. 0019780305.

248. Lefort, "L'experience proletarienne," 6.

249. Ibid., 13–15.

250. Hastings-King, "L'Internationale Situationniste, Socialisme ou Barbarie, and the Crisis of the Marxist Imaginary."

251. See in the papers Lefebvre, "Marxisme et sociologie"; Lefebvre, "La notion de totalité dans les sciences sociales"; Lefebvre, "Le concept de classe sociale"; and Lefebvre, "Psychologie des classes sociales."

252. See issue no. 12/13 of the journal *Arguments* (1959), published under the title *Qu'est-ce que la classe ouvrière française?*; Mallet, *The New Working Class;* Belleville, *Une nouvelle classe ouvrière;* and Touraine, *Post-Industrial Society;* see also the section "La 'nouvelle classe ouvrière' et la démocratie urbaine," in Lefebvre, "Les nouveaux ensembles urbains," 125–28.

253. See also Dupeux, *French Society, 1789–1970,* 223ff.; Katsiaficas, *The Imagination of the New Left,* 95ff.

254. See Hamon, *Les nouveaux comportements politiques de la classe ouvrière,* 42.

255. The account of Stefan Hołówko, a Polish architect working in the office of Coulon, Douillet, Maneval, the designers of the new town, reported to the Polish architectural public about Mourenx as a "proletarian" city; see Hołówko, "Mourenx—Ville Nouvelle." For Lefebvre's increasing criticism of Mallet, see Lefebvre, "Henri Lefebvre ouvre le débat sur la théorie de l'autogestion," 63ff.

256. Lefebvre, "Les nouveaux ensembles urbains," 117–18.

257. Negri, "Archaeology and Project," 209.

258. Toscano, "Factory, Territory, Metropolis, Empire," 200; Alquati, *Sulla FIAT, e altri scritti;* see also Rieland, *Organisation und Autonomie;* Wright, *Storming Heaven;* and Aureli, *The Project of Autonomy.*

259. See Castells et al., *Crise du logement et mouvements sociaux urbains;* and Castells et al., *Monopolville.*

260. See Lefebvre, *The Right to the City,* 179.

261. See Bodeman, "The Naked Proletarian and the Organicity of Classes."

262. See Balibar, *The Philosophy of Marx,* 39.

263. Linden, *Workers of the World,* 1–14.

264. Trebitsch, "Preface: Presentation: Twenty Years After," xx.

265. Hess, *Henri Lefebvre et l'aventure du siècle,* 202; see also Lefebvre, "Les entretiens philosophiques de Varsovie"; Lefebvre, "Suplément à l'exposé de A. Banfi," 43–45; Lefebvre, "Interventions sur les exposés de MM. A. Banfi et H. Lefebvre," 96. For an account of his contacts with Lukács, see Lefebvre, *Lukács 1955.*

266. Lefebvre, "Marksizm i myśl francuska." (The original French text cannot be found in the archives of *Twórczość* in Warsaw.) This issue of *Twórczość* gathered texts by thirty-two French intellectuals, including Jean-Paul Sartre, Albert Camus, Antonin Artaud, Georges Bataille, Samuel Beckett, René Char, Robert Desnos, Paul Eluard, and Edgar Morin; among the contributors, only Lefebvre and Louis Aragon were members of the PCF; see "Od redakcji," *Twórczość* 4 (1957), 8; see also Lefebvre, "Filozofia spirytualistyczna we Francji." For the development of Lefebvre's arguments from "Marksizm i myśl francuska," see his *Problèmes actuels du marxisme* and *La somme et le reste.*

267. See Kelly, "French Intellectuals and Zhdanovism."

268. Lefebvre, "Marksizm i myśl francuska," 17–23.

269. Ibid., 19–20.

270. Ibid., 20–21; see also Lefebvre, "Autocritique."

271. Sher, *Praxis,* xi. The main writers who were part of the Praxis Group include: Danko Grlić, Mihailo Marković, Milan Kangrga, Gajo Petrović, Predrag Vranicki, Branko Bošnjak, and Rudi Supek (ibid.); see also Müller, *Praxis und Hoffnung;* and Petrović, ed., *Revolutionäre Praxis.*

272. The particiants included Kostas Axelos, Shlomo Avineri, Ernst Bloch, Erich Fromm, Lucien Goldman, Jürgen Habermas, Serge Mallet, Herbert Marcuse, Pierre Naville, Alfred Sohn-Rethel, Enzo Paci, and also Agnes Heller, Leszek Kołakowski, and Karel Kosík, among others; see Supek, "Dix ans de l'école d'été de Korčula (1963–1973)." Lefebvre published two articles in this journal, in which careful reviews of his books appeared (*Sociologie de Marx, Critique de la vie quotidienne,* vol. 2). See Lefebvre, "Sur quelques critères du développement social et du socialisme" published in 1964 in the Yugoslav edition of *Praxis;* and Lefebvre, "Socjalizam za vrijeme odmora." For the reviews, see *Praxis: Revue philosophique,* édition internationale 2–3 (1965): 388–92; and *Praxis: Revue philosophique,* édition internationale 3 (1967): 453–55.

273. Lefebvre, *Le mode de production étatique,* 341.

274. Trebitsch, "Henri Lefebvre et l'autogestion"; Lefebvre, "La planification démocratique."

275. Lefebvre, *Le mode de production étatique.*

276. See Balandier and Szelényi, "Gestion régionale et classe sociale"; and Szelényi, "Au-delà de l'analyse de classes."

277. Lefebvre, "Sur quelques critères du développement social et du socialisme," 157ff., 161.

278. Lefebvre, *The Production of Space,* 54.

279. E-mail exchange with Bohdan Jałowiecki, summer 2009.

280. Jałowiecki, *Społeczne wytwarzanie przestrzeni,* 6.

281. Ibid., 11ff.; Lefebvre, "L'espace."

282. Jałowiecki, *Społeczne wytwarzanie przestrzeni,* 8–9.

283. Ibid., 195.

284. Ibid., 237–38.

285. Verdery, *What Was Socialism, and What Comes Next?* chapter 1.

286. Jałowiecki, *Społeczne wytwarzanie przestrzeni,* 198–99.

287. Ibid., 207.

288. See Stanek, "Die Produktion des städtischen Raums durch massenmediale Erzähl-praktiken"; and Stanek, "Simulation or Hospitality."

289. Lefebvre, *Critique of Everyday Life,* 1:49; Lefebvre, *The Production of Space,* 54.

290. Lourau, *Sociologue à plein temps,* 55.

291. Jałowiecki, *Społeczne wytwarzanie przestrzeni,* 202.

292. Verdery, *What Was Socialism, and What Comes Next?* 57.

293. See also Balandier and Szelényi, "Gestion régionale et classe sociale."

294. Lefebvre, *Critique of Everyday Life,* 3:52.

295. Lefebvre, "Henri Lefebvre ou le fil du siècle."

296. Amiot, *Contre l'État, les sociologues,* 125.

297. Lefebvre, *Henri Lefebvre: La ville/À voix nue.*

298. Amiot, *Contre l'État, les sociologues,* 8.

299. Lefebvre, "La planification démocratique," 73.

300. Amiot, *Contre l'État, les sociologues,* 53ff.

301. Ibid., 62–63.

302. Claude Gruson, quoted ibid., 79. See also Avermaete, *Another Modern,* 39ff.

303. Amoit, *Contre l'État, les sociologues.*

304. Fourcaut, "Trois discours, une politique?"

305. Newsome, "The 'Apartment Referendum' of 1959."

306. Amiot, *Contre l'État, les sociologues,* 96–97.

307. Christian Topalov, a talk given during a debate on the socioeconomy of the urban (Paris, 12 May 1981), quoted ibid., 288.

308. Lefebvre, "L'urbanisme aujourd'hui," 225ff.; see also Lefebvre, "Á propos de la recherche interdisciplinaire en sociologie urbaine et en urbanisme."

309. *Urbanose 15: Entretien avec Henri Lefebvre,* dir. Michel Régnier, 1972.

310. Lefebvre, *La production de l'espace,* 72; Lefebvre, *The Right to the City,* 83, 149; Lefebvre, *The Production of Space,* 94, 362.

311. Lefebvre, "Le nécessaire et le possible dans la formation du mondial."

312. Lefebvre, *La production de l'espace,* 72; Kopp, *Changer la vie, changer la ville;* Granet, *Changer la ville;* see also Kofman and Lebas, "Lost in Transposition," 38 fn. 23; and the interview with Richard, "La politique architecturale et urbaine de Valéry Giscard d'Estaing, entretien avec Pierre Richard," in Andrieux and Seitz, eds., *Pratiques architecturales et enjeux politiques,* 101–6.

313. In the 1968 programmatic essay "Propositions de recherches sur la vie urbaine," the concept of "way of life" was related by the ISU to three postulates: accounting for the inequalities, distortions, irregularities, and changes within the urban reality; clarifying the relationships between the ways of life and urbanization without recourse to a causal determination; and incorporating this concept into a larger theory of the city. See Lefebvre, "Propositions de recherches sur la vie urbaine," 153ff.

314. See Cohen, "Grenoble 1974: Eurocommunism Meets Urbanism"; Cohen, "Grenoble 1974: Pour un urbanisme. . . ," 59; see also "Pour un urbanisme—rapports, communications, débats."

315. Busquet, "Idéologie urbaine et pensée politique dans la France de la période 1958–1981"; Costes, *Le droit à la ville d'Henri Lefebvre,* 121.

316. Valéry Giscard d'Estaing, "Écrits et conférences: Pour une politique de l'architecture," quoted in Lengereau, "Du coup d'arrêt de la circulaire Guichard au 'cadre de vie' giscardien," 47.

317. Garnier and Goldschmidt, *La comédie urbaine ou la cité sans classes.*

318. Paquot, "Rédecouvrir Lefebvre," 14; Le ministre de l'aménagement du territoire, de l'équipement, du logement et du tourisme, "Circulaire du 21 mars 1973"; see also Guichard, "Les villes à la française."

319. Lefebvre, *The Urban Revolution,* 21.

320. Lefebvre, *Critique of Everyday Life,* 3:105.

321. Ibid., 105–6.

322. Lefebvre, "Marksizm i myśl francuska," 14–15.

323. Ibid., 14–15.

324. See Pudal, *Un monde défait,* 22ff.

325. Lefebvre, "Marksizm i myśl francuska," 15.

326. Ibid., 26. See also Lefebvre's filmed lecture on art and sociology, given on 1 December 1977 at the École sociologique interrogative, opened in 1974 by the artists Hervé Fischer, Fred Forest, and Jean-Paul Thénot of the collective of "sociological art," Institut national de l'audiovisuel (Paris), Fonds Fred Forest.

327. Giraudoux, introduction to the 1943 French edition of the Athens Charter, in *Le Corbusier,* xvii; see also Chombard-Gaudin, ed., *Jean Giraudoux et le débat sur la ville 1928–1944;* Paquot, "Rédecouvrir Lefebvre"; and Chemetov, "D'Athènes à La Courneuve, à qui la faute?" 50.

328. Lefebvre, "Henri Lefebvre ou le fil du siècle."

329. Busquet, "Idéologie urbaine et pensée politique dans la France de la période 1958–1981."

330. Garnier, "La vision urbaine de Henri Lefebvre," 131.

331. On Delebarre's example, see Garnier, "La vision urbaine de Henri Lefebvre," 131. The aims of the Banlieues 89 program, formulated by Pierre Mauroy, included the reflection on the possible future of the periphery of Paris, the inclusion of the suburbs in the "urban civilization" of the capital, and the implementation of a certain number of exemplary actions. More than a hundred projects were supported financially by the Comité interministériel des villes between 1984 and 1985. Lefebvre did not participate in the program, but the impact of his ideas was evident: Castro quoted Lefebvre in his 1994 book *Civilisation urbaine ou barbarie?* and his program to "re-create the city" in order to foster "citizenship" and "democracy" refers to Lefebvre's vocabulary. See Moiroux, "Banlieues 89, un événement fondateur?"; and Castro, *Civilisation urbaine ou barbarie?*

332. Garnier and Goldschmidt, *La comédie urbaine ou la cité sans classes,* 135.

333. Boltanski and Chiapello, *The New Spirit of Capitalism.*

334. Ibid., 194–99, 489–90.

335. Ibid., 38–39.

336. Ibid.

337. Jean-Pierre Garnier, discussion during the conference "Rethinking Theory, Space and Production: Henri Lefebvre Today," Delft University of Technology, 13 November 2008; see also Garnier's *Une violence éminemment contemporaine.*

338. Schnaidt, "Le droit à la ville," 212.

339. Foucault, *Security, Territory, Population;* Foucault, *The Birth of Biopolitics.*

340. Joseph, "Le droit a la ville, la ville a l'oeuvre."

341. Balibar, "From Class Struggle to Classless Struggle," 155–56.

342. Ibid.

343. See Dikeç, *Badlands of the Republic.*

344. See de Rudder et al., eds., *Loi d'orientation pour la ville,* 27, 65ff.; Dikeç, "Justice and the Spatial Imagination"; and Gilbert and Dikeç, "Right to the City: Politics of Citizenship."

345. Gregory, *Geographical Imaginations;* Dear, *The Postmodern Urban Condition;* Dear, "Les aspects postmodernes de Henri Lefebvre." See also Soja, *Thirdspace;* Hamel and Poitras, "Henri Lefebvre, penseur de la postmodernité"; and Soja, "The Socio-Spatial Dialectic." For an overview, see Elden, "Politics, Philosophy, Geography"; and Schmid, *Stadt, Raum und Gesellschaft.*

346. Borries, *Who's Afraid of Niketown?;* Boyer, "Cities for Sale." See also Kouvelakis, "Henri Lefebvre, Thinker of Urban Modernity," 720.

347. Brenner and Theodore, eds., *Spaces of Neoliberalism.*

348. Fezer and Heyden, eds., *Hier entsteht.*

349. Borries, *Who's Afraid of Niketown?*

350. Fraser, *Justice Interruptus;* Ost, *The Defeat of Solidarity.*

351. Sloterdijk, *Critique of Cynical Reason.*

352. Lefebvre, *Henri Lefebvre: La ville/À voix nue: Grands entretiens d'hier et d'aujourd'hui.*

353. Sloterdijk, *Critique of Cynical Reason.*

354. Lefebvre, *Henri Lefebvre: La ville/À voix nue: Grands entretiens d'hier et d'aujourd'hui.* In *Le temps des méprises,* Lefebvre said also that he was situating himself "in the lineage of heretics considered peripheral" (60).

355. See Hess, *L'analyse institutionnelle;* Lourau, *L'analyse institutionnelle.*

356. Lefebvre, "De Marx à Nietzsche."

2. RESEARCH

1. Lefebvre, *The Production of Space,* 40.

2. Shields, *Lefebvre, Love and Struggle;* Elden, *Understanding Henri Lefebvre;* Schmid, *Stadt, Raum und Gesellschaft;* Merrifield, *Henri Lefebvre.*

3. Lefebvre, *The Production of Space,* 38–39.

4. See also Raymond, "Habitat, modèles culturels et architecture," 228.

5. The three volumes about the *pavillon* were based on three hundred interviews carried out in eight towns, which include Enghien and Aulnay, in the Parisian agglomeration; Bron, near Lyon; Lens as an example of an industrial city; holiday towns (Ronce-les-Bains in the commune of La Temblance); pensioners' *pavillon* settlements in the Côte d'Azur (Antibes, Cannet); and a "neutral city" (Crépy-en-Valois). The study *La copropriété* was developed on the basis of two hundred interviews in neighborhoods in two larger cities (Grenoble and Rennes) and in four towns in the suburbs of Paris (Asnières, Montrouge, Bougival, Celle-Saint-Cloud). The case studies for the research in *Habitat et pratique de l'espace* were chosen in order to cover a variety of alternatives, in terms of not only the mixture of ownership but also architectural (formal) solutions. That study is based on 150 interviews with the inhabitants of the Unité d'habitation by Le Corbusier in Marseille, the neighborhood La Grande Borne in Grigny by Émile Aillaud, the Mont-Mesly in Créteil, the Village-Expo in Saint-Michel-sur-Orge, and two *pavillon* neighborhoods in Aulnay sous Bois and Enghien, both in the *banlieue* of Paris. See Haumont et al., *L'habitat pavillonnaire;* Raymond, *La politique pavillonnaire;* Haumont, *Les pavillonnaires;* and Haumont and Raymond, *Habitat et pratique de l'espace.*

6. Haumont, *Les Pavillonnaires,* 9.

7. Lefebvre, "Autour des deux dates 1937–1957," 408.

8. Raymond, *La politique pavillonnaire.*

9. See Magri, "Le pavillon stigmatisé."

10. Kaës, *Vivre dans les grands ensembles,* 306–7; Chombart de Lauwe, *Des hommes et des villes,* 138.

11. Magri, "Le pavillon stigmatisé," 172.

12. Haumont et al., *L'habitat pavillonnaire,* 135.

13. Raymond et al., "Avant-propos de la quatrième edition," 1.

14. Lefebvre, "L'urbanisme aujourd'hui"; see also Paquot, "Habitat et 'habiter.'"

15. Lefebvre, *The Urban Revolution,* 81.

16. Mumford, *The CIAM Discourse on Urbanism, 1928–1960,* 221.

17. Ibid., 226. See also Smithson, ed., *Team 10 Primer.*

18. Shadrach Woods quoted in Avermaete, *Another Modern,* 47.

19. Mumford, *The CIAM Discourse on Urbanism;* Pedret, "Preparing CIAM X 1954–1955"; Avermaete, *Another Modern.*

20. Avermaete, *Another Modern,* 134 ff.

21. Ibid.

22. Haumont, *Les pavillonnaires,* 17.

23. This method was spelled out in 1968 by Henri Raymond in his book *Une méthode de dépouillement et d'analyse de contenu appliquée aux entretiens non directives.* Or, as Lefebvre put it, "To inhabit is a situation that implies the relationships with groups of objects, classes of acts, and people; this situation *produces* certain relationships rather than receiving them or passively perceiving them." See Lefebvre "Éléments d'une théorie de l'objet," 277.

24. Haumont et al., *L'habitat pavillonnaire,* 86.

25. Haumont et al., *La copropriété,* 107; see also Haumont et al., *L'habitat pavillonnaire,* 79; for Chombart's uses of this concept, see his "Sciences humaines, planification et urbanisme," 194.

26. See Raymond, "Habitat, modèles culturels et architecture," 217; and Bourdieu, *Outline of a Theory of Practice,* 72.

27. See Haumont, *Les Pavillonnaires,* 227–28; see also Haumont et al., *La copropriété.*

28. Haumont, "Les pavillonnaires et la pratique de l'habitat."

29. Ibid.; Haumont, *Les Pavillonnaires,* 227–28; see also Haumont et al., *La copropriété.*

30. Henri Raymond, interview with the author, Paris, autumn 2007.

31. Lefebvre, "Preface to the Study of the Habitat of the 'Pavillon,'" 130–33.

32. Lefebvre, "Besoins profonds, besoins nouveaux de la civlisation urbaine," 200–201.

33. Lefebvre, preface to Haumont et al., *L'habitat pavillonnaire,* 23 (this part of the preface is missing in Elden et al., *Henri Lefebvre: Key Writings*).

34. Lefebvre, "Preface to the Study of the Habitat of the 'Pavillon,'" 122.

35. Lefebvre, preface to Haumont et al., *L'habitat pavillonnaire,* 23.

36. Henri Raymond, interview with the author.

37. Maïté Clavel, interview with the author, Paris, summer 2007.

38. For example, Lefebvre argued that the inhabitants' dissatisfaction with the *grands ensembles* generated a series of mechanisms of defense that could not be identified by means of interviews; see Lefebvre, "Propositions pour un nouvel urbanisme," 191. See also Lefebvre, "Psychologie des classes sociales"; and Lefebvre, "Les nouveaux ensembles urbains."

39. Lefebvre, "Preface to the Study of the Habitat of the 'Pavillon,'" 124.

40. According to Jean-Pierre Frey, Georges-Hubert de Radkowski joined the IUUP with the support of Lefebvre (interview with the author, Paris, summer 2008); see Radkowski, *Anthropologie de l'habiter;* and Schérer, *Utopies nomades.*

41. Lefebvre, preface to *L'habitat pavillonnaire,* 23.

42. Lefebvre, "L'urbanisme aujourd'hui," 222.

43. Lefebvre, *The Production of Space,* 164–65.

44. Lefebvre, "Preface to the Study of the Habitat of the 'Pavillon,'" 130.

45. Ibid., 123.

46. See also Paquot, *Demeure terrestre,* 118.

47. Lefebvre, "Preface to the Study of the Habitat of the 'Pavillon,'" 122.

48. Ibid., 121–22.

49. See Paquot, *Demeure terrestre.*

50. See Dal Co, *Figures of Architecture and Thought.*

51. Lefebvre, *Métaphilosophie,* 133–34.

52. Lefebvre, preface to *L'habitat pavillonnaire,* 23.

53. Lefebvre, "Preface to the Study of the Habitat of the 'Pavillon,'" 131.

54. Ibid., 130.

55. Lefebvre, *The Production of Space,* 165.

56. Lefebvre, "Preface to the Study of the Habitat of the 'Pavillon,'" 130.

57. Ibid.

58. Chombart wrote, "Our various surveys about the urban environment have brought to light not only a lack of space, only too evident in times of housing crisis, but also an arduously felt absence of appropriation of space" (Chombart de Lauwe, "Sciences humaines, planification et urbanisme," 194).

59. Lefebvre, "L'urbanisme aujourd'hui," 222.

60. Boudon, "Étude socio-architecturale des quartiers modernes Frugès construites à Pessac par Le Corbusier"; Boudon, *Lived-in Architecture.* In an interview with the author, Philippe Boudon said that Lefebvre presided over the committee as a replacement of Jean Margot-Duclos.

61. Rapoport, *House Form and Culture,* 4.

62. Ibid., 47.

63. Ibid.

64. For Lefebvre's critique of Rapoport, see *The Production of Space,* 123, 166, 305.

65. Lefebvre, "Preface to the Study of the Habitat of the 'Pavillon,'" 131.

66. Although Boudon refers to Lefebvre in several of his texts, including his article "Habitat ouvert ou fermé?" and the book *Richelieu Ville Nouvelle,* in an interview with

the author he said that the theories of Lefebvre were not known to him before the study. However, he added that he was aware of urban sociology through conversations with his brother, a sociologist, and stressed the role of the trained interviewer in the Pessac research.

67. Giedion, *Bauen in Frankreich,* 85ff.

68. Boudon, *Lived-in Architecture,* 152.

69. Ibid., 91.

70. Henri Lefebvre, preface to Boudon, *Lived-in Architecture,* n.p.

71. Depaule et al., "Pessac," 15–16.

72. For a discussion about the relationship between the architectural and cultural models, see Raymond, *L'architecture, les aventures spatiales de la raison,* which originated in his doctoral dissertation supervised by Lefebvre.

73. See Lefebvre's foreword to the second edition of *Critique of Everyday Life,* 1:3–99.

74. See Monnier and Klein, eds., *Les années ZUP;* and Besset, *New French Architecture.*

75. *Die neue Stadt* was a summary of the research report "Projekt einer Studienstadt im Raume Otelfingen im Furttal, Kt. Zuerich," authored by the Fachgruppe Bauplanung der Studiengruppe "Neue Stadt," headed by Ernst Egli.

76. For a discussion, see Degen, "50 Jahre Raumplanung in der Schweiz mit spezieller Betrachtung des Kantons Zürich"; and Ganz, "Nonkonformes von vorgestern."

77. Eisinger, *Die Stadt der Architekten,* 72–73.

78. Egli et al., *Die neue Stadt,* 25.

79. Ibid., 53.

80. Lefebvre, "Utopie expérimentale," 133.

81. Maslow, *Motivation and Personality.*

82. Egli et al., *Die neue Stadt,* 25.

83. Ibid., 16, 25.

84. Ibid., 32.

85. Ibid.; see also Eisinger, *Die Stadt der Architekten,* 78–80.

86. Egli et al., *Die neue Stadt,* 21.

87. See Léger et al., "Nine Points on Monumentality (1944)." See also Zucker, ed., *New Architecture and City Planning;* and Giedion, *Architecture, You and Me.*

88. Egli et al., *Die neue Stadt,* 62.

89. "Editorial Notes: Critique of Urbanism," 105.

90. Lefebvre, "Utopie expérimentale," 135.

91. Werner Aebli in Egli et al., *Die neue Stadt,* 18.

92. See Gozzi et al., *Niveaux optima des villes.*

93. Werner Aebli in Egli et al., *Die neue Stadt,* 16. Referring to the study *Niveaux optima des villes,* by Gozzi et al., Lefebvre questioned the fundamental calculation of the authors, who estimated the necessary functions on the basis of the population numbers, without taking into consideration the social structure (Lefebvre, "Utopie expérimentale," 139–40).

94. Lefebvre, *Critique of Everyday Life,* vol. 1.

95. See also Bertrand, "Qu'en est-il donc du besoin?"

96. Lefebvre, *Critique of Everyday Life,* 1:173–74.

97. See also Lefebvre, "Lefebvre parle de Marcuse."

98. Baudrillard, "The Ideological Genesis of Needs," 82.

99. See, for example, Auzelle, "Plaidoyer pour une organization consciente de l'espace," 4.

100. Moles, "Theory of Complexity and Technical Civilization," 16.

101. Ibid.

102. Moles, "Functionalism in Crisis," 24.

103. Chombart de Lauwe, *Famille et habitation,* 1:16–18; Chombart de Lauwe, *Des hommes et des villes.*

104. Chombart de Lauwe, *Famille et habitation,* 1:18.

105. Chombart de Lauwe, "Sociologie de l'habitation"; Chombart de Lauwe et al., "Logement et comportement des ménages dans trois cités nouvelles de l'agglomération bordelaise"; Cupers, "Concerning the User."

106. Chombart de Lauwe, *Famille et habitation,* 1:17–18;

107. Chombart de Lauwe, *Des hommes et des villes,* 145; Chombart de Lauwe, "Sciences humaines, planification et urbanisme," 195.

108. Paquot, "Des 'besoins' aux 'aspirations.'"

109. Lefebvre, "Propositions pour un nouvel urbanisme," 194.

110. Lefebvre, "La planification démocratique," 92–93.

111. Lefebvre, "Propositions pour un nouvel urbanisme," 195.

112. Bedos et al., eds., *Les besoins fonctionnels de l'homme,* 4, 9; see Le Corbusier, *Toward an Architecture,* 182; see also the discussion after the seminar 1bis, 6 October 1968, annex no. 1, in "Dimensions neuro-physiologique et neuro-psychologique," ed. Sturge-Moore, 149.

113. Bedos et al., eds., *Les besoins fonctionnels de l'homme,* 4.

114. Lefebvre, *The Production of Space,* 116. Jean-Charles Depaule stressed that such concepts as that of the "cultural model," applied by the ISU, are an alternative to the concepts of form and function. During the seminar "Modèles culturels Habitat" at the Institut de l'environnement (1976), he argued, "To speak about cultural models or habitus in housing means to go beyond both the concept of function and that of needs and to assert that the sociability of everyday life corresponds to the forms that imply social relations, sexuality, relations within the family, education, culinary habits, et cetera." See Depaule, "Quelques remarques sur l'usage de 'L'Habitat pavillonnaire' dans le projet," 129.

115. Several architects embraced Lefebvre's critique of the concept of need, not rarely in an attempt to operationalize the concept of dwelling *(habitation)* as opposed to that of accommodation *(loger),* as it was put forward in Émile Aillaud's essay "Habiter, et non pas loger."

116. "Un 'café-club' au prochain salon des arts ménagers."

117. Lefebvre, "Bistrot-club," 143.

118. Ibid.; Situationist International, "The Geopolitics of Hibernation," 105.

119. Michel, "Le 'BISTROT-CLUB' pour animer les nouvelles cités."

120. Situationist International, "The Geopolitics of Hibernation," 106.

121. Ibid.

122. Lefebvre, *Espace et politique,* 11; Haumont et al., *L'habitat pavillonnaire,* 67.

123. Lefebvre, *Espace et politique,* 12. During the CRAUC seminar, Dameron opposed the space of the inhabitant ("lived space, characterized by marking and appropriation") to both the "real space" and the "represented space of the architect" (Bedos et al., eds., *Les besoins fonctionnels de l'homme,* 6), and Nicole Haumont argued that the study of the practices of the appropriation of space by means of marking allows "a knowledge of the habitat that overcomes a simple study of adaptation to a functional space" (Carporzen, ed., "Marquage et appropriation de l'espace," 41). These statements draw on the ISU research conducted two years earlier on the *pavillon* as an "object of appropriation" (Haumont et al., *L'habitat pavillonnaire,* 67), and the minutes of the seminar reveal a significant impact of *L'habitat pavillonaire* on the research of the participating architects and sociologists; see Bedos et al., "Représentation et appropriation de l'espace"; and Bedos et al., "Appropriation de l'espace par les objects."

124. Haumont et al., *L'habitat pavillonnaire,* 72.

125. Ibid., 73.

126. Raymond, "Habitat, modèles culturels et architecture," 221.

127. Ibid., 223–25.

128. Haumont and Raymond, *Habitat et pratique de l'espace,* 166.

129. Ibid., 169ff.

130. Ibid., 170.

131. Huet, "Modèles culturels et architecture," 38.

132. Lefebvre, "Utopie expérimentale," 134.

133. Lefebvre, *The Urban Revolution,* 97.

134. Lefebvre and Coornaert, "Ville, urbanisme et urbanisation," 92–94.

135. See Heuvel and Risselada, eds., *Team 10, 1953–81.*

136. See Lefebvre's discussion with Antoine Haumont about Christopher Alexander, in Sturge-Moore, ed., "Architecture—mythe—idéologie," 124.

137. Alexander, "A City Is Not a Tree," 75.

138. See Lefebvre's comments in Sturge-Moore, ed., "Architecture—mythe—idéologie," 112.

139. Alexander, "A City Is Not a Tree," 80, 75–76.

140. Huizinga, *Homo Ludens;* Caillois, *Man, Play and Games;* Debord, *Mémoires,* n.p.; Lefebvre, "Utopie expérimentale," 138.

141. Lefebvre, "Les nouveaux ensembles urbains," 115.

142. Nicole Beaurain, interview with the author, Paris, spring 2008.

143. In addition to the works named in the text, see Lefebvre, "Mourenx—ville nouvelle"; and Lefebvre, *Pyrénées.* Other accounts include the discussion in *Les nouveaux comportements politiques de la classe ouvrière,* 40–42; in the personal "Notes on a New City," written in 1960 and published in Lefebvre, *Introduction à la modernité,* as well as numerous references to the city in *Critique of Everyday Life,* 2:80, 362; in the fourth interview in a series of five with Gilbert-Maurice Duprez, broadcast as *Henri Lefebvre: La ville/À voix nue;* and in the retrospective *Le temps des méprises,* 222. This research was reflected in several of Lefebvre's studies on architecture and urbanism, including his "Propositions pour un nouvel urbanisme."

144. Blazy, *Mourenx ville nouvelle du complexe de Lacq,* 13. Gas was discovered in Lacq by the Société nationale des pétroles d'Aquitaine, which was joined by the major factories of the region and the Société civile immobilière de la caisse de dépôts et consignations (SCIC), a subsidiary of the Caisse des dépôts. The SCIC was established with the aim of developing housing with state funds, and it formed a new deposit fund called the Société civile immobilière de Lacq et de sa région. The SCIC was also the developer of Mourenx. On the SCIC, see Pares, *La SCIC au service du pays.*

145. Blazy, *Mourenx ville nouvelle du complexe de Lacq,* 14–15.

146. Ibid.; see also Peaucelle, *Éléments pour une mémoire collective de Mourenx;* and Blazy, *Mourenx ville nouvelle du complexe de Lacq.*

147. Lefebvre, "Les nouveaux ensembles urbains," 119.

148. Peaucelle, *Éléments pour une mémoire collective de Mourenx.*

149. Ibid.

150. Lefebvre, "Les nouveaux ensembles urbains," 124; see also Lefebvre, "La sexualité," 141.

151. Lefebvre, *Pyrénées,* 123. Even if the main wave of returning white settlers (*pieds-noirs*) came after the 1962 Evian Treaty, the first refugees had already arrived by the late 1950s; see Peaucelle, *Éléments pour une mémoire collective de Mourenx.*

152. Lefebvre, *Introduction à la modernité,* 124.

153. Lefebvre, "Les nouveaux ensembles urbains," 126.

154. Peaucelle, *Éléments pour une mémoire collective de Mourenx.*

155. Lefebvre, "Mourenx—ville nouvelle," 207.

156. Lefebvre, "Les nouveaux ensembles urbains," 126ff.

157. Ibid., 122; see also Haumont et al., *Habitat et pratique de l'espace,* 170–71.

158. Lefebvre, "Mourenx—ville nouvelle," 207; Merlin, *Les villes nouvelles,* 255.

159. See n. 144.

160. Lefebvre, "Mourenx—ville nouvelle," 207.

161. See the study of the Institut national d'études démographiques: Girad, *Désirs des français en matière d'habitation urbaine,* which was one of the points of departure for the ISU study of the *pavillon.*

162. Magri, "Le pavillon stigmatisé," 175–76. For the prewar discussions, see Mumford, *The CIAM Discourse on Urbanism, 1928–1960,* 57.

163. Fourcaut, "Trois discours, une politique?" 40.

164. Newsome, "The 'Apartment Referendum' of 1959."

165. Pierre Sudreau, quoted in Fourcaut, "Trois discours, une politique?" 42.

166. Ibid., 43.

167. Castells, *The City and the Grassroots,* 80.

168. Expressions from the journals *Le Parisien libéré* (5 December 1960), *L'Aurore* (2 July 1962), and *Le Figaro* (15 January 1965), quoted in Viellard-Baron "Sarcelles," 53.

169. Choay, *L'urbanisme,* 7–8.

170. Lefebvre, "Preface to the Study of the Habitat of the 'Pavillon,'" 130.

171. Lefebvre, preface to *L'habitat pavillonnaire,* 23.

172. Lefebvre, "Les nouveaux ensembles urbains," 123.

173. See ibid. For an account of a monument as a "poly-," "trans-," or "suprafunctional" element, see Lefebvre, "Espace et idéologie," 111; and Lefebvre, *Critique of Everyday Life,* 2:308.

174. Lefebvre, *Introduction à la modernité,* 124; Lefebvre, *The Production of Space,* 223; Lefebvre, *Critique of Everyday Life,* 2:292.

175. Lefebvre, *Critique of Everyday Life,* 2:297. See also Lefebvre, "Éléments d'une théorie de l'objet," 283ff.; and Lefebvre, "Introduction à la psycho-sociologie de la vie quotidienne," 95.

176. Lefebvre, "Introduction à la psycho-sociologie de la vie quotidienne," 94.

177. Lefebvre, "Preface to the Study of the Habitat of the 'Pavillon,'" 131.

178. Lefebvre, *The Production of Space,* 310.

179. Lefebvre, "Preface to the Study of the Habitat of the 'Pavillon,'" 131ff.

180. Lefebvre, *The Production of Space,* 232.

181. Lefebvre, "Mourenx—ville nouvelle," 218.

182. Lefebvre, *Introduction à la modernité,* 124; Lefebvre, "La vie sociale dans la ville," 146.

183. See Lefebvre, *Introduction à la modernité,* 124.

184. See Lefebvre, "Claude Lévi-Strauss et le nouvel éléatisme," 271.

185. A similar critique, relating specifically to the work of Althusser, was developed by Lefebvre in the essay "Les paradoxes d'Althusser"; see also Kurzweil *The Age of Structuralism,* 75.

186. Lefebvre, *Everyday Life in the Modern World,* 59; Lefebvre, *The Urban Revolution,* 164; see also the work of Maïté Clavel, who defended her dissertation on French state urbanism under the supervision of Lefebvre at the university in Nanterre in 1972: Clavel, "L'aménagement étatique de l'espace"; Clavel, *L'aménagement étatique de l'espace;* Clavel, "Institutions urbaines et ideologie."

187. Lefebvre, *Pyrénées,* 121. This was developed by Kristin Ross, who argued that with the end of the French colonial empire the effort that once went into maintaining and disciplining colonial people and their situation became instead invested in a particular "level" of metropolitan existence: everyday life. See Ross, *Fast Cars, Clean Bodies,* 77.

188. Lefebvre, "Claude Lévi-Strauss et le nouvel éléatisme," 283.

189. Ibid., 303.

190. See Lefebvre, *Everyday Life in the Modern World,* 45ff.

191. Ibid.; see also Adorno and Horkheimer, *Dialectic of Enlightenment.* On a broader cultural level, Lefebvre argued that the structuralist conceptualization of the relationship between signifier and signified reflects the technological and social changes of the early twentieth century, as well as shifts in traditional conventions of perception (*Everyday Life in the Modern World,* 113).

192. Baudrillard, "The Ideological Genesis of Needs," 67.

193. Ibid., 66.

194. Ibid., 75.

195. Ibid.

196. For an opposite argument, see Moles, "Functionalism in Crisis," 24.

197. Choay, *L'urbanisme,* 77; Choay, "Urbanism and Semiology," 36.

198. Lefebvre, *The Production of Space,* 270; Eco, "Function and Sign," 22.

199. Baudrillard, *The System of Objects,* 67.

200. Lefebvre, "Claude Lévi-Strauss et le nouvel éléatisme," 291.

201. Baudrillard, *The System of Objects,* 23.

202. See Moles, "Objet et communication," 2.

203. Ross, *Fast Cars, Clean Bodies,* 105ff.

204. Lefebvre, "Preface to the Study of the Habitat of the 'Pavillon,'" 132.

205. Eleb, "Modernity and Modernisation in Postwar France," 503, 498.

206. Lefebvre, "Preface to the Study of the Habitat of the 'Pavillon,'" 133.

207. Ibid., 132.

208. Hjemslev quoted in Barthes, *The Fashion System,* 3.

209. Ibid., 26.

210. See Haumont et al., *L'habitat pavillonnaire,* 82, 95ff.

211. Ibid.

212. Ibid., 85.

213. Ibid.

214. Lefebvre, "Preface to the Study of the Habitat of the 'Pavillon,'" 133.

215. Haumont et al., *L'habitat pavillonnaire,* 85.

216. Ibid.

217. See ibid.

218. Ibid., 84–85.

219. Ibid., 81.

220. Ibid., 91.

221. This argument follows that of Jean Piaget against linguistic nativism; see Piaget, *Le structuralisme.*

222. Haumont et al., *L'habitat pavillonnaire,* 86.

223. See ibid., 90–91.

224. See Baudrillard, review of Lefebvre's *Position.*

225. Lefebvre, "Claude Lévi-Strauss et le nouvel éléatisme," 301.

226. Ibid., 128. Lefebvre confessed that the concept of the everyday and its critique originated from his astonishment at the tone of his wife when she showed a box of laundry soap and said, "This is an excellent product" (Lefebvre, *Le temps des méprises,* 34). In *The System of Objects,* Baudrillard claimed that advertising is an integral part in the system of objects, not only because it relates to consumption and tells us "what it is that we consume *through* objects," but also "because it itself becomes an object to be consumed" (178–79). To explore how "the language of advertising is reflected in us" was the aim of Georges Perec's 1965 novel *Things,* and he was accompanied in this aim by such novelists as Simone de Beauvoir and Christine Rochefort; see Ross, *Fast Cars, Clean Bodies,* 58–60; Perec, *Things;* and Lefebvre, *Everyday Life in the Modern World,* 133.

227. Lefebvre, *Everyday Life in the Modern World,* 126.

228. Haumont et al., *L'habitat pavillonnaire,* 65. A similar situation was reported in Boudon, *Lived-in Architecture,* 84.

229. Haumont et al., *L'habitat pavillonnaire,* 122.

230. Ibid., 70.

231. See Lefebvre, *Everyday Life in the Modern World,* 188.

232. Ibid., 86.

233. See also Segaud in Sturge-Moore, ed., "Architecture—mythe—idéologie," 72ff.

234. Lefebvre, *Everyday Life in the Modern World,* 165.

235. Lane, *Pierre Bourdieu,* 46.

236. See Lefebvre, *Everyday Life in the Modern World.* See also Lefebvre's discussion with Roland Barthes and Jean Duvignaud about fashion, "La mode—stratégie du désir."

237. Jay, *Marxism and Totality,* 297.

238. Lefebvre, *Sociology of Marx,* 23. See also Jay, *Marxism and Totality,* 298.

239. Lefebvre, "La notion de totalité dans les sciences sociales," 55.

240. See Lefebvre, "Claude Lévi-Strauss et le nouvel éléatisme," 296, 310; and Merrifield, *Henri Lefebvre,* 92. Almost as a warning against too quick identification of interstices with progressive politics, Lefebvre's example was taken from economy: he pointed out that between haute couture and its opposite—mass-produced clothing—is a realm that is based on the features of both of them and takes advantage precisely of this ambiguity; it is the prêt-à-porter. See Lefebvre, *Everyday Life in the Modern World,* 166.

241. Baudrillard, review of Lefebvre's *Position: Contre les technocrates.*

242. Lefebvre, "Preface to the Study of the Habitat of the 'Pavillon,'" 133.

243. Haumont et al., *L'habitat pavillonnaire,* 129. For the shift in domestic labor in France, see Duchen, "Occupation Housewife"; Ross, *Fast Cars, Clean Bodies,* 105ff.; and Baudrillard, *The System of Objects,* 48.

244. Lefebvre, *Everyday Life in the Modern World,* 121.

245. Lefebvre, "Preface to the Study of the Habitat of the 'Pavillon,'" 133.

246. This is why Lefebvre writes against structuralism: "Everyday insignificance can only become meaningful when transformed into something other than everyday life; in other words, it is not possible to construct a theoretical and practical system such that the details of everyday life will become meaningful in and by this system" (*Everyday Life in the Modern World,* 98).

247. Lefebvre, "Preface to the Study of the Habitat of the 'Pavillon,'" 133.

248. Ibid.; see also Lefebvre, *The Production of Space,* 163.

249. See Carporzen, "Marquage et appropriation de l'espace," 32.

250. Lefebvre, "Éléments d'une théorie de l'objet," 278.

251. Lefebvre, *The Production of Space,* 33.

252. This genealogy is often complicated; Christian Schmid demonstrated that Lefebvre's concept of space as consisting of three moments was preceded by an attempt to theorize a duality of mental and social, or an "ideal" and "real" space, in his *Espace et politique* and in *La survie du capitalisme;* see Schmid, *Stadt, Raum und Gesellschaft,* 205.

253. Lefebvre, *The Production of Space,* 60.

254. Schmid, *Stadt, Raum und Gesellschaft,* 318ff.; Schmid, "Henri Lefebvre's Theory of the Production of Space"; Elden, *Understanding Henri Lefebvre,* 148.

255. Shields, *Lefebvre, Love and Struggle;* Elden, *Understanding Henri Lefebvre;* Schmid, *Stadt, Raum und Gesellschaft;* Merrifield, *Henri Lefebvre.*

256. Shields, *Lefebvre, Love and Struggle,* 160ff.

257. Elden, *Understanding Henri Lefebvre,* 190.

258. Merrifield, *Henri Lefebvre,* 109–10.

259. Schmid, *Stadt, Raum und Gesellschaft,* 205.

260. Ibid., 208.

261. Ibid., 209–10.

262. Schmid, "Theorie," 165. See also Schmid, "The Dialectics of Urbanization in Zurich"; Schmid, "The City as a Contested Terrain"; and Schmid, "A New Paradigm of Urban Development for Zurich."

263. Trebitsch, "Preface: Presentation: Twenty Years After," xxiv.

264. Lefebvre, *The Production of Space,* 413, 389, 171.

265. Ibid., 38; Lefebvre, *La production de l'espace,* 48.

266. Weyl, *Symmetry;* Lefebvre, *The Production of Space,* 173.

267. Lefebvre, *The Production of Space,* 8; Lefebvre, *La production de l'espace,* 15.

268. Lefebvre, *La production de l'espace,* 15.

269. Lefebvre, "Utopie expérimentale," 134.

270. Lefebvre, *The Production of Space,* 33; Lefebvre, *La production de l'espace,* 42.

271. Lefebvre, *The Production of Space,* 346.

272. Ibid., 413–14; see also ibid., 24–25 fn. 30.

273. Ibid., 38.

274. Ibid., 33; Lefebvre, *La production de l'espace,* 43.

275. Lefebvre, *The Production of Space,* 38; Lefebvre, *La production de l'espace,* 48.

276. Lefebvre, *The Production of Space,* 45.

277. Deleuze and Foucault, "Intellectuals and Power," 206; Debord, *Society of the Spectacle.* See also Christofferson, *French Intellectuals against the Left.*

278. See Lefebvre, *Espace et politique,* 12 ff.

279. Lefebvre, *The Production of Space,* 39.

280. Ibid., 41.

281. Ibid., 39, 117, 164–65, 230. For a critique, see Casey, "The Production of Space or the Heterogeneity of Place," 76.

282. Lefebvre, *The Production of Space,* 33, 41–42.

283. Lefebvre, "La vie sociale dans la ville," 146–47; Lefebvre, "Á propos de la recherche interdisciplinaire en sociologie urbaine et en urbanisme," 254.

284. Lefebvre, *The Production of Space,* 40; translation modified.

285. Lefebvre, "Á propos de la recherche interdisciplinaire en sociologie urbaine et en urbanisme," 254; Lefebvre, "La vie sociale dans la ville," 147.

3. CRITIQUE

1. Lefebvre, *La ville/À voix nue.*

2. See Lefebvre, *Le temps des méprises,* 218–19.

3. Balibar, *The Philosophy of Marx;* Althusser, *For Marx.*

4. See Osborne, "The Reproach of Abstraction."

5. For discussion of space as concrete abstraction in capitalism, see Gottdiener, *The Social Production of Urban Space,* 128 ff.; Gottdiener, "A Marx for Our Time"; Shields, *Lefebvre, Love and Struggle,* 159 ff.; Elden, *Understanding Henri Lefebvre,* 189 ff.; Harvey, *The Urban Experience;* and Schmid, *Stadt, Raum und Gesellschaft.* See also Stanek, "Space as Concrete Abstraction."

6. See Cunningham, "The Concept of Metropolis."

7. Lefebvre, *The Production of Space,* 413, 299.

8. Ibid., 11.

9. Ibid., 413.

10. Ibid., 39; Schmid, *Stadt, Raum und Gesellschaft,* 205 ff.

11. See Lefebvre, *The Production of Space,* 14, 41, 226, 298, 356, 413.

12. Ibid., 7.

13. Busbea, *Topologies,* 11.

14. Lefebvre, *The Production of Space,* 3–5. See also Lefebvre, "La production de l'espace."

15. Lefebvre, *The Production of Space,* 334–35; Lefebvre, *The Right to the City.*

16. Moles and Rohmer, *Psychologie de l'espace,* 8.

17. Lefebvre, *The Production of Space,* 8.

18. Norberg-Schulz, *Existence, Space and Architecture,* 11.

19. Ibid., 16.

20. Lefebvre, *The Production of Space,* 298.

21. Zevi, *Architecture as Space,* 23.

22. Ibid., 220; Lefebvre, *The Production of Space,* 127.

23. Zevi, *Architecture as Space,* 224.

24. Trystram, ed., *Fondation Royaumont pour le progrès des sciences de l'homme.*

25. Ibid.

26. See the conclusions of the seminar 1bis, by Max Querrien, in "Dimensions neuro-physiologique et neuro-psychologique," ed. Sturge-Moore, 149. See also Grenzling, "Méthodologie d'expérimentation en architecture," 7.

27. Lefebvre, *The Production of Space,* 26–27.

28. Hegel, "Wer denkt abstrakt?"

29. Osborne, "The Reproach of Abstaction," 25.

30. Ilyenkov, *The Dialectics of the Abstract and the Concrete in Marx's Capital.* See also Lefebvre, "Éléments d'une théorie de l'objet," 268ff.

31. See Burbidge, *Historical Dictionary of Hegelian Philosophy;* and Inwood, *A Hegel Dictionary.*

32. Hegel, *Aesthetics,* 1:108.

33. Inwood, *A Hegel Dictionary,* 31.

34. Lefebvre, *The Production of Space,* 15–16.

35. Inwood, *A Hegel Dictionary,* 311.

36. See Wandschneider, "Zur Struktur Dialektischer Begriffsentwicklung."

37. Lefebvre, *The Production of Space,* 226–27.

38. Ibid., 15–16. For a discussion, see Dimendberg, "Henri Lefebvre on Abstract Space."

39. Lefebvre, *The Production of Space,* 72.

40. Lefebvre, *La production de l'espace,* 23. Note that the English translation of this passage in *The Production of Space* (15), which renders "l'universalité concrète" as "abstract universality," is misleading.

41. Lefebvre, *The Production of Space,* 70; for a problematization of the opposition between work and product, see ibid., 73ff.

42. Lefebvre, *Critique of Everyday Life,* 2:237.

43. Schmid, *Stadt, Raum und Gesellschaft,* 85ff.

44. Lefebvre, *The Production of Space,* 26, 101–2.

45. Lefebvre, *La pensée marxiste et la ville,* 42.

46. Ibid., 47–48.

47. Lefebvre, *The Production of Space,* 68.

48. Ibid., 71.

49. Avineri, *Hegel's Theory of the Modern State,* 90; Balibar, *The Philosophy of Marx.*

50. Lefebvre, *The Production of Space,* 71.

51. Balibar, *The Philosophy of Marx*, 30ff.

52. Lefebvre, *The Production of Space*, 42.

53. Lefebvre, *Critique of Everyday Life*, 3:134–35.

54. Lefebvre, *The Production of Space*, 288.

55. Ibid., 73.

56. Ibid., 411, 37.

57. Ibid., 137, 142; see also Lefebvre, *The Right to the City*, 102.

58. See Haumont et al., *L'habitat pavillonnaire*, 74ff. In fact, Marx described alienation in a very similar way: the worker feels free only in his basic functions—"eating, drinking, procreating, or at most in his dwelling and in dressing-up"—which become "animal" when separated from his other activities: "Certainly eating, drinking, procreating, etc., are also genuinely human functions. But in the abstraction which separates them from the sphere of all other human activity and turns them into sole and ultimate ends, they are animal"; see Marx, *Economic and Philosophic Manuscripts of 1844*.

59. Lefebvre, "Propositions pour un nouvel urbanisme," 185.

60. Lefebvre, *The Production of Space*, 86; this differentiation was also used to describe two facets of everyday life in *Critique of Everyday Life:* the concrete, linked with society by a variety of social practices, and the abstract, isolated from these practices and restricted to the levels of the imaginary and ideology (Lefebvre, *Critique of Everyday Life* 3:136).

61. See also Baudrillard, *The System of Objects,* 3ff.; and Busbea, *Topologies,* 18.

62. Lefebvre, preface in *Lived-in Architecture,* n.p.

63. Bedos et al., eds., *Les besoins fonctionnels de l'homme,* 33; Depaule, "L'architecture sauvage," 7–9.

64. Haumont et al., *L'habitat pavillonnaire,* 130.

65. Lefebvre, preface to the study of Boudon, in Lefebvre, *Du rural à l'urbain,* 233; this statement is less direct in the English translation (Lefebvre, preface in *Lived-in Architecture,* n.p.).

66. Lefebvre, *The Production of Space,* 37.

67. Ibid., 419.

68. Lefebvre, *Le mode de production étatique,* 59.

69. Ibid., 61.

70. Marx, *Grundrisse*; Lefebvre, *The Production of Space,* 69.

71. Marx, *Grundrisse*.

72. These concepts are dependent on the Hegelian differentiation between concrete and abstract. It was shown by Hiroshi Uchida, in his book *Marx's Grundrisse and Hegel's Logic,* that the "Introduction" to *Grundrisse* reflects Hegel's theory of the concept.

73. Marx, *Grundrisse*.

74. Marx, *A Contribution to the Critique of Political Economy*.

75. Lefebvre, *The Production of Space,* 352ff.

76. Ibid., 123–24.

77. Lefebvre, *Pignon*, 12.

78. Ibid., 17–18.

79. Ibid., 20–21.

80. Ibid., 14.

81. Lefebvre, "Les institutions de la société 'post technologique,'" 134. This paper was presented at the 1972 Universitas Symposium at the MoMA, organized by Emilio Ambasz; see Scott, "On the 'Counter-Design' of Institutions." Elsewhere, Lefebvre writes that Picasso, Klee, and the members of the Bauhaus have discovered that "one can represent objects in space in a way that they don't have a face or a privileged façade"; see Lefebvre, *Les contradictions de l'État moderne*, 289.

82. Tafuri, *Theories and History of Architecture*, 33–39, 84.

83. Hilberseimer, *Grossstadt Architektur*, 100.

84. Forty, *Words and Buildings*, 256–75; Moravánszky, "Die Wahrnehmung des Raumes."

85. Moravánszky, "Die Wahrnehmung des Raumes."

86. Lefebvre, *The Production of Space*, 124.

87. Ibid., 126.

88. Tafuri, "Toward a Critique of Architectural Ideology," 22.

89. Lefebvre, in Sturge-Moore, ed., "Architecture—mythe—idéologie," 58.

90. Lefebvre, *The Production of Space*, 304; see Lefebvre, "Constituez vous en avant-garde."

91. Lefebvre, *The Production of Space*, 269.

92. Ibid., 307.

93. Lefebvre, "Constituez vous en avant-garde."

94. Kopp, "De la Charte d'Athènes aux grands ensembles," 11; Schnaidt, "Les architec-nochrates [sic]"; Schnaidt, "Le droit à la ville," 210–12.

95. Lefebvre, *Le mode de production étatique*, 64. Lefebvre's distinction between "mental" (technological, scientific, geometrical) and "social" (relating to cosmology, art, religion) representations of space introduced in this passage is not easy to follow (ibid.).

96. Marx, *Grundrisse*.

97. Balibar, *The Philosophy of Marx*, 67.

98. Lefebvre, *La pensée marxiste et la ville*, 9–26.

99. Ibid.

100. See Lefebvre, *The Production of Space*, 313, 232ff.; see also Sohn-Rethel, *Intellectual and Manual Labour*.

101. See Moos, *Fernand Léger*.

102. Cohen and Lortie, *Des fortifs au périf*.

103. Moley, *Les abords du chez-soi*, 42.

104. Lefebvre, "Propositions pour un nouvel urbanisme," 187.

105. Moley, *Les abords du chez-soi*, 42ff.

106. Lefebvre, "La notion de totalité dans les sciences sociales," 61.

107. Marx, *Capital*.

108. Ibid.

109. Lefebvre, *The Production of Space*, 338–39.

110. Sohn-Rethel, *Intellectual and Manual Labour*, 49.

111. Lefebvre, *The Production of Space*, 110–11.

112. Ibid., 200.

113. Casey, "The Production of Space or the Heterogeneity of Place," 73–74.

114. Lefebvre, *The Production of Space*, 316, 342.

115. Ibid., 91.

116. Perec, *Things*, 92–93.

117. Lefebvre, *The Production of Space*, 355–66.

118. Ibid., 366.

119. Ibid., 52.

120. Mumford, *The Culture of Cities*, 185.

121. Lefebvre, *Les contradictions de l'État moderne*, 309.

122. Lefebvre, *The Production of Space*, 413. Both processes—of fragmenting space and of erasing differences—can be executed only by force, writes Lefebvre (ibid., 308). That is why he claims, "*There is a violence intrinsic to abstraction,* and to abstraction's practical (social) use," which involves a "reductive practice" of imposing an order and constituting the elements of that order (ibid., 289, 107).

123. Ibid., 90.

124. Kirsch, "The Incredible Shrinking World?" 549. Kirsch has noticed that Lefebvre understood this domination as a part of the rise of abstract space in a "historical–materialist (and not merely philosophical) development," thus theorized as a concrete abstraction (546, 550).

125. Haumont et al., *La copropriété*.

126. Lefebvre, *Le mode de production étatique*, 259ff.; see also Brenner and Elden, "Henri Lefebvre on State, Space, Territory."

127. Lefebvre, "L'espace," 39, 44.

128. Le Corbusier, *Toward an Architecture*, 86, 96, 116, 117, 129, etc.

129. See Bedos et al., eds., *Les besoins fonctionnels de l'homme*, 8; see also Raymond and Segaud, "Analyse de l'espace architectural."

130. Busbea, *Topologies*.

131. Lefebvre, *The Production of Space*, 337.

132. Ibid., 285–87; see also Schmid, *Stadt, Raum und Gesellschaft*, 263ff.

133. Lefebvre, *The Production of Space*, 341–42.

134. Marx, *Capital*.

135. Ibid.

136. Lefebvre, *The Production of Space*, 53.

137. Ibid., 73.

138. On the instrumentalization of abstract space in the processes of capitalist production, see ibid., 288. On the relative character of space, see Schmid, *Stadt, Raum und Gesellschaft;* Harvey, *The Urban Experience;* and Smith, *Uneven Development.*

139. Lefebvre, *The Production of Space,* 331.

140. Lefebvre, *The Right to the City,* 89.

141. Ibid., 135.

142. Lefebvre, *The Production of Space,* 101; compare Lefebvre, *The Right to the City,* 138.

143. Lefebvre, *The Right to the City,* 134; Lefebvre, *The Production of Space,* 101.

144. Lefebvre, *The Production of Space,* 386, 331.

145. Christaller, *Central Places in Southern Germany;* Engels, *The Housing Question;* Schmid, *Stadt, Raum und Gesellschaft,* 186–87.

146. Lefebvre, *The Production of Space,* 399.

147. Ibid., 392.

148. Ibid., 39.

149. Ibid., 354. Lefebvre wrote that his argument was inspired by Marx's theorizing of the relationships among capital, land, and labor. In a passage from *Espace et politique,* when describing the relationship of "unity and confrontation" among the moments of space, Lefebvre claimed, "Our hypothesis of jointed–disjointed space is based directly on the tripartite or trinity scheme of the capitalist society in Marx" (Lefebvre, *Espace et politique,* 43; see also Lefebvre, *The Production of Space,* 323–25). This formulation is confusing: the *trinity formula* was a scheme introduced by classical economy, and the passage from the third volume of *Capital,* referred to by Lefebvre, reveals that Marx opposed the reductive use of this formula by previous economists. In particular, he rejected the identification of the triad of capital, land, and labor with the three sources of value and opposed the argument that capital generates interests, land–annuity, and labor–wages. Clearly, this is a mystification, writes Marx, because value is produced by human labor and nothing else. The claim that these three are independent sources of value has social and political consequences, naturalizing capital as the means of production, land as real estate, and labor as paid work. Accordingly, not only is their social character concealed, but also class divisions appear as natural and scientifically explained: the three sources of value seem to imply three classes: the aristocracy as the class of landowners, the bourgeoisie as the class of capital owners, and the proletarians as the class of laborers. By contrast, when labor is considered as the only source of value, the relationship among the three elements is destabilized and open to change, as is the relationship among social classes (Marx, *Capital*).

150. Soja, *Thirdspace,* 53ff.

151. Lefebvre, *The Production of Space,* 320.

152. See Althusser, "Contradiction and Overdetermination"; Balibar, *The Philosophy of Marx.*

153. Ilyenkov, *The Dialectics of the Abstract and the Concrete in Marx's Capital.*

154. Ibid.

155. Balibar, *The Philosophy of Marx,* 92–93. On the idealist character of the distinction between use and exchange value, which is the fundament of Ilyenkov's reconstruction, see Derrida, *Specters of Marx.*

156. Lefebvre, *The Production of Space,* 66.

157. Ibid., 65.

158. Ibid., 65–66; Lefebvre, "Perspectives de la sociologie rurale."

159. Rémi Hess in his essay on Lefebvre's method (1991) quoted him attributing the regressive–progressive method to Marx; see Hess, "La méthode d'Henri Lefebvre."

160. Burke, *The French Historical Revolution,* 23.

161. Lefebvre, "Perspectives de la sociologie rurale," 65–66.

162. Ibid., 73.

163. Ibid., 74.

164. Lefebvre, "What Is the Historical Past?" 34.

165. Lefebvre, *The Urban Revolution,* 24.

166. Lefebvre, *La pensée marxiste et la ville,* 45, 31.

167. Ibid., 84–86.

168. Cohen, *Karl Marx's Theory of History,* 50ff.; Lefebvre, *La pensée marxiste et la ville,* 85–86. Lefebvre argues, "Like the land, the city is a force of production (and not just a means of production, a tool)" (ibid.). By contrast, in *The Production of Space,* he wrote that space is a "means of production" (349). Although Marx himself was sometimes ambiguous about the relationship of these two terms (see the discussion in Cohen, *Karl Marx's Theory of History,* 38), Lefebvre's differing wording suggests a shift in the accents of his argument: while in *The Production of Space* he stresses both the political and economic instrumentality, in *La pensée marxiste et la ville* he argues that space is not just a tool.

169. Lefebvre, *La pensée marxiste et la ville.*

170. Ibid., 54.

171. Ibid., 129ff.

172. Ibid., 134.

173. Ibid., 135.

174. Lefebvre, *The Production of Space,* 347.

175. Lefebvre, *La pensée marxiste et la ville,* 138.

176. Ibid., 143.

177. Ibid., 145. The conclusion that the capitalist centers need to secure the market—both internally and overseas—sheds light on Lefebvre's intuition about the colonial character of the "new towns" of the *trente glorieuses.* He writes, "Social space itself is produced, at the same time as it is supervised and controlled, in the suburbs of the big cities and in spatial planning. If thus the bourgeoisie of a country loses external markets, it transports colonialism inside this country"; ibid.

178. Marx, *Critique of the Gotha Programme*; Lefebvre, *La pensée marxiste et la ville,* 148.

179. Lefebvre, *The Right to the City,* 148.

180. Negri, "The Multitude and the Metropolis."

181. Lefebvre, *La pensée marxiste et la ville,* 166.

182. Ibid., 154–55; Lefebvre, *The Production of Space,* 336.

183. Lefebvre, *The Production of Space,* 335; Harvey, *The Condition of Postmodernity;* Harvey, *Social Justice and the City* (1973).

184. Kipfer et al., "On the Production of Henri Lefebvre," 7.

185. Lefebvre, *The Production of Space,* 104; see also Lefebvre, *La survie du capitalisme.*

186. Lefebvre, *La pensée marxiste et la ville,* 166.

187. Ibid., 167ff.; see also Lefebvre, *The Production of Space,* 352ff.

188. Lefebvre, *La pensée marxiste et la ville,* 159, 166.

189. See Lefebvre, *The Right to the City,* 120.

190. Lefebvre, *La pensée marxiste et la ville,* 159.

4. PROJECT

1. Sturge-Moore, ed., "Architecture et sciences sociales," 4.

2. Tafuri, "Architecture et semiologie."

3. Ibid., 18.

4. Lefebvre, "L'espace spécifique de l'architecture," 62.

5. Ibid., 64.

6. Ibid.; see also Lefebvre, "Habiter," 18.

7. Tafuri, "Towards a Critique of Architectural Ideology," 32.

8. See also ibid., 28.

9. Tafuri, *Theories and History of Architecture,* 228.

10. Jameson's taxonomy could not have been appreciated by Tafuri, who, after the publication of the volume in which Jameson's essay was included, wrote to the editor, "If American culture wants to understand me, why not make an effort to abandon facile typologies (Marxism, negative thought, etc.)?"; see Manfredo Tafuri, letter to Joan Ockman, 29 April 1985, quoted in Ockman, "Venice and New York," 67.

11. Jameson, "Architecture and the Critique of Ideology," 72; Toscano, "Factory, Territory, Metropolis, Empire," 204.

12. Jameson, "Architecture and the Critique of Ideology," 72. One of the main discussions in *Theories and History of Architecture* is a polemics with the argument that structuralism is "a new Eleaticism," thus unable to provide a methodology for historical research. The immediate source for this argument seems to be the Italian translation of François Furet's essay "Les intellectuels français et le structuralisme"; see also Lefebvre, "Claude Lévi-Strauss et le nouvel éléatisme."

13. See also Lefebvre, *The Production of Space,* 232–33.

14. Guilbaud et al., "International Competition for the New Belgrade Urban Structure Improvement," 1; I would like to thank Ljiljana Blagojević for making this document available to me before it was published. See also Lefebvre, "Quand la ville se perd dans une métamorphose planétaire"; and Lefebvre, "Les illusions de la modernité."

15. Lefebvre, *Critique of Everyday Life,* 2:178–19.

16. Ibid., 348.

17. Ibid.

18. Ibid., 118–19; see also Lefebvre, *The Urban Revolution,* 5; and Simondon, "The Genesis of the Individual."

19. Sadler, *The Situationist City,* 44. For a discussion on the relationship between Lefebvre and the situationists, see Ross, "Henri Lefebvre on the Situationist International"; Violeau, *Situations construites;* Merrifield, *Henri Lefebvre;* and Merrifield, "Lefebvre and Debord."

20. Lefebvre, *The Right to the City,"* 155; Dessauce, ed., *The Inflatable Moment.*

21. Busbea, *Topologies.*

22. Schnaidt, "Le droit à la ville," 211; see also Violeau, *Les architectes et mai 68.*

23. Lefebvre, *The Urban Revolution,* 131; Lefebvre, *The Right to the City,* 173.

24. Lefebvre, *The Production of Space,* 413.

25. Ibid., 52.

26. Lefebvre, "Sur quelques critères du développement social et du socialisme," 164–65.

27. Situationist International, "Definitions," 52.

28. Lefebvre in Ross, "Henri Lefebvre on the Situationist International."

29. Ibid.

30. Kotányi and Vaneigem, "Basic Program of the Bureau of Unitary Urbanism," 87.

31. Lefebvre, "Introduction," *Actualité de Fourier,* 14.

32. Fischbach, *La production des hommes.*

33. Schérer and Hocquenghem, "Fourier théoricien de la production," 96; Schérer, *Utopies nomades.*

34. Lefebvre, interview for *Un certain regard: Charles Fourier.*

35. Bollerey, *Architekturkonzeptionen der utopischen Sozialisten,* 124ff.

36. Ibid. See also Lefebvre, "Introduction," *Actualité de Fourier,* 14.

37. Lefebrve, Interview on *Un Certain Regard: Charles Fourier.*

38. For a discussion, see Papayanis, *Planning Paris before Haussmann,* 171.

39. See Garnier, *Une cité industrielle;* Zola, *Work;* Giedion, *Space, Time and Architecture,* 820.

40. Serenyi, "Le Corbusier, Fourier and the Monastery of Ema"; Guerrand, "Aux origines de la cité radieuse"; Bollerey, *Architekturkonzeptionen der utopischen Sozialisten;* Vidler, "The Idea of Unity and Le Corbusier's Urban Form"; Vidler, "Asylums of Libertinage."

41. Barthes, *Sade, Fourier, Loyola,* 90.

42. Benjamin, *The Arcades Project,* 642.

43. Fourier, *Des modifications à introduire dans l'architecture des villes,* 5ff. For discussion, see Bollerey, *Architekturkonzeptionen der utopischen Sozialisten,* 100–107.

44. Fourier, *Des modifications à introduire dans l'architecture des villes,* 17.

45. Ibid., 20.

46. Perreymond, "Études sur la ville de Paris."

47. Perreymond, quoted in Papayanis, *Planning Paris before Haussmann,* 187.

48. Fourier, quoted in Manuel, *The Prophets of Paris,* 207.

49. Ibid., 220ff.

50. Fourier, *Des modifications à introduire dans l'architecture des villes,* 23, 38.

51. Ibid., 29.

52. Ibid., 38.

53. Ibid., 39.

54. Manuel, *The Prophets of Paris,* 225.

55. Barthes, *Sade, Fourier, Loyola,* 99–100.

56. Raymond "L'utopie concrète." See also Raymond, "Hommes et dieux à Palinuro."

57. Furlough, "Packaging Pleasures." See also Peyre and Raynouard, *Histoire et légendes du Club Méditerranée.*

58. Raymond "L'utopie concrète," 282.

59. Furlough, "Packaging Pleasures," 65.

60. Lefebvre, *The Production of Space,* 383.

61. See Lefebvre, interview on *Paris Paris où le temps d'une génération 1936–1957.*

62. Lefebvre, *The Production of Space,* 384.

63. Ibid., 372. See also Kipfer, "How Lefebvre Urbanized Gramsci."

64. The first version of the text on the Commune ("La signification de la Commune") was published in the journal *Arguments* 27–28 (1962): 11–19. See also Lefebvre, "L'avis du sociologue: État ou non-État," and the discussion during the colloquium on the Commune (Paris, 21–23 May 1971), in *Colloque universitaire pour la commémoration du centenaire de la Commune de 1871,* 173–77, and 184–90. See also Hess, *Henri Lefebvre et l'aventure du siècle,* 195.

65. Lefebvre, *The Explosion,* 117–18.

66. Lefebvre, *La proclamation de la Commune,* 11.

67. Rémi Hess, interview with the author, Paris, summer 2007.

68. Lefebvre, *The Explosion,* 104.

69. Chauveau, "Logement et habitat populaire de la fin de deuxième guerre mondiale aux années 1960," 138.

70. See also McDonough, "Invisible Cities: Henri Lefebvre's *The Explosion.*"

71. "Domaine universitaire de Nanterre," 130.

72. Lefebvre, "Introduction à l'espace urbain," 25. The concept of the space of catastrophe was inspired by the catastrophe theory by René Thom, a mathematician and a colleague from the University of Strasbourg.

73. Althusser, "Contradiction and Overdetermination."

74. Lefebvre, *The Production of Space*, 358.

75. Ibid., 365.

76. Ibid., 129.

77. Lefebvre, *The Explosion*, 105.

78. Ibid., 105; Lefebvre, *The Urban Revolution*, 128. Lefebvre's concept of heterotopia differed from Foucault's introduced in a lecture in March 1967. Lefebvre started to use the concept in 1968, in *The Urban Revolution* and during the CRAUC seminar, inspired by the work of the linguist Algirdas Julius Greimas; see Lefebvre, *The Urban Revolution*, 190; and Schmid, *Stadt, Raum und Gesellschaft*, 277. See also Foucault, "Of Other Spaces."

79. Lefebvre, *The Explosion*, 104.

80. Ibid.

81. Lefebvre, interview on *Enquêtes sur les causes des manifestations*.

82. Lefebvre, *The Explosion*, 106.

83. Ibid.

84. Ibid., 105.

85. See Duteuil, *Nanterre 1965–66–67–68*.

86. Lefebvre, "La sexualité," 137ff.

87. Leaflet, reprinted in Duteuil, *Nanterre 1965–66–67–68*, 73.

88. Lefebvre, *The Explosion*, 109; Lefebvre in Sturge-Moore, ed., "Architecture—mythe—idéologie," 43.

89. Kopp, *Town and Revolution*, 12.

90. Ibid., 115.

91. Kopp in Sturge-Moore, ed., "Architecture—mythe—idéologie," 140.

92. See Lefebvre, *The Explosion*, 124.

93. Ibid., 109.

94. Ibid., 108.

95. Lefebvre, *The Production of Space*, 356.

96. Lefebvre, *The Explosion*, 119, 123.

97. Dreyfus-Armand, "Le mouvement du 22 mars," 125.

98. Lefebvre, *The Explosion*, 123.

99. Lefebvre, "Espace et ideologie,"114–15.

100. Lefebvre, *The Explosion*, 105.

101. Ibid.

102. Lefebvre, *La proclamation de la Commune*, 32.

103. Ibid., 134.

104. Ibid., 139–40. See also Castells, *The City and the Grassroots*, chapter 3.

105. Ibid., 394.

106. The students in Nanterre directly referred to the Commune, which, according to one of the leaflets distributed on the campus was "the last big revolutionary movement . . . accomplished by direct action," that is to say, without political intermediaries (reprinted by Jean-Pierre Duteuil, *Nanterre 1965–66–67–68*, 45).

107. See also Unwin, "A Waste of Space?"

108. Lefebvre, *The Production of Space*, 332.

109. On this understanding of the mode of production, see Lefebvre, *Critique of Everyday Life*, 3:134.

110. The references include D'Arcy Thompson's *On Growth and Form*; and, in particular, Hermann Weyl's *Symmetry*.

111. Lefebvre, *The Production of Space*, 172–73.

112. Ibid., 195.

113. Ibid., 171, 205; see also Lefebvre, *Rhythmanalysis*.

114. See Lefebvre, *The Production of Space*, 192. The anthropological research by Marcel Mauss, Claude Lévi-Strauss, Edward Evans-Pritchard, and Amos Rapoport are significant references for *The Production of Space*.

115. Ibid., 190.

116. Ibid., 194.

117. Ibid., 13–14.

118. Ibid., 46.

119. See Shields, *Lefebvre, Love and Struggle*, 170; see also Schmid, *Stadt, Raum und Gesellschaft*, 137 ff.

120. Lefebvre, *The Production of Space*, 116.

121. Ibid., 42.

122. Ibid., 229, 110, 212.

123. See Šubrt, "The Problem of Time from the Perspective of the Social Sciences"; and Gurvitch, *La multiplicité des temps sociaux*. The interest in nonsynchronicities and persistences constantly reappears in Lefebvre's books; see *Critique of Everyday Life*, 2:133, 315 ff.

124. Lefebvre, *The Production of Space*, 164.

125. Ibid., 334.

126. Ibid., 229.

127. Ibid.

128. Ibid., 423.

129. Ibid., 220.

130. See ibid., the chapter "From Absolute Space to Abstract Space."

131. See Schmid, *Stadt, Raum und Gesellschaft*, 257 ff.

132. Lefebvre, *The Production of Space*, 226.

133. Maïté Clavel, interview with the author, Paris, summer 2007.

134. Cohen, "La coupure entre architectes et intellectuels, ou les enseignements de l'italophilie"; Dessauce, ed., *The Inflatable Moment*; Lefebvre, *Critique of Everyday Life*, 3:45–46.

135. Lefebvre, *The Urban Revolution*, 21.

136. Lefebvre, "Utopie expérimentale," 136–37; Lefebvre, *The Urban Revolution*, 21–22.

137. Lefebvre, *The Production of Space*, 386.

138. Lefebvre in Sturge-Moore, ed., "Architecture—mythe—idéologie," 117.

139. Lefebvre, *The Production of Space,* 385.

140. See Bedos et al., eds., *Les besoins fonctionnels de l'homme,* 33; see also Depaule, "Les sauvages de l'architecture"; for a recent account, see Depaule, "Savoirs et manières de faire architecturaux."

141. Arthaud, *Les palais du rêve.*

142. See Haumont et al., *L'habitat pavillonnaire.*

143. Lefebvre, *The Production of Space,* 222; Barthes, "Sémiologie et urbanisme."

144. Lefebvre, *The Production of Space,* 221.

145. Ibid.

146. Ibid., 162.

147. Lefebvre, *Critique of Everyday Life,* 2:334.

148. Lefebvre, *The Production of Space,* 7; Lefebvre, *The Right to the City,* 115.

149. Lefebvre, *The Production of Space,* 399.

150. See ibid., 12; see also Brenner, "The Urban Question as a Scale Question."

151. Lefebvre, *The Production of Space,* 294. For discussion, see Schmid, *Stadt, Raum und Gesellschaft,* 323–29.

152. Lefebvre, *Critique of Everyday Life,* 2:119.

153. Ibid., 139ff.

154. Lefebvre, *The Urban Revolution,* 78ff.; Lefebvre, *Critique of Everyday Life,* 2:90.

155. Lefebvre, *The Urban Revolution,* 78ff., 87.

156. Ibid., 79ff.

157. Ibid., 80.

158. Ibid., 80ff.

159. Lefebvre, *The Production of Space,* 12. This position was particularly visible in the discussion after Lefebvre's talk "L'urbanisme aujourd'hui" in 1967, in which he urged the distinction of architecture (as the microsociological level of dwelling) from urbanism (as the macrosociological level of the urban society). This was opposed by the architect Jean Balladur, who claimed that this division is "an expression of the contradictions of our society" (see Lefebvre, "L'urbanisme aujourd'hui," in *Les cahiers du Centre d'études socialistes,* 19). Lefebvre responded that he wanted not to separate architecture from urbanism but to stress that they are two levels that are necessarily related (Lefebvre, "L'urbanisme aujourd'hui," in *Du rural à l'urbain,* 225). See also Lefebvre, "Espace architectural, espace urbain," 44.

160. Moley, *Les abords du chez-soi;* Frey, "Prolégomènes à une histoire des concepts de morphologie urbaine et de morphologie sociale."

161. Moley, *Les abords du chez-soi.*

162. For a recent account on Chombart and Auzelle, see the fourth chapter of Rosemary Wakeman's *The Heroic City,* in particular pages 170–88.

163. Smithson, ed., *Team 10 Primer;* Banham, *Megastructure.* See also Welter, "In-Between Space and Society."

164. Moley, *Les abords du chez-soi,* 6ff.

165. Haumont et al., *L'habitat pavillonnaire,* 131; Raymond, "Habitat, modèles culturels et architecture," 226–28. See also Haumont and Raymond, *Habitat et pratique de l'espace,* 166, 170.

166. See Lefebvre, "La vie sociale dans la ville," 149.

167. Lefebvre, *The Production of Space,* 40.

168. The interviews were carried out in Grenoble and Rennes (two cities of considerable size, in which co-ownership was more widespread than in other French cities), as well as four locations of differing social status in the suburbs of Paris (Asnières, Montrouge, Bougival, and Celle-Saint-Cloud).

169. See Haumont et al., *La copropriété,* 99, 49ff.

170. Ibid., 176.

171. See ibid., 46.

172. Ibid., 179.

173. Ibid., 183–84.

174. Lefebvre, *The Production of Space,* 375.

175. Lefebvre, "Quartier et vie de quartier." The study consists of three parts and, besides Lefebvre's essay, it includes two texts by his collaborators: "Ville et quartier," by Monique Coornaert and Claude Harlaut; and "Les quartiers dans trois communes de la banlieue parisienne," by Antoine Haumont.

176. Coornaert et al., *Le quartier et la ville,* 33.

177. Ibid., 15.

178. Ibid., 71.

179. Ibid., 35–36.

180. Ibid., 44.

181. Ibid., 42–44.

182. Ibid., 44.

183. See Bardet, "Les échelons communautaires dans les agglomérations urbaines." In this essay, the six scales of community life that Bardet distinguishes are three hypo-urban scales (patriarchal, domestic, and parochial) and three hyper-urban scales (urban, regional–metropolitan, and capital–metropolitan).

184. Lefebvre, *The Production of Space,* 118.

185. Lefebvre, "L'espace specifique de l'architecture," 69.

186. Lefebrve, "Espace architectural, espace urbain," 40–43.

187. Lefebvre, interview, *Ricardo Bofill invité d'Inter-Actualités.*

188. Lefebvre, *Le temps des méprises,* 247.

189. Banham, *Megastructure.* Banham's criteria follow the list of Ralph Wilcoxon's "Megastructure Bibliography"; ibid., 8.

190. Banham, *Megastructure,* 81–83, 106.

191. James, *Ricardo Bofill.*

192. Taller de arquitectura, "Réaliser l'utopie," 88.

193. Albers, *Zur Entwicklung der Stadtplanung in Europa,* 109–11.

194. Lefebvre in Ross, "Henri Lefebvre on the Situationist International."

195. Bofill and Taller de arquitectura, "Prologo."

196. Bofill and Taller de arquitectura, "Necesidad de nuevos métodos operativos."

197. Bofill et al., *Hacia una formalización,* 2; the English translation is presented according to the leaflet attached to this publication.

198. See Bofill and Taller de arquitectura, "Problemas estructurales"; and Bofill and Taller de arquitectura, "Estudio geométrico previo al diseño de viviendas."

199. Bofill et al., *Hacia una formalización,* 26.

200. Ibid., 30.

201. Bofill and Taller de arquitectura, "Prologo."

202. Ibid.

203. Bofill and Taller de arquitectura, "La forma de la vivienda." This approach was expressed in the typology of dwellings, which include "unconventional apartments" (on several stories, without a preconceived division of functions and intended for "creative" professionals); economical "typical apartments," founded on the distinction between small individual and larger communal rooms; and "special apartments," expressing traditional customs (including a reduction of the dimensions of bedrooms and an enlargement of the kitchen, designed as the communal space and the work place for the wife not working outside the home); see Bofill and Taller de arquitectura, "Estudio geométrico previo al diseño de viviendas."

204. Bofill and Taller de arquitectura, "Necesidad de nuevos métodos operativos." The authors postulate the use of in-place carpeting and other "modern" furnishings instead of cupboards, wardrobes, three-seater sofas, umbrella stands, armchairs, and so on; see Bofill and Taller de arquitectura, "Estudio geométrico previo al diseño de viviendas."

205. Bofill, *L'architecture d'un homme,* 107.

206. Interview with Ricardo Bofill, Barcelona, autumn 2008.

207. Bofill, *L'architecture d'un homme,* 108. For a brief recounting of the history and an interview with Ricardo Bofill, see the article "La 'ciudad en el espacio,' un proyecto."

208. Lefebvre, "L'espace specifique de l'architecture," 69.

209. Ricardo Bofill, interview with the author.

210. Bofill and Taller de arquitectura, "Problemas estructurales."

211. Lefebvre, *The Urban Revolution,* 21. See also Schuman, "Utopia Spurned." For Lefebvre's critique of postmodern architecture, see Lefebvre, "Espace architectural, espace urbain"; and Guilbaud et al., "International competition for the New Belgrade Urban Structure Improvement."

212. Bofill et al., *Hacia una formalización,* cover.

213. Lefebvre, "Quartier et vie de quartier," 11.

214. Ibid.

215. See Lefebvre, *The Production of Space,* 363; Lefebvre, "Espace architectural, espace urbain," 44.

216. Lefebvre in Sturge-Moore, ed., "Architecture—mythe—idéologie," 43–44.

217. Nieuwenhuys, "New Babylon," 154; Nieuwenhuys, "On Traveling," 201.

218. Nieuwenhuys, "New Babylon," 155; Nieuwenhuys, "Description of the Yellow Sector," 134.

219. Situationist International, "Definitions," 51–52.

220. Nieuwenhuys, "Unitary Urbanism," 132.

221. Ibid., 134.

222. Description of the seminar by Hubert Tonka, manuscript, Rijksbureau voor Kunsthistorische Documentatie, The Hague, Constant Archive, box 319.

223. Constant Nieuwenhuys, letter to the students of Institut d'urbanisme de Paris, 5 October 1969, Rijksbureau voor Kunsthistorische Documentatie, The Hague, Constant Archive, box 320.

224. See Wigley, *Constant's New Babylon,* 12; see also Heynen, "New Babylon"; and McDonough, "Metastructure."

225. Wigley, *Constant's New Babylon,* 37–38.

226. Nieuwenhuys, "New Babylon—Ten Years On," 222.

227. For a discussion, see Wigley, *Constant's New Babylon,* 35ff.

228. Nieuwenhuys, "New Babylon: Outline of a Culture," 160.

229. Nieuwenhuys, "New Babylon—Ten Years On," 224.

230. Wigley, *Constant's New Babylon,* 68.

231. Nieuwenhuys, "Another City for Another Life," 115.

232. Guy Debord, quoted in Levin, "Geopolitics of Hibernation," 13.

233. Debord and Wolman, "A User's Guide to Détournement (1956)," 19.

234. Nieuwenhuys, "New Babylon: Outline of a Culture," 161.

235. Brenner, "The Urban Question as a Scale Question," 367.

236. Lefebvre, *Les contradictions de l'État moderne,* 272.

237. Ibid., 273.

238. See Smith, "Geography, Difference and the Politics of Scale"; Smith, "Remaking Scale"; Swyngedouw, "Neither Global nor Local"; and Jessop, *The Future of the Capitalist State.*

239. Brenner et al., "State Space in Question," 1–26.

240. Brenner, "The Urban Question as a Scale Question," 368, 374.

241. See Lefebvre, "Bistrot-club"; and Lefebvre, "Constituez vous en avant-garde."

242. Lefebvre, "Constituez vous en avant-garde," n.p.

243. Ibid.

244. Ajzenberg, introduction to *Du contrat de citoyenneté.*

245. Renaudie, "Sur l'urbain," 194.

246. Lefebvre, "Du pacte social au contrat de citoyenneté," 32. In these statements, Lefebvre's very strong ties to his native region, the Béarn, and to his compatriots, such as Georges Lapassade and René Lourau, might resonate.

247. Ibid., 33–36.

248. Lefebvre, *The Right to the City,* 173; Lefebvre, "Le droit à la ville," 34–35.

249. Lefebvre, "Quand la ville se perd dans une métamorphose planétaire," 17; Lefebvre, "Les illusions de la modernité," 17. See also Harvey, "The Right to the City"; and *Droit de cité.*

250. See Guilbaud et al., "International Competition for the New Belgrade Urban Structure Improvement." See also Blagojević, "The Right to New Belgrade."

251. Serge Renaudie, e-mail correspondence with the author, spring 2008.

252. See Guilbaud et al., "International Competition for the New Belgrade Urban Structure Improvement," 12, 16.

253. Ibid., 16.

254. Ibid., 27–28.

255. Ibid., 5.

256. Blagojević, "The Right to New Belgrade"; for an overview of the planning history of New Belgrade, see Blagojević, "New Belgrade."

257. Petrović, "A Study for the Restructuring of the Center of New Belgrade and the Sava Amphitheatre."

258. Blagojević, "New Belgrade."

259. Guilbaud et al., "International Competition for the New Belgrade Urban Structure Improvement," 2–3. The jury awarded two *ex-aequo* first prizes, one to the Polish architects Krzysztof Domaradzki, Olgierd Roman Dziekoński, and Zbigniew Garbowski, and the other to the Slovakian architect Jaroslav Kachlik (Blagojević, "The Right to New Belgrade").

260. Blagojević, "The Right to New Belgrade."

261. Brenner, "State Theory in the Political Conjuncture," 789.

262. Henri Lefebvre, lecture at the "Rencontres pour la ville," organized by the French Communist Party, 19–20 November 1982, published in *Société française: Cahiers de l'Institut de recherches marxistes,* 15.

263. Ibid.

264. Lefebvre, "Une interview d'Henri Lefebvre," 123–25. Lefebvre was a member of the editorial board of *Autogestion* (in 1970 the journal changed its name to *Autogestion et socialisme*); see Trebitsch, "Henri Lefebvre et l'autogestion."

265. Lefebvre, "Du pacte social au contrat de citoyenneté," 35.

266. Lefebvre, "Henri Lefebvre ouvre le débat sur la théorie de l'autogestion," 65.

267. Ibid., 67.

268. See ibid., 67ff.

269. Edvard Kardelj, the main ideologue of Yugoslav self-management, quoted in Mušič, "The New System of Social Planning in Yugoslavia and Perspectives of Urban Planning," 2:303. See also Brborić, *Democratic Governance in the Transition from Yugoslav Self-Management to a Market Economy;* and Kardelj, *Über das System der selbstverwaltenden Planung.*

270. Mušič, "The New System of Social Planning in Yugoslavia," 304. See also Mušič, "Urban Planning, Participation, and Self-Management," 303ff.

271. Blau and Rupnik, *Project Zagreb,* 205ff., 248ff.

272. Brborić, *Democratic Governance in the Transition from Yugoslav Self-Management to a Market Economy.*

273. Ibid.

274. Lefebvre, "Comments on a New State Form," 135.

275. Ibid.

276. Guilbaud et al., "International Competition for the New Belgrade Urban Structure Improvement," 5.

277. Ibid., 6; translation modified according to the French text also presented in *Autogestion.*

278. See Erić, *Differentiated Neighborhoods.*

279. On "progressive nostalgia," see Viktor Misiano, introduction to "English Digest 2005–2007."

280. Lefebvre, "Henri Lefebvre ouvre le débat," 66.

281. Hubert Tonka interviewed by Pawley and Tschumi, "The Beaux Arts since 1968," 566.

282. Aubert quoted in Violeau, "Utopie: In acts . . . ," 50. See also Baudrillard, *Utopia Deferred.*

283. Luxemburg, *Social Reform or Revolution.*

284. Interview with Claude Schnaidt, in Schnaidt, *Autrement dit,* 575.

285. Tafuri, "Towards a Critique of Architectural Ideology," 30.

286. Le Corbusier, *Toward an Architecture,* 307.

287. Lefebvre, "Henri Lefebvre ouvre le débat." See also Elden, *Understanding Henri Lefebvre,* 228.

288. Lefebvre, "La planification démocratique," 83.

289. Ibid.

290. See also Lefebvre, "Henri Lefebvre ouvre le débat," 62.

291. Constant, quoted in Levin, "The Geopolitics of Hibernation," 30.

292. Taller de arquitectura, "Réaliser l'utopie," 88; see also Kofman and Lebas, "Recovery and Reappropriation in Lefebvre and Constant," 88–89.

293. Lefebvre, "La dictature de l'oeil et du phallus," 52.

294. Ibid.

295. Ibid.

AFTERWORD

1. Henri Lefebvre, "Vers une architecture de la jouissance" (1973), 2.

2. Ibid., 3.

3. Ibid., 217.

□□□ Bibliography

LIBRARIES AND ARCHIVES

Archives, Espaces et sociétés, Paris

Archives, Musée national des arts et traditions populaires (MNATP), Paris

Archives, Taller de arquitectura, Barcelona

Archives Jean Dieuzaide, Toulouse

Archives nationales, Fontainebleau

Bibliothèque de documentation internationale contemporaine, Paris—Nanterre

Bibliothèque de géographie—Sorbonne, Paris

Bibliothèque nationale, Paris

Centre d'archives d'architecture du XXe siècle, Paris

Centre de documentation de l'urbanisme, Paris

Centre de recherche sur l'habitat, Paris

Fonds ancien, Institut d'urbanisme de Paris

Gemeentemuseum, The Hague

GTA Archiv, Institut Geschichte und Theorie der Architektur, Eidgenössische
   Technische Hochschule, Zurich

Institut national de l'audiovisuel, Paris

Nederlands Instituut voor Beeld en Geluid, Hilversum

Norbert Guterman Archive, Butler Library, Columbia University, New York

Private archives of companions and colleagues of Henri Lefebvre

Rijksbureau voor Kunsthistorische Documentatie, The Hague

Trésor, Delft University of Technology, Delft

WORKS BY HENRI LEFEBVRE

Lefebvre, Henri. "Á propos de la recherche interdisciplinaire en sociologie urbaine et en urbanisme." In Henre Lefebvre, *Du rural à l'urbain,* 253–65. Paris: Anthropos, 1970. Originally published in *Utopie* 2 (1968).

———. "Á propos d'un nouveau modèle étatique." *Dialectiques* 27 (1979): 47–55.

———. *Au-delà du structuralisme.* Paris: Anthropos, 1971.

———. "Autocritique: Contribution à l'effort d'éclaircissement idéologique." *La nouvelle critique* 4 (1949): 41–57.

———. "Autour des deux dates 1937–1957." In *Paris—Paris 1937–1957,* 404–9. Paris: Centre Georges Pompidou, 1981.

———. "Les autres Paris." *Espaces et sociétés* 13–14 (1974–75): 185–92.

———. "L'avis du sociologue: État ou non-État." In *Colloque universitaire pour la commémoration du centenaire de la Commune de 1871,* 173–77. Paris: Éditions ouvrières, 1972. *Le Mouvement Social,* special issue (79) (April–June 1972).

———. "Besoins profonds, besoins nouveaux de la civlisation urbaine." In Henri Lefebvre, *Du rural à l'urbain,* 197–206. Paris: Anthropos, 1970.

———. "Bistrot-club: Noyau de vie sociale." In Henri Lefebvre, *Du rural à l'urbain,* 141–43. Paris: Anthropos, 1970. Originally published in *Informations bimestrielles du syndicat des architectes de la Seine,* February 1962.

———. "Les classes sociales dans les campagnes: La Toscane et la 'mezzadria classica.'" In Henri Lefebvre, *Du rural à l'urbain,* 41–62. Originally published in *Cahiers internationaux de sociologie* 10 (1951): 70–93.

———. "Claude Lévi-Strauss et le nouvel éléatisme." In Henri Lefebvre, *Au-delà du structuralisme,* 261–312. Paris: Anthropos, 1971. Originally published in *L'homme et la société* 1 (1966): 21–31, and 2 (1966): 81–103; also reprinted in Henri Lefebvre, *L'idéologie structuraliste* (Paris: Le Seuil, 1975).

———. "Comments on a New State Form." In *State, Space, World: Selected Essays by Henri Lefebvre,* ed. Neil Brenner and Stuart Elden, 124–37. Minneapolis: University of Minnesota Press, 2009. Translation of "Á propos d'un nouveau modèle étatique," *Dialectiques* 27 (1979): 47–55.

———. "Les communautés paysannes pyrénéennes (origines, développement, déclin). Étude de sociologie historique, thèse principale de doctorat d'État présentée devant la Faculté des Lettres de l'Université de Paris. PhD diss.," vol. 1, University of Paris–Sorbonne, 1954.

———. "La communauté villageoise." *La Pensée* 66 (1956): 29–36.

———. "Le concept de classe sociale: Un dialogue entre G. Gurvitch et H. Lefebvre." *Critique* (1955): 558–69.

———. "Les conditions sociales de l'industralisation." In *Industrialisation et technocratie,* ed. Georges Gurvitch, 118–40. Paris: Colin, 1949.

———. "Constituez vous en avant-garde." *Archivari: Revue trimestrielle d'architecture* 4 (1984): n.p.

———. *Les contradictions de l'État moderne: La dialectique et/de l'État.* Vol. 4 of *De l'État.* Paris: UGE, 1978.

———. *Contribution à l'esthétique.* Paris: Éditions sociales, 1955.

———. *De l'État.* 4 vols. Paris: UGE, 1976–78.

———. *Critique of Everyday Life,* vol. 1: *Introduction.* Translated by John Moore. 1991; New York: Verso, 2008. Originally published as *Critique de la vie quotidienne,* vol. 1: *Introduction* (Paris: Grasset, 1947).

———. *Critique of Everyday Life,* vol. 2: *Foundations for a Sociology of the Everyday.* Translated by John Moore. London: Verso, 2002. Originally published as *Critique de la vie quotidienne,* vol. 2: *Fondements d'une sociologie de la quotidienneté* (Paris: L'Arche, 1961).

———. *Critique of Everyday Life,* vol. 3: *From Modernity to Modernism: Towards a Metaphilosophy of Daily Life.* Translated by John Moore. London: Verso, 2005. Originally published as *Critique de la vie quotidienne,* vol. 3: *De la modernité au modernisme: Pour une métaphilosophie du quotidien* (Paris: l'Arche, 1981).

———. "De Marx à Nietzsche." Interview. *Le Monde,* 29 January 1971, 16.

———. "Les deux niveaux de la sociologie." In "Marquage et appropriation de l'espace," ed. Jean-François Carporzen. In *Les besoins fonctionnels de l'homme en vue de leur projection ultérieure sur le plan de la conception architecturale: Compte rendu de fin du contrat,* ed. Françoise Bedos, Michel Dameron, Claude Leroy, Henri Raymond, and Léonie Sturge-Moore, annex no. 1, 3. Paris: Centre de recherche d'architecture, d'urbanisme et de construction, 1970.

———. *Dialectical Materialism.* Translated by John Sturrock. London: Cape, 1968. Originally published as *Le matérialisme dialectique* (Paris: Alcan, 1939).

———. "La dictature de l'oeil et du phallus." *Actuel* 18 (1972): 48–52.

———. Discussion. In *La dépolitisation, mythe ou réalité?* ed. Georges Vedel, 267–68. Paris: Colin, 1962.

———. Discussion. In *Les nouveaux comportements politiques de la classe ouvrière: Entretiens de Dijon,* by Léo Hamon, 40–42. Paris: Presses universitaires de France, 1962.

———. Discussion. In *Structuralisme et marxisme,* ed. Jean-Marie Auzias et al., 85–137. Paris: Union générale d'éditions, 1970.

———. Discussion, "Structures familiales comparées." In *Villes et campagnes: Civilisation urbaine et civilisation rurale en France,* ed. Georges Friedmann, 327–62. Paris: Colin, 1953.

———. "Une discussion philosophique en U.R.S.S. Logique formelle et logique dialectique." *La pensée* 59 (1955): 5–20.

———. "Le droit à la ville." *L'homme et la société* 6 (1967): 29–35.

———. "Du pacte social au contrat de citoyenneté." In Lefebvre and the Groupe de Navarrenx, *Du contrat de citoyenneté,* 15–37. Paris: Syllepse etc., 1990.

———. *Du rural à l'urbain.* Paris: Anthropos, 1970.

———. "Éléments d'une théorie de l'objet." In Henri Lefebvre, *Du rural à l'urbain,* 267–85. Paris: Anthropos, 1970. Originally published in *Opus International* 10–11 (1969): 16–22.

———. "Engels et l'utopie." *Espaces et sociétés* 4 (1971): 3–12.

———. "Entretien avec Henri Lefebvre." *AMC: Architecture mouvement continuité* 14 (1986): 6–9.

———. "Les entretiens philosophiques de Varsovie." *Comprendre: Revue de politique de la culture* 19 (1958): 237–45.

———. "L'espace." In Henri Lefebvre, *Le droit à la ville,* vol. 2: *Espace et politique,* 33–44. Paris: Anthropos, 2000.

———. "Espace architectural, espace urbain." In *Architectures en France: Modernité, post-modernité,* 40–46. Paris: Centre Georges Pompidou, 1981.

———. "Espace et ideologie." In "Architecture—mythe—idéologie," ed. Léonie Sturge-Moore. Report of third seminar, 8–9 February 1969. In *Les besoins fonctionnels de l'homme en vue de leur projection ultérieure sur le plan de la conception architecturale: Compte rendu de fin du contrat,* ed. Françoise Bedos, Michel Dameron, Claude Leroy, Henri Raymond, and Léonie Sturge-Moore, annex no. 1, 110–15. Paris: Centre de recherche d'architecture, d'urbanisme et de construction, 1970.

———. *Espace et politique.* Vol. 2 of *Le droit à la ville.* Paris: Anthropos, 2000 [1972].

———. "L'espace spécifique de l'architecture." In *Architecture et sciences sociales: Séminaire annuel, 22–26 juin 1972, Port Grimaud,* ed. Léonie Sturge-Moore, 60–69. Paris, 1972. Centre de recherche sur l'habitat, Paris.

———. *L'État dans le monde moderne.* Vol. 1 of *De l'État.* Paris: UGE, 1976.

———. *Everyday Life in the Modern World.* Trans. Sacha Rabinovitch. New Brunswick, N.J.: Transaction Publishers, 1984. Originally published as *La vie quotidienne dans le monde moderne* (Paris: Gallimard, 1968). Originally published in English translation (London: Allen Lane, 1971).

———. "Evolution or Revolution: Conversation with Leszek Kołakowski." In *Reflexive Water: The Basic Concerns of Mankind,* ed. Fons Elders, 199–267. London: Souvenir, 1974.

———. *The Explosion: Marxism and the French Revolution.* Translated by Alfred Ehrenfeld. New York: Monthly Review Press, 1969. Originally published as *L'irruption de Nanterre au sommet* (Paris: Anthropos, 1968).

———. "Filozofia spirytualistyczna we Francji." *Myśl filozoficzna* 24, no. 4 (1956): 69–96.

———. *La fin de l'historie.* Paris: Éditions de minuit, 1970.

———. *Frédéric Nietzsche.* Paris: Éditions Syllepse, 2003. Originally published by Éditions sociales internationales, Paris, 1939.

———. "Habiter: L'éveil et le réveil de la pensée architecturale." In *Construire pour habiter: Catalogue d'exposition,* ed. Elisabeth Allain-Dupré Fabry and Armelle Lavalou, 18. Paris: Éditions l'Equerre-Plan construction, 1982.

——. *Henri Lefebvre: Key Writings.* Edited by Stuart Elden, Elizabeth Lebas, and Eleonore Kofman; translated by Imogen Forster, Norbert Guterman, Elizabeth Lebas, and John Sturrock. New York: Continuum, 2003.

——. *Henri Lefebvre: La ville/À voix nue: Grands entretiens d'hier et d'aujourd'hui.* France Culture, 1–4 March 1994 (rebroadcast), interview by Gilbert-Maurice Duprez. Conducted and originally broadcast in 1970; also rebroadcast as *Henri Lefebvre: Mémorables,* France Culture, 7–11 October 2002.

——. *Henri Lefebvre: Writings on Cities.* Edited and translated by Elisabeth Lebas and Eleonore Kofman. Oxford: Blackwell, 1996.

——. "Henri Lefebvre ou le fil du siècle." On *Océaniques des idées,* Broadcast on Canal 3, 27 June 1988.

——. "Henri Lefebvre ouvre le débat sur la théorie de l'autogestion." *Autogestion* 1 (1966): 59–70.

——. *Henri Lefebvre, philosophe.* Interview. France Culture, 20 August 1991.

——. "Humanisme et urbanisme: Quelque propositions." *Architecture, Formes, Fonctions* 14 (1968): 22–26.

——. *L'idéologie structuraliste.* Paris: Le Seuil, 1975.

——. "Les illusions de la modernité." *Le monde diplomatique,* "Manière de voir" 13 (1991): 14–17.

——. "Informatique et urbanisation en Californie." In *Crise de l'urbain, futur de la ville: Colloque de Royaumont 1984,* ed. Jacques Le Goff and Louis Guieysse, 19–22. Paris: Économica, 1985.

——. "Les institutions de la société 'post technologique.'" In Henri Lefebvre, *Le droit à la ville,* vol. 2: *Espace et politique,* 99–140. Paris: Anthropos, 2000.

——. "Interventions sur les exposés de MM. A. Banfi et H. Lefebvre." In *Entretiens philosophiques de Varsovie: Les rapports de la pensée et de l'action,* 93–96. Institut international de philosophie, 17–26 juillet 1957. Wrocław: Wydawnictwo Polskiej Akademii Nauk, 1958.

——. "Une interview d'Henri Lefebvre." *Autogestion et socialisme* 33–34 (1976): 115–26.

——. Interview on *Un certain regard: Charles Fourier.* Documentary directed by José-Maria Berzosa. Broadcast on Canal 1, 6 September 1972. Institut national de l'audiovisuel, Paris.

——. Interview on *Enquêtes sur les causes des manifestations.* Broadcast on Canal 1, 11 May 1968. Institut national de l'audiovisuel, Paris.

——. Interview on *Paris Paris où le temps d'une génération 1936–1957.* Broadcast on Antenne 2, 4 and 11 September 1983.

——. Interview on *Ricardo Bofill invité d'Inter-Actualités.* Broadcast on France Inter, 10 May 1975.

——. "An Interview with Henri Lefebvre." *Environment and Planning D: Society and Space* 5 (1987): 27–38. Translated by Eleonore Kofman from "Entretien avec Henri Lefebvre," *Villes en parallèle* 7 (1983): 51–63.

——. "Introduction." In *Actualité de Fourier: Colloque d'Arc-et-Senans,* ed. Henri Lefebvre, 9–20. Paris: Éditions Anthropos, 1975.

——. "Introduction à l'espace urbain." *Metropolis: Urbanisme, planification régionale, environnement* 22 (1976): 24–31.

——. *Introduction à la modernité: Préludes.* Paris: Éditions de Minuit, 1962.

——. "Introduction à la psycho-sociologie de la vie quotidienne." In Henri Lefebvre, *Du rural à l'urbain,* 89–107. Paris: Anthropos, 1970. Originally published in *Encyclopédie de la psychologie,* 102–7 (Paris: Fernand Nathan, 1960).

——. *Le langage et la societé.* Paris: Gallimard, 1966.

——. Lecture at "Rencontres pour la ville." *Société française: Cahiers de l'Institut de recherches marxistes,* special supplement issue, 6 (1982): 14–15.

——. "Lefebvre parle de Marcuse." *La quinzaine littéraire* 52 (1968): 3–5.

——. *Logique formelle, logique dialectique.* Paris: Éditions sociales, 1947.

——. *Lukács 1955.* Paris: Aubier, 1986.

——. *Manifeste différentialiste.* Paris: Gallimard, 1970.

——. "Marksizm i myśl francuska." *Twórczość* 4 (1957): 9–32.

——. "Marxisme: Cours donné à la Faculté de Droit, dans le cadre de l'Institut d'études politiques." Strasbourg, n.d. Centre de recherche sur l'habitat, Paris.

——. "Marxisme et sociologie." *Cahiers internationaux de sociologie* 3, no. 4 (1948): 48–74.

——. *Le matérialisme dialectique.* Paris: Alcan, 1939.

——. *Métaphilosophie.* Paris: Syllepse, 2000. Originally published by Éditions de minuit, Paris, 1965.

——. "M. Merleau-Ponty et la philosophie de l'ambiguïtë." *La pensée,* part 1, 68 (1956): 44–58; part 2, 73 (1957): 37–52.

——. *Le mode de production étatique.* Vol. 3 of *De l'État.* Paris: UGE, 1977.

——. "La mode—stratégie du désir." Interview with H. Lefebvre, Roland Barthes, and Jean Duvignaud. *Le Nouvel observateur,* 23 March 1966, 28–29.

——. "Il modello californiano, gli Stati Uniti e il nuovo ordine mondiale." *Il ponte* 40, (1984): 71–76.

——. "Le mondial et le planetaire." *Espaces et sociétés* 8 (1973): 15–22.

——. "Mourenx—ville nouvelle." In *15 jours en France . . . ,* 207–25. Paris: La documentation française, 1965.

——. "La musique et la ville." *Musique en jeu* 24 (1976): 75–81.

——. *Le nationalisme contre les nations.* Paris: Méridiens Klincksieck, 1988. Originally published by Éditions sociales internationales, Paris, 1937.

——. "Le nécessaire et le possible dans la formation du mondial." www.unu.edu/unu-press. For a detailed summary of this talk, see *Science and Technology in the Transformation of the World: First International Seminar of the Series on The Transformation of the World; Belgrade, 22–26 October 1979,* ed. Miroslav Pečujlić, Gregory Blue, and

Anouar Abdel-Malek, 10–15 (New York: United Nations University, St. Martin's Press, 1982).

——. "La notion de totalité dans les sciences sociales." *Cahiers internationaux de sociologie* 18–19 (1955): 55–77.

——. "Les nouveaux ensembles urbains (un cas concret: Lacq–Mourenx et les problèmes urbains de la nouvelle classe ouvrière)." In Henri Lefebvre, *Du rural à l'urbain,* 109–28. Paris: Anthropos, 1970. Originally published in *La Revue française de sociologie* 1, no. 1–2 (1960): 186–201.

——. "Une nouvelle positivité de l'urbain." Interview with Serge Renaudie and Catherine Régulier. *M, Mensuel, Marxisme, Mouvement* 17 (1988): 62–66.

——. *Oratorio reportage: Claude-Nicolas Ledoux ou la ville idéale.* Documentary directed by Raoul Sangla. Broadcast on France 2, 21 November 1969. Institut national de l'audiovisuel.

——. "Les paradoxes d'Althusser." In Henri Lefebvre, *Au-delà du structuralisme,* 371–471. Paris: Anthropos, 1971. Originally published in *L'homme et la société* 13 (1969): 3–37; also reprinted in Henri Lefebvre, *L'idéologie structuraliste* (Paris: Le Seuil 1975).

——. *La pensée marxiste et la ville.* Paris: Casterman, 1972.

——. "Perspectives de la sociologie rurale." In Henri Lefebvre, *Du rural à l'urbain,* 63–78. Paris: Anthropos, 1970. Originally published in *Cahiers internationaux de la sociologie* 14 (1953): 122–40.

——. *Pignon.* Paris: Le musée de poche, 1956.

——. "La planification démocratique." *La nouvelle revue marxiste* 2 (1961): 71–93. Republished in Henri Lefebvre, *Au-delà du structuralisme* (Paris: Anthropos, 1971), 137–64.

——. *Position: Contre les technocrates.* Paris: Gonthier, 1967.

——. Preface. In *L'habitat pavillonnaire,* by Antoine Haumont, Nicole Haumont, Henri Raymond, and Marie-Geneviève Raymond, 3–24. Paris: Centre de recherche d'urbanisme, 1966.

——. Preface. In *L'idéologie libérale: L'individu et sa propriété,* by André Vachet, xi–xiv. Paris: Éditions Anthropos, 1970.

——. Preface. In *Lived-in Architecture: Le Corbusier's Pessac Revisited,* by Philippe Boudon (unpaginated). London: Lund Humphries, 1972. Translation of *Pessac de Le Corbusier* (Paris: Dunod, 1969).

——. Preface. In *Matériau/technologie/forme,* 8–15. Paris: Centre de création industrielle, 1974.

——. "Preface to the Study of the Habitat of the 'Pavillon.'" In *Henri Lefebvre: Key Writings,* 130–33. Edited by Stuart Elden, Elizabeth Lebas, and Eleonore Kofman. New York: Continuum, 2003. Originally published as the preface to *L'habitat pavillonnaire,* by Antoine Haumont, Nicole Haumont, Henri Raymond, and Marie-Geneviève Raymond, 3–24 (Paris: Centre de recherche d'urbanisme, 1966).

——. *La présence et l'absence: Contribution à la théorie des représentations.* Tournai: Casterman, 1980.

——. *Problèmes actuels du marxisme.* Paris: Presses universitaires de France, 1958.

——. "Problèmes de sociologie rurale: La communauté paysanne et ses problèmes historico-sociologiques." In Henri Lefebvre, *Du rural à l'urbain,* 7–20. Originally published in *Cahiers internationaux de sociologie* 6 (1949): 78–100.

——. *La proclamation de la Commune.* Paris: Gallimard, 1965.

——. "La production de l'espace." *L'homme et la société* 31–32 (1974): 15–32.

——. *La production de l'espace.* Paris: Anthropos, 2000 [1974].

——. *The Production of Space.* Translated by Donald Nicholson-Smith. Oxford: Blackwell, 1991. Originally published as *La production de l'espace.* Paris: Anthropos, 1974.

——. "Propositions de recherches sur la vie urbaine." *Revue française de sociologie* 9, no. 2 (1968): 151–66.

——. "Propositions pour un nouvel urbanisme." In Henri Lefebvre, *Du rural à l'urbain,* 183–95. Paris: Anthropos, 1970. Originally published in *L'architecture d'aujourd'hui* 132 (1967): 14–16.

——. "Psychologie des classes sociales." In *Traité de sociologie,* ed. Georges Gurvitch, vol. 2, 364–86. Paris: Presses universitaires de France, 1958.

——. *Pyrénées.* Lausanne, France: Éditions Rencontre, 1965.

——. "Quand la ville se perd dans une métamorphose planétaire." *Le monde diplomatique* (May 1989): 16–17.

——. "Quartier et vie de quartier." In Monique Coornaert, C. Marlaut, Antoine Haumont, and Henri Lefebvre, *Le quartier et la ville,* 9–12. Paris: Les Cahiers de l'IAURP, 1967. Reprinted in Henri Lefebvre, *Du rural à l'urbain,* 207–15 (Paris: Anthropos, 1970).

——. "Réflexions sur la politique de l'espace," *Espaces et sociétés* 1 (1970): 3–12.

——. "Une république pastorale: La vallée du Campan: Organisation, vie et historie d'une communauté pyrénéenne: Textes et documents accompagnés de commentaires et d'une Étude de sociologie historique." PhD diss., vol. 2, University Paris–Sorbonne, 1954.

——. *Rhythmanalysis: Space, Time, and Everyday Life.* Translated by Stuart Elden and Gerald Moore. London: Continuum, 2004. Originally published as *Éléments de rythmanalyse: Introduction à la connaissance des rythmes* (Paris: Éditions Syllepse, 1992).

——. *The Right to the City.* In *Henri Lefebvre: Writings on Cities,* 63–182. Translated by Elisabeth Lebas and Eleonore Kofman. Oxford: Blackwell, 1996. Originally published as *Le droit à la ville* (Paris: Anthropos, 1968).

——. "La sexualité." In "Dimensions neuro-physiologique et neuro-psychologique. Système nerveux—organes sensoriels—perception—fonctions symboliques—sommeil," ed. Léonie Sturge-Moore. Report of seminar 1bis, "Les besoins fonctionnels de l'homme en vue de leur projection ultérieure sur le plan de la conception architecturale," conducted by Michel Dameron and Henri Lefebvre, 6 October 1968. In *Les besoins fonctionnels de l'homme en vue de leur projection ultérieure sur le plan de la conception architecturale: Compte rendu de fin du contrat,* annex no. 1, ed. Françoise Bedos, Michel Dameron, Claude Leroy, Henri Raymond, and Léonie Sturge-Moore, 137–44. Paris: Centre de recherche d'architecture, d'urbanisme et de construction, 1970.

——. "La signification de la Commune." *Arguments* 27–28 (1962): 11–19.

——. *Sociology of Marx.* Translated by Norbert Guterman. London: Allen Lane the Penguin Press, 1968. Originally published as *Sociologie de Marx* (Paris: Presses universitaires de France, 1966).

——. "Socjalizam za vrijeme odmora." *Praxis,* édition yougoslave 1 (1965): 164–66.

——. *La somme et le reste.* Paris: La Nef de Paris, 1959.

——. "La splendeur de la ville." *Archivari: Revue trimestrielle d'architecture* 2 (1984): n.p.

——. *State, Space, World: Selected Essays.* Edited by Neil Brenner and Stuart Elden; translated by Gerald Moore, Neil Brenner, and Stuart Elden. Minneapolis: University of Minnesota Press, 2009.

——. "La structure sociale de l'Ardèche." *Emancipation: Bulletin mensuel du syndicat de l'enseignement laïque Ardèche* (October 1931): 8–10.

——. "Suplément à l'exposé de A. Banfi." In *Entretiens Philosophiques de Varsovie: Les rapports de la pensée et de l'action: Institut international de philosophie, 17–26 juillet 1957,* 43–45. Wrocław: Wydawnictwo Polskiej Akademii Nauk, 1958.

——. "Sur quelques critères du développement social et du socialisme." *Praxis: Revue philosophique,* édition internationale 2 (1965): 156–67.

——. *La survie du capitalisme: La reproduction des rapports de production.* Paris: Anthropos, 1973.

——. "La technologie, le communication: Éléments déterminant du troisième millénaire." *Metropolis* 90–91 (1990): 9–10.

——. *Le temps des méprises.* Paris: Stock, 1975.

——. "Théorie de la rente foncière et sociologie rurale." In Henri Lefebvre, *Du rural à l'urbain,* 79–87. Paris: Anthropos, 1970. Originally published in *Transactions of the Third Congress of Sociology Amsterdam, August, 22–29, 1956,* ed. International Sociological Association (London, 1957), vol. 2, part 3, 244–50.

——. *Théorie marxiste de l'État de Hegel à Mao.* Vol. 2 of *De l'État.* Paris: UGE, 1976.

——. "L'urbanisme aujourd'hui: Mythes et réalités: Débat entre Henri Lefebvre, Jean Balladur et Michel Ecochard." In Henri Lefebvre, *Du rural à l'urbain,* 217–27. Paris: Anthropos, 1970. Originally published in *Cahiers du Centre d'études socialistes* 72–73 (1967).

——. *The Urban Revolution.* Translated by Robert Bononno. Minneapolis: University of Minnesota Press, 2003. Originally published as *La révolution urbaine* (Paris: Gallimard, 1970).

——. "Utopie expérimentale: Pour un nouvel urbanisme." In Henri Lefebvre, *Du rural à l'urbain,* 129–40. Paris: Anthropos, 1970. Originally published in *Revue française de sociologie* 2, no. 3 (1961): 191–98.

——. *La vallée de Campan: Étude de sociologie rurale.* Paris: Presses universitaires de France, 1963.

——. *Vers le cybernanthrope.* Paris: Denoël-Gonthier, 1971.

——. *La vie quotidienne dans le monde moderne.* Paris: Gallimard, 1968.

——. "La vie sociale dans la ville." In Henri Lefebvre, *Du rural à l'urbain,* 145–52. Paris: Anthropos, 1970.

——. "La ville et l'urbain." *Espaces et sociétés* 2 (1971): 3–7.

——. "What Is the Historical Past?" *New Left Review* 90, no. 1 (1975): 27–34. Originally published as "Qu'est-ce que le passé historique?" *Les temps modernes* 161 (1959): 159–69.

——, ed. *Actualité de Fourier: Colloque d'Arc-et-Senans.* Paris: Éditions Anthropos, 1975.

Lefebvre, Henri, and Monique Coornaert. "Ville, urbanisme et urbanisation." In *Perspectives de la sociologie contemporaine, hommage à Georges Gurvitch,* ed. Georges Balandier, Roger Bastide, Jacques Berque, and Pierre George, 85–105. Paris: Presses universitaires de France, 1968.

Lefebvre, Henri, and the Groupe de Navarrenx. *Du contrat de citoyenneté.* Paris: Syllepse etc., 1990.

Lefebvre, Henri, Pierre Guilbaud, and Serge Renaudie. "International Competition for the New Belgrade Urban Structure Improvement." In *Autogestion, or Henri Lefebvre in New Belgrade,* ed. Sabine Bitter and Helmut Weber, 1–71. Berlin: Sternberg Press, 2009.

Lefebvre, Henri, and Catherine Régulier. *La révolution n'est plus qu'elle était.* Paris: Éditions Libres-Hallier, 1978.

OTHER SOURCES

Abassi, Rouhollah. "Introduction à la sociologie urbaine de la ville de Téhéran." PhD diss., University Paris 10, 1969.

Adorno, Theodor W., and Max Horkheimer. *Dialectic of Enlightenment.* London: Allen Lane, 1973 [1944].

Aillaud, Émile. "Habiter, et non pas loger." *Urbanisme* 136 (1973): 41.

Ajzenberg, Armand. Introduction to Henri Lefebvre and the Groupe de Navarrenx, *Du contrat de citoyenneté,* 11–14. Paris: Syllepse etc., 1990.

Ajzenberg, Armand, Lucien Bonnafé, and René Lourau. "Des points où enfoncer le clou à grands coups de marteau, et d'autres où passer énergiquement la faucille." *M, Mensuel, Marxisme, Mouvement* 50 (1991): 16–19.

Albers, Gerd. *Zur Entwicklung der Stadtplanung in Europa: Begegnungen, Einflüsse, Verflechtungen.* Wiesbaden, Germany: Vieweg, 1997.

Alexander, Christopher. "A City Is Not a Tree." In *Design after Modernism: Beyond the Object,* ed. John Thackara, 67–84. London: Thames and Hudson, 1988 [1967]. Published in French in *AMC: Architecture mouvement continuité* 1 (1967): 3–11.

Alquati, Romano. *Sulla FIAT, e altri scritti.* Milan: Feltrinelli, 1975.

Alquier, François. "Contribution à l'étude de la rente foncière sur les terrains urbains." *Espaces et sociétés* 2 (1971): 75–87.

Althusser, Louis. "Contradiction and Overdetermination." www.marxists.org. Published also in Louis Althusser, *For Marx,* 87–128 (New York: Verso, 2005 [1965]).

——. *For Marx.* New York: Verso, 2005 [1965].

——. *Philosophy of the Encounter: Later Writings, 1978–87.* London: Verso, 2006 [1994].

Amiot, Michel. *Contre l'État, les sociologues: Éléments pour une histoire de la sociologie urbaine en France, 1900–1980.* Paris: Éditions de l'École des hautes études en sciences sociales, 1986.

Andreotti, Libero, and Xavier Costa, eds. *Situationists: Art, Politics, Urbanism.* Barcelona: Museu d'Art contemporani de Barcelona, 1996.

——, eds. *Theory of the Dérive and Other Situationist Writings on the City.* Barcelona: Museu d'Art contemporani de Barcelona, 1996.

Andrieux, Jean-Yves, and Frédéric Seitz, eds. *Pratiques architecturales et enjeux politiques: France 1945–1995.* Paris: Picard, 1998.

Antoine, Serge, Henri Beauge, and Jean Blanc, eds. *Les journées nationales d'études sur les parcs naturels régionaux: Compte rendu des conférences et débats.* Paris: La documentation française, 1967.

Arnade, Peter, Martha Howell, and Walter Simons. "Fertile Spaces: The Productivity of Urban Space in Northern Europe." *Journal of Interdisciplinary History* 4 (2002): 515–48.

——, eds. "Productivity of Urban Space in Northern Europe." *Journal of Interdisciplinary History* 4 (2002).

Arthaud, Claude. *Les palais du rêve.* Paris: Arthaud et Paris–Match, 1970.

Ascher, François. "Contribution à l'analyse de la production du cadre bâti." *Espaces et sociétés* 6–7 (1972): 89–113.

——. "Quelques critique de 'l'économie urbaine.'" *Espaces et sociétés* 4 (1971): 25–40.

Aureli, Pier Vittorio. *The Project of Autonomy: Politics and Architecture Within and Against Capitalism.* New York: Princeton Architectural Press, 2008.

Auzelle, Robert. "Plaidoyer pour une organization consciente de l'espace." *L'architecture d'aujourd'hui* 104 (1962): 1–7.

Auzelle, Robert, Jean Gohier, and Pierre Vetter. *323 citations sur l'urbanisme.* Paris: Vincent et Fréal, 1964.

Avermaete, Tom. *Another Modern: The Post-War Architecture and Urbanism of Candilis—Josic—Woods.* Rotterdam: NAi Publishers, 2005.

Avineri, Shlomo. *Hegel's Theory of the Modern State*. London: Cambridge University Press, 1974.

Bachelard, Gaston. *The Poetics of Space*. Boston: Beacon Press, 1969 [1957].

Baird, George, and Charles Jencks. *Meaning in Architecture*. London: Barrie and Barrie and Rockliff the Cresset Press, 1969.

Balandier, Anne, and Iván Szelényi. "Gestion régionale et classe sociale: Le cas de l'Europe de l'Est." *Revue française de sociologie* 17, no. 1 (1976): 13–52.

Balibar, Étienne. "From Class Struggle to Classless Struggle." In Étienne Balibar and Immanuel Wallerstein, *Race, Nation, Class: Ambiguous Identities,* 153–84. London: Verso, 1991 [1988].

——. *The Philosophy of Marx*. London: Verso, 2007 [1993].

Balibar, Étienne, and Immanuel Wallerstein. *Race, Nation, Class: Ambiguous Identities*. London: Verso, 1991 [1988].

Banham, Reyner. *Megastructure: Urban Futures of the Recent Past*. London: Thames and Hudson, 1976.

Bardet, Gaston. "Les échelons communautaires dans les agglomérations urbaines." In Bardet, *Pierre sur pierre,* 233–49. Paris: Éditions L.C.B., 1945.

Barthes, Roland. *The Fashion System*. Berkeley: University of California Press, 1990 [1967].

——. *Sade, Fourier, Loyola*. Berkeley: University of California Press, 1976 [1970].

——. "Sémiologie et urbanisme." *L'architecture d'aujourd'hui* 153 (1970–71): 11–13.

Baudrillard, Jean. "The Ideological Genesis of Needs." In Jean Baudrillard, *For a Critique of the Political Economy of the Sign,* 63–87. St. Louis, Mo.: Telos Press, 1981 [1969].

——. Review of Henri Lefebvre's *Position: Contre les technocrates. Cahiers internationaux de sociologie* 44 (1968): 176–78.

——. "Le système des objets." PhD diss., University Paris 10, 1966.

——. *The System of Objects*. London: Verso, 2005 [1968].

——. *Utopia Deferred: Jean Baudrillard, Writings for Utopie (1967–1978)*. Cambridge, Mass.: MIT Press, 2006.

Bauhain, Claude. "L'image de l'espace." PhD diss., University Paris 10, 1970.

Bauhain, Claude, Nicole Haumont, Marion Segaud, and Henri Raymond. *Espace urbain et image de la ville*. Paris: ISU, 1970.

Bedos, Françoise, Claude Berthelot, and Claude Leroy. "Appropriation de l'espace par les objects: Chambres de l'Institut Marcel Rivière." In *Les besoins fonctionnels de l'homme en vue de leur projection ultérieure sur le plan de la conception architecturale: Compte rendu de fin du contrat,* ed. Françoise Bedos, Michel Dameron, Claude Leroy, Henri Raymond, and Léonie Sturge-Moore, annex no. 4. Paris: Centre de recherche d'architecture, d'urbanisme et de construction, 1970.

Bedos, Françoise, Michel Dameron, Claude Leroy, Henri Raymond, and Léonie Sturge-Moore, eds. *Les besoins fonctionnels de l'homme en vue de leur projection ultérieure* sur le plan de la conception architecturale: Compte rendu de fin du contrat, annex no. 1. Paris: Centre de recherche d'architecture, d'urbanisme et de construction, 1970.

Bedos, Françoise, Alberto Eiguer, and Claude Leroy. "Représentation et appropriation de l'espace: Plan de l'Institut Marcel Rivière." In Les besoins fonctionnels de l'homme en vue de leur projection ultérieure sur le plan de la conception architecturale: Compte rendu de fin du contrat, ed. Françoise Bedos, Michel Dameron, Claude Leroy, Henri Raymond, and Léonie Sturge-Moore, annex no. 3. Paris: Centre de recherche d'architecture, d'urbanisme et de construction, 1970.

Belina, Bernd, and Boris Michel. "Raumproduktionen." In Raumproduktionen: Beiträge der Radical Geography—eine Zwischenbilanz, 7–34. Münster: Westfälisches Dampfboot, 2007.

———, eds. Raumproduktionen: Beiträge der Radical Geography—eine Zwischenbilanz. Münster: Westfälisches Dampfboot, 2007.

Belleville, Pierre. Une nouvelle classe ouvrière. Paris: R. Julliard, 1963.

Bellos, David. Georges Perec: Une vie dans les mots: Biographie. Paris: Éditions du Seuil, 1994.

Benjamin, Walter. The Arcades Project. Cambridge, Mass.: Belknap Press, 1999 [1982].

Berdoulay, Vincent, and Nicholas Entrikin. "The Pyrenees as Place: Lefebvre as Guide." Progress in Human Geography 29, no. 2 (2005): 129–47.

Bernard-Simonet, Helene. "Le problème des régions rurales dans les pays industrialises: Un exemple en France: Le pays d'Albion." PhD diss., University Paris 10, 1972.

Bertrand, M. "Qu'en est-il donc du besoin?" In Besoin(s)—analyse et critique de la notion, ed. Institut français d'architecture, 21–36. Paris: Institut Français d'Architecture, 1975.

Besset, Maurice. New French Architecture. Teufen, Switzerland: Niggli, 1967.

Bidart, Pierre, Gérard Collomb, Jacques Allières, and Jean Guibal. Pays aquitains: Bordelais, Gascogne, Pays Basques, Béarn, Bigorre. Vol. 18 of L'architecture rurale française. Paris: Berger–Levrault, 1984.

Bidet, Jacques, and Stathis Kouvelakis, eds. Critical Companion to Contemporary Marxism. Leiden: Brill, 2008.

Bitter, Sabine, and Helmut Weber, eds. Autogestion, or Henri Lefebvre in New Belgrade. Berlin: Sternberg Press, 2009.

Blagojević, Ljiljana. "New Belgrade: The Capital of No-City's-Land." In Differentiated Neighborhoods, ed. Zoran Erić, 22–33. Beograd: Museum of Contemporary Art, 2009.

———. "The Right to New Belgrade: The Problematic of the New Urban." Paper presented at the conference "Rethinking Theory, Space and Production: Henri Lefebvre Today." Delft University of Technology, 11–13 November 2008.

Blain, Catherine, ed. L'Atelier de Montrouge: La modernité à l'oeuvre, 1958–1981: Exposition, Paris, Cité de l'architecture et du patrimoine, 19 mars—11 mai 2008. Paris: Cité de l'architecture et du patrimoine, 2008.

Blanchot, Maurice. Friendship. Stanford, Calif.: Stanford University Press, 1997 [1971].

Blau, Eve, and Ivan Rupnik. *Project Zagreb: Transition as Condition, Strategy, Practice.* Barcelona: Actar, 2007.

Blazy, Louis. *Mourenx ville nouvelle du complexe de Lacq: Éclosion, floraison.* Mourenx, France: Impr. Aquitaine communication, 1988.

Blin, Pascale. *L'AUA: Mythe et réalités: L'Atelier d'urbanisme et d'architecture, 1960–1985.* Paris: Electa Moniteur, 1988.

Bloch, Ernst. *Heritage of Our Times.* Oxford: Polity, 1991 [1935].

——. "Non-Synchronism and the Obligation to Its Dialectics." *New German Critique* 11 (1977 [1935]): 22–38.

Bloch, Marc. *Feudal Society.* London: Routledge and Kegan Paul, 1961 [1939–40].

——. *French Rural History.* London: Routledge and Kegan Paul, 1966 [1931].

——. "La lutte pour l'individualisme agraire dans la France du XVIIIe siècle." *Annales d'histoire économique et sociale* 2, no. 7 (1930): 329–83; no. 8 (1930): 511–56.

Bobroff, Jacqueline. "Politique urbaine et traitement des quartiers anciens (le cas de Montauban)." PhD diss., University Paris 10, 1980.

Bockock, Robert. *Consumption.* London: Routledge, 1993.

Bodeman, Y. Michael. "The Naked Proletarian and the Organicity of Classes: A Re-Appraisal of the Marxist Conception." In *Rethinking Marx,* ed. Sakari Hänninen and Leena Paldán, 146–51. Berlin: Argument-Verlag, 1984.

Bodiguel, Jean-Luc. "La DATAR: Quarante ans d'histoire." *Revue française d'administration publique* 119 (2006): 401–14.

Boëll, Denis-Michel, Jacqueline Christophe, and Régis Meyran, eds., *Du folklore à l'ethnologie.* Paris: Maison des sciences de l'homme, 2009.

Bofill, Ricardo. *L'architecture d'un homme: Entretiens avec François Hérbert-Stevens.* Paris: Arthaud, 1978.

Bofill, Ricardo, Xavier Bagué, Ramón Collado, Peter Hodgkinson, and Emanuel Yanowsky. *Hacia una formalización.* Barcelona: Blume, 1968.

Bofill, Ricardo, and Taller de arquitectura. "Ejemplo de una agrupación urbana superior a los 50,000 habitantes." In "Proyecto genérico," in *Hacia una formalización de la ciudad en el espacio,* by Ricardo Bofill and Taller de arquitectura (unpaginated). 1968. Archives of Taller de arquitectura, Barcelona.

——. "Estudio geométrico previo al diseño de viviendas." In "Experiencia 1," in *Hacia una formalización de la ciudad en el espacio,* by Ricardo Bofill and Taller de arquitectura (unpaginated). 1968. Archives of Taller de arquitectura, Barcelona.

——. "La forma de la vivienda." In "Proyecto genérico," in *Hacia una formalización de la ciudad en el espacio,* by Ricardo Bofill and Taller de arquitectura (unpaginated). 1968. Archives of Taller de arquitectura, Barcelona.

——. *Hacia una formalización de la ciudad en el espacio.* 1968. Archives of Taller de arquitectura, Barcelona.

———. "Necesidad de nuevos métodos operativos." In "Proyecto genérico," in *Hacia una formalización de la ciudad en el espacio,* by Ricardo Bofill and Taller de arquitectura (unpaginated). 1968. Archives of Taller de arquitectura, Barcelona.

———. "Plantas de las viviendas, con situación de los bajantes en cuadro." In "Experiencia 1," in *Hacia una formalización de la ciudad en el espacio,* by Ricardo Bofill and Taller de arquitectura (unpaginated). 1968. Archives of Taller de arquitectura, Barcelona.

———. "Problemas de significado y estructurales." In "Experiencia 1," in *Hacia una formalización de la ciudad en el espacio,* by Ricardo Bofill and Taller de arquitectura (unpaginated). 1968. Archives of Taller de arquitectura, Barcelona.

———. "Problemas estructurales." In "Proyecto genérico," in *Hacia una formalización de la ciudad en el espacio,* by Ricardo Bofill and Taller de arquitectura (unpaginated). 1968. Archives of Taller de arquitectura, Barcelona.

———. "Prologo." In "Proyecto genérico," in *Hacia una formalización de la ciudad en el espacio,* by Ricardo Bofill and Taller de arquitectura (unpaginated). 1968. Archives of Taller de arquitectura, Barcelona.

———. "Prototipo y visualización de un ejemplo." In "Experiencia 1," in *Hacia una formalización de la ciudad en el espacio,* by Ricardo Bofill and Taller de arquitectura (unpaginated). 1968. Archives of Taller de arquitectura, Barcelona.

———. "Towards a Formalization of the City in Space." English translation attached to *Hacia una formalización de la ciudad en el espacio,* by Ricardo Bofill and Taller de arquitectura (unpaginated). 1968. Archives of Taller de arquitectura, Barcelona.

———. "Visualización." In "Proyecto genérico," in *Hacia una formalización de la ciudad en el espacio,* by Ricardo Bofill and Taller de arquitectura (unpaginated). 1968. Archives of Taller de arquitectura, Barcelona.

Bollerey, Franziska. *Architekturkonzeptionen der utopischen Sozialisten: Alternative Planung und Architektur für den gesellschaftlichen Prozess.* Berlin: Ernst und Sohn, 1991.

Boltanski, Luc, and Eve Chiapello. *The New Spirit of Capitalism.* London: Verso, 2005.

Borries, Friedrich von. *Who's Afraid of Niketown? Nike Urbanism, Branding and the City of Tomorrow.* Rotterdam: Episode, 2004.

Boucheret, J.-M., J.-P. Dreyfus, Antoine Haumont, and Henri Raymond. *Les equipements dans la région parisienne.* Paris: ISU, 1969.

Boucheret, J. M., D. Druenne, A. Gotman, Antoine Haumont, and J. M. Léger. *L'espace du travail dans la ville.* Paris: ISU, 1973.

Boudon, Philippe. "Étude socio-architecturale des quartiers modernes Frugès construites à Pessac par Le Corbusier." Master's thesis, Institut d'urbanisme de l'Université de Paris, 1967.

———. "Habitat ouvert ou fermé?" *L'architecture d'aujourd'hui* 148 (1970): 14–17.

———. *Lived-in Architecture: Le Corbusier's Pessac Revisited.* London: Lund Humphries, 1972. Translation of *Pessac de Le Corbusier* (Paris: Dunod, 1969).

———. *Pessac de Le Corbusier.* Paris: Dunod, 1969.

———. *Richelieu Ville Nouvelle.* Paris: Dunod, 1978.

Bourdieu, Pierre. *Outline of a Theory of Practice.* Cambridge: Cambridge University Press, 2003 [1972].

Boyer, M. Christine. "Cities for Sale: Merchandising History at South Street Seaport." In *Variations on a Theme Park: The New American City and the End of Public Space,* ed. Michael Sorkin, 181–204. New York: Hill and Wang, 1992.

———. *CyberCities: Visual Perception in the Age of Electronic Communication.* New York: Princeton Architectural Press, 1996.

Braudel, Fernand. *Capitalism and Material Life, 1400–1800.* London: Weidenfeld and Nicolson, 1973 [1967].

———. *The Mediterranean and the Mediterranean World in the Age of Philip II.* London: Collins, 1972–73 [1949].

Brborić, Branka Likić. *Democratic Governance in the Transition from Yugoslav Self-Management to a Market Economy: The Case of the Slovenian Privatization Debates 1990–1992.* Uppsala, Sweden: Uppsala University, 2003.

Brenner, Neil. "Global, Fragmented, Hierarchical: Henri Lefebvre's Geographies of Globalization." *Public Culture* 10/11 (1997): 135–67.

———. "State Theory in the Political Conjuncture: Henri Lefebvre's 'Comments on a New State Form.'" *Antipode* 33, no. 5 (2001): 783–808.

———. "The Urban Question as a Scale Question: Reflections on Henri Lefebvre, Urban Theory and the Politics of Scale." *International Journal of Urban and Regional Research* 24 (2000): 361–78.

Brenner, Neil, and Stuart Elden. "Henri Lefebvre in Contexts: An Introduction." *Antipode* 33, no. 5 (2001): 763–68.

———. "Henri Lefebvre on State, Space, Territory." *International Political Sociology* 3 (2009): 353–77.

———. "Introduction: State, Space, World: Lefebvre and the Survival of Capitalism." In *State, Space, World: Selected Essays,* by Henri Lefebvre, ed. Neil Brenner and Stuart Elden, 1–48. Minneapolis: University of Minnesota Press, 2009.

Brenner, Neil, Bob Jessop, Martin Jones, and Gordon MacLeod. "State Space in Question." In *State/Space: A Reader,* ed. Neil Brenner, Bob Jessop, Martin Jones, and Gordon MacLeod, 1–26. Oxford: Blackwell, 2003.

———, eds. *State/Space: A Reader.* Oxford: Blackwell, 2003.

Brenner, Neil, and Nik Theodore, eds. *Spaces of Neoliberalism: Urban Restructuring in North America and Western Europe.* Malden, Mass.: Blackwell, 2004.

Brillat-Savarin, Jean-Antheleme. *Brillat-Savarin's Physiologie du goût: A Handbook of Gastronomy.* London: Nimmo and Bain, 1884 [1825].

Broadbent, Geoffrey, Richard Bunt, and Charles Jencks, eds. *Signs, Symbols, and Architecture*. Chichester, U.K.: Wiley, 1980.

Broekman, Jan, Ante Pažanin, and Bernhard Waldenfels. *Phänomenologie und Marxismus*. 4 vols. Frankfurt am Main: Suhrkamp, 1977–79.

Bruneton-Governatori, Ariane, and Denis Peaucelle. *Bâtiment A, rue des Pionniers*. Mourenx, France: Éditions Lacq odyssée, 1997.

Burbidge, John W. *Historical Dictionary of Hegelian Philosophy*. Lanham, Md.: Scarecrow Press, 2001.

Burckhardt, Lucius, Max Frisch, and Markus Kutter. *Achtung: Die Schweiz: Ein Gespräch über unsere Lage und ein Vorschlag zur Tat*. Basel: Werner, 1955.

Burke, Peter. *The French Historical Revolution: The Annales School, 1929–89*. Cambridge: Polity, 1990.

Burkhard, Bud. *French Marxism between the Wars: Henri Lefebvre and the "Philosophies."* Amherst, N.Y.: Humanity Books, 2000.

Burlen, Catherine. "Pratique idéologique et discours des architectes: De l'image à la parole." PhD diss., University Paris 10, 1975.

——. "La réalisation spatiale du désir et l'image spatialisée du besoin." In *Les besoins fonctionnels de l'homme en vue de leur projection ultérieure sur le plan de la conception architecturale: Compte rendu de fin du contrat*, annex no. 7, ed. Françoise Bedos, Michel Dameron, Claude Leroy, Henri Raymond, and Léonie Sturge-Moore. Paris: Centre de recherche d'architecture, d'urbanisme et de construction, 1970.

Busbea, Larry. *Topologies: The Urban Utopia in France, 1960–1970*. Cambridge, Mass.: MIT Press, 2007.

Busquet, Grégory. "Henri Lefebvre, les situationnistes et la dialectique monumentale: Du monument social au monument spectacle." *Homme et la société* 146 (2002): 41–60.

——. "Idéologie urbaine et pensée politique dans la France de la période 1958–1981." PhD diss., University Paris 12—Val de Marne, 2007.

Bykhovskii, B. "'Itog i ostatok' ili balans renegata." *Voprosy filosofii* 7 (1964).

Caillois, Roger. *Man, Play and Games*. London: Thames and Hudson, 1962 [1958].

Carporzen, Jean-François, ed. *Marquage et appropriation de l'espace*. Report of the second seminar "Les besoins fonctionnels de l'homme en vue de leur projection ultérieure sur le plan de la conception architecturale," conducted by Michel Dameron and Henri Lefebvre, Centre de recherche d'architecture, d'urbanisme et de construction, 14–15 December 1968. In *Les besoins fonctionnels de l'homme en vue de leur projection ultérieure sur le plan de la conception architecturale: Compte rendu de fin du contrat*, ed. Françoise Bedos, Michel Dameron, Claude Leroy, Henri Raymond, and Léonie Sturge-Moore, annex no. 1. Paris: Centre de recherche d'architecture, d'urbanisme et de construction, 1970.

Casey, Edward. "Between Geography and Philosophy: What Does It Mean to Be in the Place-World?" *Annals of the Association of American Geographers* 91, no. 4 (2001): 683–93.

———. "The Production of Space or the Heterogeneity of Place: A Commentary on Edward Dimendberg and Neil Smith." In *The Production of Public Space*, ed. Andrew Light and Jonathan Smith, 71–80. Lanham, Md.: Rowman and Littlefield, 1998.

Castells, Manuel. *The City and the Grassroots: A Cross-Cultural Theory of Urban Social Movements*. London: Edward Arnold, 1983.

———. "Lutte de classes et contradictions urbaines: L'émergence des mouvements sociaux urbains dans le capitalisme avancé." *Espaces et sociétés* 6–7 (1972): 3–8.

———. "La rénovation urbaine aux Etats-Unis." *Espaces et sociétés* 1 (1970): 107–37.

———. "L'urbanisation dépendante en Amérique latine." *Espaces et sociétés* 3 (1971): 5–23.

———. *The Urban Question: A Marxist Approach*. London: Edward Arnold, 1977 [1972].

Castells, Manuel, Eddy Cherki, Francis Godard, and Dominique Mehl. *Crise du logement et mouvements sociaux urbains: Enquête sur la région parisienne*. Paris: École des hautes études en sciences sociales, 1978.

Castells, Manuel, Francis Godard, and Vivian Balanowski. *Monopolville: Analyse des rapports entre l'entreprise, l'État et l'urbain à partir d'une enquête sur la croissance industrielle et urbaine de la région de Dunkerque*. Paris: Mouton, 1974.

Castex, Jean, Jean-Charles Depaule, and Philippe Panerai. *Formes urbaines: De l'îlot à la barre*. Paris: Dunod, 1977.

Castro, Roland. *Civilisation urbaine ou barbarie?* Paris: Plon, 1994.

Cattiau, Robert. "Histoire générale des festivals et essai d'une phénoménologie des festivals français." Master's thesis, Institut d'urbanisme de l'Université de Paris, 1967.

Certeau, Michel de. *The Practice of Every Day Life*. Berkeley: University of California Press, 1998 [1980].

Chamboredon, Jean-Claude, and Madeleine Lemairelien. "Proximité spatiale et distance sociale: Les grands ensembles et leur peuplement." *Revue française de sociologie* 11 (1970): 3–33.

Chauveau, Geneviève. "Logement et habitat populaire de la fin de deuxième guerre mondiale aux années 1960." In *Un siècle de banlieue parisienne (1859–1964): Guide de recherche*, ed. Annie Fourcaut, 130–63. Paris: L'Harmattan, 1988.

Chemetov, Paul. "D'Athènes à La Courneuve, à qui la faute?" *Urbanisme* 322 (2002): 50–51.

———. "Henri Lefebvre nous parle . . . des villes méditerranéennes." *M, Mensuel, Marxisme, Mouvement* 50 (1991): 40–41.

Chevalier, Gérard. *Sociologie critique de la politique de la ville: Une action publique sous influence*. Paris: L'Harmattan, 2005.

Chevalier, Louis. "Le problème de la sociologie des villes." In *Traité de sociologie*, ed. Georges Gurvitch, vol. 1, 293–314. Paris: Presses universitaires de France, 1958.

Choay, Françoise. "Urbanism and semiology." In *Meaning in Architecture,* ed. Charles Jencks and George Baird, 27–38. London: Barrie and Rockliff, Cresset Press, 1969.

——. *L'urbanisme: Utopies et réalités: Une anthologie.* Paris: Éditions du Seuil, 1965.

Chombard-Gaudin, Cécile, ed. *Jean Giraudoux et le débat sur la ville 1928–1944.* Paris: Grasset, 1993.

Chombart de Lauwe, Paul-Henry. *Un anthropologue dans le siècle: Entretiens avec Thierry Paquot.* Paris: Descartes, 1996.

——. *Des hommes et des villes.* Paris: Payot, 1965.

——. *Famille et habitation.* 2 vols. Paris: Centre national de la recherche scientifique, 1959–60.

——. *Paris, essais de sociologie 1952–1964.* Paris: Éditions ouvrières, 1965.

——. *Paris et l'agglomération parisienne.* 2 vols. Paris: Presses universitaires de France, 1952.

——. "Sciences humaines, planification et urbanisme." *L'architecture d'aujourd'hui* 91–92 (1960): 194–96.

——. "Sociologie de l'habitation: Méthodes et perspectives de recherches." *Urbanisme* 65 (1959): 3–12.

——. *La vie quotidienne des familles ouvrières.* Paris: Centre national de la recherche scientifique, 1956.

Chombart de Lauwe, Paul-Henry, Louis Couvreur, and Jacques Jenny. "Logement et comportement des ménages dans trois cités nouvelles de l'agglomération bordelaise." *Cahiers du centre scientifique et technique du batiment* 30 (1958).

Christaller, Walter. *Central Places in Southern Germany.* Englewood Cliffs, N.J.: Prentice-Hall, 1966 [1933].

Christofferson, Michael Scott. *French Intellectuals against the Left: The Antitotalitarian Moment of the 1970's.* New York: Berghahn Books, 2004.

"La 'ciudad en el espacio,' un proyecto." *ABC* (Madrid), 23 May 1975.

Claval, Paul. *Histoire de la géographie française de 1870 à nos jours.* Paris: Nathan, 1998.

Clavel, Maïté. "L'aménagement étatique de l'espace." PhD diss., University Paris 10, 1972.

——. *L'aménagement étatique de l'espace.* Paris: Hachette, 1973.

——. "Henri Lefebvre: Une pensée critique de l'espace conçu et aménagé." Paper presented at the conference "L'aménagement du territoire: Changement de temps, changement d'espace," Centre culturel international de Cerisy-la-Salle, 27 September–2 October 2006.

——. "Institutions urbaines et ideologie." In "Architecture—mythe—idéologie," ed. Léonie Sturge-Moore, 93–101. In *Les besoins fonctionnels de l'homme en vue de leur projection ultérieure sur le plan de la conception architecturale: Compte rendu de fin du contrat,* ed. Françoise Bedos, Michel Dameron, Claude Leroy, Henri Raymond, and Léonie Sturge-Moore. Paris: Centre de recherche d'architecture, d'urbanisme et de construction, 1970.

——. *Sociologie de l'urbain.* Paris: Anthropos, 2002.

——. "La ville comme œuvre." *Urbanisme* 319 (2002): 37–40.

Clerc, Paul, ed. *Grands ensembles, banlieues nouvelles: Enquête démographique et psycho-sociologique.* Paris: Presses universitaires de France, 1967.

Cohen, Gerald Allan. *Karl Marx's Theory of History: A Defence.* Oxford: Clarendon Press, 1978.

Cohen, Jean-Louis. "La coupure entre architectes et intellectuels, ou les enseignements de l'italophilie." In *In extenso: Recherches à l'École d'architecture Paris–Villemin.* Paris: École d'architecture Paris–Villemin, 1984.

——. "Grenoble 1974: Eurocommunism Meets Urbanism." Paper delivered at the conference "Rethinking Theory, Space and Production: Henri Lefebvre Today," 13 November 2008, Delft University of Technology.

——. "Grenoble 1974: Pour un urbanisme . . ." In *Organiser la ville hypermoderne—François Ascher, Grand Prix de l'urbanisme 2009,* ed. Ariella Masboungi and Olivia Barbet-Massin, 58-59. Marseille: Parenthèses, 2009.

——. "Infortune transalpine: Aldo Rossi en France." In *L'architecture et la ville: Mélanges offerts à Bernard Huet,* ed. Emmanuelle Sarrazin, 57–59. Paris: École d'architecture Paris–Belleville, 2000.

——. "Transalpine Architektur: Der französische Italianismus zwischen 1965 und 1980." *Archithese* 4 (1988): 68–73.

Cohen, Jean-Louis, and André Lortie. *Des fortifs au périf: Paris, les seuils de la ville.* Paris: Édition du Pavillon de l'Arsenal, 1991.

Coit, Catherine. "Silences et révoltes des usagers (une comparaison des mouvements sociaux urbains aux États-Unis, en France, en Grande-Bretagne et en Italie)." PhD diss., University Paris 10, 1977.

Combes, Francis, and Patricia Latour. *Conversation avec Henri Lefebvre.* Paris: Messidor, 1991.

Coornaert, Monique. "Ville et quartier." *Cahiers internationaux de sociologie* 40 (1966): 89–102.

Coornaert, Monique, Claude Marlaut, Antoine Haumont, and Henri Lefebvre. *Le quartier et la ville.* Paris: Les cahiers de l'IAURP, 1967.

Coquery, Michel. "L'urbanisation française." *Annales de géographie* 74, no. 406 (1965): 740–46.

Cossalter, Chantal. "D'un espace l'autre." PhD diss., University Paris 10, 1976.

Costes, Laurence. *Le droit à la ville d'Henri Lefebvre: Étude de sociologie urbaine.* Paris: Ellipses, 2009.

Coudroy de Lille, Laurent, Grégory Busquet, and Claire Carriou. *Un ancien institut: Une histoire de l'Institut d'urbanisme de Paris.* Paris: Institut d'urbanisme—Ville de Créteil, 2005.

Couvidat, Yann. "L'exemple de la baie de San Francisco." In *Crise de l'urbain, futur de la ville: Colloque de Royaumont 1984,* ed. Jacques Le Goff and Louis Guieysse, 23–25. Paris: Économica, 1985.

Crawford, Margaret. Reviews of *Postmodern Cities and Spaces,* ed. Katherine Gibson and Sophie Watson; and *Writings on Cities,* by Henri Lefebvre. *Harvard Design Magazine* (Winter–Spring 1998): 84–85.

Cunningham, David. "The Concept of Metropolis: Philosophy and Urban Form." *Radical Philosophy* 133 (2005): 13–25.

Cupers, Kenny. "Concerning the User: The Experiment of Modern Urbanism in Postwar France, 1955–1975." 2009 draft of forthcoming PhD diss., Harvard University.

Dal Co, Francesco. *Figures of Architecture and Thought: German Architecture Culture, 1880–1920.* New York: Rizzoli, 1990.

Dear, Michael. "Les aspects postmodernes de Henri Lefebvre." *Espaces et sociétés* 76 (1999): 31–40.

———. *The Postmodern Urban Condition.* Oxford: Blackwell, 2000.

Debord, Guy-Ernest. *Mémoires: Structures portantes d'Asger Jorn.* Copenhagen: Internationale situationniste, 1959.

———. "Perspectives for Conscious Changes in Everyday Life." In *Situationist International Anthology,* ed. Ken Knabb, 90–99. Berkeley, Calif.: Bureau of Public Secrets, 2006.

———. *Society of the Spectacle.* Detroit: Black and Red, 1970 [1967].

Debord, Guy, and Gil Wolman. "A User's Guide to Détournement (1956)." In *Situationist International Anthology,* ed. Ken Knabb, 14–20. Berkeley, Calif.: Bureau of Public Secrets, 2006.

De Carlo, Giancarlo. "Editoriale: La testata, i contenuti e gli assunti, la struttura della rivista." *Spazio e società* 1 (1978): 3–8.

Degen, Hans. "50 Jahre Raumplanung in der Schweiz mit spezieller Betrachtung des Kantons Zürich." *DISP Journal* 139 (1999): 49–56.

Delannoi, Gil. "Arguments, 1956–1962, ou la parenthèse de l'ouverture." *Revue française de science politique* 34, no. 1 (1984): 127–45.

Deleuze, Gilles, and Michel Foucault. "Intellectuals and Power." In Michel Foucault, *Language, Counter-Memory, Practice: Selected Essays and Interviews,* 205–17. Oxford: Basil Blackwell, 1977.

Dembelle, Kary. "Sociologie politique des paysans du Mali." PhD diss., University Paris 10, 1970.

de Michelis, Marco, and Marco Venturi. "Le centre de direction de Bologne: Ou comment le P.C.I. gère le problème urbain." *Espaces et sociétés* 2 (1971): 45–52.

Depaule, Jean-Charles. "L'architecture sauvage." In *Les besoins fonctionnels de l'homme en vue de leur projection ultérieure sur le plan de la conception architecturale: Compte rendu de fin du contrat,* annex no. 5, ed. Françoise Bedos, Michel Dameron, Claude Leroy, Henri Raymond, and Léonie Sturge-Moore. Paris: Centre de recherche d'architecture, d'urbanisme et de construction, 1970.

———. "L'architecture sauvage." In "Marquage et appropriation de l'espace," ed. Jean-François Carporzen, 7–11, report of seminar, 14–15 December 1968. In *Les besoins fonctionnels de l'homme en vue de leur projection ultérieure sur le plan de la conception architecturale: Compte rendu de fin du contrat,* annex no. 1, ed. Françoise Bedos, Michel Dameron, Claude Leroy, Henri Raymond, and Léonie Sturge-Moore. Paris: Centre de recherche d'architecture, d'urbanisme et de construction, 1970.

———. "Quelques remarques sur l'usage de 'L'habitat pavillonnaire' dans le projet." In *Modèles culturels habitat: Séminaire de l'Institut de l'environnement de Nanterre, 4 février 1976,* ed. Institut de l'environnement, 127–36. Paris: Centre d'études et de recherches architecturales, 1977.

———. "Les sauvages de l'architecture." PhD diss., University Paris 10, 1979.

———. "Savoirs et manières de faire architecturaux: Populaires versus savants." *Les cahiers de la recherche architecturale et urbaine* 15 (2004): 13–28.

Depaule, Jean-Charles, Laurent Bony, and Patrick Pincemaille. "Pessac." In *Les besoins fonctionnels de l'homme en vue de leur projection ultérieure sur le plan de la conception architecturale: Compte rendu de fin du contrat,* annex no. 6, ed. Françoise Bedos, Michel Dameron, Claude Leroy, Henri Raymond, and Léonie Sturge-Moore, 1–24. Paris: Centre de recherche d'architecture, d'urbanisme et de construction, 1970.

Derrida, Jacques. *Specters of Marx: The State of the Debt, the Work of Mourning, and the New International.* New York: Routledge, 1994 [1993].

de Rudder, Véronique, Ghislaine Garin-Ferraz, and Bénédicte Haquin, eds. *Loi d'orientation pour la ville: Séminaire chercheurs, décideurs.* Paris: Plan construction et architecture, 1992.

Deshays, Gerard. "Urbanisme et terrorisme." PhD diss., University Paris 10, 1984.

Desportes, Marc, and Antoine Picon. *De l'espace au territoire: L'aménagement en France, XVIe–XXe siècles.* Paris: Presses de l'École nationale des Ponts et chaussées, 1997.

Dessauce, Marc, ed. *The Inflatable Moment: Pneumatics and Protest in '68.* New York: Princeton Architectural Press, 1999.

Devisme, Laurent. *Actualité de la pensée d'Henri Lefebvre à propos de l'urbain: La question de la centralité.* Tours, France: Maison des sciences de la ville, 1998.

———. "Henri Lefebvre, curieux sujet, non?" *Urbanisme* 319 (2001): 44.

———. *La ville décentrée: Figures centrales à l'épreuve des dynamiques urbaines.* Paris: Harmattan, 2005.

Diener, Roger, Jacques Herzog, Marcel Meili, Pierre de Meuron, and Christian Schmid. *Switzerland: An Urban Portrait.* Basel: Birkhäuser, 2006.

Dikeç, Mustafa. *Badlands of the Republic: Space, Politics, and French Urban Policy.* Malden, Mass.: Blackwell Publishing, 2007.

———. "Justice and the Spatial Imagination." *Environment and Planning A* 33 (2001): 1785–805.

Dimendberg, Edward. "Henri Lefebvre on Abstract Space." In *The Production of Public Space,* ed. Andrew Light and Jonathan Smith, 17–47. Lanham, Md.: Rowman and Littlefield, 1998.

Dissard, Françoise, and Jean-Paul Trystram, eds. *Sociologie et urbanisme.* 2 vols. Vol. 1: *Essai de synthèse et notes de sociologie.* Vol. 2: *Méthodologie et bibliographie.* Paris: Ministère de la construction, 1965.

"Domaine universitaire de Nanterre." *Techniques et Architecture* (February 1968): 130–31.

Dosse, François. *Histoire du structuralisme.* 2 vols. Paris: Éditions la Découverte, 1991–92.

Dreyfus-Armand, Geneviève. "Le mouvement du 22 mars: Entretien avec Daniel Cohn-Bendit." *Matériaux pour l'histoire de notre temps* 11 (1988): 124–29.

Droit de cité. Special issue of *Revue Rue Descartes* 63 (2009).

Duchen, Claire. "Occupation Housewife: The Domestic Ideal in 1950s France." *French Cultural Studies* 2, part 1, no. 4 (1991): 1–11.

Dupeux, Georges. *French Society, 1789–1970.* London: Methuen, 1976.

Duteuil, Jean-Pierre. *Nanterre 1965–66–67–68: Vers le mouvement du 22 mars.* Mauléon, France: Acratie, 1988.

Duvignaud, Jean. "Ledrut, l'espace, la ville." *Espaces et sociétés* 57–58 (1989): 193–96.

Eco, Umberto. "Function and Sign: The Semiotics of Architecture." In *Signs, Symbols, and Architecture,* ed. Geoffrey Broadbent, Richard Bunt, and Charles Jencks, 11–69. Chichester, U.K.: Wiley, 1980.

"Editorial Notes: Critique of Urbanism." In *Guy Debord and the Situationist International: Texts and Documents,* ed. Tom McDonough, 103–14. Cambridge, Mass.: MIT Press, 2002.

Editors of *Fortune* magazine, eds. *The Exploding Metropolis.* Garden City, N.Y.: Doubleday, 1958.

Egli, Ernst, Werner Aebli, Eduard Brühlmann, Rico Christ, and Ernst Winkler. *Die neue Stadt: Eine Studie für das Furttal.* Zurich: Verlag Bauen und Wohnen, 1961.

Egli, Ernst, and Fachgruppe Bauplanung der Studiengruppe "Neue Stadt." Research report: "Projekt einer Studienstadt im Raume Otelfingen im Furttal, Kt. Zuerich." *Studienprojekt einer neuen Stadt im Furttal,* vol. 1, and *Bericht über die Grundlagen einer neuen Schweizer Stadt: Untersuchung der wirtschaftlichen, rechtlichen und organisatorischen Fragen einer neuen Stadt,* vol. 2. 1958–63. Archive of the Institute of Theory and History of Architecture (GTA), ETH Zurich.

Eisinger, Angelus. *Die Stadt der Architekten: Anatomie einer Selbstdemontage.* Gütersloh, Germany: Bauverlag, 2006.

Elden, Stuart. "Between Marx and Heidegger: Politics, Philosophy and Lefebvre's 'The Production of Space.'" *Antipode* 36 (2004): 86–105.

——. "Politics, Philosophy, Geography: Henri Lefebvre in Recent Anglo-American Scholarship." *Antipode* 33 (2001): 809–25.

——. "Some Are Born Posthumously: The French Afterlife of Henri Lefebvre." *Historical Materialism* 14 (2006): 185–202.

——. *Understanding Henri Lefebvre: Theory and the Possible.* London: Continuum, 2004.

Elders, Fons. *Internationaal Filosofenprojekt: Henri Lefebvre.* Utrecht, the Netherlands: Bureau Vormingswerk Rijksuniversiteit Utrecht, n.d.

Eleb, Monique. "Modernity and Modernisation in Postwar France: The Third Type of House." *Journal of Architecture* 9, part 4 (2004): 495–514.

Emmerich, D.-G. Review of Henri Lefebvre's *Le droit à la ville. L'architecture d'aujourd'hui* 144 (1968): xxxvi–vii.

Engels, Friedrich. *The Condition of the Working Class in England.* Oxford: Basil Blackwell, 1958 [1845].

——. *The Housing Question.* London: Lawrence and Wishart, 1942 [1872–73].

"Entwicklung des Lehrprogramms der Hochschule für Gestaltung." *Archithese* 15 (1975): 45–46.

Erić, Zoran. *Differentiated Neighborhoods.* Belgrade, Serbia: Museum of Contemporary Art, 2009.

Febvre, Lucien. *Philippe II et la Franche-Comté, la crise de 1567, ses origines et ses conséquences: Étude d'histoire politique, religieuse et sociale.* Paris: H. Champion, 1911.

——. *The Problem of Unbelief in the Sixteenth Century: The Religion of Rabelais.* Cambridge, Mass.: Harvard University Press, 1982 [1942].

Ferrand-Bechmann, Dan. "À propos de Henri Lefebvre et Henri Raymond: Témoignage pour l'histoire de la sociologie." *La somme et le reste: Études lefebvriennes—Réseau mondial* 13 (2008): 15–17.

Fezer, Jesko, and Mathias Heyden, eds. *Hier entsteht: Strategien partizipativer Architektur und räumlicher Aneignung.* Berlin: b_books, 2004.

Fischbach, Franck. *La production des hommes: Marx avec Spinoza.* Paris: Presses universitaires de France, 2005.

Fontaine, Pierre François Léonard. *Le Palais-Royal: Domaine de la Couronne.* Paris, 1837.

Forty, Adrian. *Words and Buildings: A Vocabulary of Modern Architecture.* London: Thames and Hudson, 2000.

Foucault, Michel. *The Birth of Biopolitics: Lectures at the Collège de France, 1978–79.* Basingstoke, U.K.: Palgrave Macmillan, 2008 [2004].

——. *Language, Counter-Memory, Practice: Selected Essays and Interviews.* Oxford: Basil Blackwell, 1977.

——. "Of Other Spaces." *Diacritics* 16 (Spring 1986): 22–27. Originally published as "Espaces autres," *AMC: Architecture mouvement continuité* 5 (1984): 46–49.

——. *Security, Territory, Population: Lectures at the Collège de France, 1977–78.* Basingstoke, U.K.: Palgrave Macmillan, 2007 [2004].

Fourcaut, Annie. "Trois discours, une politique?" *Urbanisme* 322 (2002): 39–45.

——, ed. *Banlieue rouge: 1920–1960: Années Thorez, années Gabin: Archétype du populaire, banc d'essai des modernités.* Paris: Éditions Autrement, 1992.

——, ed. *Un siècle de banlieue parisienne (1859–1964): Guide de recherche.* Paris: L'Harmattan, 1988.

Fourier, Charles. *Des modifications à introduire dans l'architecture des villes.* Paris: Librairie Phalanstérienne, 1849.

——. *Oeuvres complètes.* 5 vols. Paris: Anthropos, 1971 [1846].

Francastel, Pierre. *Art and Technology in the Nineteenth and Twentieth Centuries.* New York: Zone Books, 2003 [1956].

Fraser, Nancy. *Justice Interruptus: Critical Reflections on the "Postsocialist" Condition.* New York: Routledge, 1997.

Frey, Jean-Pierre. "Prolégomènes à une histoire des concepts de morphologie urbaine et de morphologie sociale." In *Les identités urbaines, échos de Montréal,* ed. Lucie Morisset and Luc Noppen, 19–35. Québec: Éditions Nota bene, 2003.

Frey, Jean-Pierre, and Henri Raymond. *Paroles d'un sociologue: Vers une histoire architecturale de la société.* Paris: L'Harmattan, 2006.

Friedmann, Georges, ed., *Villes et campagnes: Civilisation urbaine et civilisation rurale en France.* Paris: A. Colin, 1953.

Furet, François. "Les intellectuels français et le structuralisme." *Preuves* 192 (1967): 3–12.

Furlough, Ellen. "Packaging Pleasures: Club Méditerranée and French Consumer Culture, 1950–1968." *French Historical Studies* 18, no. 1 (1993): 65–81.

Ganas, Pierre. *Henri Lefebvre (1901–1991): Philosophe mondialement connu, Pyrénéen ignoré.* Navarrenx, France: Cercle historique de l'Arribère, 2005.

Ganz, Martin. "Nonkonformes von vorgestern: 'Achtung: Die Schweiz.'" In *Bilder und Leitbilder im sozialen Wandel,* ed. Andreas Balthasar, Monika Bucheli, and Bernhard Degen, 373–414. Zurich: Schweizerisches Sozialarchiv, 1991.

Gardiner, Michael. *Critiques of Everyday Life.* London: Routledge, 2000.

Garnier, Jean-Pierre. *Une violence éminemment contemporaine: Essais sur la ville, la petite-bourgeoisie intellectuelle et l'effacement des classes populaires.* Marseille: Agone, 2010.

——. "La vision urbaine de Henri Lefebvre." *Espaces et sociétés* 76 (1994): 123–45.

Garnier, Jean-Pierre, and Denis Goldschmidt. *La comédie urbaine ou la cité sans classes.* Paris: F. Maspero, 1978.

Garnier, Tony. *Une cité industrielle: Étude pour la construction des villes.* Paris: Vincent, 1917.

Gauchet, Marcel. "Changement de paradigme dans les sciences sociales." *Le Débat* 50 (1988): 165–70.

Gaviria, Mario. *España a go-go: Turismo charter y neocolonialismo de espacio.* Madrid: Turner, 1974.

Giedion, Sigfried. *Architecture, You and Me: The Diary of a Development.* Cambridge, Mass.: Harvard University Press, 1958.

———. *Bauen in Frankreich: Eisen, Eisenbeton.* Leipzig: Klinkhardt und Biermann, 1928.

———. *Space, Time and Architecture: The Growth of a New Tradition.* Cambridge, Mass.: Harvard University Press, 1970 [1941].

Gilbert, Liette, and Mustafa Dikeç. "Right to the City: Politics of Citizenship." In *Space, Difference, Everyday Life: Reading Henri Lefebvre,* ed. Kanishka Goonewardena, Stefan Kipfer, Richard Milgrom, and Christian Schmid, 250–63. London: Routledge, 2008.

Girad, Alain. *Désirs des français en matière d'habitation urbaine: Une enquête par sondage.* Paris: Presses universitaires de France, 1947.

Giraudoux, Jean. Introduction to the 1943 French edition of the Athens Charter. In *Le Corbusier: The Athens Charter,* xv–xix. New York: Grossman Publishers, 1973.

Gombin, Richard. "French Leftism." *Journal of Contemporary History* 7, no. 1–2 (1972): 27–50.

Goonewardena, Kanishka, Stefan Kipfer, Christian Schmid, and Richard Milgrom, eds. *Space, Difference, Everyday Life: Reading Henri Lefebvre.* London: Routledge, 2008.

Gottdiener, Mark. "A Marx for Our Time: Henri Lefebvre and the Production of Space." *Sociological Theory* 11, no. 1 (1993): 129–34.

———. *The Social Production of Urban Space.* Austin: University of Texas Press, 1985.

Gozzi, J., P. Pinchemel, and A. Vakili. *Niveaux optima des villes: Essai de définition d'après l'analyse des structures urbaines du Nord et du Pas-de-Calais.* Liège, Belgium: CERES, 1959.

Granet, Paul. *Changer la ville.* Paris: Club français du livre, 1975.

Granger, Jean-Maurice. "Ecosystème socio-culturel et planification intégrale." PhD diss., University Paris 10, 1969.

Grawitz, Madeleine, and Roger Pinto. *Méthodes des sciences sociales.* 2 vols. Paris: Dalloz, 1964.

Gregory, Derek. *Geographical Imaginations.* Cambridge, Mass.: Blackwell, 1994.

Gregory, Derek, and John Urry. *Social Relations and Spatial Structures.* Basingstoke, U.K.: Macmillan, 1985.

Grenzling, Claude. "Méthodologie d'expérimentation en architecture." In "Architecture—mythe—idéologie," ed. Léonie Sturge-Moore. Report of third seminar, 8–9 February 1969. In *Les besoins fonctionnels de l'homme en vue de leur projection ultérieure sur le plan de la conception architecturale: Compte rendu de fin du contrat,* ed. Françoise Bedos, Michel Dameron, Claude Leroy, Henri Raymond, and Léonie Sturge-Moore, annex no. 1. Paris: Centre de recherche d'architecture, d'urbanisme et de construction, 1970.

Guerrand, Roger-Henri. "Aux origines de la cité radieuse: L'architecture phalanstérienne." *AMC: Architecture mouvement continuité* 12 (1968): 18–24.

Guichard, Olivier. "Les villes à la française." *Urbanisme* 136 (1973): 2–3.

Guilbaud, Pierre, Henri Lefebvre, and Serge Renaudie. "International Competition for the New Belgrade Urban Structure Improvement." In *Autogestion, or Henri Lefebvre in New Belgrade,* ed. Sabine Bitter and Helmut Weber, 1–32. Berlin: Sternberg Press, 2009.

Gurvitch, Georges. *La multiplicité des temps sociaux.* Paris: Centre de documentation universitaire, 1958.

——. *La vocation actuelle de la sociologie: Vers une sociologie différentielle.* Paris: Presses universitaires de France, 1950.

——, ed. *Industrialisation et technocratie.* Paris: Colin 1949.

Hamel, Pierre, and Claire Poitras. "Henri Lefebvre, penseur de la postmodernité." *Espaces et sociétés* 76 (1994): 41–58.

Hamon, Léo. *Les nouveaux comportements politiques de la classe ouvrière: Entretiens de Dijon.* Paris: Presses universitaires de France, 1962.

"Hans Ulrich Obrist in Conversation with Raoul Vaneigem." *e-flux* 5 (2009), www.e-flux.com.

Harvey, David. *The Condition of Postmodernity.* Oxford: Blackwell, 1990.

——. "Possible Urban Worlds: A Review Essay." *City and Community* 3 (2004): 83–89.

——. "The Right to the City." *New Left Review* 53 (2008): 23–40.

——. *Social Justice and the City.* London: Edward Arnold, 1973.

——. *The Urban Experience.* Oxford: Basil Blackwell, 1989.

——. *The Urbanization of Capital.* Oxford: Basil Blackwell, 1985.

Hastings-King, Stephen. "L'Internationale Situationniste, Socialisme ou Barbarie, and the Crisis of the Marxist Imaginary." *SubStance* 28, no. 3 (1999): 26–54.

Haumont, Antoine. "Paris: La vie quotidienne." *La documentation française* 3982–83 (1973).

Haumont, Antoine, Nicole Haumont, and Henri Raymond. *La copropriété.* Paris: Centre de recherche d'urbanisme, 1971.

Haumont, Antoine, Nicole Haumont, Henri Raymond, and Marie-Geneviève Raymond. *L'habitat pavillonnaire.* Paris: Centre de recherche d'urbanisme, 1966.

Haumont, Nicole. *Les locataires.* Paris: Institut de sociologie urbaine, 1976.

——. *Les pavillonnaires: Étude psycho-sociologique d'un mode d'habitat.* Paris: Centre de recherche d'urbanisme, 1966.

——. "Les pavillonnaires et la pratique de l'habitat." *Urbanisme* 151 (1975): 68–72.

Haumont, Nicole, and Henri Raymond. *Habitat et pratique de l'espace: Étude des relations entre l'intérieur et l'extérieur du logement.* Paris: Institut de sociologie urbaine, 1973.

Hays, K. Michael, ed. *Architecture Theory since 1968.* Cambridge, Mass.: MIT Press, 1998.

Hegel, Georg Wilhelm Friedrich. *Aesthetics: Lectures on Fine Art.* 2 vols. Oxford: Clarendon Press, 1988 [1835].

——. "Wer denkt abstrakt?" www.marxists.org. Also published in *Gesammelte Schriften,* ed. Manfred Baum and Kurt Rainer Meist, vol. 5, 381–87. Hamburg: Felix Meiner, 1998 [1807].

Heidegger, Martin. "Building Dwelling Thinking." In Martin Heidegger, *Poetry, Language, Thought,* 141–60. New York: Harper Colophon Books, 2001 [1951].

———. *Poetry, Language, Thought.* New York: Harper Colophon Books, 2001.

Hess, Rémi. *L'analyse institutionnelle.* Paris: Presses universitaires de France, 1993.

———. *Henri Lefebvre et l'aventure du siècle.* Paris: Métailié, 1988.

———. *Henri Lefebvre et la pensée du possible: Théorie des moments et construction de la personne.* Paris: Économica–Anthropos, 2009.

———. "La méthode d'Henri Lefebvre." www.multitudes.samizdat.net, 6 July 2004.

Heuvel, Dirk van den, and Max Risselada, eds. *Team 10, 1953–81: In Search of a Utopia of the Present.* Rotterdam: Netherlands Architecture Institute, 2005.

Heynen, Hilde. "New Babylon: The Antinomies of Utopia." In Hilde Heynen, *Architecture and Modernity: A Critique,* 151–74. Cambridge, Mass.: MIT Press, 1999.

Highmore, Ben. *Everyday Life and Cultural Theory: An Introduction.* London: Routledge, 2002.

Hilberseimer, Ludwig. *Grossstadt Architektur.* Stuttgart: Hoffmann, 1927.

Hirsch, Bernard. *Oublier Cergy . . . : L'invention d'une ville nouvelle: Cergy–Pontoise 1965–75.* Paris: Presses de l'École nationale des Ponts et Chaussées, 1990.

Hołówko, Stefan. "Mourenx—ville nouvelle." *Architektura* 9 (1960): 363–66.

Huet, Bernard. "Modèles culturels et architecture." In *Modèles culturels habitat: Séminaire de l'Institut de l'environnement de Nanterre, 4 février 1976,* ed. Institut de l'environnement, 27–41. Paris: Centre d'études et de recherches architecturales, 1977.

Huizinga, Johan. *Homo Ludens: A Study of the Play-Element in Culture.* London: Routledge and Kegan, 1949 [1938].

Ilyenkov, Evald. *The Dialectics of the Abstract and the Concrete in Marx's Capital.* www.marxists.org. Published also by Progress Publishers, Moscow, 1982 [1960].

Institut de l'environnement, ed. *Modèles culturels habitat: Séminaire de l'Institut de l'environnement de Nanterre, 4 février 1976.* Paris: Centre d'études et de recherches architecturales, 1977.

Institut de sociologie urbaine. *Choisy-le-Roi.* N.d. Centre de recherche sur l'habitat, Paris.

———. *Les modes de vie: Approchés et directions de recherches.* Paris: Insitut de sociologie urbaine, 1975.

———. "Organisation urbaine et comportements sociaux." 1964. Centre de recherche sur l'habitat, Paris.

"L'Institut d'urbanisme en autogestion." *Urbanisme* 106 (1968): 11–13.

Institut français d'architecture, ed. *Besoin(s)—analyse et critique de la notion.* Paris: Institut français d'architecture, 1975.

Het Internationaal Filosofen Project: Arne Naess, Leszek Kołakowski, Henri Lefebvre, Freddy Ayer. Directed by Louis van Gasteren. 1971, NOS, the Netherlands.

Inwood, Michael James. *A Hegel Dictionary.* Cambridge, Mass.: Blackwell, 1992.

Jacobs, Jane. *The Death and Life of Great American Cities.* New York: Random, 1961.

Jaisson, Marie. "Temps et espace chez Maurice Halbwachs (1925–1945)." *Sciences Humaines: Revue d'histoire des sciences humaines* 1 (1991): 163–78.

Jałowiecki, Bohdan. *Społeczne wytwarzanie przestrzeni.* Warsaw: Wyd. Ksi□□ka i Wiedza, 1988.

James, Warren A. *Ricardo Bofill: Taller de Arquitectura: Buildings and Projects 1960–1985.* New York: Rizzoli, 1988.

Jameson, Fredric. "Architecture and the Critique of Ideology." In *Architecture, Criticism, Ideology,* ed. Joan Ockman, 51–87. Princeton, N.J.: Princeton Architectural Press, 1985.

——. *Postmodernism, or the Cultural Logic of Late Capitalism.* London: Verso, 1991.

Jay, Martin. *Marxism and Totality: The Adventures of a Concept from Lukács to Habermas.* Cambridge: Polity, 1984.

Jencks, Charles. *Architecture 2000: Predictions and Methods.* London: Studio Vista, 1971.

Jessop, Bob. *The Future of the Capitalist State.* London: Polity, 2002.

——. *State Power: A Strategic–Relational Approach.* Cambridge: Polity, 2008.

Jolé, Michèle. "Henri Lefebvre à Strasbourg." *Urbanisme* 319, no. 7–8 (2001): 40–43.

——. "La sociologie urbaine à Strasbourg avec Henri Lefebvre: Un apprentissage du difficile rapport de la théorie à l'action." *Revue des sciences sociales* 40 (2008): 134–41.

Joseph, Isaac. "Le droit à la ville, la ville à l'oeuvre: Deux paradigmes de la recherche urbaine." *Les annales de la recherche urbaine* 64 (1994): 4–10.

Kaës, René. *Vivre dans les grands ensembles.* Paris: Éditions ouvrières, 1963.

Kardelj, Edvard. *Über das System der selbstverwaltenden Planung: Brioni-Diskussionen.* Belgrade, Yugoslavia: Sozialistische Theorie und Praxis, 1976.

Katsiaficas, George. *The Imagination of the New Left: A Global Analysis of 1968.* Boston: South End Press, 1987.

Kelly, Michael. "French Intellectuals and Zhdanovism." *French Cultural Studies* 22, no. 8 (1997): 17–28.

Kipfer, Stefan. "How Lefebvre Urbanized Gramsci: Hegemony, Everyday Life, and Difference." In *Space, Difference, Everyday Life: Reading Henri Lefebvre,* ed. Kanishka Goonewardena, Stefan Kipfer, Christian Schmid, and Richard Milgrom, 193–211. London: Routledge, 2008.

Kipfer, Stefan, Kanishka Goonewardena, Christian Schmid, and Richard Milgrom. "On the Production of Henri Lefebvre." In *Space, Difference, Everyday Life: Reading Henri Lefebvre,* ed. Kanishka Goonewardena, Stefan Kipfer, Christian Schmid, and Richard Milgrom, 1–23. London: Routledge, 2008.

Kipfer, Stefan, and Richard Milgrom. "Henri Lefebvre: Urbanization, Space and Nature." *Capitalism, Nature, Socialism* 13 (2002): 37–41.

Kipfer, Stefan, Christian Schmid, Kanishka Goonewardena, and Richard Milgrom. "Globalizing Lefebvre?" In *Space, Difference, Everyday Life: Reading Henri Lefebvre,* ed. Kanishka Goonewardena, Stefan Kipfer, Christian Schmid, and Richard Milgrom, 285–305. London: Routledge, 2008.

Kirsch, Scott. "The Incredible Shrinking World? Technology and the Production of Space." *Environment and Planning D: Society and Space* 13, no. 5 (1995): 529–55.

Kleinspehn, Thomas. *Der verdrängte Alltag: Henri Lefèbvres marxistische Kritik des Alltagslebens.* Giessen, Germany: Focus-Verlag, 1975.

Knabb, Ken, ed. *Situationist International Anthology.* Berkeley, Calif.: Bureau of Public Secrets, 2006.

Kofman, Eleonore, and Elizabeth Lebas. "Lost in Transposition—Time, Space and the City." In *Henri Lefebvre: Writings on Cities,* ed. and trans. Elisabeth Lebas and Eleonore Kofman, 3–60. Oxford: Blackwell, 1996.

——. "Recovery and Reappropriation in Lefebvre and Constant." In *Non-Plan: Essays on Freedom Participation and Change in Modern Architecture and Urbanism,* ed. Jonathan Hughes and Simon Sadler, 80–89. Oxford: Architectural Press, 2000.

Kopp, Anatole. *Changer la vie, changer la ville: De la vie nouvelle aux problèmes urbains, U.R.S.S. 1917–1932.* Paris: Union générale d'éditions, 1975.

——. "De la Charte d'Athènes aux grands ensembles." *Le carre bleu* 1 (1980): 6–11.

——. *Town and Revolution: Soviet Architecture and City Planning, 1917–1935.* New York: G. Braziller, 1970 [1967].

Kosík, Karel. *Dialectics of the Concrete: A Study on Problems of Man and World.* Dordrecht, the Netherlands: D. Reidel Publishing Co., 1976 [1963].

Kotányi, Attila, and Raoul Vaneigem. "Basic Program of the Bureau of Unitary Urbanism." In *Situationist International Anthology,* ed. Ken Knabb, 86–89. Berkeley, Calif.: Bureau of Public Secrets, 2006.

Kouvelakis, Stathis. "The Crises of Marxism and the Transformation of Capitalism." In *Critical Companion to Contemporary Marxism,* ed. Jacques Bidet and Stathis Kouvelakis, 23–38. Leiden: Brill, 2008.

——. "Henri Lefebvre, Thinker of Urban Modernity." In *Critical Companion to Contemporary Marxism,* ed. Jacques Bidet and Stathis Kouvelakis, 711–27. Leiden: Brill, 2008.

Kurzweil, Edith. *The Age of Structuralism: Lévi-Strauss to Foucault.* New York: Columbia University Press, 1996.

Lane, Jeremy. *Pierre Bourdieu: A Critical Introduction.* Sterling, Va.: Pluto Press, 2000.

——. "Towards a Poetics of Consumerism: Gaston Bachelard's 'Material Imagination' and a Narratives of Post-War Modernisation." *French Cultural Studies* 17, no. 1 (2006): 19–34.

Laude, Claudine. "Le Centre d'études sociologiques en 1959." *Revue française de sociologie* 32 (1991): 405–9.

Lauga, Pierre. *La révolution urbaine, ou l'architecture au secours de l'économie politique.* Paris: Éditions Je sers, 1946.

Lebovics, Herman. *True France: The Wars over Cultural Identity 1900–1945.* Ithaca, N.Y.: Cornell University Press, 1992.

Le Corbusier. *The Athens Charter.* New York: Grossman, 1973 [1941].

——. *Toward an Architecture.* London: Frances Lincoln, 2008 [1923].

Ledrut, Raymond. *L'espace social de la ville: Problèmes de sociologie appliquée à l'aménagement urbain.* Paris: Éditions anthropos, 1968.

———. "The Social Space of a Town." *Society and Leisure* 1 (1971): 21–31.

———. *Sociologie urbaine.* Paris: Presses universitaires de France, 1968.

Lefebvre, Jean-Pierre. *Une expérience d'écologie urbaine.* Paris: Éditions du Linteau, 1999.

———. *Quel altermonde?* Paris: L'Harmattan, 2004.

———. "Sur la ville, entretien avec Jean-Pierre Lefebvre." In *Sodédat 93, un laboratoire urbain,* supplement to *L'architecture d'aujourd'hui* 295 (1994): 4–8.

———. "Sur 'L'unique et l'homogène dans la production de l'espace,' communication de Jorge Hajime Oseki, Université de Sao Paulo, au colloque du centenaire d'Henri Lefebvre." *La somme et le reste: Études lefebvriennes–réseau mondial* 3 (2004): 15–19.

Lefort, Claude. "L'experience proletarienne." *Socialisme ou Barbarie* 11 (1952): 1–19.

Léger, Fernand, José Luis Sert, and Sigfried Giedion. "Nine Points on Monumentality (1944)." In *Architecture Culture 1943–1968: A Documentary Anthology,* ed. Joan Ockman, 48–54. New York: Rizzoli, 1993.

Lengereau, Éric. "Du coup d'arrêt de la circulaire Guichard au 'cadre de vie' giscardien." *Urbanisme* 322 (2002): 47–49.

———. *L'État et l'architecture: 1958–1981, une politique publique?* Paris: Picard, 2001.

Lenin, Vladimir Ilyich. "What Is to Be Done?" www.marxists.org. Also published in Vladimir Ilyich Lenin, *Collected Works,* vol. 5, 347–530 (Moscow: Foreign Languages Publishing House, 1961).

Leroy, Claude, Françoise Bedos, and Claude Berthelot. "Appropriation de l'espace par les objects (Chambres de l'Institut Marcel Rivière)." In *Les besoins fonctionnels de l'homme en vue de leur projection ultérieure sur le plan de la conception architecturale: Compte rendu de fin du contrat,* annex no. 4, ed. Françoise Bedos, Michel Dameron, Claude Leroy, Henri Raymond, and Léonie Sturge-Moore. Paris: Centre de recherche d'architecture, d'urbanisme et de construction, 1970.

Leroy, Claude, Françoise Bedos, and Alberto Eiguer. "Représentation et appropriation de l'espace (Plan de l'Institut Marcel Rivière)." In *Les besoins fonctionnels de l'homme en vue de leur projection ultérieure sur le plan de la conception architecturale: Compte rendu de fin du contrat,* annex no. 3, ed. Françoise Bedos, Michel Dameron, Claude Leroy, Henri Raymond, and Léonie Sturge-Moore. Paris: Centre de recherche d'architecture, d'urbanisme et de construction, 1970.

Lethierry, Hughes. *Penser avec Henri Lefebvre: Sauver la vie et la ville?* Lyon, France: Chronique sociale, 2009.

Levin, Thomas Y. "Geopolitics of Hibernation: The Drift of Situationist Urbanism." In *Situationists: Art, Politics, Urbanism,* ed. Libero Andreotti and Xavier Costa, 111–46. Barcelona: Museu d'Art Contemporani de Barcelona, 1996.

Lévy, Marie-Françoise. "Paul-Henry Chombart de Lauwe, un sociologue à la télévision 1957–1960." *Espaces et sociétés* 103 (2001): 85–95.

Lichtheim, George. *Marxism in Modern France*. New York: Columbia University Press, 1966.

Lier, Henri van. *Le nouvel âge*. Paris: Casterman, 1962.

Light, Andrew, and Jonathan Smith, eds. *The Production of Public Space*. Lanham, Md.: Rowman and Littlefield, 1998.

Linden, Marcel van der. *Workers of the World: Essays toward a Global Labor History*. Leiden: Brill, 2008.

Lion, Yves. *Yves Lion: Études, réalisations, projets 1974–1985*. Paris: Electa Moniteur, 1985.

Lojkine, Jean. "Y a-t-il une rente foncière urbaine?" *Espaces et sociétés* 2 (1971): 89–94.

Lourau, René. "L'analyse institutionnelle." PhD diss., University Paris 10, 1969.

——. *L'analyse institutionnelle*. Paris: Éditions de Minuit, 1991.

——. *Sociologue à plein temps: Analyse institutionnelle et pédagogie*. Paris: Épi, 1976.

Lucan, Jacques. *France: Architecture 1965–1988*. Paris: Electa Moniteur, 1989.

Luxemburg, Rosa. *Social Reform or Revolution*. www.marxists.org. Published also by Militant Publications, London, 1986 [1900].

Macherey, Pierre. *Petits riens: Ornières et dérives du quotidien*. Lormont, France: Le Bord de l'eau, 2009.

Magri, Susanna. "Le pavillon stigmatisé: Grands ensembles et maisons individuelles dans la sociologie des années 1950 à 1970." *L'année sociologique* 58, no. 1 (2008): 171–202.

Mallet, Serge. *The New Working Class*. Nottingham, U.K.: Bertrand Russell Peace Foundation for Spokesman Books, 1975 [1963].

"Manifeste pour la création d'un mensuel." GTA Archiv, Institut Geschichte und Theorie der Architektur, Eidgenössische Technische Hochschule, Zürich, Claude Schnaidt files, letters: Henri Lefebvre.

Manuel, Frank E. *The Prophets of Paris*. Cambridge, Mass.: Harvard University Press, 1962.

Marcuse, Herbert. *One-Dimensional Man: Studies in the Ideology of Advanced Industrial Society*. London: Routledge and Kegan Paul, 1964.

Martin, Corinne, and Thierry Paquot. "Rencontre avec Nicole Beaurain." *Urbanisme* 319 (2001): 42–43.

Martins, José de Souza. *A aparição do demônio na fábrica: Origens sociais do eu dividido no subúrbio operário*. São Paulo, Brazil: Editora 34, 2008.

——. *A sociabilidade do homem simples*. São Paulo, Brazil: Hucitec, 2000.

——. *Subúrbio*. São Paulo, Brazil: Hucitec, 1992.

——, ed. *Henri Lefebvre e o retorno da dialética*. São Paulo, Brazil: Hucitec, 1996.

Marx, Karl. *Capital: A Critique of Political Economy*. www.marxists.org. Published also by Lawrence and Wishart, London, 1974 [vol. 1, 1867].

——. *A Contribution to the Critique of Political Economy*. www.marxists.org. Published also by Progress Publishers, Moscow, 1970 [1859].

——. *Critique of the Gotha Programme*. www.marxists.org. Published also by Progress Publishers, Moscow, 1960 [1890–91].

——. *Economic and Philosophic Manuscripts of 1844*. www.marxists.org. Published also by Foreign Languages Publishing House, Moscow, 1959 [1932].

——. *Grundrisse: Foundations of the Critique of Political Economy*. www.marxists.org. Published also by Penguin, Harmondsworth, U.K., 1973 [1939].

——. *Morceaux choisis*. Paris: Gallimard, 1934.

——. "Notes sur les besoins, la production et la division du travail." *La revue marxiste* (June 1929): 513–38.

——. "Travail et propriété privée." *La revue marxiste* 1 (1929): 7–28.

Maslow, Abraham Harold. *Motivation and Personality*. New York: Harper and Bros., 1954.

McDonough, Tom. "Invisible Cities: Henri Lefebvre's *The Explosion*." *Art Forum* 46, no. 9 (2008): 314–21.

——. "Metastructure: Experimental Utopia and Traumatic Memory in Constant's New Babylon." *Grey Room* 33 (2008): 84–95.

——, ed. *Guy Debord and the Situationist International: Texts and Documents*. Cambridge, Mass.: MIT Press, 2002.

Merlin, Pierre. *L'aménagement du territoire*. Paris: Presses universitaires de France, 2002.

——. *Les villes nouvelles: Urbanisme régional et aménagement*. Paris: Presses universitaires de France, 1969.

Merrifield, Andy. *Henri Lefebvre: A Critical Introduction*. London: Routledge, 2006.

——. "Henri Lefebvre: A Socialist in Space." In *Thinking Space,* ed. Mike Crang and Nigel Thrift, 167–82. London: Routledge, 2000.

——. "Lefebvre and Debord: A Faustian Fusion." In *Space, Difference, Everyday Life: Reading Henri Lefebvre,* ed. Kanishka Goonewardena, Stefan Kipfer, Richard Milgrom, and Christian Schmid, 176–89. London: Routledge, 2008.

——. "Lefebvre, Anti-Logos, and Nietzsche: An Alternative Reading of 'The Production of Space.'" *Antipode* 27 (1995): 294–303.

——. "Place and Space: A Lefebvrian Reconciliation." *Transactions of the Institute of British Geographers* 18, no. 4 (1993): 516–31.

Meyer, Kurt. *Henri Lefebvre: Ein romantischer Revolutionär*. Vienna: Europaverlag, 1973.

——. *Von der Stadt zur urbanen Gesellschaft: Jacob Burckhardt und Henri Lefebvre*. Munich: Wilhelm Fink, 2007.

Michel, Jacques. "Le 'BISTROT-CLUB' pour animer les nouvelles cités." *Le Monde,* 22 December 1961.

Le ministre de l'aménagement du territoire, de l'équipement, du logement et du tourisme. "Circulaire du 21 mars 1973: Relative aux formes d'urbanisation dites 'grands ensembles' et à la lutte contre la ségrégation sociale par l'habitat." *Urbanisme* 136 (1973): 76. Originally published in *Journal officiel de la Republique française,* 5 April 1973, 3864.

Misiano, Viktor. Introduction to "English Digest 2005–2007." *Moscow Art Magazine* (2007): n.p.

Moiroux, Françoise. "Banlieues 89, un événement fondateur?" *Urbanisme* 332 (2003): 43–46.

Moles, Abraham. "Functionalism in Crisis." *Ulm* 19–20 (1967): 24–25.

——. "Objet et communication." *Communications* 13 (1969): 1–21.

——. "Theory of Complexity and Technical Civilization." *Ulm* 12 (1965): 11–16.

Moles, Abraham, and Elisabeth Rohmer. *Psychologie de l'espace.* Paris: Casterman, 1972.

Moley, Christian. *Les abords du chez-soi, en quête d'espaces intermédiaires.* Paris: Éditions de la Villette, 2006.

Monnier, Gérard. "La croissance et l'innovation typologique." In *Les années ZUP: Architectures de la croissance, 1960–1973,* ed. Gérard Monnier and Richard Klein, 280–92. Paris: Picard, 2002.

Monnier, Gérard, and Richard Klein, eds. *Les années ZUP: Architectures de la croissance 1960–1973.* Paris: Éditions A&J Picard, 2002.

Moos, Stanislaus von. *Fernand Léger: La ville: Zeitdruck, Grossstadt, Wahrnehmung.* Frankfurt am Main: Fischer, 1999.

Moravánszky, Ákos. "Die Wahrnehmung des Raumes." In *Architekturtheorie im 20. Jahrhundert: Eine kritische Anthologie,* ed. Ákos Moravánszky, 121–46. Vienna: Springer, 2003.

——, ed. *Architekturtheorie im 20. Jahrhundert: Eine kritische Anthologie.* Vienna: Springer, 2003.

Moulin, Raymonde. "Avons-nous encore besoin d'architectes?" *Esprit* 385 (1969): 389–407.

Müller, Horst. *Praxis und Hoffnung: Studien zur Philosophie und Wissenschaft gesellschaftlicher Praxis von Marx bis Bloch und Lefebvre.* Bochum, Germany: Germinal Verlag, 1986.

Müller-Schöll, Ulrich. *Das System und der Rest: Kritische Theorie in der Perspektive Henri Lefebvres.* Mössingen–Talheim, Germany: Talheimer, 1999.

Mumford, Eric. *The CIAM Discourse on Urbanism, 1928–1960.* Cambridge, Mass.: MIT Press, 2000.

Mumford, Lewis. *The Culture of Cities.* London: Routledge, 1997 [1938].

Mušič, Vladimir-Braco. "The New System of Social Planning in Yugoslavia and Perspectives of Urban Planning." In *Learning from Past Experience: Housing and Planning in the Eighties: Papers and Proceedings: International Congress Göteborg,* vol. 2, 303–9. Göteborg, Sweden, 1979.

——. "Urban Planning, Participation, and Self-Management." In *Urban Policy and Urban Development in the 80's: Danish Experience in a European Context,* ed. Christian Wichmann Matthiessen, 63–68. Copenhagen: Geografisk Centralinstitut, 1983.

Negri, Antonio. "Archaeology and Project: The Mass Worker and the Social Worker." In *Revolution Retrieved: Writings on Marx, Keynes, Capitalist Crisis and New Social Subjects (1967-83),* 199–228. London: Red Notes, 1988.

——. "The Multitude and the Metropolis." www.generation-online.org, 2002.

——. *Revolution Retrieved: Writings on Marx, Keynes, Capitalist Crisis and New Social Subjects (1967-83)*. London: Red Notes, 1988.

Newsome, W. Brian. "The 'Apartment Referendum' of 1959: Toward Participatory Architectural and Urban Planning in Postwar France." *French Historical Studies* 28, no. 2 (2005): 329–58.

Nieuwenhuys, Constant. "Another City for Another Life." In Mark Wigley, *Constant's New Babylon: The Hyper-Architecture of Desire,* 115–16. Rotterdam: 010 Publishers, 1998.

——. "Description of the Yellow Sector." In Mark Wigley, *Constant's New Babylon: The Hyper-Architecture of Desire,* 122. Rotterdam: 010 Publishers, 1998.

——. "New Babylon." In *Theory of the Dérive and Other Situationist Writings on the City,* ed. Libero Andreotti and Xavier Costa. Barcelona: Museu d'Art Contemporani de Barcelona, 1996.

——. "New Babylon: Outline of a Culture." In Mark Wigley, *Constant's New Babylon: The Hyper-Architecture of Desire,* 160–65. Rotterdam: 010 Publishers, 1998.

——. "New Babylon—Ten Years On." In Mark Wigley, *Constant's New Babylon: The Hyper-Architecture of Desire,* 222–26. Rotterdam: 010 Publishers, 1998.

——. "On Traveling." In Mark Wigley, *Constant's New Babylon: The Hyper-Architecture of Desire,* 200–201. Rotterdam: 010 Publishers, 1998.

——. "Unitary Urbanism." In Mark Wigley, *Constant's New Babylon: The Hyper-Architecture of Desire,* 131–35. Rotterdam: 010 Publishers, 1998.

Norberg-Schulz, Christian. *Existence, Space, and Architecture.* London: Studio Vista, 1971.

Ockman, Joan. "Lessons from Objects: Perriand from the Pioneer Years to the 'Epoch of Realities.'" In *Charlotte Perriand: An Art of Living,* ed. Mary McLeod, 154–81. New York: Abrams, 2003.

——. "Venice and New York." *Casabella* 619–20 (1995): 56–73.

——, ed. *Architecture Culture 1943–1968: A Documentary Anthology.* New York: Rizzoli, 1993.

Orville, Paul. "Paris XX arrondissement, les incidences de certains types d'habitation sur la délinquance juvénile." Master's thesis, Institut d'urbanisme de l'Université de Paris, 1967.

Osborne, Peter. "The Reproach of Abstraction." *Radical Philosophy* 127 (2004): 21–28.

Ost, David. *The Defeat of Solidarity: Anger and Politics in Postcommunist Europe.* Ithaca, N.Y.: Cornell University Press, 2005.

Papayanis, Nicholas. *Planning Paris before Haussmann.* Baltimore, Md.: Johns Hopkins University Press, 2004.

Paquot, Thierry. *Demeure terrestre: Enquête vagabonde sur l'habiter.* Paris: Éditions de l'imprimeur, 2005.

——. "Des 'besoins' aux 'aspirations': Pour une critique des grands ensembles." *Urbanisme* 322 (2002): 79–80.

——. "Habitat et 'habiter.'" *Urbanisme* 298 (1998): 46–48.

———. "Rédecouvrir Lefebvre." *Rue Descartes* 63 (2009): 8–16.

Pares, René. *La SCIC au service du pays.* Paris: S.C.I.C., 1992.

Pawley, Martin, and Bernard Tschumi. "The Beaux Arts since 1968." *Architectural Design* 41 (1971): 536–66.

Peaucelle, Denis. *Éléments pour une mémoire collective de Mourenx: 1957–1965.* Mourenx, France: Association Lacq Odyssée, 1985.

Pedret, Annie. "Preparing CIAM X 1954–1955." www.team10online.org.

Perec, Georges. *Things: A Story of the Sixties and a Man Asleep.* London: Collins Harvill, 1990 [1965].

Perreymond. "Études sur la ville de Paris." *Revue générale de l'architecture et des travaux publics* 3 (December 1842): cols. 540–44, 570–79; 4 (January 1843): cols. 25–37; 4 (February 1843): 72–88; 4 (September 1843): cols. 413–29; 4 (October 1843): cols. 449–69; 4 (November 1843): cols. 517–28.

Petrović, Gajo, ed. *Revolutionäre Praxis: Jugoslawischer Marxismus der Gegenwart.* Freiburg i. Br., Germany: Rombach, 1968.

Petrović, Miloš R. "A Study for the Restructuring of the Center of New Belgrade and the Sava Amphitheatre." *Ekistics: The Problems and Science of Human Settlements* 52, no. 311 (1985): 217–31.

Peyre, Christiane, and Yves Raynouard. *Histoire et légendes du Club Méditerranée.* Paris: Seuil, 1971.

Pflieger, Géraldine. *De la ville aux réseaux: Dialogue avec Manuel Castells.* Lausanne, Switzerland: Presses polytechniques et Universitaires Romandes, 2006.

P. G. "Formes de croissance des villes." *Population* 8 (1953): 201.

Piaget, Jean. *Le structuralisme.* Paris: Presses universitaires de France, 1968.

Pierre, Roger. *La Drôme et l'Ardèche entre deux guerres 1920–1939.* Valence, France: Notre temps, 1977.

Pile, Steve. *The Body and the City: Psychoanalysis, Space and Subjectivity.* London: Routledge, 1996.

"Pour un urbanisme—rapports, communications, débats: Texte intégral du colloque, Grenoble, 6–7 avril 1974." *La nouvelle critique* 78 bis (1974).

Prigge Walter. "Die Revolution der Städte lesen." In *Stadt-Räume: Die Zukunft des Städtischen,* ed. Martin Wentz, 99–112. Frankfurt am Main: Campus Verlag, 1991.

———. *Peripherie ist überall.* Frankfurt am Main: Campus Verlag, 1998.

———. "Urbi et Orbi—zur Epistemologie des Städtischen." In *Capitales Fatales: Urbanisierung und Politik in den Finanzmetropolen Frankfurt und Zürich,* ed. Hansruedi Hitz, Roger Keil, Ute Lehrer, Klaus Ronneberger, Christian Schmid, and Richard Wolff, 176–87. Zurich: Rotpunkt, 1995.

Programme du 7ième congrès CIAM: Mis en application de la Charte d'Athènes. Paris, 1948.

Pudal, Bernard. *Un monde défait: Les communistes français de 1956 à nos jours.* Broissieux, France: Éditions du Croquant, 2009.

15 jours en France . . . Paris: La documentation française, 1965.

Radkowski, Georges-Hubert de. *Anthropologie de l'habiter: Vers le nomadisme.* Paris: Presses universitaires de France, 2002.

Rafatdjou, Makan, and Sylvian Sangla. "Henri Lefebvre: Présences d'une recherche." *Société française* 56 (1996): 22–28.

Ragon, Michel. *Histoire mondiale de l'architecture et de l'urbanisme modernes.* 3 vols. Paris: Casterman, 1971–78.

Rame, Bernard. "Étude des obstacles à la diffusion culturelle au Havre et ses prolongents." PhD diss., University Paris 10, 1970.

Rapoport, Amos. *House Form and Culture.* Englewood Cliffs, N.J.: Prentice-Hall, 1969.

Raymond, Henri. "Analyse de contenu et entretien non directif: Application au symbolisme de l'habitat." *Revue française de sociologie* 9, no. 2 (1968): 167–79.

———. "L'architecture: Approche d'un concept." Doctorat d'État, University Paris 10, 1980.

———. *L'architecture, les aventures spatiales de la raison.* Paris: Centre Georges Pompidou, 1984.

———. *La gare dans le mode de vie et l'espace suburbain.* Paris: Institut de sociologie urbaine, 1974.

———. "Habitat, modèles culturels et architecture." In *Architecture, urbanistique et société,* ed. Henri Raymond, Jean-Marc Stébé, and Alexandre Mathieu-Fritz, 213–29. Paris: Harmattan, 2001. Originally published in *L'architecture d'aujourd'hui* 174 (1974): 50–53.

———. "Hommes et dieux à Palinuro (Observations sur une société de loisirs)." *Esprit* 274 (1959): 1030–40.

———. *Une méthode de dépouillement et d'analyse de contenu appliquée aux entretiens non directives.* Paris: Institut de sociologie urbaine, 1968.

———. "Modèles culturels." In *Modèles culturels habitat: Séminaire de l'Institut de l'environnement de Nanterre, 4 février 1976,* ed. Institut de l'environnement, 71–83. Paris: Centre d'études et de recherches architecturales, 1977.

———. *Paroles d'habitants: Une méthode d'analyse.* Paris: l'Harmattan, 2001.

———. "Urbanisation et changement social." In *Les champs de la sociologie française contemporaine,* ed. Henri Mendras and Michel Verret, 63–73. Paris: Colin, 1988.

———. "L'utopie concrète: Recherches sur un village de vacances." In *Architecture, urbanistique et société,* ed. Henri Raymond, Jean-Marc Stébé, and Alexandre Mathieu-Fritz, 271–84. Paris: Harmattan, 2001. Originally published in *Revue française de sociologie* 1 (1960): 323–33.

Raymond, Henri, Nichole Haumont, Marie-Geneviève Dezès, and Antoine Haumont. "Avant-propos de la quatrème edition." In Antoine Haumont, Nicole Haumont, Henri Raymond, and Marie-Geneviève Raymond, *L'habitat pavillonnaire,* 1–6. 4th ed. Paris: L'Harmattan, 2001.

Raymond, Henri, and Marion Segaud. "Analyse de l'space architectural: Le Corbusier." In *Les besoins fonctionnels de l'homme en vue de leur projection ultérieure sur le plan de la conception architecturale: Compte rendu de fin du contrat,* annex no. 2, ed. Françoise Bedos, Michel Dameron, Claude Leroy, Henri Raymond, and Léonie Sturge-Moore. Paris: Centre de recherche d'architecture, d'urbanisme et de construction, 1970.

Raymond, Henri, Jean-Marc Stébé, and Alexandre Mathieu-Fritz. *Architecture, urbanistique et société*. Paris: Harmattan, 2001.

Raymond, Marie-Geneviève. *La politique pavillonnaire*. Paris: Centre de recherche d'urbanisme, 1966.

Renaudie, Serge. "Sur l'urbain." In Lefebvre and the Groupe de Navarrenx, *Du contrat de citoyenneté*, 185–96. Paris: Syllepse etc., 1990.

Rieffel, Rémy. *La tribu des clercs: Les intellectuels sous la Ve République*. Paris: Calman-Lévy, 1993.

Rieland, Wolfgang. *Organisation und Autonomie: Die Erneuerung der italienischen Arbeiterbewegung*. Frankfurt am Main: Verlag Neue Kritik, 1977.

Rivière, Georges-Henri. "Le chantier 1425: Un tour d'horizon, une gerbe de souvenirs." *Ethnologie française* 3, no. 1–2 (1973): 9–12.

———. "Formes: Notes sur les caractères esthétiques de la maison rurale française." *Techniques et architecture* 1–2 (1947): 25–35.

———. "Musée rural—musée de terroir." In *Logis et loisirs: Urbanisme 37: 5e congrès CIAM, Paris 1937,* 83–85. Boulogne-sur-Seine, France: Éditions de L'architecture d'aujourd'hui, 1937.

———. "Recherches et Musées d'ethnographie française depuis 1939, Communicated by Georges Henri Rivière, Conservateur du Musée des arts et traditions populaires, to the Royal Anthropological Institute, 17 April 1946." *Man* 47 (1947): 7–10.

Roberts, John. "Philosophizing the Everyday: The Philosophy of Praxis and the Fate of Cultural Studies." *Radical Philosophy: A Journal of Socialist and Feminist Philosophy* 98 (1999): 16–29.

Röhr, Friedemann, and Lieselotte Röhr. "Die kapitalistische Stadt: Ökonomie und Politik der Stadtentwicklung (Rezension)." *Architektur der DDR* 4 (1979): 244–45.

———. "Urbane Revolution und städtischer Raum." *Architektur der DDR* 12 (1981): 754–57.

Ronneberger, Klaus. "Contours and Convolutions of Everydayness: On the Reception of Henri Lefebvre in the Federal Republic of Germany." *Capitalism Nature Socialism* 13, no. 50 (2002): 42–57.

Ross, Kristin. *Fast Cars, Clean Bodies: Decolonization and the Reordering of French Culture*. Cambridge, Mass.: MIT Press, 1996.

———. "Henri Lefebvre on the Situationist International." www.notbored.org. Published also in *October* 79 (1997): 69–83.

Rossi, Aldo. *The Architecture of the City*. Cambridge, Mass.: MIT Press, 1982 [1966].

Sadler, Simon. *The Situationist City*. Cambridge, Mass.: MIT Press, 1990.

Sag, Jean-Pierre. "Contribution à l'étude des formes et techniques de la participation dramatique à la résidence universitaire d'Antony." PhD diss., University Paris 10, 1973.

Schérer, René. *Utopies nomades*. Paris: Séguier, 1996.

Schérer, René, and Guy Hocquenghem. "Fourier théoricien de la production." In *Actualité de Fourier: Colloque d'Arc-et-Senans,* ed. Henri Lefebvre, 95–106. Paris: Éditions anthropos, 1975.

Schmid, Christian. "The City as a Contested Terrain." In *Possible Urban Worlds: Urban Strategies at the End of the 20th Century,* ed. International Network for Urban Research and Action, 188–91. Basel: Birkhäuser, 1998.

———. "The Dialectics of Urbanization in Zurich." In *Possible Urban Worlds: Urban Strategies at the End of the 20th Century,* ed. International Network for Urban Research and Action, 216–25. Basel: Birkhäuser, 1998.

———. "Henri Lefebvre's Theory of the Production of Space: Towards a Three Dimensional Dialectic." In *Space, Difference, Everyday Life: Reading Henri Lefebvre,* ed. Kanishka Goonewardena, Stefan Kipfer, Richard Milgrom, and Christian Schmid, 27–45. London: Routledge, 2008.

———. "A New Paradigm of Urban Development for Zurich." In *The Contested Metropolis: Six Cities at the Beginning of the 21st Century,* ed. Raffaele Paloscia, 236–46. Basel: Birkhäuser, 2004.

———. *Stadt, Raum und Gesellschaft: Henri Lefebvre und die Theorie der Produktion des Raumes.* Stuttgart: Steiner, 2005.

———. "Theorie." In *Die Schweiz: Ein städtebauliches Portrait,* ed. Roger Diener, Jacques Herzog, Marcel Meili, Pierre de Meuron, and Christian Schmid, 163–223. Basel: Birkhäuser, 2006. Translated as *Switzerland: An Urban Portrait* (Basel: Birkhäuser, 2006).

Schmidt, Hajo. *Sozialphilosophie des Krieges: Staats- und subjekttheoretische Untersuchungen zu Henri Lefebvre und Georges Bataille.* Essen, Germany: Klartext-Verlag, 1990.

Schnaidt, Claude. "Les architecnochrates." *AMC: Architecture mouvement continuité* 13 (1969): 15–16.

———. *Autrement dit: Écrits 1950–2001.* Paris: Infolio édition, 2004.

———. "Le droit à la ville." In *Autrement dit: Écrits 1950–2001,* 200–212. Gollion: Infolio édition, 2004.

Schuman, Tony. "Utopia Spurned: Ricardo Bofill and the French City Tradition." *Journal of Architectural Education* 1 (1986): 20–29.

Scott, Felicity D. "On the 'Counter-Design' of Institutions: Emilio Ambasz's Universitas Symposium at MoMA." *Greyroom* 14, no. 1 (2003): 46–77.

Scott-Brown, Denise, and Robert Venturi. "Levittown et après." *L'architecture d'aujourd'hui* 163 (1972): 38–42.

Scovazzi, Emma. "Esquisses sur le développement urbain de l'Amérique du sud de colonisation espagnole et de l'Argentine." PhD diss., University Paris 10, 1972.

Segaud, Marion. "Le Corbusier, mythe et idéologie de l'espace." PhD diss., University Paris 10, 1969.

Serenyi, Peter. "Le Corbusier, Fourier and the Monastery of Ema." *Art Bulletin* 49 (1967): 227–86.

Serres, Michel. *Hermès II: L'interférence.* Paris: Minuit, 1972.

Sher, Gerson. *Praxis: Marxist Criticism and Dissent in Socialist Yugoslavia.* Bloomington: Indiana University Press, 1977.

Sheringham, Michael. *Everyday Life: Theories and Practices from Surrealism to the Present.* New York: Oxford University Press, 2006.

Shields, Rob. *Lefebvre, Love and Struggle: Spatial Dialectics.* London: Routledge, 1996.

Siegel, Horst. "Novi Beograd—Neu-Belgrad—ein Stadtteil für 200 000 Einwohner." *Deutsche Architektur* 3 (1965): 138–47.

Simondon, Gilbert. *Du mode d'existence des objets techniques.* Paris: Aubier, 1958.

———. "The Genesis of the Individual." In *Incorporations,* ed. Jonathan Crary and Sanford Kwinter, 297–319. New York: Zone Books, 1992 [1964].

Situationist International. "Definitions." In *Situationist International Anthology,* ed. Ken Knabb, 51–52. Berkeley, Calif.: Bureau of Public Secrets, 2006.

———. "The Geopolitics of Hibernation." In *Situationist International Anthology,* ed. Ken Knabb, 100–107. Berkeley, Calif.: Bureau of Public Secrets, 2006.

Sloterdijk, Peter. *Critique of Cynical Reason.* Minneapolis: University of Minnesota Press, 1987 [1983].

Smith, Neil. "Geography, Difference and the Politics of Scale." In *Postmodernism and the Social Sciences,* ed. Joe Doherty, Elspeth Graham, and Mo Malek, 57–79. New York: St. Martin's Press, 1992.

———. "Remaking Scale: Competition and Cooperation in Pre-National and Post-National Europe." In *Competitive European Peripheries,* ed. Heikki Eskelinen and Folke Snickars, 59–74. Berlin: Springer Verlag, 1995.

———. *Uneven Development: Nature, Capital and the Production of Space.* Oxford: Blackwell, 1984.

Smithson, Alison, ed. *Team 10 Primer.* London: Standard Catalogue Co., 1962.

Soboul, Albert. *The Parisian Sans-Culottes and the French Revolution 1793–94.* Westport, Conn.: Greenwood Press, 1979 [1958].

Sociologie comparée de la famille contemporaine. Paris: Centre national de la recherche scientifique, 1955.

Sohn-Rethel, Alfred. *Intellectual and Manual Labour: A Critique of Epistemology.* London: Macmillan, 1978 [1970].

Soja, Edward. *Postmetropolis.* Oxford: Blackwell, 2000.

———. *Postmodern Geographies: The Reassertion of Space in Critical Social Theory.* London: Verso, 1989.

———. "The Socio-Spatial Dialectic." *Annals of the Association of American Geographers* 70, no. 2 (1990): 207–25.

———. *Thirdspace: Journeys to Los Angeles and Other Real-and-Imagined Places.* Oxford: Blackwell, 1996.

Solà-Morales, Manuel de. "Another Modern Tradition: From the Break of 1930 to the Modern Urban Project." *Lotus* 64 (1989): 6–31.

Solinas, A. Y. "Essai d'organisation touristique à Castel Sardo [Sardaigne], Italie." Master's thesis, Institut d'urbanisme de l'Université de Paris, 1967. Fonds ancien, Institut d'urbanisme de Paris.

Solzhenitsyn, Alexander. *The Gulag Archipelago.* London: Collins/Fontana, 1974 [1973].

Stalin, Joseph. *Dialectical and Historical Materialism.* Foreign Languages Publishing House, 1939 [1938].

Stanek, Łukasz. "Lessons from Nanterre." *Log* (Fall 2008): 59–67.

——. "Die Produktion des städtischen Raums durch massenmediale Erzählpraktiken: Der Fall Nowa Huta." In *Sozialistische Städte zwischen Herrschaft und Selbstbehauptung Kommunalpolitik, Stadtplanung und Alltag in der DDR,* ed. Heinz Reif and Christoph Bernhardt, 274–98. Stuttgart: Franz Steiner Verlag, 2008.

——. "Simulationen: Identitätspolitik und Raumkonsum in Nowa Huta." In *Industriestadtfuturismus—100 Jahre Wolfsburg/Nowa Huta,* ed. Martin Kaltwasser, Ewa Majewska, and Kuba Szreder, 294–309. Frankfurt am Main: Revolver, 2007.

——. "Simulation or Hospitality—beyond the Crisis of Representation in Nowa Huta." In *Visual and Material Performances in the City,* ed. Lars Frers and Lars Meier, 135–53. Aldershot, U.K.: Ashgate, 2007.

——. "Space as Concrete Abstraction: Hegel, Marx, and Modern Urbanism in Henri Lefebvre." In *Space, Difference, Everyday Life: Reading Henri Lefebvre,* ed. Kanishka Goonewardena, Stefan Kipfer, Christian Schmid, and Richard Milgrom, 62–79. London: Routledge, 2008.

Staniszkis, Jadwiga. *Postkomunizm: Próba opisu.* Gdańsk: Idee–Słowo/Obraz Terytoria, 2001.

St. John Wilson, Colin. *The Other Tradition of Modern Architecture: The Uncompleted Project.* London: Academy, 1995.

Sturge-Moore, Léonie, ed. "Architecture et sciences sociales: Séminaire annuel, 22–26 juin 1972, Port Grimaud: Compte rendu des communications et des interventions." Paris, 1972. Centre de recherche sur l'habitat, Paris.

——, ed. "Architecture—mythe—idéologie." Report of third seminar, 8–9 February 1969. In *Les besoins fonctionnels de l'homme en vue de leur projection ultérieure sur le plan de la conception architecturale: Compte rendu de fin du contrat,* ed. Françoise Bedos, Michel Dameron, Claude Leroy, Henri Raymond, and Léonie Sturge-Moore, annex no. 1. Paris: Centre de recherche d'architecture, d'urbanisme et de construction, 1970.

——, ed. "Dimensions neuro-physiologique et neuro-psychologique: Système nerveux—organes sensoriels—perception—fonctions symboliques—sommeil." Report of seminar 1bis, 6 October 1968. In *Les besoins fonctionnels de l'hommeen vue de leur projection ultérieure sur le plan de la conception architecturale: Compte rendu de fin de contrat,* ed. Françoise Bedos, Michel Dameron, Claude Leroy, Henri Raymond, and Léonie Sturge-Moore, annex no. 1. Paris: Centre de recherche d'architecture, d'urbanisme et de construction, 1970.

Šubrt, Jiří. "The Problem of Time from the Perspective of the Social Sciences." *Czech Sociological Review* 9 (2001): 211–24.

Supek, Rudi. "Dix ans de l'école d'été de Korčula (1993–1973)." *Praxis: Revue philosophique,* édition internationale 1–2 (1974): 8–9.

Swyngedouw, Erik. "Neither Global Nor Local: 'Glocalization' and the Politics of Scale." In *Spaces of Globalization,* ed. Kevin R. Cox, 137–66. New York: Guilford Press, 1997.

——. "Territorial Organization and the Space/Technology Nexus." *Transactions of the Institute of British Geographers,* n.s. 17, no. 4 (1992): 417–33.

Szelényi, Iván. "Au-delà de l'analyse de classes: Quelques dilemmes pour la sociologie urbaine." *Sociologie du travail* 2 (1979): 201–14.

"Table et index pour l'année 1950." *Politique étrangère* 15 (1950).

Tafuri, Manfredo. *Architecture and Utopia: Design and Capitalist Development.* Cambridge, Mass.: MIT Press, 1976 [1973].

——. "Architecture et semiologie." In *Architecture et sciences sociales: Séminaire annuel 22–26 juin, 1972, Port Grimaud: Compte rendu des communications et des interventions,* ed. Léonie Sturge-Moore, 7–13. Paris, 1972. Centre de recherche sur l'habitat, Paris.

——. *Theories and History of Architecture.* London: Granada, 1980 [1968].

——. "Toward a Critique of Architectural Ideology." In *Architecture Theory since 1968,* ed. Michael K. Hays, 6–35. Cambridge, Mass.: MIT Press, 1998 [1969].

Taller de arquitectura. "Réaliser l'utopie." *Techniques et architecture* 306 (1975): 88–97.

Thoenig, Jean-Claude. *L'ère des technocrates: Le cas des Ponts et chaussées.* Paris: Éditions d'organisation, 1973.

Thompson, D'Arcy Wentworth. *On Growth and Form.* Cambridge: Cambridge University Press, 1917.

Tolan, Barlas. "Problématique de l'urbanisation en Turquie: Aspects sociaux." PhD diss., University Paris 10, 1971.

Tonka, Hubert. "Pratique urbaine de l'urbanisme." *Urbanisme* 106 (1968): 6–11.

Toscano, Alberto. "Factory, Territory, Metropolis, Empire." *Angelaki* 9, no. 2 (2004): 197–216.

Tosel, André. "Henri Lefebvre ou le philosophe vigilant (1936-1946)." In *Marx contemporain: Acte 2,* 77–108. Paris: Syllepses, 2008.

Touraine, Alain. *Post-Industrial Society: Tomorrow's Social History: Classes, Conflicts and Culture in the Programmed Society.* London: Wildwood House, 1971 [1969].

Treanton, Jean-René. "Les premières années du Centre d'études sociologiques (1946-1955)." *Revue française de sociologie* 32, no. 3 (1991): 390–91.

Trebitsch, Michel. "Henri Lefebvre et l'autogestion." In *Autogestion: La dernière utopie?* ed. Frank Georgi, 65–77. Paris: Publications de la Sorbonne, 2003.

——. Preface. In Henri Lefebvre, *Critique of Everyday Life,* vol. 1: *Introduction,* ix–xxviii. London: Verso, 1991.

——. Preface. In Henri Lefebvre, *Le nationalisme contre les nations.* Paris: Méridiens Klincksieck, 1988.

———. "Preface: Presentation: Twenty Years After." In Henri Lefebvre, *Critique of Everyday Life*, vol. 3: *From Modernity to Modernism (Towards a Metaphilosophy of Daily Life)*, vii–xxxiv. London: Verso, 2005.

———. "Preface: The Moment of Radical Critique." In Henri Lefebvre, *Critique of Everyday Life*, vol. 2: *Foundations for a Sociology of the Everyday*, ix–xxix. London: Verso, 2002.

Treusch-Dieter, Gerburg. "Revolution der Städte? Zu Henri Lefèbres 'Revolution der Städte' und 'Stadt im marxistischen Denken.'" *Arch+* 34 (1977): 58–62.

Trystram, Jean-Paul, ed. *Fondation Royaumont pour le progrès des sciences de l'homme: Sociologie et urbanisme*. Paris: Épi, 1970.

———, ed. *Sociologie et développement urbain*. 2 vols. Vol. 1: *Introduction, Aix-en-Provence, Le Havre, Toulouse*. Vol. 2: *Bordeaux, Lille, Rennes, Stasbourg*. Paris: Ministère de l'équipement, 1965–66.

Uchida, Hiroshi. *Marx's Grundrisse and Hegel's Logic*. London: Routledge, 1988.

"Un 'café-club' au prochain salon des arts ménagers." *Techniques et architecture* 1 (1961): 39.

"Unités pédagogiques d'architecture—France." *AMC: Architecture mouvement continuité* 13 (1969): 22–36.

Unwin, Tim. "A Waste of Space? Towards a Critique of the Social Production of Space." *Transactions of the Institute of British Geographers* 25, no. 1 (2000): 11–29.

"L'urbanisme aujourd'hui: Mythes et réalités: Débat entre Henri Lefebvre, Jean Balladur et Michel Ecochard." Special issue of *Les Cahiers du Centre d'études socialistes* 72–73 (1967).

Vailland, Roger, and Shadrach Woods. "Retour à la sauvagerie." *L'architecture d'aujourd'hui* 132 (1967): 6–7.

Vaneigem, Raoul. "Comments against Urbanism." *October* 79 (1997): 123–28.

———. *The Revolution of Everyday Life*. Seattle: Left Bank, 1983 [1967].

Venturi, Robert. *Complexity and Contradiction in Architecture*. Garden City, N.Y.: Doubleday, 1966.

Verdery, Katherine. *What Was Socialism, and What Comes Next?* Princeton, N.J.: Princeton University Press, 1996.

Vidler, Anthony. "Asylums of Libertinage: Sade, Fourier, Ledoux." *Lotus International* 44 (1984): 28–29.

———. "The Idea of Unity and Le Corbusier's Urban Form." *Architects' Year Book* 12 (1968): 225–35.

Viellard-Baron, Hevré. "Sarcelles: Un cas toujours exemplaire?" *Urbanisme* 322 (2002): 53–56.

"Village-Expo." *La vie urbaine: Urbanisme—habitation—aménagement du territoire: Organe de l'Institut d'urbanisme de l'Université de Paris* 4 (1966): 317–18.

Villes nouvelles, recherches pour une ville future: Grand prix international d'urbanisme et d'architecture. Paris: Construction et humanisme, 1970.

Violeau, Jean-Louis. *Les architectes et mai 68*. Paris: Éditions recherches, 2005.

———. *Situations construites*. Paris: Sens et Tonka, 2005.

———. "Utopie: In acts . . ." In *The Inflatable Moment: Pneumatics and Protest in '68,* ed. Marc Dessauce, 37–59. New York: Princeton Architectural Press, 1999.

———. "Why and How 'to Do Science'? On the Often Ambiguous Relationship between Architecture and the Social Sciences in France in the Wake of May '68." *Footprint* 1 (2007): 7–22.

Wakeman, Rosemary. *The Heroic City: Paris, 1945–1958*. Chicago: University of Chicago Press, 2009.

Wandschneider, Dieter. "Zur Struktur Dialektischer Begriffsentwicklung." In *Das Problem der Dialektik,* ed. Dieter Wandschneider, 114–69. Bonn: Bouvier, 1997. Also available at www.phil-inst.rwth-aachen.de.

Welter, Volker. "In-Between Space and Society—on some British Roots of Team 10's Urban Thought in the 1950s." In *Team 10, 1953–81: In Search of a Utopia of the Present,* ed. Dirk van den Heuvel and Max Risselada, 258–63. Rotterdam: Netherlands Architecture Institute, 2005.

Werlen, Benno. *Society, Action and Space: An Alternative Human Geography*. London: Routledge, 1993.

Weyl, Hermann. *Symmetry*. Princeton, N.J.: Princeton University Press, 1952.

Wigley, Mark. *Constant's New Babylon: The Hyper-Architecture of Desire*. Rotterdam: 010 Publishers, 1998.

Wirth, Louis. "Urbanism as a Way of Life." *American Journal of Sociology* 44, no. 1 (1938): 1–24.

Woud, Auke van der, ed. *Het nieuwe bouwen internationaal: CIAM: Volkshuisvesting, stedebouw/Het nieuwe bouwen international: CIAM: Housing, Town Planning*. Delft: Delft University Press, 1983.

Wright, Steve. *Storming Heaven: Class Composition and Struggle in Italian Autonomist Marxism*. London: Pluto Press, 2002.

Zach, Juliane, ed. *Eilfried Huth: Varietät als Prinzip*. Berlin: Gebr. Mann, 1996.

Zevi, Bruno. *Architecture as Space: How to Look at Architecture*. New York: Horizon Press, 1974 [1948].

Zola, Émile. *Work*. London: Chatto and Windus, 1901 [1901].

Zucker, Paul, ed. *New Architecture and City Planning: A Symposium*. New York: Philosophical Library, 1944.

by Denise E. Carlson

Note: All geographic names are located in France unless otherwise indicated.

Orville, Paul, 24
Otto, Frei, 169
overdetermination: concept of, 157, 180
ownership: of land, 57–58, 78, 204, 247; of means of production, 66, 157, 162, 220, 243–44, 246

Palais idéal, Hauterives (Cheval), 196
Palais-Royal, Paris, 171, 172
Palinuro, 177; photo of, 178
Parent, Claude, 47
Paris, 19, 39, 48, 147, 153, 171, 262n104, 276n5; collective housing in, 106, 116, 117, 300n168; design competitions for, 40, 42–47; Haussmann's reorganization of, 174, 186, 191, 195; neighborhoods in, 9, 106; periphery of, 33, 82, 150, 190; Perreymond's design for, 174, 175; shantytowns of, 180, 182, 183, 186; social/spatial segregation of, xiv, 74. *See also* Nanterre university
Paris Commune (1871), xiii, 19, 158, 179–80, 181, 191, 240, 297n106
Parmenides, 120
Parti communiste français. *See* French Communist Party
Parti communiste international, 58
particularity: moment of, xiii, 139, 141
Parti socialiste (Socialist Party, PS), 68
Parti socialiste unifié (United Socialist Party, PSU), 59, 72, 242
passion: concept of, 75, 174–76
pavillonaires. See inhabitants: of the *pavillon*
PCF. *See* French Communist Party
peasants, 5–17, 18, 57–59, 62–63
perceived space (*l'espace perçu*), 146, 153, 188; in Lefebvre's theory of space, xii, 81, 128, 129, 131–32, 169; moments of space and, 135, 136, 149–50, 194, 200, 247

perception, 58, 75, 146–47, 150, 194, 199, 224, 284n191
Perec, Georges, 18, 153, 285n226
periphery. *See* center-periphery relationships; Paris: periphery of
Perreymond, 171, 174, 175
Pessac neighborhood (Le Corbusier), 29–30, 89, 94, 144; Boudon's research on, 25, 89–93, 143, 278n66
Petrović, Miloš R., 235
Peyre, Christiane, 18
phalanstery, 40, 171, 173, 176, 245
phenomenology, 24, 86, 105, 128, 129, 135, 136, 261n87
Philosophes group, 4, 9
philosophy, 64, 88, 129, 132, 135; Lefebvre's engagement with, 82, 169, 240. *See also* idealism, German; Romanticism, German
Picard, Michel, 260n72
Picasso, Pablo, 146, 290n81
Piganiol, Pierre: photo of, 42
Pignon, Édouard, 146
Pincemaille, Patrick, 93
Pingusson, Georges-Henri, 33, 39
planners/planning, 28, 40, 62, 66, 84, 130–31, 148, 198, 293n177; capitalist, 245–46; French, 22–24, 68–73, 262n104; functionalist, 119, 170; state, ix, 23, 28, 68–73, 74, 76, 80, 88, 105, 132; urban, ix, 19–20, 68, 76, 206, 222; in Yugoslavia, 243–44
pleasure, 169, 171, 175, 176–77, 222
Poland, 66–67, 77
politics, 28, 73, 102, 167, 186, 231, 245; of class, 57–59; economy and, 39, 69, 73, 285n240; of everyday life, 170; of housing, 126; of representation, 131; of scale, 220–33, 242–43; of self-management, 109, 242; of space, x, 39, 66; of urbanism, 71, 73–74, 245. *See also* Communist

□ □ □

Łukasz Stanek is a researcher and teacher at the
Institute of History and Theory of Architecture at the Swiss
Federal Institute of Technology (ETH) in Zurich.

□ □ □